D1568647

BULGARIA, HUNGARY, ROMANIA, THE CZECH REPUBLIC, AND SLOVAKIA

BULGARIA, HUNGARY, ROMANIA, THE CZECH REPUBLIC, AND SLOVAKIA

EDITED BY LORRAINE MURRAY, EDITOR, GEOGRAPHY

Britannica®
Educational Publishing

IN ASSOCIATION WITH

ROSEN
EDUCATIONAL SERVICES

Published in 2014 by Britannica Educational Publishing
(a trademark of Encyclopædia Britannica, Inc.)
in association with Rosen Educational Services, LLC
29 East 21st Street, New York, NY 10010.

Distributed exclusively by Rosen Educational Services.
For a listing of additional Britannica Educational Publishing titles, call toll free (800) 237-9932.

First Edition

Britannica Educational Publishing
J.E. Luebering: Director, Core Reference Group
Adam Augustyn: Assistant Manager, Core Reference Group
Marilyn L. Barton: Senior Coordinator, Production Control
Steven Bosco: Director, Editorial Technologies
Lisa S. Braucher: Senior Producer and Data Editor
Yvette Charboneau: Senior Copy Editor
Kathy Nakamura: Manager, Media Acquisition
Lorraine Murray: Editor, Geography

Rosen Educational Services
Jeanne Nagle: Senior Editor
Nelson Sá: Art Director
Cindy Reiman: Photography Manager
Brian Garvey: Designer, Cover Design
Introduction by Richard Barrington

Library of Congress Cataloging-in-Publication Data

Bulgaria, Hungary, Romania, the Czech Republic, and Slovakia/edited by Lorraine Murray.
    pages cm.—(The Britannica guide to countries of the European Union)
"In association with Britannica Educational Publishing, Rosen Educational Services."
Includes bibliographical references and index.
ISBN 978-1-61530-968-9 (library binding)
1. Europe, Central—Encyclopedias. I. Murray, Lorraine.
DAW1051.B85 2014
943.7003—dc23

                                                        2013011132

Manufactured in the United States of America

On the cover p. iii: (map contour and stars), back cover, multiple interior pages (stars)
©iStockphoto.com/pop_jop; cover, multiple interior pages *(background graphic) Mina De La
O/Digital Vision/Getty Images*

On page xiv: Map of Central Europe, showing the countries covered in this book: Bulgaria,
Hungary, Romania, the Czech Republic, and Slovakia. *PILart/Shutterstock.comw*

CONTENTS

33

50

58

71

74

78

93

110

112

ZIPS

ATHIAN

Pressburg

KINGDOM
OF
HUNGARY

Buda Pest

hérvár

Kalocsa

TRANSYLVA

Pécs Szeged

Herma

Bras

b

A

Belgrade

WALA
(to Hunga

SNIA

Danub

arajevo

KINGDOM
OF
SERBIA

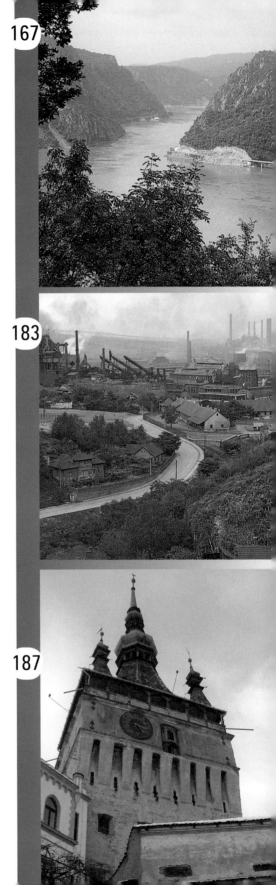

167

183

187

201

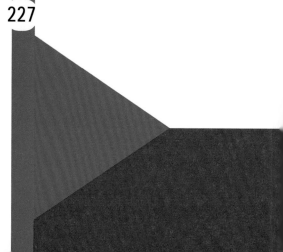

211

227

237

243

253

286

310

329

Reykjavik
Iceland

Norway

Finland

Sweden

Helsinki

Oslo
Stockholm

Tallinn
Estonia

Moscow

Riga Latvia

Lithuania
Vilnius

Denmark
Copenhagen

Minsk

Belarus

United
Kingdom

Dublin
Ireland

Netherlands
Amsterdam

Berlin

Warsaw

Poland

Kyiv

Ukraine

London

Brussels
Belgium

Germany

Prague
Czech
Republic

Slovakia

Chisinau

Luxembourg

Bratislava

Moldova

Paris

Vienna
Austria

Budapest

Hungary

Romania

France

Switzerland
Bern

Liechtenstein
Vaduz

Slovenia

Ljubljana

Bucharest

Zagreb

Belgrade

Croatia

Bosnia and
Herzegovina

Serbia

Bulgaria

Sarajevo

Sofia

Monaco

San Marino

Montenegro

Kosovo

Skopje

Podgorica

Macedonia

Portugal

Andorra

Italy

Vatican City
Rome

Tirana

Lisbon

Madrid

Albania

Spain

Greece

Athens

Malta
Valletta

When one looks at a map, it can be tempting to assume the borders defining various countries have been in place forever. After all, the physical features of a map—the mountains, rivers, and coastlines—do not change much through the centuries. As for the question of countries as political entities, however, political affiliations and world events can alter their identities as well as their physical borders. Such has been the case in eastern Europe. This book takes a look at five countries in this region—Bulgaria, Hungary, Romania, the Czech Republic, and Slovakia—exploring both what they are like today and how they have become what they are through the course of their histories.

Situated in the southeast portion of the Balkan Peninsula, with Turkey just to the south, Bulgaria lies on the historical route taken by travelers between Europe and Asia--be they invaders or simply traders. As a result, Bulgaria's culture is a mix of Eastern and Western influences. The physical terrain also is varied, composed of everything from rugged mountains to tranquil beaches on the Black Sea.

Less varied is the demographic profile of Bulgaria. The great majority of the population consists of ethnic Bulgarians, and the majority of the people belong to the Bulgarian Orthodox Church, which practices an Eastern Orthodox form of Christianity. Since 1991, this population has been governed by a parliamentary system featuring a directly elected president and a prime minister elected by the National Assembly (parliament). This democratic state is the outcome of a long and often convoluted history that began with the Slavic invasions of the peninsula in the 6th and 7th centuries CE and the formation of a tribal confederation known as Great Bulgaria in the 7th century. The spread of Christianity to Bulgaria shortly thereafter helped foster institutions of learning and helped unite the Bulgars with the Slavs.

Bulgaria in its first centuries was far from a peaceful place. Conflicts with outsiders, especially the forces of the Byzantine Empire, weakened the country. Subsequent centuries would see invasions by Mongols and Serbs, but the conquerors who had the greatest lasting impact were the Ottoman Turks. At its peak, the Ottoman Empire had made significant inroads into Europe. Given its location just north of Turkey, Bulgaria was a prime target for conquest and usurpation. Bulgaria fell to the Ottoman Empire in the late 14th century and would remain under its control until late in the 19th century.

The country gained independence in 1878, but further troubles lay ahead. Continuing battles with the Ottoman Empire were followed by war against Greece and Serbia over disputed territories, and then came World War I, which Bulgaria entered as an ally of the eventual loser, Germany. The period between the world wars was marked by a series of coups and revolts in Bulgaria. The country's troubles continued throughout World War II, when Bulgaria once again chose to support what would prove to be the losing side, that of the Axis alliance.

The ultimate result of Bulgaria's support of the Axis powers in World War II was its occupation by Soviet troops at the end of the war and the installation of communist rule soon afterward that lasted until the early 1990s. Though today a free and independent state that was granted membership in the European Union in 2007, Bulgaria has continued to struggle with both internal conflicts and disputes with neighbouring countries. In short, while a new era may have begun in Bulgaria, the country has not left its troubled history behind entirely.

Just as much of Bulgaria's history has been determined by its proximity to Russia and Turkey, Hungary's location has played a significant role in its history, including a drastic reduction in territory following World War I. Hungary is much farther west than Bulgaria, bordering on Austria. Appropriately, given its physical closeness to the West, Hungary was one of the first countries in the eastern European communist bloc to implement market-based economic reforms, which date back to the late 1960s. This has culminated in a favourable business environment that attracts foreign investment and has nurtured a large number of entrepreneurial start-ups.

A common thread that runs through the history of many European countries is that of recurring struggles over royal succession. The Hungarian kingdom dates back to the 10th century, but by the 16th century disputes over this throne, in addition to invasion by the Ottoman Empire, threatened the country's very existence. Hungary spent much of the 16th and 17th centuries split into three separate parts, with the largest part of its territory under foreign domination by the Ottoman Turks.

Another common theme in European history is the intertwining of royal lines from different countries—often through marriage. This often took place for strategic purposes; that is, to form international alliances by means of uniting different royal families. It was in this way that the Habsburgs of Austria first gained a claim to the Hungarian throne in the 1520s. Once Hungary, at the end of the 17th century, regained its territory that was under Ottoman rule, the Habsburgs imposed German as the official language and made the country virtually a part of Austria. However, a combination of declining Austrian power and a rising spirit of nationalism within Hungary led to a series of revolts. This ultimately resulted in an 1867 compromise that created the dual monarchy of Austria-Hungary, under which the two countries shared one ruler.

The association pulled Hungary into World War I on the side of Austria, which proved to have drastic consequences. After the war Hungary lost much of its territory and population to other countries, leaving it greatly weakened. Yet another setback came with World War II, when Hungary joined the Axis powers and again was defeated. Like virtually all of eastern Europe, Hungary emerged from World War II under Soviet control and with a communist government. The postwar story of Hungary was one that largely revolved around hardship and survival. Thus, while the country's emergence from communist rule in 1989 can be seen as a triumph, Hungary's hard-won freedom may be considered simply the latest step in that long struggle.

Romania shares a border with both Hungary and Bulgaria (as well as Serbia, Ukraine, and Moldova). Given its proximity to these two countries, it should come as no surprise that Romania shares some of the same elements of its neighbours' history. It is widely believed that the country's ethnic roots can be traced back to the mixing of heritage settlers from the Roman Empire with members of the Dacian tribes who inhabited the area. Following the Roman Empire's withdrawal of its government from the area of present-day Romania that was known as the province of Dacia in the 3rd century, the region spent most of the next millennium dominated by a variety of outside invaders. Not until the 14th century did the Romanian principalities of Walachia and Moldavia first gain independence from Hungary, at that time the dominant power in the region. Although these principalities were soon invaded by the Ottoman Empire, they were able to retain some level of autonomy by paying annual tribute to that empire.

The rise of Russia as a regional power in the 19th century marked a transition for Romania from Ottoman domination to Russian domination. Up until then, Romania had not yet existed as a single, independent political entity. Only in the latter half of the 19th century did Walachia and Moldavia free themselves of Russian interference and declare themselves to be the new country of Romania. Its territory expanded greatly as a result of its role on the winning side in World War I.

The remainder of the 20th century saw a series of challenges for Romania. The country drifted from democracy to dictatorship after World War I and then became a communist state after World War II. The return of Romania to democracy at the end of the 1980s and its admittance to the European Union in 2007 may be seen as two of the more triumphant moments in Romania's development.

While Romania was formed from the union of separate principalities and territories, the Czech Republic and Slovakia are countries created from a relatively recent split of a formerly singular country. These two countries, which sit side by side near the centre of Europe, were joined for most of the 20th century as Czechoslovakia, a country itself formed in 1918 from three regions with separate and distinct political and social histories. The area that is now the Czech Republic actually comprises two regions that were once the separate states of Bohemia and Moravia. These two states had similar cultures and at times were governed jointly. Slovakia, on the other hand, was ruled by Hungary for almost 1,000 years prior to 1918 and was known as Upper Hungary for much of that time.

What brought Bohemia, Moravia, and Slovakia together was a mutual desire for independence. While Slovakia was dominated by Hungary, a large German minority exerted a significant influence in Bohemia and Moravia, and these two regions were under Austrian Habsburg rule for centuries. After their loss in World War I devastated the power of Germany, Hungary, and Austria, Czech and Slovak leaders saw an opportunity to win independence and worked together to strengthen their cause.

As a result, the new country of Czechoslovakia was founded in 1918. The union, however, was not an easy one. By the late 1930s, German aggression in central Europe heightened tensions that led Slovak leaders to call for a split from the Czech region. The split finally occurred when German troops occupied the regions of Bohemia and Moravia in March 1939. When World War II broke out later that year, Czech and Slovak factions joined forces again in resistance against the Germans. They enlisted the support of the Soviet Union in their cause, which eventually led to Czechoslovakia's existence as a communist state after the war.

Czechoslovakia remained united under communist rule until 1989, when a nationwide wave of prodemocracy protests led to the peaceful downfall of communism known as the Velvet Revolution. Shortly after the country's first free elections in 1990, political tensions led to an ultimately amicable split of the Czechoslovak federation.

The formal separation occurred on January 1, 1993. Though each subsequently faced its share of political and economic challenges, the Czech Republic and Slovakia were able to advance reforms and stabilize sufficiently to be granted admission into the European Union in 2004.

The histories of Bulgaria, Hungary, Romania, the Czech Republic, and Slovakia have been marked by violent upheavals stemming from internal divisions, disputes with neighbouring countries, and invasion by outside powers. These upheavals have frequently changed the shape of Europe's borders over the last several centuries, and in the process had a profound effect on the lives of tens of millions of people. It remains to be seen if the future of these countries will be noticeably different from their often turbulent pasts. Perhaps a favourable omen can be found in the awarding of the 2012 Nobel Peace Prize to the European Union, which was rewarded for its work in promoting the reconciliation of international disputes. With each of the countries' admittance to the European Union following their transitions from communism, they may have found the route to a more stable future.

BULGARIA: THE LAND AND ITS PEOPLE

Occupying the eastern portion of the Balkan Peninsula in southeastern Europe, Bulgaria was founded in the 7th century and is one of the oldest states on the European continent. It is intersected by historically important routes from northern and eastern Europe to the Mediterranean basin and from western and central Europe to the Middle East. Even before the creation of the Bulgarian state, the empires of ancient Rome, Greece, and Byzantium were strong presences, and people and goods traveled the land with frequency.

The flag of Bulgaria. Encyclopaedia Britannica, Inc.

Nearly rectangular in outline, Bulgaria is bounded by Romania to the north, with most of the border marked by the lower Danube River. The Black Sea lies to the east, Turkey and Greece to the south, Macedonia to the southwest, and the federated country of Serbia and Montenegro to the west. The capital city, Sofia, lies in a mountainous basin in the west.

RELIEF

Within a relatively small compass, the Bulgarian landscape exhibits striking topographic variety. Open expanses of lowland alternate with broken mountain country, cut by deep river gorges and harbouring upland basins such as that in which Sofia lies. Three basic

Physical map of Bulgaria. Encyclopaedia Britannica, Inc.

structural and physiographic divisions run east-west, splitting the country into the traditional regions of North Bulgaria, including the Danubian Plain and the Balkan Mountains; South Bulgaria, including the Rila-Rhodope Massif; and a transitional area between them.

All but a short section of the northern frontier of Bulgaria is marked by the lower Danube River. The abrupt and often steep banks on the Bulgarian side contrast with the swamps and lagoons of the Romanian side. Extending southward from the Danube to the foothills of the Balkan Mountains is the fertile, hilly Danubian Plain. The average elevation of the region is 584 feet (178 metres), and it covers some 12,200 square miles (31,600 square kilometres). Several rivers cross the plain, flowing northward from the Balkans to join the Danube.

The Balkan Mountains border the Danubian Plain on the south. Their rounded summits have an average height of 2,368 feet (722 m) and rise to 7,795 feet (2,376 m) at Mount Botev, the highest peak.

The mountain chain is larger than the adjacent ranges that run parallel in a transitional region of complex relief. Block faulting—the raising or lowering of

Steppe grasslands at Point Kaliakra, Bulgaria, on the northwestern shore of the Black Sea. Oleg Polunin

great structural segments along regular lines of crustal weakness—has produced there the Sredna Mountains, the Vitosha Massif near Sofia, a number of sheltered structural basins, and the Upper Thracian and Tundzha lowlands.

Another mountain mass covers southern Bulgaria. This includes the Rhodope Mountains (Bulgarian: Rodopi; Greek: Rhodopis), which rise to 7,188 feet (2,190 m) at Golyam Perelik Peak; the Rila Mountains, rising to 9,596 feet (2,925 m) at Musala Peak, which is the highest point in the country and indeed in the whole Balkan Peninsula; the Pirin Mountains, with Vikhren Peak reaching 9,560 feet (2,914 m); and a frontier range known as the Belasitsa Mountains. These majestic ranges discharge meltwater from montane snowfields throughout the summer, and their sharp outlines, pine-clad slopes, and, in the Rila and Pirin ranges, several hundred lakes of glacial origin combine to form some of the most beautiful Bulgarian landscapes.

Trending north-south at the eastern fringe of three principal regions is the narrow Black Sea coastal region. With the exception of the fine harbours of Varna and Burgas, the coast has few bays, but it does have extensive stretches of sandy beach that are features of a number of picturesque seaside resorts.

DRAINAGE

Bulgaria has a complex drainage pattern characterized, with the notable exception of the Danube, by relatively short rivers. The major rivers are the Maritsa (Marica), Iskŭr, Struma, Arda, Tundzha,

The Danube River basin and its drainage network. Encyclopaedia Britannica, Inc.

and Yantra. Overall, more than half of the runoff drains to the Black Sea, and the rest flows to the Aegean Sea.

Bulgaria's numerous lakes may be coastal (such as the large lakes around Varna and Burgas, both on the Black Sea), glacial (such as those in the southern mountains), structural, or karst in origin. The country has some 500 mineral springs, half of which are warm or hot (reaching 217 °F [103 °C] at Sapareva Banya, in the west). Numerous dams have been constructed in the mountains.

SOILS

The varied Bulgarian natural environment has produced about 20 soil types and subtypes, which may be grouped into three main regions. Northern Bulgaria is characterized by the fertile black-earth soils known as chernozems and also by gray soils of forest origin. Southern Bulgaria has forest soils with acidic (cinnamonic) traces—by far the most extensive single category—as well as the modified chernozems known as chernozem-smolnitzas (a dark-coloured zonal soil with a deep and rich humus horizon). The rugged high mountain regions have brown forest, dark mountain forest, and mountain meadow soils.

CLIMATE

Most of Bulgaria has a moderate continental climate, which is tempered by Mediterranean influences in the south. The average annual temperature is 51 °F (10.5 °C), but this conceals a wide variation; temperatures as low as -37 °F (-38 °C) and as high as 113 °F (45 °C) have been recorded. Mean annual precipitation ranges from about 18 inches (450 millimetres) in the northeast to more than 47 inches (1,190 mm) in the highest mountains. The lowlands receive snowfall from mid-October to mid-May, with an annual average of 25–30 days of snow cover. Hailstorms occur between May and August.

PLANT AND ANIMAL LIFE

The relatively large number of Bulgarian plant and animal species reflects the country's location adjoining several of the great Eurasian biogeographic zones. During the Pleistocene Epoch (i.e., about 2,600,000 to 11,700 years ago), life in the region was not destroyed by advancing glaciers as occurred in much of Europe but was actually enriched by the immigration of species from the north, some of which still survive. Influences from the steppes of western Asia also penetrated the region at that time. Nonetheless, most of the plant and animal life is central European, mixed with a type that blends Arctic and alpine characteristics in the high mountains. Steppe species are most characteristic in the northeast and southeast, while the south is rich in sub-Mediterranean and Mediterranean species.

Rila National Park is a refuge for local fauna, such as suslik, rock partridges, chamois, capercaillie, chough, accentor, wall creeper, owls, bats, and martens.

About one-third of the nesting birds in Bulgaria can be found in the park, as well as one-third of invertebrates. Fish species include the Balkan trout and common minnow.

The Bulgarian government has introduced a number of conservation measures, including steps to protect soil, water, and air from pollution and to establish protected areas of outstanding interest to naturalists. The Srebarna Nature Reserve, a freshwater lake and bird sanctuary adjoining the Danube River, was named a UNESCO World Heritage site in 1983 and then placed on UNESCO's endangered list in 1992 after environmental decline; improvements were seen in the early 21st century.

ETHNIC GROUPS AND LANGUAGES

Ethnically, the population is fairly homogeneous, with Bulgarians making up more than four-fifths of the total. Slavic tribes who settled in the eastern part of the Balkan Peninsula in the 6th century BCE assimilated to a large extent the local Thracian culture, which had roots in the 4th century BCE, and formed a basic ethnic group. The Bulgars, who established the first Bulgarian state in 681, formed another component. With the gradual obliteration of fragmented Slavic tribes, Bulgars and Slavs coalesced into a unified people who became known as Bulgarians.

CYRILLIC ALPHABET

The writing system known as the Cyrillic alphabet was developed in the 9th–10th century CE for Slavic-speaking peoples of the Eastern Orthodox faith; it is the alphabet currently used for Russian and other languages of the republics that once formed the Soviet Union and for Bulgarian and Serbian. Based on the medieval Greek uncial script, the Cyrillic alphabet was probably invented by later followers of the 9th-century "apostles to the Slavs," St. Cyril (or Constantine), for whom it was named, and St. Methodius. As the Slavic languages were richer in sounds than Greek, 43 letters were originally provided to represent them; the added letters were modifications or combinations of Greek letters, or (in the case of the Cyrillic letters for ts, sh, and ch) they were based on Hebrew. The earliest literature written in Cyrillic was a translation of the Bible and various church texts.

The modern Cyrillic alphabets—Russian, Ukrainian, Bulgarian, and Serbian—have been modified somewhat from the original, generally by the loss of some superfluous letters. Modern Russian has 32 letters (33, with inclusion of the soft sign—not strictly a letter), Bulgarian 30, Serbian 30, and Ukrainian 32 (33). Modern Russian Cyrillic has also been adapted to many non-Slavic languages, sometimes with the addition of special letters.

The Turks, Bulgaria's largest minority, comprise about one-tenth of the citizenry and live in some regions of the northeast and in the eastern Rhodope Mountains region. Roma (Gypsies) are another sizable minority. Macedonians, often tabulated as ethnic Bulgarians, claim minority status. There are a few thousand Armenians, Russians, and Greeks (mostly in the towns), as well as Romanians and Tatars (mostly in the villages).

The Bulgarian language belongs to the South Slavic group, along with Serbo-Croatian and Slovene; closely related to Bulgarian is Macedonian. A number of dialects remain in common speech. Bulgarian is written in the Cyrillic alphabet.

RELIGION

With the reforms of the 1990s, following the communist period of state-sponsored atheism, full freedom of religion was established. There is no official religion, and the majority of religious Bulgarians are adherents of the Bulgarian Orthodox Church. Minority religious groups include Muslims, Protestants, Catholics, Jews, and Gregorian Armenians. Within the Protestant minority are Great Commission Christians, Pentecostals, and Evangelicals. The Catholic minority are followers of the Bulgarian Catholic Church, which, in contrast to the Roman Catholic Church, uses a Byzantine rite in liturgy.

The variety of religious traditions in Bulgaria can be traced in UNESCO World Heritage sites, from the Thracian cult tombs of the 3rd and 4th centuries BCE near the villages of Sveshtari and Kazanlak to the Horseman of Madara statue near Shumen that symbolizes Bulgaria's conversion to Christianity in the 9th century. The Rila Monastery was founded in the 10th century by St. John of Rila, who was canonized by the Bulgarian Orthodox Church. The wooded hills of the environs surrounding the monastery shelter several small monasteries, churches, and chapels housing a variety of religious art. To the northeast is the most famous of these sites, the Hermitage of St. John of Rila, a church that was erected about 1746 and rebuilt by 1820. The church stands near the cave in which the hermit lived and was buried (his remains were later moved). Both the cave and the church are pilgrimage destinations. In the northeast, the rock-hewn churches of Ivanavo date to the 12th century. The Boyana Church, erected outside Sofia in the 10th–19th centuries, features religious artwork of the medieval period.

SETTLEMENT PATTERNS

Bulgarian settlements have been officially classified into more than 250 larger urban areas and 4,000 smaller villages. The latter includes hundreds of small hamlets, clusters of farmsteads, and, deep in the mountains, a handful of historic monasteries. Many Bulgarian towns have roots in the Middle Ages and some even in antiquity, although a large number of modern settlements were created in the communist era of the mid-to-late 20th

RILA MONASTERY

Located in the Rhodope Mountains of southwestern Bulgaria, Rila Monastery is a historic monastery and cultural site. It is situated in a valley of the Rila massif, some 70 miles (110 km) south of Sofia. Rila is a symbol of Bulgarian national identity, and it is the most prominent monastery of the Bulgarian Orthodox Church.

Rila Monastery, southwestern Bulgaria. © Magdalena Yaramova/Fotolia

The first Christian monastery in Bulgaria, Rila was founded by the hermit John of Rila (Yoan of Rila, in Bulgarian Ivan Rilski), who is the traditional patron saint of Bulgaria. Rila grew rapidly in power and influence from the 13th to the 14th century. After a devastating fire, it was rebuilt and fortified (*c.* 1334–35) in its present location by the feudal lord Khrelio (also spelled Hrelyo or Hreljo).

The main sections standing today were constructed in the early to mid-19th century in an irregularly shaped polygon. Within its imposing frame are hundreds of dormitory rooms and halls, as well as archives and museums of history and ethnography. The relics of St. John of Rila are also on display. Smooth stone walls around the exterior rise four to five stories (some 65 feet [20 m]) and are topped by a clay tile roof. The white brick archways and polished wooden balconies of the interior of the polygon surround a spacious courtyard paved with flagstones. In the centre of the courtyard is a domed church, which is admired for its colourful frescoes and its iconostasis (sanctuary partition) of carved wood. Next to the church stands the 74-foot- (23-m-) high Tower of Khrelio (built *c.* 1334–35), which contains a vaulted chapel on its top story.

century. The urban population overtook the rural for the first time in 1969, and by the turn of the 21st century, it comprised about two-thirds of the total population. Despite the pressure of urban population growth, many Bulgarian towns preserve their ancient charm and are rich in cultural monuments; located as they are in remote areas, they offer a slower pace of life than can be found in the cities.

SOFIA

The capital of Bulgaria, Sofia (Bulgarian: Sofiya), is situated near the geographical centre of the Balkans region, in the Sofia Basin, a troughlike valley in the western part of the country. The Serdi (Sardi), a Thracian tribe, established a settlement in the region in the 8th century BCE. This community was conquered soon after 29 BCE by the Romans, who named it Serdica (Greek: Sardica). It flourished during the reign of the emperor Trajan (98–117) and reached its greatest height under the emperor Constantine I the Great; in 342 or 343 it was the site of an important meeting of Christian bishops, the Council of Sardica. From the 4th century it was part of the Western Roman Empire, but with the decline of Rome passed to Byzantium; it was plundered by Attila and the Huns in 441–447. During the 6th century Byzantine influence increased under the emperor Justinian, and the restored Church of St. Sofia, which later gave the town its name, survives from this period. In 809 the Bulgarian khan Krum seized the town and incorporated it in the Bulgarian state; it was given the Slav name Sredets (Greek: Triaditsa). It was under Byzantine rule from 1018 until 1185, when the second Bulgarian Empire was established.

Sofia fell to the Turks in 1382; the Ottoman governor of Rumelia took up residence there, and the town gradually acquired a distinctive Oriental appearance. It was liberated from Ottoman rule by Russian troops on January 4, 1878, and was designated the Bulgarian capital on April 3, 1879.

After World War II the city was further industrialized. The chief industries are engineering, metallurgy, food processing, and the manufacture of textiles and clothing. Printing is important; the rubber, footwear, furniture and woodworking, and chemical industries are also well represented.

An agricultural zone characterized by fruit and vegetable growing and by dairy farming surrounds Sofia, and it is connected with neighbouring towns by roads. Sofia is also the centre of Bulgarian air and rail traffic. Local transport is served by tramways, trolleybuses, and buses, while several cable lifts ascend the neighbouring Vitosha Mountains.

Among the many educational institutions in Sofia are the Bulgarian Academy of Sciences, the Academy of Agricultural Sciences, and the University of Sofia (1888), the oldest establishment of higher learning in Bulgaria. The city also contains the Cyril and Methodius National Library, the Ivan Vazov National Theatre and Opera House, an astronomical observatory, and a number of museums. In addition to the restored St. George, Boyana, and St. Sofia churches, historical monuments include two mosques, one housing a fine archaeological collection, and the Alexander Nevsky Cathedral, erected to commemorate the gratitude of the Bulgarian people to the Russian liberators of 1878.

Sofia, the capital, is the largest city and dominates the economic and cultural life of the country. Plovdiv, another major industrial and cultural centre, is located in the south-central region; it enjoys a scenic location on the Maritsa River and is host to an annual international trade fair. Varna focuses industry, transport, and tourism on the shores of the Black Sea. The nearby seaside resorts of Zlatni Pyassŭtsi ("Golden Sands") and Albena attract an international tourist trade. Burgas is Bulgaria's largest port on the Black Sea, while Ruse, on the Danube in the north, is the largest river port; there the Friendship Bridge leads to the Romanian city of Giurgiu. Stara Zagora, which lies on the southern flanks of the central Sredna Mountains, is notable for its archaeological and architectural remains.

Following World War II, Bulgarian villages underwent a transformation from the sleepy, underdeveloped, and poverty-stricken settlements that had typified much of the region for centuries. Almost all of the rural population now live in villages that are supplied with water and electricity and that have paved streets; a majority of the houses are recent constructions that replace older lath-and-plaster buildings. In addition to updated residences, processing plants have been built in many villages, so that rural areas have become increasingly industrialized.

DEMOGRAPHIC TRENDS

As a result of socioeconomic changes after World War II, notably the introduction of free medical care and the improvement of working conditions, Bulgaria's death rate dropped greatly, but it began to rise again in the 1970s as the proportion of older people in the population rose. At the turn of the 21st century the death rate not only was above the world average but also was about one-third greater than the birth rate, which was significantly below the global norm. Though the rate of infant mortality was reduced, Bulgaria had a negative natural-growth rate.

During World War II the government—in opposition to the demands of Nazi Germany, Bulgaria's wartime ally—saved virtually all of Bulgaria's 50,000 Jews from deportation, but after the war about 48,000 of them emigrated to Israel. A large number of Turks also left the country; 155,000 were expelled in 1949–51 by the communist government, and about 300,000 emigrated in 1989, though almost half of the latter group returned after 1991, with the end of communism. Throughout the 1990s migration was pronounced.

Internally, the movement of population has been from rural areas to larger towns and cities. In the 50-year period from 1949 to 1999, for example, the population of Sofia doubled; Plovdiv's population increased more than ninefold; and the populations of Varna and that of Ruse rose more than elevenfold.

Bulgaria's geographic variety is reflected in the distribution of its population. The most densely populated areas are the Danubian Plain, the Upper Thracian Basin, the Burgas Plain, and the intermontane basins of southwestern Bulgaria. Areas of lowest density are the eastern and southeastern parts of the country, such as in the Strandzha and Dobruja regions and the higher mountain areas.

Urbanization continues to have an effect on the demographic structure; a large segment of the urban population is of a young working—and childbearing—age, leading to natural growth of the towns and cities. Because relatively more older adults remain in the villages, the birth rate there continues to be lower and the death rate higher. These effects thus amplify the shift of population from rural areas to urban centres.

CHAPTER 2

THE BULGARIAN ECONOMY

The rapid industrialization of Bulgaria since World War II and the economic transition it underwent with the demise of the communist regime had a profound effect on Bulgarian society. Liberalization of price controls in the early 1990s led to a marked rise in prices. As a result, inflation rose and strikes became more frequent. The growing pains of the private sector and the strict financial discipline required to ease the heavy foreign debt also resulted in periods of high unemployment and decreased social services. Against this backdrop the Bulgarian government pursued economic stability with the assistance of international financial institutions, and with the introduction of the currency board in 1997 and other reforms, inflation was dramatically reduced by the end of the decade. By the beginning of the 21st century, with the government aggressively privatizing state-run industries, the restructured Bulgarian economy was revving up (aided in 2007 by the country's ascension to full membership in the EU). GDP increased at an average annual rate of more than four percent during the first decade of the new century.

AGRICULTURE

Agriculture accounts for less than one-tenth of the national income of Bulgaria. Cereal crops are grown on almost three-fifths of the sown land. Wheat is by far the most important, followed by corn (maize) and barley; rye, oats, soybeans, and rice also are grown. Tobacco, which is of a good-quality Oriental type and is grown mainly in the south, is an especially important industrial crop. The state-run tobacco company, Bulgartabac, was sold to a Russian firm in 2011.

Sunflower seed is the chief oilseed crop; after extraction of the oil, the pulp is made into cattle feed. Sunflowers, like sugar beets, grow mainly in the north. Bulgaria has become a leading exporter of grapes and tomatoes. There is stock breeding of cattle, sheep, pigs, and poultry. The forestry industry claims nearly 4,000,000 hectares (9,900,000 acres) of land.

A cooperative movement in agriculture developed before World War II. After the war, cooperative farms were established in the fashion of Soviet kolkhozy on most arable land. The cooperative and state farms later merged into large state and collective units. These were further consolidated in 1970–71 into even larger groupings, called agro-industrial complexes, that took advantage of integrated systems of automation, supply, and marketing.

In 1990 the government lifted restrictions on private farming, and almost all agricultural land was restored thereafter to private ownership while loans for the establishment of small farms and food-processing facilities were made available.

RESOURCES AND POWER

Bulgaria is relatively well-endowed with a variety of both metallic and nonmetallic minerals. Geologic exploration has identified about 40 coal basins, which together contain almost 3 billion tons of proven recoverable reserves. Of the

Farm in the Sredna Mountains, Bulgaria. Art Resource, New York

reserves, virtually all is lignite. The main mining areas are in the Pernik basin southwest of Sofia, in the Maritsa basin (at two locations: south of Stara Zagora and further southwest, at Dimitrovgrad), and in the northwest at Lom on the Danube. Lignite and brown coal fire the country's thermal power stations and are used as fuel and raw material for many of Bulgaria's industries.

Although deposits of anthracite and bituminous coal have been almost exhausted in Bulgaria, other deposits of black coking coal have been found in the northeast, in the Dobruja region. One of the largest reserves is near Sofia, at Kremikovtsi, the site of the country's largest metallurgical plant. Smaller quantities of iron ore are mined in the northwest

KOLKHOZ

The term kolkhoz (plural: kolkhozy) is an abbreviated form of the Russian *kollektivnoye khozyaynstvo* ("collective farm"), which, in the former Soviet Union, was a cooperative agricultural enterprise operated on state-owned land by peasants from a number of households who belonged to the collective. The workers were paid as salaried employees on the basis of the quality and quantity of labour contributed. Conceived as a voluntary union of peasants, the kolkhoz became the dominant form of agricultural enterprise as the result of a state program of expropriation of private holdings embarked on in 1929. Operational control was maintained by state authorities through the appointment of kolkhoz chairmen (nominally elected) and (until 1958) through political units in the machine-tractor stations (MTSs), which provided heavy equipment to kolkhozy in return for payments in kind of agricultural produce. Individual households were retained in the kolkhozy, and in 1935 they were allowed garden plots.

An amalgamation drive beginning in 1949 increased the pre-World War II average of about 75 households per kolkhoz to about 340 households by 1960. In 1958 the MTSs were abolished, and the kolkhozy became responsible for investing in their own heavy equipment. By 1961 their production quotas were established by contracts negotiated with the State Procurement Committee, in accordance with centrally planned goals for each region; the kolkhozy sold their products to state agencies at determined prices. Produce in surplus of quotas and from garden plots was sold on the kolkhoz market, where prices were determined according to supply and demand. With the collapse of communism and the breakup of the Soviet Union in 1990–91, the kolkhozy began to be privatized.

(Montana [formerly Mikhaylovgrad]), in the central region (Troyan), and in the southeast (Yambol). There are significant deposits of nonferrous ores (copper, lead, and zinc) in the Rhodope, Balkan, and Sredna mountains.

Bulgaria is also rich in less-valuable minerals, including rock salt, gypsum, limestone, dolomite, kaolin (china clay), asbestos, and barite. The country has only small deposits of oil and natural gas, though it is hoped that offshore exploration of the Black Sea will reap new deposits. Bulgaria relies on Russia for supplies of natural gas.

About one-half of Bulgaria's energy is imported. Coal and nuclear power combine about equally to provide nearly nine-tenths of the country's electrical production. The major source of energy within Bulgaria is the Maritsa lignite field, which provides fuel for large thermoelectric plants at Dimitrovgrad and Maritsa-Iztok; there are also thermal power stations at Pernik, Sofia, Plovdiv, and Burgas. Bulgaria's first and only nuclear power station, at Kozloduy, was constructed with Soviet aid and began operation in 1974; two reactors were closed there in 2002 and another two were shut down in 2006.

MANUFACTURING

Before World War II, Bulgarian industries were of minor importance. Under the socialist system industrialization became one of the principal aims of economic policy, with particular emphasis on basic industries such as electric power, ferrous and nonferrous metallurgy, and chemicals. Central planning of management, production, and investment channeled a large portion of national resources into industry. The industrial base remained important even after Bulgaria discarded socialism for a market economy at the end of the 20th century.

Before World War II, shipbuilding at Varna and foundries at Sofia, Plovdiv, Ruse, and Pernik were the most important metallurgical industries. Those developed after the war include iron and steel works at Pernik, utilizing local brown coal and iron ore from the Sofia district; a large steel project at Kremikovtsi; a lead and zinc works at Kŭrdzhali; and a copper and sulfuric acid plant at Pirdop.

A chemical industry was developed at Dimitrovgrad, and chemical plants were also built at Stara Zagora, Vratsa, Devnya, and Vidin, as well as a petrochemical plant at Burgas. The biotechnology sector is increasingly important in the economy, as is machine building; their relative share of industrial production has jumped dramatically. Machine building and metal processing are widely dispersed throughout the country; the largest plants are located in Sofia, Varna, Ruse, Burgas, and Plovdiv. In general, the production of chemicals and rubber is centred on Sofia, Dimitrovgrad, Varna, Devnya, and Plovdiv.

Since the 1960s three other industries have had marked regional development: food, beverage, and tobacco processing, textiles, and tourism. While food processing and beverage production are found throughout the country, three main industrial regions may be defined. The first, in the south, includes the towns of Plovdiv, Krichim, Pazardzhik, Asenovgrad, and Pŭrvomay, which primarily specialize in canning and tobacco processing. The second region, in northern Bulgaria (comprising Gorna Oryakhovitsa, Veliko Tŭrnovo, and Lyaskovets), concentrates on canning, sugar refining, and meat processing. A third region, to the northwest (Pleven, Dolna Mitropoliya, and Cherven Bryag), has become important for flour, paste products, poultry processing, canning, sugar refining, and the processing of vegetable oils.

Fishing and fish breeding have also become important industries. As the production of wine increased at the end of the 20th century, it became an important export item.

Before World War II, textile industries were mainly found where the demand for textiles was constant (Sofia, Plovdiv, and Varna) or where raw materials were available (Sliven and Vratsa). Under the communists' five-year plans, large new mills were built at Sofia, Sliven, and Plovdiv, and the total output of textile fabrics rose tremendously.

FINANCE

Until the reform movement of the late 1980s, the Bulgarian economy was based solely on state ownership of all means of production. In the early 1990s Bulgaria began a process of transition toward a market-oriented economy. The government initiated a program of privatized ownership, in addition to freeing prices and restructuring credit, banking, and other monetary institutions. Large-scale privatization of many industries was prevalent by the end of the century, when about three-fifths of the gross domestic product (GDP) was produced by the private sector.

These reforms enabled Bulgaria to receive financial assistance from Western countries, although they also produced unemployment and inflation. Beginning in 1997 the reform process sped up. By the end of the decade, more than half of the state-owned enterprises had been privatized, and annual inflation, under regulation by a new currency board, had been lowered.

The national budget continues to finance some capital investments, enterprises under direct central management, and a number of social and cultural institutions (e.g., higher education). It also covers defense and the central government. The state social insurance budget covers expenditure for matters such as employees' pensions, temporary incapacity to work, maternity leave, maintenance of rest homes, and family allowances. Social security and medical care reforms are monitored by the International Monetary Fund (IMF) and the World Bank. About one-fourth of the total budgetary expenditure funds social services.

In the early 1990s the banking system, formerly under the direction of the government, underwent significant reform. Legislation passed in June 1991 ended government direction of the Bulgarian National Bank but retained a measure of bank accountability to the National Assembly. In addition, a new tier of commercial banks and other lending institutions was introduced. In 1997, with the advent of the currency board, the national currency (lev) was tied to the German mark. Bulgaria put its plans to adopt the euro on hold in 2012 in response to the economic problems that befell the euro zone beginning in 2008.

TRADE AND TOURISM

Almost two-thirds of all exports are capital goods, such as machinery and equipment, and one-fourth are consumer goods, mainly of agricultural origin (such as fruit, wine, cigarettes, dairy products, and meat). About two-fifths of all imports are capital goods. The Soviet Union, until its dissolution in the early 1990s, was Bulgaria's main trading partner, but now Bulgarian trade is oriented to the rest of the countries of the European Union (EU).

Tourism in Bulgaria has grown markedly since the 1960s. Roughly 750,000 annual foreign arrivals were arriving in Bulgaria in 2005. In addition to the popular Black Sea resorts, tourists visit

Detail of a ceiling in Rila Monastery, Bulgaria. The historic monastery is one of the country's primary tourist destinations. © Corbis

historical centres such as Sofia, Plovdiv, and Rila Monastery and winter sports centres such as Borovets in the Rhodope Mountains. Pirin National Park, which occupies 67,700 acres (27,400 hectares) in the Pirin Mountains, was designated a UNESCO World Heritage site in 1983.

LABOUR AND TAXATION

The manufacturing and mining sector employs as many Bulgarians as agriculture does (each employs about one-fifth of the total labour force). Almost one-fourth of the active workforce is employed in trade and services. The percentage of female workers has risen to almost half of the total labour force, and women have greater representation in the service industry.

Bulgaria has thousands of local trade-union organizations made up of more than 100,000 separate subgroups. Only an insignificant portion of the country's workforce does not belong to a trade union. Until the late 1980s all trade unions belonged to the Central Council of Trade Unions (Tsentralen Sŭvet na Profesionalnite Sŭyuzi), founded in 1944 and allied with the Bulgarian Communist Party. It was reconstituted in 1989 as the Confederation of Independent Bulgarian Trade Unions (S'uz na Nezavisemite B'lgarski Profs'uze).

The main sources of revenue under the socialist system were the turnover tax (which taxed products at every stage of production and distribution) and deductions made from the profits of public enterprises. The advent of privatization and the harmonization of national legislation with EU standards led to a reform of the tax system and the tax administration, including the introduction of a value-added tax.

TRANSPORTATION AND TELECOMMUNICATIONS

The development of the Bulgarian economy has required an expansion of the transportation system. Road transport accounts for a large percentage of all freight carried as well as for most passenger traffic. The European International Highway links Sofia with Istanbul, and the main railway lines connect Sofia with the Black Sea coast. Bulgaria is intersected by major European transportation corridors, such as one from Thessaloníki, Greece, to northern Europe and another linking the Adriatic coast with the Black Sea coast.

The Danube is used for both internal and international traffic, with Ruse, Svishtov, and Lom the main river ports. The chief seaports are Varna and Burgas on the Black Sea, providing regular international merchant service. Bulgaria has international airports at Sofia, Varna, and Burgas.

The length of telephone and telegraph trunk lines and the number of radio and television transmitters were in decline by the end of the 1990s, following a mid-decade peak. The use of mobile cellular telephones rose dramatically in the same period, as did the number of Internet users.

CHAPTER 3

BULGARIAN GOVERNMENT AND SOCIETY

In July 1991 the National Assembly adopted a new constitution establishing a parliamentary government and guaranteeing direct presidential elections, separation of powers, and freedom of speech, press, conscience, and religion. New laws allowed for the return of the properties that had been confiscated by the previous communist governments. Other laws aimed at meeting EU standards were passed, including those regarding competition, foreign investment, intellectual property rights, and a commercial code.

Under the terms of the 1991 constitution, Bulgaria is a parliamentary republic, i.e., the prime minister is elected by the majority party (or coalition of parties) in the National Assembly (parliament). The president, who is elected for a five-year term, is the head of state. The president schedules national referenda and elections for the National Assembly, serves diplomatic and other functions, and promulgates and can veto laws.

According to the constitution, the nation's governing body, the Council of Ministers, is proposed by the president in consultation with the various groups of the National Assembly and with the majority party's candidate for prime minister. Comprising the prime minister, deputy prime ministers, and ministers, the Council of Ministers is charged with coordinating and overseeing the implementation of policies on both domestic and foreign issues in accordance with the constitution and laws of Bulgaria.

The National Assembly, a unicameral, representative body composed of 240 members, constitutes the legislative branch of the government. It passes and amends laws, ratifies treaties, levies taxes, and retains the power to pass a motion of no confidence in the Council of Ministers or the prime minister, thereby compelling the resignation of the council. Members of the National Assembly serve four-year terms.

LOCAL GOVERNMENT

Township councils embody state power at the local government level. The members of the township councils are elected by the inhabitants of the township to four-year terms. Executive power at the level of local government lies with the

Political map of Bulgaria. Encyclopaedia Britannica, Inc.

elected mayor of a township. Between the township and state levels of government is the oblast, or province, government.

JUSTICE

The court system consists of the Supreme Court of Cassation, the Supreme Administrative Court, local courts, courts of appeal, and military courts. The constitution provides that specialized courts may also be established. At the head of the prosecutorial structure is the prosecutor general.

The High Judicial Council, consisting of 25 members, appoints judges, prosecutors, and investigators. The members of this council are appointed by the National Assembly and judicial authorities. The Constitutional Court, composed of 12 justices (each of whom serves a nine-year term), is charged with interpreting the constitution and ruling on the legality of measures passed by the National Assembly. The parliament, the

president, and the supreme courts each appoint four justices.

POLITICAL PROCESS

Prior to the overthrow of the veteran Communist Party leader Todor Zhivkov in November 1989, the ruling party had been the Bulgarian Communist Party (Bŭlgarska Komunisticheska Partiya; BKP), founded in 1891 as the Bulgarian Social Democratic Party. After Zhivkov's fall, the party gave up its guaranteed right to rule, adopted a new manifesto, streamlined its leadership, and changed its name to the Bulgarian Socialist Party (BSP). Despite these reforms, the opposition Union of Democratic Forces (UDF) won leadership of the Bulgarian government by a small margin over the BSP in elections held in 1991 and 1997. The National Movement for Simeon II (NDSV), a new party centred on the former king of Bulgaria (but not seeking restoration of the crown), controlled the

TODOR ZHIVKOV

Todor Zhivkov (born Todor Khristov Zhivkov; September 7, 1911, Pravets, near Botevgrad, Bulgaria—died August 5, 1998, Sofia, Bulgaria) was the first secretary of the ruling Bulgarian Communist Party's Central Committee (1954–89) and president of Bulgaria (1971–89). He led Bulgaria for 35 years and was the longest-serving leader in any of the Soviet-bloc nations of eastern Europe.

The son of poor peasants, Zhivkov rose in the Communist Party and during World War II helped organize the resistance movement known as the People's Liberation Insurgent Army. After the war and the institution of a Soviet-sponsored communist government in Bulgaria, Zhivkov held increasingly important posts, including the command of the People's Militia, which arrested thousands of political opponents. In March 1954 he was made first secretary of the Central Committee—the youngest leader of any nation in the Soviet bloc—and, as a protégé of the Soviet leader Nikita S. Khrushchev, emerged as the strongman in the internal party struggles that followed.

From 1962 to 1971 Zhivkov served as premier of Bulgaria and in the latter year was elected president of the State Council formed by Bulgaria's new constitution. In 1965 he survived an attempted coup d'état by dissident party members and military officers—the first ever within a communist regime. Zhivkov hewed closely to the Soviet line in both domestic and foreign affairs. He collectivized his country's agriculture, firmly repressed internal dissent, and cultivated close ties with Khrushchev's successor, Leonid Brezhnev.

In 1989 when communist governments across eastern Europe began to collapse, a coup arose within his own party, and Zhivkov resigned all his posts in November of that year. He was subsequently expelled from the Bulgarian Communist Party in December and was placed under arrest in January 1990. Zhivkov was convicted of embezzlement in 1992 and sentenced to seven years' imprisonment. He was allowed to serve his sentence under house arrest on account of his failing health, and in 1998 he was reinstated as a member of the Communist Party's successor organization, the Socialist Party.

government from 2001 to 2005, after which a coalition headed by the BSP took power. In 2009, a new populist centre-right party, Citizens for the European Development of Bulgaria (Grazhdani za Evropeisko Razvitie Balgariya; GERB) swept into power.

Scores of minor political parties and other organizations, including labour, religious, environmental, and ethnic groups, were created in the early 1990s and each gravitated toward one of the two main parties. Notable among the other political parties was the Movement for Rights and Freedoms, backed mainly by ethnic Turks.

SECURITY

The president is the commander in chief of the Bulgarian armed forces, whose main defense capabilities lie in a ground force, an air force, and a navy. With the demise of the Warsaw Treaty Organization (Warsaw Pact) in 1991, Bulgaria assumed responsibility for its own defense policies. A radical military reform program was implemented to meet the requirements for accession to the North Atlantic Treaty Organization (NATO) in 2004. The military and the police are under civilian control. The streamlining of the armed forces has resulted in considerable downsizing.

HEALTH AND WELFARE

Before World War II a rather developed system of welfare and medical insurance existed in the country. With the establishment of the communist regime, social and medical insurance were abolished, medical care was entirely nationalized and offered at no cost, and all social funds were absorbed by the state budget. However, in spite of the highly educated medical personnel, the quality of medical care deteriorated considerably owing to organizational chaos.

Reforms in medical care and social welfare followed the fall of communism but did not gain momentum until the late 1990s. Free medical care remains, but a wider range of options is now available because of the reintroduction of medical insurance and the return of private medical practice.

Social welfare laws reestablished funding for social concerns. Separate from, though for a time supported by, the state budget, these funds are governed by a special National Social Insurance Institute. Its moneys derive from social and retirement insurance and health insurance payments from employers, as well as nontax revenues, loans, and additional voluntary payments by the insured. They provide coverage for illness, work-related injuries, maternity compensation, retirement, and death.

HOUSING

With the establishment of the communist regime after World War II, a vast number of properties, including apartments and houses, were nationalized, though, owing to a strong traditional desire among the population to live in private homes, private ownership of houses was permitted within narrow limits and was often carried out surreptitiously. Rapid urbanization led to a severe and protracted housing shortage.

After 1990 a widespread restitution returned homes to many people. The restrictions imposed on the right of ownership were abolished, and a large number of renters of state-owned apartments were given the chance to buy them. Individual housing construction was also stimulated. As a result, by the turn of the century, most of the population lived in privately owned homes.

EDUCATION

Primary and secondary education are the responsibility of a hierarchy of educational councils. Higher education is governed by the Ministry of Public Education. Education is free at all levels, and an eight-year elementary program is obligatory for children. Since 1959 general education has included polytechnical subjects and vocational training.

"St. Clement of Ohrid" University of Sofia (founded in 1888 as the Sofia Higher Institute and named for the 9th-century Christian scholar) is the oldest body of higher learning in Bulgaria and was the only university until 1971, when teacher-training institutes in Plovdiv and Veliko Tŭrnovo were elevated to university status. Among the universities licensed at the end of the century are the American University in Blagoevgrad and the New Bulgarian University in Sofia. There are numerous technical institutes as well as schools for the arts.

CHAPTER 4

BULGARIAN CULTURAL LIFE

Contemporary Bulgarian culture is a lively blend of millennium-old folk traditions and a more formal culture that played a vital role in the emergence of national consciousness under Ottoman rule and in the development of a modern state.

Because Bulgaria's population is largely homogeneous, the degree of cultural variation even at the regional level is small. The state encourages cultural development at all levels of society and supports the dissemination of culture, particularly through schools, libraries, museums, publishing, and state radio and television. Bulgaria's numerous theatre troupes, opera companies, and orchestras began fusing together into larger, more competitive units in the 1990s.

DAILY LIFE AND SOCIAL CUSTOMS

From 1946 until 1990 daily life in Bulgaria was outwardly dominated by the socialist political system. A network of mass organization, controlled by the state and the Communist Party, attempted to penetrate every sphere of private life. The state sought to inculcate (habitually instill) a new mode of thinking and manner of action based above all on the need for and benefit of social labour. Beneath the surface, however, daily life long has been dominated by a much older tradition and cultural legacy. For example, the Bulgarian family kept many of its traditional forms of organization. Many households consist of an extended family comprising parents and one of their married sons—usually the youngest—or daughters.

Participants in the Bulgarian kouker festival, a traditional ritual held to ward off evil spirits and bring good fortune during the year. Martin Dimitrov/E+/Getty Images

Under the communist government, religious functions were declared entirely separate from state functions. Indeed, the postwar constitution prohibited the use of religion or religious organizations for political purposes. After 1990 the Bulgarian constitution provided for religious freedom, but in practice this freedom was granted only to mainstream, registered religions. The practice of non-registered religions was prohibited.

FESTIVALS

Bulgarians participate in many festivals, including the International Folklore Festival, held early in August in Burgas; the Varna Summer International Festival, primarily a music festival, held in July; and Sofia Musical Weeks, a springtime celebration of classical music. Historical plays are popular, particularly when staged outdoors in summer against the backdrop of important monuments or buildings associated with events in the country's history. Local festivals provide an opportunity for new musical and literary works to be performed.

The blossoming of the roses in the Karlovo and Kazanlŭk valleys is celebrated through May and June; the oil-bearing roses are collected for the production of attar of roses, an essential oil distilled from fresh petals that is exported worldwide.

THE ARTS

The early impetus of Bulgarian traditions in the arts was cut short by the Ottoman occupation in the 14th century, and many early masterpieces were destroyed. Native artistic life emerged again in Bulgaria during the national revival in the 19th century. Among the most influential works were the secular and realist paintings of Zahari Zograph in the first half of the century and Hristo Tsokev in the second half. At the end of the 19th century and beginning of the 20th century, Bulgarian painters such as Anton Mitov and the Czech-born Ivan Mrkvichka produced memorable works, many of them depicting the daily life of the Bulgarian people.

In the early decades of the 20th century, further development of both style and subject matter took place, and the foundations were laid for later artists such as Vladimir Dimitrov, an extremely gifted painter specializing in the rural scenes of his native country; Tsanko Lavrenov, a noted graphic artist and art critic who also painted scenes of old Bulgarian towns; Zlatyo Boyadjiev, noted for his village portraits; and Ilya Petrov, who painted scenes and themes from Bulgarian history. After World War II, Socialist Realism dominated Bulgarian artistic circles. Its influence was seen in the broad historical themes that were adopted by artists in genres ranging from cartoons to still-life paintings and regional landscapes. At the beginning of the 21st century, the best-known contemporary Bulgarian artist was Christo, an environmental sculptor known for wrapping famous structures, such as the Pont Neuf in Paris and

The Pont Neuf in Paris, re-envisioned by the Bulgarian artist Christo, in 1985. Michel Baret/Gamma-Rapho/Getty Images

the Reichstag in Berlin, in fabric and plastic.

The first performances of Bulgarian classical music date from the 1890s, and the earliest Bulgarian opera, by Emanuil Manolov, was performed in 1900. He, along with other Bulgarian composers, concentrated on solo and choral vocal works. Between World War I and World War II, several symphonies and works for ballet, in addition to choral and opera works, were created by such composers as Lyubomir Pipkov, Petko Stainov, and Pancho Vladigerov. Bulgarian composers in the second half of the 20th century experimented with new tonality in vocal and instrumental music. Recordings and concert tours abroad won much wider audiences for traditional Bulgarian vocal music.

Opera remains popular, and Bulgaria has produced many world-class performers, including bass singers Boris Christoff and Nikolai Ghiaurov. Pianist Milcho Leviev, saxophonist Yuri Yunakov, and clarinetist Ivo Papazov gained acclaim for their blending of American jazz with traditional Bulgarian folk music. In the 1990s the Bulgarian State Radio and Television Female Vocal Choir achieved international stardom for the recording *Le Mystère des voix bulgares*, a collection of folk tunes sung a cappella in a style marked by strong dissonances and lack of vibrato.

The Bulgarian theatre is also a popular source of entertainment. World classics and modern foreign dramas are typically produced, as well as both modern and traditional Bulgarian plays, including those by Ivan Vazov and poet Peyo Yavorov (pseudonym of Peyo Kracholov).

Bulgaria's literary tradition can be traced to the 9th century, when Saints Cyril and Methodius created an alphabet for Old Bulgarian, which is the basis of the Old Church Slavonic language. They translated most of the Old and New Testament into it and used it to write some original theological treatises. Both the Cyrillic and Glagolitic alphabets were in early use. During Ottoman domination, literature was preserved only in the monasteries and churches. With the national revival in the 19th century, Bulgarian literature flowered once more and was used as a spiritual means of supporting the country's liberation.

At the end of the 19th century and again in the period between the two world wars, native authors attempted to fit the Bulgarian literary tradition into the European system of standards.

Perhaps the most important work during the national revival was Vazov's *Pod igoto* (1893; *Under the Yoke*, 1894), which detailed Bulgarian concerns under Ottoman rule and the events of the 1876 uprising. The writings of Vazov, who worked in a multitude of genres, served to define much of the Bulgarian character and influenced generations of Bulgarian writers. These included poets such as Petko Slaveykov, Peyo Yavorov, and Dimcho Debelyanov, as well as such belletrists as Aleko Konstantinov, Yordan Yovkov, and Elin Pelin. Among those writers who gained fame in the second half of the 20th century were poet Atanas Slavov, novelist and playwright Yordan Radichkov, and Blaga Dimitrova, a poet and novelist who served briefly as the vice president of Bulgaria. More-contemporary Bulgarian writers of note include Maria Stankova, Emil Andreev, Georgi Tenev, and Milen Ruskov.

Bulgaria's film industry expanded considerably following World War II, but it nearly collapsed in the mid-1990s. Bulgarian audiences take interest in both domestic and foreign films, and the country's feature and documentary films have been widely exported. Animated cartoons also are popular. Many of the motion pictures were produced at the state-run Boyana Film Studios near Sofia. The successor to that historic institution, the Nu Boyana Film Studios, on the outskirts of Sofia, now draws filmmakers from all over the world to its facilities. Sofia also holds an annual international film festival.

PETKO RACHEV SLAVEYKOV

The writer Petko Slaveykov (born November 17, 1827, Turnovo, Bulgaria—died July 1, 1895, Sofia, Bulgaria) helped to enrich Bulgarian literature by establishing a modern literary language and introducing contemporary ideas from other European countries. Slaveykov became an itinerant schoolteacher at age 17. His early poems were lyrical and patriotic (*Smesena kitka* ["Mixed Bouquet"] and *Pesnopoyka* ["Songbook"], both 1852), and, by reestablishing the vernacular as a medium for literature (the language of his translation of the Bible in 1862 was based on Bulgarian dialects), he prepared for the flowering of native poetry. As a patriot and politician, he helped to shape resurgent Bulgaria, producing political pamphlets notorious for their outspokenness against Turkish oppression and against the spiritual domination of the Greek patriarchate.

In 1863 Slaveykov moved to Istanbul, where he contributed to Bulgarian émigré reviews and edited satirical and political periodicals. After Bulgaria's liberation (1878) he became an active politician, both as president of the constituent assembly and as cofounder of the Democratic Party. Following the 1881 coup d'état, Slaveykov went to Plovdiv, then still under Turkish rule, and there edited the newspaper *Nezavisimost* ("Independence"). Pencho Petkov Slaveykov, his son, was also a noted writer.

CULTURAL INSTITUTIONS

Bulgaria has thousands of libraries. Among its major state libraries are the Cyril and Methodius National Library and the Central Library of the Bulgarian Academy of Sciences, both in Sofia. There are also a few thousand *chitalishtes*, cultural centres similar to reading rooms, which are found in even the smallest villages.

Some of the most notable of the country's many museums are in Sofia: the National Archaeological Institute and Museum, the National History Museum, the National Art Gallery, the Museum of Socialist Art, and the National Ethnographic Museum. Other important archaeological museums are found in Plovdiv, Stara Zagora, Burgas, and Varna. The highest research institution in the country, the Bulgarian Academy of Sciences, is involved in international cooperative projects and has cultural agreements with other European countries.

SPORTS AND RECREATION

In international sports competition, Bulgarians have excelled in tennis, wrestling, boxing, and gymnastics, but the country's greatest repute may be in weight lifting. Through the 1980s Bulgaria produced many world and Olympic champions in the sport, to the credit of coach Ivan Abadjiev, who developed innovative training practices. Several

HRISTO STOICHKOV

The Bulgarian football (soccer) player Hristo Stoichkov (born February 8, 1966, Plovdiv, Bulgaria) was an explosive striker noted for his fierce competitiveness. Stoichkov began his soccer career early. By age 12 he was playing for Maritza Plovdiv in the Bulgarian second division, where his goal-scoring prowess earned him a contract with the powerful CSKA Sofia in 1984. The following year Stoichkov and five others received lifetime bans for fighting during a match. The bans were lifted 10 months later, however, after Bulgaria qualified for the 1986 World Cup. Stoichkov did not play for that World Cup team, but in 1987 he made the first of 60 appearances as a Bulgarian international. His professional career skyrocketed in 1989 when he tallied 38 goals for Sofia and shared the award for Europe's leading scorer.

In 1991 Stoichkov signed with FC Barcelona. That year he helped the team win its first of four consecutive Spanish league championships. In 1992 Barcelona won the European Cup. Two years later Stoichkov was named European Player of the Year. Known as "the Raging Bull" for his emotional intensity, Stoichkov was a huge fan favourite, though he often battled with the team's coach, Johan Cruyff. Many were stunned when Stoichkov shifted teams in the middle of the 1994–95 season, moving to Parma in the Italian first division. After playing there for one season, he returned to Barcelona and helped the team win the Spanish league championship in 1998. He subsequently played for a succession of teams, including several Major League Soccer teams in the United States.

Stoichkov was at his best during Bulgaria's remarkable 1994 World Cup run. In five previous appearances, Bulgaria had failed to gain a World Cup victory (10 losses, 6 ties), but after the fall of the communist regime in 1989, the country's best players were free to hone their talents against the world's finest in leagues in western Europe. To qualify for the tournament, Bulgaria defeated heavily favoured France. Bulgaria then qualified for the final 16 by beating Greece and Argentina in group play. Led by Stoichkov, Bulgaria made it to the semifinals, which included a quarterfinal victory over defending champion Germany. Only a hard-fought loss to Italy kept Bulgaria from reaching the finals. With his six goals, Stoichkov was the leading goal scorer of the tournament.

After his retirement from play in 2003, Stoichkov became a coach, and in 2004 he was named head of the Bulgarian national team. Poor results and frequent clashes with players, however, led to his resignation in 2007.

Bulgarian athletes have accomplished the rare feat of lifting more than three times their own body weight. Among them was Bulgarian-born Turkish champion Naim Suleymanoglu, who up until 1986 competed for Bulgaria.

Fans of football (soccer), the most popular sport in Bulgaria, were buoyed by the success of the national team in the 1994 World Cup, when it advanced to the semifinal match behind the leadership of forward Hristo Stoichkov. The premier league in Bulgaria has 16 teams, of which four play in Sofia: CSKA, Levski, Salvia, and Lokomotiv.

Bulgarian athletes have considerable facilities at their disposal, including Vasil Levski Stadium, Universiada Hall, Festivalna Hall, and Students' Sports Complex in Sofia and the Palace of Sport and Culture in Varna; many regional centres also have sports complexes for local use. The major sports event in the country is the National Spartakiad, which involves mass participation of teams, clubs, and individuals in athletics (track and field) and other activities. The Committee for Youth, Physical Education, and Sports is the main governmental body charged with sports administration in the country.

MEDIA AND PUBLISHING

Broadcasting is the responsibility of the Committee for Television and Radio. In addition to national and regional programs, Bulgarian Radio broadcasts in several languages to foreign countries. Bulgarian National Television produces a variety of programming, including news coverage and documentaries, sports broadcasts, and programs focusing on arts and education or aimed at children and youths or at visiting tourists. Since the end of 1989, mass media, including printed matter, have not been censored, and free media outlets (newspapers, radio stations, and private television channels) have flourished. In a one-year span, from 1999 to 2000, the number of radio and television stations doubled.

CHAPTER 5

BULGARIA: PAST AND PRESENT

Evidence of human habitation in the area of Bulgaria dates from sometime within the Middle Paleolithic Period (Old Stone Age; 100,000 to 40,000 BCE). Agricultural communities, though, appeared in the Neolithic Period (New Stone Age), and in the Bronze Age the lands were inhabited by Thracian tribes. The Thracians were eventually expelled or absorbed by Greek, Persian, and Roman colonies, but traces of their culture remain in their monuments devoted to horse worship and in the mummer (Bulgarian: *kuker*) tradition that still survives in southwestern Bulgaria.

In Roman times Bulgaria was divided between the provinces of Moesia (to the north of the Balkan Mountains) and Thrace (to the south of the Balkans) and was crossed by the main land route from the West to the Middle East. The ruins of Roman towns and settlements are numerous, and extensive sites have been excavated at Plovdiv in the southwest, Varna in the northeast, and other locations. Situated on the Black Sea, the ancient city of Nesebŭr, now a UNESCO World Heritage site, was the Thracian settlement of Mesembria for centuries before it became a Greek colony in the 6th century BCE.

THE BEGINNINGS OF MODERN BULGARIA

The story of the modern Bulgarian people begins with the Slavic invasions of the Balkan Peninsula in the 6th and 7th centuries CE, a time when Byzantium was absorbed in prolonged conflict with Persia and could not resist the incursions

NESEBŬR

Nesebŭr, known until 1934 as Mesembria, is a historic town and resort in eastern Bulgaria, located on the Black Sea coast. Nesebur is situated on an island connected to the mainland by a narrow strip of land. The Greek colony of Mesembria was founded on the site late in the 6th

Nesebŭr, Bulgaria. Wizzard

century BCE and thrived on the trade between Greece and Thrace. It was relatively unimportant during the Roman occupation but regained its former prosperity during Byzantine times. Nesebŭr's gradual decline under the Turks was accelerated by the development of the nearby port of Burgas after 1878.

Narrow, cobbled streets, stone and wooden houses, and trim courtyards sheltering fig trees and arbors are characteristic of Nesebur. The town also contains more than 40 churches, many of which are now in ruins. The oldest, the now-roofless Old Metropolitan Church, dates from the 6th century; the most recent is the late 12th-century New Metropolitan Church. Beach facilities for tourists have been developed on the mainland.

from the north. Ancient sources refer to two Slavic tribes north of the Danube at this time, the Slavenae and the Antae. Evidence suggests that the Slavenae, to the west, were the ancestors of the Serbs and Croats, while the Antae moved into the regions of Bulgaria, Macedonia, and northern Greece. The Slavic tribes tilled the soil or practiced a pastoral way of life and were organized in patriarchal communities.

The name Bulgaria comes from the Bulgars, a people who are still a matter of academic dispute with respect to their origin (Turkic or Indo-European) as well as to their influence on the ethnic mixture and the language of present-day Bulgaria. They are first mentioned under this name in the sources toward the end of the 5th century CE. Living at that time on the steppes to the north of the Black Sea, the Bulgar tribes were composed of skilled, warlike horsemen governed by khans (chiefs) and boyars (nobles).

The Bulgars were subdued by the Avars in the 6th century, but in 635 Khan Kubrat led a successful revolt and organized an independent tribal confederation known as Great Bulgaria. After Kubrat's death in 642, the Bulgars were attacked by the Khazars and dispersed. According to Byzantine sources, the Bulgars split into five groups, each under one of Kubrat's sons. One of these sons, Asparukh (or Isperikh), moved into Bessarabia (between the Dniester and Prut rivers) and then crossed to the south of the Danube, where his people conquered or expelled the Slavic tribes living north of the Balkan Mountains. The Byzantine emperor Constantine IV led an army against the Bulgars but was defeated, and in 681 Byzantium recognized by treaty Bulgar control of the region between the Balkans and the Danube. This is considered to be the starting point of the Bulgarian state.

THE FIRST BULGARIAN EMPIRE

Asparukh and his successors established their court, which they built of stone, at Pliska, northeast of modern Shumen, and a religious centre at nearby Madara. Archaeological evidence suggests that the Bulgars kept their settlements distinct from those of the Slavs, from whom they accepted tribute. They maintained a mixed pastoral and agricultural economy, although much of their wealth continued to be acquired through warfare. Asparukh's successor, Tervel (701–718), helped to restore Emperor Justinian II to the Byzantine throne and was rewarded with the title "caesar."

On the whole, however, relations with Byzantium were hostile, and the 8th century was marked by a long series of raids and larger campaigns in which the Byzantine forces were usually victorious. Bulgaria recovered under Khan Krum (reigned 803–814), who, after annihilating an imperial army, took the skull of Emperor Nicephorus I, lined it with silver, and made it into a drinking cup. Under Krum's successors Bulgaria enjoyed an extended period of peace with Byzantium and expanded its control over Macedonia and parts of what are now Serbia and Croatia.

THE SPREAD OF CHRISTIANITY

Internally, the 8th and 9th centuries saw the gradual assimilation of the Bulgars by the Slavic majority. There are almost no sources that describe this process, but it was certainly facilitated by the spread of Christianity, which provided a new basis for a common culture. Boris I of Bulgaria (852–889) was baptized a Christian in 864, at a time when the conflict between the Roman church and the Eastern church in Constantinople was becoming more open and intense. Although Boris's baptism was into the Eastern church, he subsequently wavered between Rome and Constantinople until the latter was persuaded to grant de facto autonomy to Bulgaria in church affairs.

The spread of Christianity was facilitated by the work of Saints Cyril and Methodius, who had invented an alphabet in which to write the Slavic language

SAINTS CYRIL AND METHODIUS

The outstanding scholars, theologians, and linguists Cyril (born c. 827, Thessalonica, Macedonia —died February 14, 869, Rome) and Methodius (born c. 815, Thessalonica—died April 6, 884, Moravia; feast day for both, Western Church February 14; Eastern Church May 11) were brothers who for christianizing the Danubian Slavs and for influencing the religious and cultural development of all Slavic peoples received the title "the apostles of the Slavs." They were honoured by Pope John Paul II in his 1985 encyclical Slavorum Apostoli.

In 860, Cyril (originally named Constantine), who had gone on a mission to the Arabs and been professor of philosophy at the patriarchal school in Constantinople, worked with Methodius, the abbot of a Greek monastery, for the conversion of the Khazars northeast of the Black Sea. In 862, when Prince Rostislav of Great Moravia asked Constantinople for missionaries, the emperor Michael III and the patriarch Photius named Cyril and Methodius. In 863, they started their work among the Slavs, using Slavonic in the liturgy. They translated the Holy Scriptures into the language later known as Old Church Slavonic (or Old Bulgarian) and invented a Slavic alphabet based on Greek characters that in its final Cyrillic form is still in use as the alphabet for modern Russian and a number of other Slavic languages.

The brothers accepted Pope St. Nicholas I's invitation to Rome (867) to explain their conflict with the German archbishop of Salzburg and bishop of Passau, who claimed control of the same Slavic territory and who wanted to enforce the exclusive use of the Latin liturgy. Cyril and Methodius arrived in Rome (868), where the new pope, Adrian II, took their side, formally authorizing the use of the Slavic liturgy. When Cyril died, Adrian sent Methodius back to the Slavs as his legate and archbishop of Sirmium.

Methodius's ecclesiastical province included all of Moravia. When Rostislav's nephew and successor, Svatopluk, failed to support Methodius, he was tried in 870 by the German clergy, brutally treated, and jailed until liberated by the intervention of Pope John VIII. In 880 Methodius was again summoned to Rome about the Slavic liturgy, obtaining once more papal approval of his use of the vernacular.

When Methodius's suffragan bishop, Wiching, continued to make trouble, Methodius tried to strengthen his position in the Eastern Church by visiting Constantinople in 882. After Methodius's death, Pope Stephen V forbade the use of the Slavonic liturgy; and Wiching, as successor, forced the disciples of Cyril and Methodius into exile. The posthumous influence of Cyril and Methodius reached distant Kiev in Russia and left traces among the Slavs of Croatia, Bohemia, and Poland. Soon canonized by the Eastern church, they were celebrated by the Roman Catholic church in 1880.

(known as Old Church Slavonic or Old Bulgarian) and almost completed the translation of the Bible (most parts of both the Old and the New Testament) into the vernacular of the land. They also developed a Slavonic liturgy in Moravia. When Moravia committed to Rome and expelled the disciples of Cyril and Methodius, many of them resettled in Bulgaria, where they were welcomed by Boris and undertook the translation of church books and the training of priests. St. Clement and St. Naum are credited with preparing more than 3,000 priests at the religious educational centre (in effect the first Slavic university) they established on the shores of Lake Ohrid (Okhrid) in Macedonia.

Bulgaria's conversion had a political dimension, for it contributed both to the growth of central authority and to the merging of Bulgars and Slavs into a unified Bulgarian people. Boris adopted Byzantine political conceptions, referring to himself as ruler "by the grace of God," and the new religion provided justification for suppressing those boyars of Bulgar origin who clung to paganism and the political and social order with which it was linked. In 889 Boris, whose faith apparently was deep and genuine, abdicated to enter a monastery. When his eldest son, Vladimir, fell under the influence of the old boyars and attempted to reestablish paganism, Boris led a coup that overthrew him. After Vladimir was deposed and blinded, Boris convened a council that confirmed Christianity as the religion of the state and moved the administrative capital from Pliska to the Slavic town of Preslav (now known as Veliki Preslav). The council conferred the throne on Boris's third son, Simeon, and Boris retired permanently to monastic life.

REIGN OF SIMEON I

The reign of Simeon I (893–927) marked the high point of the first medieval Bulgarian state. Educated in Constantinople and imbued with great respect for the arts and Greek culture, Simeon encouraged the building of palaces and churches, the spread of monastic communities, and the translation of Greek books into Slavonic. Preslav was made into a magnificent capital that observers described as rivaling Constantinople. The artisans of its commercial quarter specialized in ceramics, stone, glass, wood, and metals, and Bulgarian tile work in the "Preslav style" surpassed its contemporary rivals and was eagerly imported by Byzantium and Kievan Rus.

Simeon was also a gifted military leader. His campaigns extended Bulgaria's borders, but he ultimately dissipated the country's strength in an effort to take Constantinople. When he died, he was master of the northern Balkans, including the Serbian lands, and styled himself "Tsar of the Bulgars and Autocrat of the Greeks," but his country was near exhaustion.

Under Simeon's successors, Bulgaria was beset by internal dissension provoked by the spread of Bogomilism (a dualist religious sect) and by assaults from Magyars, Pechenegs, the Rus, and Byzantines. The capital city was moved to Ohrid after the fall of Preslav in 971. In the campaign of 1014 the Byzantine emperor Basil II won a decisive victory over Tsar Samuel, after which he blinded as many as 15,000 prisoners taken in the battle and then released them. (For this act he became known as Basil Bulgaroctonus, or "Basil, Slayer of the Bulgars.") The shock of seeing his blinded army is said to have caused Samuel's death. Bulgaria lost its independence in 1018 and remained subject to Byzantium for more than a century and a half, until 1185.

THE SECOND BULGARIAN EMPIRE

With the collapse of the first Bulgarian state, the Bulgarian church fell under the domination of Greek ecclesiastics who took control of the see of Ohrid and attempted to replace the Bulgarian Slavic liturgy with a Greek liturgy. Bulgarian culture was by this time too deeply rooted to be easily changed, and the Byzantine Empire, beset by the attacks of the Seljuq Turks and the disturbances of the Crusaders, lacked the power to support a more forcible Hellenization.

In 1185 the brothers Ivan and Peter Asen of Tŭrnovo launched a revolt to throw off Byzantine sovereignty. The Asen brothers defeated the Byzantines and forced Constantinople to recognize Bulgarian independence. Their brother and successor, Kaloyan (reigned 1197–1207), briefly accepted the supremacy of Rome in church affairs and received a royal crown from the pope. But when Baldwin I, first Latin emperor of Constantinople, refused him recognition and declared war on Bulgaria (claiming all its territory by virtue of succession of the Byzantines), Kaloyan had a change of heart. He defeated Baldwin and afterward reverted to Orthodoxy.

The second Bulgarian empire, with its centre at Tŭrnovo, reached its height during the reign of Tsar Ivan Asen II

IVAN ASEN I

The tsar of the second Bulgarian empire from 1186 to 1196, Ivan Asen I (also called Asen I; died 1196) ruled during one of the most brilliant periods of the restored Bulgarian nation. He and his brother Peter II were founders of the Asen dynasty, which survived until the latter half of the 13th century.

Asen was a descendant of landowners and boyars from Turnovo whose family name was Belgun. In 1186, after a violent dispute with the Byzantine emperor Isaac II Angelus, Asen and Peter led a popular rising of Vlachs and Bulgars and proclaimed their independence from the Byzantines. Asen was crowned tsar as Ivan Asen I at Turnovo, and Peter became ruler of the eastern half of the kingdom, with his residence at Preslav (now Veliki Preslav). The brothers invaded Thrace but were defeated, withdrew to the north, and, in alliance with the Kumans, conquered northern Bulgaria. In 1187 they checked the Byzantine army in Thrace; and, in the armistice that followed, their younger brother Kaloyan was sent as hostage to Constantinople (now Istanbul). He escaped, however, and war broke out, to continue intermittently until the Byzantine forces were thoroughly defeated in 1196. Later in that year, Ivan Asen was killed by one of his boyars, Ivanko, who seized power at Turnovo but soon had to seek refuge in Constantinople. Asen's brother Peter ascended the throne as Peter II but was killed by the boyars in 1197. Kaloyan was then crowned tsar, reigning from 1197 to 1207.

(1218–41). Bulgaria was then the leading power in the Balkans, holding sway over Albania, Epirus, Macedonia, and Western Thrace. During this period the first Bulgarian coinage appeared, and in 1235 the head of the Bulgarian church received the title of patriarch.

The successors of Ivan Asen II, however, could not match his ability. Moreover, Bulgaria was beset by Mongol attacks from the north and by internal upheavals brought on by the growing burdens placed on the peasantry by the powerful nobles. The great peasant revolt of 1277–80 briefly allowed the swineherd Ivaylo to occupy the royal throne at Tŭrnovo until he was defeated with the aid of the Byzantines. The Asen dynasty died out in 1280 and was followed by the houses of Terter and Shishman, neither of which was very successful in restoring central authority.

The declining state reached its nadir in 1330 when Tsar Mikhail Shishman was defeated and slain by the Serbs at the Battle of Velbuzhd (modern Kyustendil). Bulgaria lost its Macedonian lands to the Serbian empire of Stefan Dušan, which then became the dominant Balkan power for the next four decades. Bulgaria appeared to be on the point of disintegration into feudal states when the invasions of the Ottoman Turks began.

OTTOMAN RULE

The Ottoman Turks first entered the Balkans as mercenaries of Byzantium in the 1340s, and they returned as invaders in their own right during the following decade. Between 1359 and 1362 Sultan Murad I wrested much of Thrace from Byzantine control and captured Adrianople (modern Edirne, Turkey), commanding the route up the Maritsa valley into the heart of the Bulgarian lands. In 1364 the Turks defeated a Crusade sent by Pope Urban V to regain Adrianople, but not before the Crusaders had committed so many atrocities against Orthodox Christians that many Bulgarians came to regard Turkish rule as preferable to alliance with the Roman Catholic West.

Although Ivan Shishman, Bulgaria's last medieval tsar, declared himself a vassal of Murad in 1371, the Ottomans continued to seek complete domination. Sofia, in the west, was seized in 1382, and Shumen, in the east, fell in 1388. A year later the defeat of the Serbs at the Battle of Kosovo sealed the fate of the entire Balkan Peninsula. In 1393, after a three-month siege, Tŭrnovo was taken and burned. Ivan Shishman allegedly died in Turkish captivity three years later. With the capture of a rump Bulgarian kingdom centred at Bdin (Vidin) in 1396, the last remnant of Bulgarian independence disappeared.

THE "TURKISH YOKE"

The five centuries from 1396 to 1878, known as the era of the "Turkish yoke," are traditionally seen as a period of darkness and suffering. Both national and ecclesiastical independence were lost.

The Bulgarian nobility was destroyed—its members either perished, fled, or accepted Islam and Turkicization—and the peasantry was enserfed to Turkish masters. The "blood tax" took a periodic levy of male children for conversion to Islam and service in the Janissary Corps of the Ottoman army.

The picture was not entirely negative, however. Once completed, the Turkish conquest included Bulgaria in a "Pax Ottomanica" that was a marked contrast to the preceding centuries of war and conflict. While Ottoman power was growing or at its height, it provided an acceptable way of life for the Bulgarian population. It was only when the empire was in its decline and unable to control the depredations of local officials or maintain reasonable order that the Bulgarians found Ottoman rule unbearable.

Bulgaria did not change radically in its religious or ethnic composition during the Ottoman period, for the Turks did not forcibly attempt to populate Bulgaria with Turks or to convert all Bulgarians to Islam. With the exception of the people of the Rhodope Mountains who were converted (and thereafter were called Pomaks) and some Catholic communities based in the northwest, the Bulgarian population remained mainly within the Orthodox church. Although Turkish administrators were established in the towns and countryside, Turkish peasants did not settle in Bulgaria in large numbers, and those who did immigrate were concentrated in the southern and eastern parts of the country and in some

JANISSARY CORPS

The elite group of troops called the Janissary Corps (Janissary also spelled Janizary, meaning "new soldier," or "troop") was part of the standing army of the Ottoman Empire from the late 14th century to 1826. Highly respected for their military prowess in the 15th and 16th centuries, the Janissaries became a powerful political force within the Ottoman state. The Janissary corps was originally staffed by Christian youths from the Balkan provinces who were converted to Islam on being drafted into the Ottoman service. Subject to strict rules, including celibacy, they were organized into three unequal divisions (*cemaat, bölükhalkı, segban*) and commanded by an *aga*. In the late 16th century the celibacy rule and other restrictions were relaxed, and by the early 18th century the original method of recruitment was abandoned. The Janissaries frequently engineered palace coups in the 17th and 18th centuries, and in the early 19th century they resisted the adoption of European reforms by the army. Their end came in June 1826 in the so-called Auspicious Incident. On learning of the formation of new, westernized troops, the Janissaries revolted. Sultan Mahmud II declared war on the rebels and, on their refusal to surrender, had cannon fire directed on their barracks. Most of the Janissaries were killed, and those who were taken prisoner were executed

of the valleys of Macedonia and Thrace. In the 15th and 16th centuries Turkish authorities permitted the immigration of Jewish refugees from the Christian West. While the majority were resettled in Constantinople and Salonika (now Thessaloníki, Greece), most Bulgarian towns acquired small Jewish communities in which newcomers mostly from Spain mixed with the already existent Jewish population.

OTTOMAN ADMINISTRATION

At the time Bulgaria was conquered, the Ottoman Empire was divided into two parts for administrative purposes. Bulgaria was part of the European section, called Rumelia, headed by a *beglerbeg* ("lord of lords") who resided in Sofia. As the empire expanded, this system proved inadequate, and in the 16th century it was replaced by territorial divisions called *vilayets* (provinces), further subdivided into *sanjaks* (districts). The borders of these units changed many times over the centuries. Bulgarian lands were assigned as fiefs to Turkish warriors, or *spahis*, who could impose taxes and other obligations on the subject population. Fiefs were also given to governors and other officeholders to provide their income, and lands in the form of *vakifs*—designated for the support of religious, educational, or charitable enterprises—were assigned to specific institutions. The *spahi* had no right of lordship or justice over the peasants living in his fief, and the Bulgarians frequently retained their traditional village administration and the customs of local law with regard to issues in which Turkish interests were not involved.

DECLINE OF THE OTTOMAN EMPIRE

The decline of the Ottoman Empire was marked by military defeats at the hands of Christian Europe and by a weakening of central authority. Both of these factors were significant for developments in Bulgaria. As the empire was thrown on the defensive, the Christian powers, first Austria and then Russia, saw the Bulgarian Christians as potential allies. Austrian propaganda helped to provoke an uprising at Tŭrnovo in 1598, and two others occurred in 1686 and 1688 after the Turks were forced to lift the Siege of Vienna. Under Catherine II (the Great), Russia began to assert itself as the protector of the Orthodox population of the Ottoman Empire, a claim that the Sublime Porte (as the government of the empire was called) was forced to recognize in the Treaty of Küçük Kaynarca in 1774.

Of greater significance, however, was the inability of the central government to keep the *spahis* and local officials under control. During the 17th and 18th centuries the *spahis* succeeded in converting their fiefs to *çiftliks*, hereditary estates that could not be regulated by the government. Owners of *çiftliks* were free to impose higher obligations on the peasantry or to drive them off the land. Turkish refugees from lands liberated by Christian states were frequently resettled on *çiftliks* in Bulgaria, increasing the pressure on the land and the burden on the peasantry. Occasionally, Turkish refugees formed marauding bands that could not be subdued by central authority and that exacted a heavy toll from their Christian victims.

One response among the Bulgarians was a strengthening of the *haiduk* tradition. The *haiduks* were guerrillas—some would say bandits—who took to the mountains to live by robbing the Turks. Although the *haiduks* lacked a strong sense of national consciousness, they kept alive a spirit of resistance and gave rise to legends that inspired later revolts.

THE NATIONAL REVIVAL

In the 19th century, growing Bulgarian discontent found direction in a movement of national revival that restored Bulgarian national consciousness and prepared the way for independence. The social foundation of this movement arose from the quickening of economic life in the late 18th and early 19th centuries and from the influence of the Enlightenment and the French Revolution, echoes of which, however faint, were heard among the people. A growing demand for cotton cloth and other products stimulated urban development. Many Bulgarian merchant houses were founded, and artisans in the towns began to form guild organizations (*esnafi*), which played an important role in sponsoring schools and providing scholarships for young Bulgarians to study abroad.

The monk Paisiy of the Khilendar Monastery on Mount Athos is recognized as the founder of the national revival. Little is known of his life except that he came from a merchant family in Bansko, a town in southwestern Bulgaria that maintained commercial relations with Vienna. In the 1760s Paisiy used texts preserved on Mount Athos to write his Slaveno-Bulgarian History. It reminded Bulgarians of the greatness of their past empires and called on them to forswear foreign customs and to take pride in their race and use their own language. Sofroniy, bishop of Vratsa, helped to spread Paisiy's influence. In his own writings he stressed the importance of education, without which his people would remain, in his words, "dumb animals."

SPREAD OF EDUCATION

The spread of education was in fact the centrepiece of the Bulgarian national revival. In 1835 Vasil Aprilov founded a Lancasterian school, based on the monitorial system of instruction, in Gabrovo. With the monk Neofit Rilski (Neophyte of Rila) as its teacher, it was the first school to teach in Bulgarian. Its work was facilitated by the appearance of a Bulgarian publishing industry and a small but influential periodical press. By the 1870s the guilds, town and village councils, and wealthy groups and individuals had founded some 2,000 schools in Bulgaria, each providing free education. The schools were supplemented with the *chitalishte*, or "reading room," an institution

MONITORIAL SYSTEM

The monitorial system, also called the Lancasterian system, is a teaching method in which the older or better scholars teach the younger or weaker pupils. In the system, as formulated by the English educator Joseph Lancaster, the superior students learned their lessons from the adult teacher in charge of the school and then transmitted their knowledge to the inferior students. By 1806 Lancaster's monitorial system for the education of poor children was the most widely emulated in the world. The method marked its success through economy (it reduced the number of adult teachers needed) and efficiency (it avoided wasting the time of children who waited for the attention of the principal teacher). Parents of the monitors, however, objected to the learning time their children were losing even though many of the monitors were paid a small weekly sum. It was found that some training of the monitors was necessary, and in about 1840 the movement began that replaced monitors with "pupil-teachers"—i.e., boys and girls who, at the age of 13, were apprenticed for a period of five years, during which time they learned the art of teaching while continuing their education under the head teacher of an elementary school. Some such programs developed into normal schools and training colleges, in which professional and academic education could be continued after the apprenticeship was completed. The rapid rise and decline of the monitorial system in the United States was an important factor in the establishment of free nondenominational school systems.

that first appeared in Svishtov in 1856 but soon spread throughout the country. More than just a small library, the *chitalishte* staged lectures, meetings, plays, concerts, debates, and social events. It was of immense importance for those who did not acquire formal education.

The influence of American Protestant missionaries in the 19th century, mainly in the western part of the country, led to the establishment in Samokov in 1856 of the American College, which was later enlarged and moved to Sofia. Many of the students at Robert College (founded 1861) in Istanbul, Turkey, were young Bulgarians who, after the liberation from Ottoman rule in 1878, took important political and economic positions in Bulgaria. Additionally, a considerable number of young Bulgarians were sent by their families or by sponsors to study in Russia, Austria-Hungary, Germany, and Switzerland.

CULTURAL MOVEMENT AGAINST GREEK INFLUENCE

The cultivation of Bulgarian national consciousness was initially a cultural rather than a political movement. Consequently, it was directed more against the "cultural yoke" of the Greeks than the "political yoke" of the Ottoman Empire. After the Turkish conquest of the Balkans, the Greek patriarch had become the representative of the *Rūm millet*, or "Roman nation," which comprised all the subject Christian nationalities.

Considered by some historians as the sui generis Bulgarian reformation, the desire to restore an independent Bulgarian church was a principal goal of the national "awakeners." Their efforts were rewarded in 1870 when the Sublime Porte issued a decree establishing an autocephalous Bulgarian church, headed by an exarch, with jurisdiction over the 15 dioceses of Bulgaria and Macedonia, in which more than two-thirds of the population defined itself as Bulgarian. Although the Greek patriarch refused to recognize this church and excommunicated its adherents, it became a leading force in Bulgarian life, representing Bulgarian interests at the Sublime Porte and sponsoring the further expansion of Bulgarian churches and schools. After the liberation of 1878, it provided a powerful means of maintaining Bulgarian national feeling in Macedonia.

NATIONAL REVOLUTION

The inability of the Sublime Porte to maintain order or to carry through its program of reform known as Tanzimat (1839–76), especially when contrasted with Greek and Serbian independence, engendered an explicitly revolutionary movement among the Bulgarians. Inspired by the *haiduk* tradition, Georgi Rakovski formed a Bulgarian legion on Serbian territory in 1862 to send armed bands to harass the Turks in Bulgaria. In 1866 Lyuben Karavelov and Vasil Levski created a Bulgarian Secret Central

Committee in Bucharest, Romania, to prepare for a national uprising. It dispatched "apostles" into Bulgaria to spread the message among the people. Levski, who worked for a democratic, independent republic, is considered to be the greatest hero of the revolutionary movement. He was captured during one of his organizing missions into Bulgaria and was hanged in Sofia in 1873.

Against the background of a wider Balkan crisis, the Bulgarian revolutionary committees laid plans for a nationwide uprising in 1876. The April Uprising broke out prematurely on April 20. (The date may also be counted as May 2, according to the New Style, or Gregorian, calendar, a reform of the Julian calendar that was proclaimed in 1582 by Pope Gregory XIII; Bulgaria began to use it informally in the late 19th century.) The rebellion was violently put down. The atrocities committed against the civilian population by irregular Turkish forces, including the massacre of 15,000 Bulgarians near Plovdiv, increased the Bulgarian desire for independence. They also outraged public opinion in Europe, where they became known as the Bulgarian Horrors. A conference of European statesmen proposed a series of reforms, and, when the sultan refused to implement them,

BULGARIAN HORRORS

The Bulgarian Horrors were the atrocities committed by the forces of the Ottoman Empire in subduing the Bulgarian rebellion of 1876. The name was given currency by the British statesman W.E. Gladstone. Publicity given to the atrocities, especially in Gladstone's pamphlet "The Bulgarian Horrors and the Question of the East" (1876), served to arouse public sympathy in Europe for the Bulgarians and other southern Slavs attempting to gain independence from the Ottoman Empire.

The Bulgarian revolt, part of the eastern crisis of 1875–78, began as an uprising that broke out in Bosnia and Herzegovina in 1875 and spread to Bulgaria the following spring. It was cruelly suppressed by the Turks, especially the poorly disciplined irregulars known as *bashi-bazouks*. About 15,000 persons were said to have been massacred at Philippopoli (now Plovdiv), and many villages and some monasteries were destroyed. Isolated risings in the mountains were crushed with equal severity.

Gladstone, then in opposition and contemplating retirement from the leadership of the Liberal Party, was moved by reports of the atrocities to write his pamphlet and to campaign vigorously against the foreign policy of the Conservative prime minister, Benjamin Disraeli, which favoured supporting the Ottoman Empire as a counterweight to Russia. Despite widespread public indignation, the European powers did little to alleviate the situation, and the climate of opinion changed after Russia attacked Turkey in 1877. The crisis ended with the Congress of Berlin in 1878, which created a small, autonomous principality of Bulgaria, still under the sovereignty of the Ottoman Empire and confined to territory north of the Balkan Mountains.

Russia declared war. In the ensuing campaign, Bulgarian volunteer forces fought alongside the Russian army, earning particular distinction in the epic battle for Shipka Pass.

TREATIES OF SAN STEFANO AND BERLIN

Advancing to the outskirts of Constantinople, the Russians dictated the Treaty of San Stefano, which called for a large independent Bulgaria within the territory of the exarchate of the Bulgarian Orthodox Church, stretching from the Danube River to the Aegean Sea and from the Vardar and Morava valleys to the Black Sea. The boundaries stated in the treaty, signed on February 19 (March 3), 1878, represented the fulfillment of Bulgaria's territorial aspirations and remained for generations the national ideal of the people. But the creation of a large Bulgaria, perceived as an outpost of Russian influence in the Balkans, was intolerable to Austria-Hungary and Britain, and they forced a revision of the Treaty of San Stefano a few months later at the Congress of Berlin.

The Treaty of Berlin, signed July 1 (July 13), 1878, created a much smaller Bulgarian principality, autonomous but under the sovereignty of the Sublime Porte, in the territory between the Danube and the Balkan Mountains and the region of Sofia, which soon became the capital. To the south the treaty created the autonomous province of Eastern Rumelia, subject to the sultan but with a Christian governor. Macedonia was returned entirely to the Ottoman Empire. The treaty also stipulated that Bulgaria would elect an assembly of notables to meet at Tŭrnovo to prepare a constitution and to choose a prince who would be confirmed by the powers.

The liberation of Bulgaria from Turkish rule also functioned as a land reform, for Russian occupation authorities and subsequent Bulgarian governments confiscated the Turkish estates and sold them in small parcels to the peasantry. Bulgaria began its independence as a nation of smallholders with one of the most egalitarian land distributions in Europe.

THE PRINCIPALITY

By the time the constituent assembly convened in Tŭrnovo in February 1879, conservative and liberal political tendencies had emerged and rapidly coalesced into parties. The Liberal Party, under Dragan Tsankov, Petko Karavelov (the brother of Lyuben Karavelov), and Petko Slaveikov, dominated the assembly and created a constitution that was one of the most democratic in Europe. It provided for a single National Assembly elected by universal male suffrage, guarantees of civil rights, and strict limits on the power of the prince.

POLITICAL DIVISIONS UNDER ALEXANDER OF BATTENBERG

The democratic character of the constitution was at variance with the views of Bulgaria's first prince, Alexander I of Battenberg (of both Austrian and Russian ancestry), and with those of the Russian advisers who played a large role in his court. The prince first formed a Conservative ministry, but he was forced by popular agitation to form a Liberal government under Tsankov. Tsankov's government undertook the construction of judicial and state apparatuses and put an end to the depredations of brigands who had remained active in the mountains after the war.

In Prince Alexander's estimation, however, the Liberals showed insufficient respect for the institution of monarchy. Moreover, Russia was concerned that the Liberals were starting to follow the same pro-Western tendencies as the Conservatives. As a result, Alexander dismissed the Liberal government in favour of a pro-Russian one led by Gen. Casimir Erenroth, a Finn in Russian service who had earlier been charged with setting up the Bulgarian army. Erenroth used rigged elections to select the Grand National Assembly, which agreed in 1881 to suspend the constitution and invest the prince with absolute power for seven years.

A period of dictatorship followed under the Russian generals Leonid N. Sobolev and Alexander V. Kaulbars. Prince Alexander, however, soon found his Russian allies harder to deal with than their Liberal predecessors. The popular sentiment against the Russian generals was growing too. In September 1883 Alexander compromised with his

opponents, dismissed the Russians, restored the constitution, and accepted a Conservative-Liberal coalition government, but the coalition was soon supplanted by an entirely Liberal government under Petko Karavelov.

Meanwhile, popular sentiment for unification with Bulgaria had been growing in Eastern Rumelia, and the restoration of the constitution provided the Eastern Rumelians with the stimulus to prepare for a seizure of power in Plovdiv. In September 1885, with the prior approval of Prince Alexander, they staged a bloodless coup d'état and declared the unification of the two states. Turkey did not resist, but Russia, incensed by such independence of action in its diplomatic sphere of influence, refused to approve, and Tsar Alexander III ordered the withdrawal of all Russian officers and advisers from the Bulgarian army.

In these circumstances, King Milan of Serbia, stating that the balance of power in the Balkans was endangered by Bulgarian unification, suddenly declared war. The Serbs advanced as far as Slivnitsa, where they were met and defeated by the untrained Bulgarian army under Prince Alexander's command. Bulgarian forces pursued the Serbs across the frontier but were stopped by the threat of Austrian intervention. Peace and the status quo were restored by the Treaty of Bucharest (February 19 [March 3], 1886) and the convention of Tophane (March 24 [April 5], 1886). Prince Alexander was appointed governor-general of Eastern Rumelia, and the Eastern Rumelian administrative and military forces were merged with those of Bulgaria.

Prince Alexander had little time to enjoy the fruits of his popular triumph. On August 9 (August 21), 1886, a group of Russophile conspirators and military officers whom Alexander had passed over for promotion seized the prince in his palace, forced him to sign a statement of abdication, transported him out of the country, and handed him over to the Russians at the Danube port of Reni. The conspiracy was countered, however, by Stefan Stambolov, president of the National Assembly, and by Lieut. Col. Sava Mutkurov, commander of the Plovdiv garrison, who took control of Sofia and recalled the prince. Alexander was not detained by the Russians, but he declared he would not remain in Bulgaria without Russian approval. When the tsar refused to give it, Alexander abdicated on August 26 (September 7), appointing a regency composed of Stambolov, Mutkurov, and Petko Karavelov.

The regency was successful in preserving order but had great difficulty in finding a new prince, for few wished to assume the throne in the face of Russian hostility. A willing candidate was at last found in the person of 26-year-old Prince Ferdinand of Saxe-Coburg-Gotha, a grandson of Louis-Philippe of France, who was then serving as an officer in the Austrian army. Ferdinand was elected prince by the Grand National Assembly in July 1887.

PRINCE FERDINAND'S RULE

Because Russia declared Ferdinand a usurper, Europe withheld recognition, the bishops of the Holy Synod would not pay him homage, and conspiracies flourished. However, Stambolov, as prime minister from 1887 to 1894, ruthlessly suppressed all opposition. Recognized as one of Europe's strongmen, he stabilized Bulgaria's international position, but his methods, which amounted to a virtual dictatorship, alienated much of the population. In 1894 Ferdinand unexpectedly made use of his constitutional right to dismiss Stambolov and replaced him with a government headed by a Conservative, Konstantin Stoilov. A year later the former prime minister was murdered in the street in Sofia.

The change of course in Sofia and the death of Tsar Alexander III facilitated a reconciliation between Bulgaria and Russia. Ferdinand gained international recognition as prince, and in 1896 Tsar Nicholas II became the godfather of Ferdinand's first son when he was baptized into the Orthodox faith.

BULGARIA AT THE END OF THE 19TH CENTURY

The first two decades following the reestablishment of the Bulgarian state were dominated by efforts at modernization in political, economic, and cultural spheres. The governments of Karavelov (1883–85), Stambolov (1887–94), and Stoilov worked to bring the country closer to Europe. As prince and later as tsar, Ferdinand also played an important role.

Sofia and other cities were modernized, railways were built, trade with European countries (especially Austria-Hungary and Germany) was rapidly developed, and laws encouraging local industry were passed. Special emphasis was put on education, and, by the turn of the century, illiteracy had practically vanished. The University of Sofia (1888) was opened, and large numbers of young Bulgarians were finding ways to study abroad, bringing back European culture and ideas. In the political sphere, parliamentary traditions were established mainly after the fashion of France and Belgium. Full reception of the Continental legal system was effected in the late 1880s and the 1890s, combining institutions from the Roman (French and Italian) and the Pandect (German) legislative systems.

This modernization exacerbated the social differences in a society that was used to being more egalitarian. The desire for reunification with the Bulgarian lands of the exarchate allowed for increases in military expenditures, which led to rising taxes. Internally, there was criticism of this growing bureaucracy and bouts of government corruption. Moreover, the shrinking of the Turkish market and the decline in world grain prices added to the economic problems of rural regions.

Following the restitution of Eastern Rumelia, differences arose among both the Conservatives and the Liberals, and new political parties were formed. In the 1890s two new leftist parties were created—the Bulgarian Social Democratic Party and the Agrarian Union (later Bulgarian National Union). While the first, led by schoolteacher Dimitŭr Blagoev, echoed to a great extent the spreading socialist ideas in Europe and Russia (Blagoev himself had studied in Russia), the Agrarian Union was somewhat unique. Established in 1899, it gained popularity among peasants as well as among educated people who maintained their roots in rural life. Its popularity was largely due to the charismatic leadership of Aleksandŭr Stamboliyski.

FOREIGN POLICY UNDER FERDINAND

The period from Stambolov's fall in 1894 to World War I is known as the era of Ferdinand's "personal regime." By encouraging the fragmentation of the political parties and by skillfully using his powers of patronage to manipulate the party chiefs, Ferdinand became the dominant political figure in the country. In 1908, in conjunction with the Austrian annexation of Bosnia and Herzegovina, he proclaimed the de jure independence of Bulgaria from the Sublime Porte and assumed the title of tsar. Three years later the Grand National Assembly amended the constitution to give him this title officially and to grant him the right to conclude treaties with foreign states without the consent of the National Assembly.

Macedonia constituted the principal objective of Ferdinand's diplomacy. On July 20 (August 2), 1903, the Internal Macedonian Revolutionary Organization (IMRO) initiated a revolt—known as the Ilinden (St. Elijah's Day) Uprising—the goal of which was to establish an independent Macedonian state. The revolt, however, was brutally suppressed, focusing attention yet again on the problems of Turkish misrule in Macedonia. In 1908 the revolution of the Young Turks led Balkan statesmen to believe that the time was fast approaching when Macedonia could be wrested from the empire. Greece and Serbia, however, laid claim to portions of Macedonia that Bulgarians regarded as rightfully theirs. It was the great mistake of Bulgarian diplomacy to organize a war against the Ottoman Empire without first clearly resolving these competing claims.

THE BALKAN WARS

In March 1911, against the background of increasing unrest in Macedonia, Ferdinand appointed a new government under Ivan Geshov to begin negotiations for an anti-Turkish alliance. In May 1912 Bulgaria signed a treaty with Serbia providing for military cooperation but leaving a large section of Macedonia as a contested zone, the fate of which would be determined after the war. A quickly made agreement with Greece also made no provision for the future distribution of territory. An arrangement between Greece and Serbia and verbal agreements with Montenegro completed the formation of the Balkan League. Montenegro declared war on the Ottoman Empire on September 25 (October 8), and the other Balkan states soon entered the conflict.

The successes of the Balkan League exceeded expectations. Bulgarian forces won major victories at Lozengrad (now Kırklareli) and Lüleburgaz and laid siege to Adrianople (now Edirne) and the Çatalca line of fortifications defending Constantinople, while the Greeks took Salonika (now Thessaloníki), and Serbian troops won a series of battles in Macedonia. The Ottoman Turks asked for an armistice, but Ferdinand insisted that the army attempt to capture Constantinople. When the assault on the Çatalca line failed, leaving the Bulgarian army in a weakened state, the tsar agreed to the armistice, and peace negotiations began in London.

On May 17 (May 30), 1913, the Ottoman Empire signed the Treaty of London, conceding all but a small strip of its European territory. But it proved impossible to divide the territory peacefully among the victors. Serbia and Greece insisted on retaining most of the Macedonian territory they had occupied, and Romania demanded compensation for its neutrality. When Geshov was not able to negotiate a compromise, he resigned in favour of Stoyan Danev, who reflected Ferdinand's desire for a military solution. On the night of June 16–17

Balkan Wars map. Encyclopaedia Britannica, Inc.

(June 29–30) Bulgarian forces began the Second Balkan War by launching a surprise assault on Greek and Serbian positions in Macedonia. As the Bulgarian attack was being repulsed, Romanian troops began an uncontested march toward Sofia from the north, and Turkey reoccupied the fortress of Adrianople.

By the Treaty of Bucharest, signed on July 28 (August 10), 1913, Romania took the rich lands of the southern Dobruja and the city of Silistra, while Serbia and Greece divided the larger part of Macedonia between them. From its gains

in the First Balkan War, Bulgaria retained only a small part of eastern Macedonia, the Pirin region, and a portion of eastern Thrace. This was poor compensation for the loss of the southern Dobruja and of the Bulgarian exarchate in Macedonia. Consequently, the desire to win back what had been lost was the main motivating factor in Bulgaria's diplomacy when World War I began.

WORLD WAR I

When World War I began, Bulgaria declared strict neutrality, but the tsar and a Germanophile government under Vasil Radoslavov encouraged both sides to bid for Bulgarian intervention. In this contest, the Central Powers (Austria-Hungary and the German Empire) could offer far more at the expense of Serbia, Greece, and, later, Romania than could the Triple Entente (an alliance of Great Britain, France, and Russia), which had to take the interests of its smaller allies into account. During the summer of 1915, when the military balance swung in Germany's favour, Bulgaria committed to the Central Powers and declared war on Serbia on October 1 (October 14). Some of the neutralist and pro-entente political figures objected, but none went as far as the Agrarian leader Stamboliyski, who threatened the tsar and issued a call for the troops to resist mobilization. For these acts he was arrested and condemned to life imprisonment.

By the autumn of 1918, approximately 900,000 Bulgarian men, nearly

40 percent of the male population, had been conscripted. The army suffered 300,000 casualties, including 100,000 killed, the most severe per capita losses of any country involved in the war. In the interior, bad weather and the absence of adult male labour cut grain production nearly in half, while those in the towns suffered from shortages of food and fuel and from runaway inflation. "Women's riots" for food began early in 1917 and continued to the end of the war. The revolutions in Russia and the hopes inspired by American intervention in the war and by U.S. Pres. Woodrow Wilson's Fourteen Points peace plan seemed to promise change for Bulgarians and further contributed to the breakdown of civilian order and military discipline. In June 1918 the replacement of the pro-German Radoslavov by Alexander Malinov, a leader of the parliamentary opposition, raised hopes for an end to the war, but instead frustration increased as Malinov yielded to Tsar Ferdinand's determination to fight on.

On September 15, 1918 (New Style), the Allied forces on the Macedonian front broke through the Bulgarian lines at Dobro Pole. The army dissolved, as many of the troops deserted to return home, and others began a march on Sofia to punish the tsar and party leaders responsible for the war. Ferdinand turned to Stamboliyski, releasing the Agrarian leader from prison in return for his promise to use his influence to restore order among the troops. Stamboliyski, however, joined the uprising and, at the village of Radomir, where rebel troops were encamped, proclaimed Bulgaria a republic. The Radomir Rebellion was short-lived, as the Agrarian-led assault on Sofia was repulsed by German and Macedonian forces that remained loyal to the tsar. But this provided only a temporary respite. The Bulgarian government asked the Allies for an armistice, which was signed on September 29. Four days later Tsar Ferdinand abdicated in favour of his son Boris III and left the country.

Bulgaria was punished for its part in World War I by the Treaty of Neuilly, which assigned the southern portion of the Dobruja region to Romania, a strip of western territory including Tsaribrod (now Dimitrovgrad) and Strumica to the Kingdom of Serbs, Croats, and Slovenes (subsequently called Yugoslavia), and the Aegean territories gained in the Balkan Wars to the Allies, who turned them over to Greece at the Conference of San Remo in 1920. Bulgaria also was disarmed and subjected to a heavy burden of reparations.

POSTWAR POLITICS AND GOVERNMENT

Defeat and the hardships of war broke the hold of Bulgaria's traditional parties on the government. In the first two postwar elections, the Agrarians, communists, and socialists together polled first 59 percent and then 65 percent of the ballots. These parties were not united, however, and a communist-led general strike in the winter of 1919–20 was ruthlessly put down by Stamboliyski, who became prime minister first in coalition with smaller conservative parties and then as head of an all-Agrarian cabinet.

PROGRAMS OF THE AGRARIAN UNION

The years from 1920 to 1923 represented a remarkable period in which the Agrarian Union sought to translate into reality the beliefs and ideas developed in its years in opposition. The Agrarian government introduced a progressive income tax and a land reform directed against the country's few large estates and against absentee ownership, sponsored the spread of cooperative organizations in agriculture and other branches of the economy, and undertook a massive expansion of the school system, providing for, among other things, free, obligatory secondary education. The Agrarians also introduced the practice of obligatory labour service, by which all young men were required to contribute a year's labour on state projects in lieu of military conscription. The Agrarian government, however, exhibited authoritarian characteristics, which disturbed the majority of the nation.

STAMBOLIYSKI'S FOREIGN POLICY

Stamboliyski abandoned the traditional Bulgarian goal of territorial expansion, which had required huge military budgets, maintaining a standing army and professional officer corps, and the patronage of the great powers. His policy aimed, above all, to cultivate good relations with the Kingdom of Serbs, Croats, and Slovenes by accepting the status quo in Macedonia.

Stamboliyski's policies alienated the old political leaders, the Military League (comprising active and reserve officers), and Tsar Boris's court. The rightist parties united in the National Alliance (later called Democratic Alliance) and planned to march on Sofia to wrest control of the country. On the left, the communists viewed the Agrarian government as their principal opponent. But the most dangerous enemies were the Military League and Internal Macedonian Revolutionary Organization (IMRO).

IMRO established effective control over the Pirin region and launched terrorist attacks across the border into Yugoslav and Greek Macedonia. It also assassinated several Agrarian leaders. Unable to rely on the Bulgarian military against the Macedonian terrorists, Stamboliyski turned to Yugoslavia (as the Kingdom of Serbs, Croats, and Slovenes was soon to be known): by signing the Treaty of Niš, he permitted Yugoslav forces to pursue the Macedonian guerrilla bands into Bulgarian territory.

This treaty, the pressures of dictatorial rule, and an overwhelming Agrarian election victory in early 1923 led Stamboliyski's opponents to plan a coup d'état. It was organized by the Military League, IMRO, and the old parties, and it probably had the support of Tsar Boris III.

When the coup was launched on the night of June 8–9, 1923, it took the Agrarian government by surprise. Stamboliyski was captured a few days later and brutally murdered, and a right-wing government under Aleksandŭr Tsankov took over.

COMMUNIST UPRISING

The Bulgarian communists, who had declared their neutrality when the coup occurred, were chastised by Moscow and directed to prepare an armed revolt against the Tsankov regime. The communists' September Uprising was ruthlessly suppressed and provided Tsankov with a pretext for outlawing the Bulgarian Communist Party in 1924, though the party would surface briefly again under another name and continued to operate underground for two decades.

The communists struck back in 1925 with a series of terrorist acts, culminating in an attempt to assassinate the tsar and leaders of the government by blowing up Sofia's Sveta Nedelya Cathedral during services. Although 123 people were killed and hundreds more wounded, the main targets escaped, and the government exacted brutal reprisals.

In the wake of the defeats suffered in 1923 and 1925, the communist leaders escaped abroad, finding positions in the Soviet Union or the Comintern (Communist International). One of them, Georgi Dimitrov, achieved international fame as the chief defendant in the Reichstag fire trial of 1933. Following Dimitrov's acquittal, Soviet leader Joseph Stalin had him appointed secretary-general of the Comintern, a position he held until that body was dissolved in 1943.

ATTEMPTS TO STABILIZE GOVERNMENT

After 1925 Bulgarian political life began a slow recovery. In January 1926 Tsankov yielded the premiership to the more moderate Andrei Liapchev. A gradual and qualified return to a free press and parliamentary politics marked his five-year tenure, although terrorist acts by IMRO continued and soured Bulgaria's relations with Yugoslavia and Greece. In 1931 a reconstituted opposition called the Popular Bloc, a coalition that included the moderate wing of the Agrarian Union, defeated the Democratic Alliance.

Coming to power during the Great Depression, the Popular Bloc government was unable to alleviate the dire economic situation and stem a rising tide of labour unrest. On the night of May 18–19, 1934, the Military League carried out a peaceful coup d'état that installed as prime minister Kimon Georgiev, a participant in the 1923 coup. Similar to Italian fascism, the ideology of the new regime was supplied by an elitist group called Zveno ("A Link in a Chain"), which drew its membership from intellectual, commercial, and military circles. Zveno advocated "national restoration" through an authoritarian, nonpartisan regime. The "divisive forces" associated with parliamentary politics were eliminated by the suspension of the constitution and the suppression of all political parties. A new assembly was created, composed of individuals without party affiliation and elected from approved government lists.

The new regime was able to suppress IMRO and restore the government's authority over Pirin Macedonia, but its political base was too narrow to allow it to consolidate power firmly. The real beneficiary of the 1934 coup was Tsar Boris III. By the end of 1935, he had filled the power vacuum. He used his own clique in the army to unseat and jail Georgiev, purged the Military League, and, by November 1935, installed a subservient government under Georgi Kyoseivanov. The relative weight of parliament was considerably diminished, and the government approximated a royal-military dictatorship, the form of government that had become prominent in eastern Europe.

WORLD WAR II

After World War II began, Bulgaria proclaimed neutrality. Tsar Boris, however, appointed a new government under a notorious Germanophile, Bogdan Filov, and moved steadily closer to the German orbit. This was especially the case after Germany and the Soviet Union, then allied by the German-Soviet Nonaggression Pact, forced Romania to restore the southern Dobruja to Bulgaria in August 1940.

BORIS'S ALLIANCE WITH GERMANY

The desire for territorial expansion at the expense of Yugoslavia and Greece and the expectation of a German victory led Boris to join the Axis on March 1, 1941. German troops used Bulgaria as a base from which to attack Yugoslavia and Greece. In return, Bulgarian forces were permitted to occupy Greek Thrace, Yugoslav Macedonia, and part of Serbia.

After the German invasion of the Soviet Union and the Japanese attack on the United States, Bulgaria yielded to German pressure to declare war on Great Britain and the United States, a move of only symbolic importance, but Tsar Boris avoided joining the war against the Soviet Union, fearing that this would lead to popular unrest. Bulgaria did not send troops to the front and was relatively untouched by military operations until the summer of 1943, when Allied bombers began to attack rail and industrial centres.

DEFENDING BULGARIAN JEWS

In 1941 anti-Semitic legislation was enacted in Bulgaria under German pressure to adopt something akin to the Nürnberg Laws. However, the legislation met with a wave of protest and was never strictly implemented. In early 1943 the government complied with German requests to secretly deport non-Bulgarian Jews from occupied territories that had not been incorporated into Bulgaria to the concentration camp at Treblinka (in Poland). The clandestine deportation of Jews from Bulgaria was also scheduled, for March 1943, but Dimitar Peshev, deputy speaker of the National

Assembly, managed to force the government to cancel it. Forty-three members of the majority backed a resolution in parliament in defense of Bulgarian Jews, a move supported by many from across the social strata. In late May, in spite of Nazi pressure, Tsar Boris canceled the deportation orders for Bulgaria's Jews.

BULGARIAN RESISTANCE TO THE AXIS ALLIANCE

Some attempts at forming a resistance were made by Agrarian leaders when Bulgaria joined the Axis. After Germany attacked the Soviet Union, however, the Bulgarian Communist Party took the initiative inside the country. Until the final stage of the war, resistance tactics emphasized sabotage and small-group operations. About 10,000 persons are estimated to have participated in or supported the resistance, making it the largest such movement among Germany's allies. Politically, the communists sought the cooperation of other opposition groups, and in August 1943 the Fatherland Front was formed, composed of communists, left-wing Agrarians, Zveno, socialists, and some independent political figures. The front's influence grew as the military situation of Germany deteriorated.

Many Bulgarians expected Tsar Boris to break with the German alliance when circumstances permitted. On August 28, 1943, however, just after a stormy encounter with Adolf Hitler at Berchtesgaden, Germany, the tsar suffered a fatal heart attack. Because his son and heir, Simeon II, was only six years old, Filov established a regency council headed by himself and appointed a new government under Dobri Bozhilov, which remained loyal to the German alliance. In May 1944, faced with the continuing German collapse and stern Allied threats that Germany's allies would be severely punished, Bozhilov resigned.

He was replaced by the right-wing Agrarian Ivan Bagrianov, who began secret negotiations for surrender with the Allies but at a snail's pace. At the end of August the sudden surrender of Romania, which brought Soviet troops to the Danube months before they had been expected, created panic in Sofia. When Bagrianov's attempt to proclaim Bulgarian neutrality was rejected as insufficient by both Britain and the Soviet Union, the prime minister resigned and was replaced by Kosta Muraviev of the Agrarian Union on September 2, 1944.

Three days later, aware that the new government was preparing to break with Germany, the Soviet Union declared war on Bulgaria and entered the country unopposed. Simultaneously, the Fatherland Front began preparations for a coup d'état. On September 8 Muraviev declared war against Germany; nonetheless, military forces organized by Zveno occupied key points in Sofia and toppled Muraviev's government in the name of the Fatherland Front. Kimon Georgiev of Zveno became the new prime minister and sought an immediate armistice with the Soviet command.

SIMEON SAXECOBURGGOTSKI

The last king of Bulgaria, who ruled as Simeon II (also known as Simeon Saxe-Coburg-Gotha or Simeon Coburgotski; born June 16, 1937, Sofia, Bulgaria), reigned as a child from 1943 to 1946. Much later, he served as the country's prime minister (2001–05).

On August 28, 1943, Simeon's father, Boris III, died under mysterious circumstances—the cause of death being reported variously as heart attack or poisoning—and the six-year-old crown prince ascended the throne, overseen by a three-man regency comprising Boris's brother Prince Cyril, former war minister Lieutenant General Nikolai Michov, and former premier Bogdan Filov. After Bulgaria quit the Axis Powers and was overrun by the Soviet Red Army, the regents were arrested, and on February 2, 1945, all three were executed as enemies of the state and as collaborators with the Germans. A second regency was established, but on September 8, 1946, the monarchy was voted out of existence, and Simeon and his mother, Queen Ioanna, went into exile. Simeon eventually settled in Madrid, marrying a Spanish heiress.

In 1996 Simeon visited Bulgaria and most of the royal property was later returned to him. In April 2001 he announced the formation of the National Movement for Simeon II, an organization that set out to field candidates in the national legislative elections scheduled in June. When the courts ruled that the party had not met all of the requirements for registration, it joined two minor parties' coalition and was thereby allowed to participate in the election. The party won 120 of the 240 seats and formed a coalition with the Movement for Rights and Freedoms, which represented the country's Turkish minority. On July 24, 2001, Simeon became the country's prime minister.

Upon taking office, Simeon took as his surname Saxecoburggotski, the Bulgarian form of the name of his royal house, Saxe-Coburg-Gotha. Saxecoburggotski, who largely appointed professionals and those lacking political experience to his cabinet, vowed to introduce economic reforms and end corruption. He also stressed the importance of preparing Bulgaria for membership in the European Union and North Atlantic Treaty Organization (NATO), and in 2004 the country became a member of the latter. In the 2005 elections Saxecoburggotski's party finished second in the voting, and he was replaced as prime minister by Sergei Stanishev of the Bulgarian Socialist Party.

THE EARLY COMMUNIST ERA

The consolidation of communist power in Bulgaria was carried out by 1948, coinciding with the completion of the peace treaty with the Allies and the presence of Soviet occupation forces. In the coalition Fatherland Front government, the communists had control of the interior and judicial ministries, which were crucial in setting up the new state.

CONSOLIDATION OF POWER

Exploiting the popular feeling that those who were responsible for Bulgaria's involvement in the war should be punished, the regime established "people's courts" to prosecute the political leaders of the wartime period. The first mass trial (December 20, 1944–February 1, 1945) resulted in death sentences for more than 100 top officials. By the time sentencing was completed in April 1945, the courts had tried 11,122 people, of whom 2,730 were condemned to death, 1,305 to life imprisonment, and 5,119 to terms of up to 20 years. (Unofficial estimates suggested that as many as 30,000 political opponents of the new regime, including anti-Nazi activists, were killed without trial.) When the army returned following the German surrender, the regime also purged the officer corps.

On November 4, 1945, Georgi Dimitrov returned to Bulgaria after 22 years of exile and became prime minister. Given the Bulgarian Communist Party's control of the instruments of power, the hopes of the noncommunist opposition rested on the Western democracies. Indeed, during the summer of 1945 the regime postponed parliamentary elections after Great Britain and the United States protested the undemocratic character of the proposed electoral laws. Bulgaria, however, was not a high priority on the diplomatic agenda of the West. As early as October 1944 British Prime Minister Winston Churchill had shown his willingness to consign the country to Soviet control during his "percentages discussion" with the Soviet premier Joseph Stalin.

Bulgarian communists and their Soviet sponsors moved more forcefully to eliminate the internal opposition. Elections held in November 1945 returned a substantial majority of communists and their allies. In September 1946 a referendum decided by a 93 percent majority proclaimed Bulgaria a republic, and Tsar Simeon II and the queen mother were required to leave the country. Elections for a Grand National Assembly to prepare a new constitution were held on October 27, 1946. The noncommunist opposition polled more than one million votes, or 28 percent of the total. When the assembly opened in November, the Agrarian leader, Nikola Petkov, emerged as the opposition's principal spokesman. However, he was charged with plotting to overthrow the government and was expelled from the Grand National Assembly along with most of his associates. In June 1947 Petkov was arrested, and on September 23 he was executed. One week later the United States extended diplomatic recognition to the new regime; Great Britain had already done so in February.

The defeat of the political opposition coincided with the elimination of pluralism in Bulgarian society. This was accelerated after the founding congress of the Cominform (Communist Information Bureau) in September 1947 in Poland, where Andrey A. Zhdanov delivered the message that Stalin desired a more rapid transformation of the socialist camp along Soviet lines.

In Bulgaria this resulted in increased pressure on the remaining noncommunist parties. The Socialist Party was formally absorbed by the Bulgarian

GEORGI MIKHAILOVICH DIMITROV

Georgi Mikhailovich Dimitrov. Encyclopædia Britannica, Inc.

The Bulgarian communist leader Georgi Mikhailovich Dimitrov (born June 18, 1882, Kovachevtsi, Bulgaria—died July 2, 1949, near Moscow, Russia, U.S.S.R.) became the post-World War II prime minister of Bulgaria. He also won worldwide fame for his defense against Nazi accusations during the German Reichstag Fire trial of 1933.

A printer and trade union leader, Dimitrov led the Bulgarian socialist parliamentary opposition to the voting of national war credits in 1915, and he played a major role in the formation of the Bulgarian Communist Party in 1919. Briefly imprisoned for sedition in 1918, he later journeyed to the Soviet Union, where he was elected to the executive committee of the Comintern (Communist International) in 1921. In 1923 he led a communist uprising in Bulgaria that provoked ferocious government reprisals. Under sentence of death, he was forced to live abroad, from 1929 in Berlin as head of the central European section of the Comintern. After the Reichstag fire of February 27, 1933, which provided Adolf Hitler, the newly appointed German chancellor, with an excuse for a decree outlawing his communist opponents, Dimitrov was accused with other communist leaders of plotting the fire.

At his trial Dimitrov thoroughly bested the Nazi prosecution and won acquittal. He settled in Moscow and, as secretary-general of the Comintern's executive committee (1935–43), encouraged the formation of popular-front movements against the Nazi menace, except when his patron, Joseph Stalin, and Hitler were cooperating. During 1944 he directed the resistance to Bulgaria's Axis satellite government, and in 1945 he returned to Bulgaria, where he was immediately appointed prime minister of a communist-dominated Fatherland Front government. Assuming dictatorial control of political affairs, he effected the communist consolidation of power that culminated in the formation of a Bulgarian People's Republic in 1946.

Communist Party in August 1948, and socialists who remained in opposition were crushed by police repression. The Agrarian leader, Georgi Traikov, repudiated his party's traditional ideology and defined a new role for it as the helpmate or "little brother" of the Bulgarian Communist Party in the countryside. By 1949 Zveno and the remaining smaller parties announced their "self-liquidation" and dissolved into the Fatherland Front, which in turn was converted into a broad "patriotic" organization under communist control.

In the Grand National Assembly a team of Soviet jurists assisted in the preparation of the "Dimitrov Constitution," enacted on December 4, 1947. Modeled closely on the Soviet constitution of 1936, it provided a legal foundation for the reconstruction of the state on communist principles.

REFORMS UNDER THE FATHERLAND FRONT

The Fatherland Front regime had launched an assault on private property almost immediately after the coup of September 9, 1944, employing a variety of legislative measures aimed at confiscating the wealth of "fascists" or "speculators."

The Dimitrov Constitution provided for even larger measures of nationalization. All large-scale industries, banks, and insurance companies were nationalized, and government monopolies were established over retail trade. By the end of 1948, approximately 85 percent of industrial production was in the hands of the state, with another 7 percent carried on by cooperative organizations. The party also created the General Workers' Trade Union, gradually forcing all workers' organizations into it. Similarly, the youth organizations of the various parties were incorporated into the Dimitrov Communist Youth League.

Exarch Stefan, head of the Bulgarian Orthodox Church, sought to adapt to the new political regime, but he resisted the efforts of the Bulgarian Communist Party to control church affairs directly. In September 1948 he resigned his office under mysterious circumstances and retired to a monastery. His successor offered no resistance to legislation adopted in March 1949 that subjected all religious orders to state supervision. At the same time, 15 pastors from evangelical Protestant churches were arrested, tried, and executed for espionage and other alleged crimes. Soon afterward a number of Bulgarian Catholic clergy were tried for spying for the Vatican and for disseminating anticommunist propaganda. Among the executed was Bishop Evgeny Bosilkov, beatified by the Vatican in 1998.

The nearly 50,000 Bulgarian Jews who survived the war were encouraged to emigrate to Israel. The regime also attempted to deport ethnic Turks and Roma (Gypsies), causing the Turkish government to seal the border.

STALINISM AND DE-STALINIZATION

Traicho Kostov, who had been particularly instrumental in supervising the destruction of the opposition, was accused of treason and of collaborating with Yugoslavia's communist leader Josip Broz Tito against Stalinism. Kostov's execution in December 1949 was followed by the purge of thousands of "Kostovites" and others alleged to be criminals and spies.

Dimitrov died in office in July 1949 and was succeeded by Vasil Kolarov, who died in early 1950, and Vulko Chervenkov. Known as Bulgaria's "Little Stalin," Chervenkov followed policies aimed at developing Bulgaria according to the Soviet model. These included rapid industrialization, the forced collectivization of agriculture, heavy reliance on the police and security apparatus, and isolation from countries outside the Soviet bloc.

Stalin's death in 1953 and the inauguration of the "New Course" in the Soviet Union had repercussions in Bulgaria. In 1954 Chervenkov accepted the Soviet model of collective leadership, remaining prime minister but yielding his post as party leader to Todor Zhivkov. The government also released several thousand political prisoners and moderated its economic policies in favour of raising living standards. The beginning of open de-Stalinization at the Soviet Union's 20th Communist Party Congress in February 1956 was followed in Bulgaria by the April Plenum of the Bulgarian Communist Party, at which Chervenkov was accused of abuse of power and later removed from the premiership. There was some relaxation of censorship, and the victims of the Kostovite trials, including Kostov himself (posthumously), began to be rehabilitated.

These developments, however, did not put an end to communist repression, and the concentration ("labour reconstruction") camps did not close until the early 1970s.

LATE COMMUNIST RULE

After becoming prime minister in 1962, Todor Zhivkov continued to hold the positions of head of state and head of party until 1989. An attempted putsch led by Gen. Ivan Todorov-Gorunya in 1965 was easily put down, and Zhivkov consistently managed to purge or undercut party leaders regarded as potential rivals.

THE ZHIVKOV ERA

During the era of Zhivkov's ascendancy, Bulgaria modeled its domestic policies on those of the Soviet Union, with long-term treaties linking Bulgaria's economic development to the Soviets'. Bulgaria gave the highest priority to scientific and technological advancement and the development of trade skills appropriate to an industrial state. In 1948 approximately 80 percent of the population drew their living from the soil, but by 1988 less than one-fifth of the labour force was engaged in agriculture, with the rest concentrated in industry and the service sector.

By the 1960s Bulgaria had abandoned the isolationism that characterized the Chervenkov period. Although remaining steadfast in its commitments to the Warsaw Pact and Comecon, Bulgaria improved relations with its Balkan neighbours, particularly Greece, and expanded its economic and cultural relations with most Western states. Relations with Yugoslavia remained strained, however, over the persistence of the Macedonian question. In 1979 Bulgaria proposed a treaty with Yugoslavia that would guarantee the inviolability of the borders established after World War II; this proposal was rejected, however, because of Bulgaria's refusal to admit the existence of a distinct Macedonian nationality. From the Bulgarian point of view, such an admission would both fly in the face of historical reality and legitimize Yugoslav claims on the Pirin region.

During the 1970s concern developed over the low birth rate of the ethnic Bulgarian population, and policies were adopted to encourage larger families, but without apparent effect. In late 1984 the government began a major campaign to "Bulgarize," or assimilate, the country's ethnic Turks. Measures aimed at the Turkish population, estimated to number approximately 800,000, included the discontinuation of Turkish-language publications and radio broadcasts and the requirement that Turks adopt Bulgarian names.

The ethnic Turkish population, however, resisted assimilation, and clashes with the authorities continued. In spite of official harassment, independent human rights groups were formed in defense of the Turks. In 1989, when the government of Turkey offered to accept refugees from Bulgaria, more than 300,000 ethnic Turks fled or were forcibly driven from the country by the communist authorities.

The era of reforms launched by Mikhail Gorbachev in the Soviet Union had a major impact on Bulgaria, inspiring greater demands for openness and democratization. The increase in Bulgarian dissidents, a declining economic situation, and internal party rivalries led Zhivkov's colleagues to force his resignation on November 10, 1989. He was later tried, sentenced, and imprisoned for embezzlement.

END OF PARTY RULE

Under growing popular pressure, Zhivkov's successors endorsed a policy of openness, pluralism, and respect for law, halted repression of the ethnic Turks, and took the first steps toward separating the Bulgarian Communist Party from the state, such as repealing its constitutional monopoly of power. After some shuffling of positions, Petar Mladenov was named head of state, Andrey Lukanov prime minister, and Alexander Lilov head of the Bulgarian Communist Party. In early 1990 the party held an extraordinary congress that enacted significant changes in party structure, and in April 1990 it renamed itself the Bulgarian Socialist Party (BSP).

In the meantime, dissident groups had taken advantage of the country's new freedoms to organize opposition political parties. Many of these joined the Union of Democratic Forces (UDF), a coalition led by the sociologist Zheliu Zhelev. By the spring of 1990, at a roundtable held between early January and May 1990, the UDF and the BSP had agreed to free elections for a Grand National Assembly that would prepare a new constitution. In these June elections the socialists won a narrow majority. In July 1990 Mladenov resigned after it was discovered that he had recommended a military crackdown on protesters in late 1989. Because their majority was too small to allow them to govern alone, in August 1990 the BSP supported the election of Zhelev as head of state.

The National Assembly adopted a new constitution on July 12, 1991, which proclaimed Bulgaria a parliamentary republic and promised citizens a broad range of freedoms. During the summer several parties withdrew from the UDF coalition, and those that remained split into two factions: UDF (liberals) and UDF (movement). In elections for the National Assembly held in October 1991, the UDF (movement) won a narrow majority of seats over the BSP, with the Movement for Rights and Freedoms (MRF; primarily representing the country's Turkish minority) gaining few seats; no other minority party gained the required minimum percentage of the vote to qualify for participation in parliament. The leader of the UDF, Philip Dimitrov, was elected prime minister and, with the support of the MRF, formed a government, without BSP participation. Under the new constitution, Zhelev was elected president for a five-year term in general elections held in January 1992.

BULGARIA'S TRANSITION

Dimitrov's government launched an ambitious reform program aimed at changing the country into a pro-Western democracy with a market economy. Chief among the reforms were the liberalization of prices, the restitution of properties commandeered during the communist regime, and the restructuring of state-owned enterprises. Efforts were made to ease the external debt, build a legal framework for the new market infrastructure, and reach out to the International Monetary Fund (IMF) and the World Bank. In 1992 Bulgaria joined the Council of Europe, and in 1993 it signed the Europe Agreement with the European Union, in which it sought membership.

Bulgaria recognized the newly independent former Yugoslav republics as states and on January 16, 1992, became the first country to recognize the Republic of Macedonia. The relationship between Bulgaria and Macedonia nevertheless continues to be complicated by the fact that Bulgaria does not recognize the existence of a separate Macedonian language or nation, claiming that Macedonian is simply a dialect of Bulgarian and that the Macedonians are really Bulgarians. In addition, successive Bulgarian governments have refused to recognize the existence of a Macedonian minority in

Bulgaria and have attempted to suppress any expression of a Macedonian national identity among its citizens. In 2000 the United Macedonian Organization (OMO) "Ilinden"–Party for Economic Enhancement and Integration of the Population (PIRIN), an organization dedicated to protecting the rights of the Macedonian minority in Bulgaria, was refused recognition as a political party, an action that was condemned in 2000 by the European Court of Human Rights.

Meanwhile, President Zhelev grew critical of the UDF and Dimitrov's government and received support from the MRF. In October 1992 Dimitrov's government was forced to resign by a vote of no confidence. In December 1992 a new government dominated by the MRF was elected with support from the BSP. For the next two years, under the leadership of Zhelev's adviser Luben Berov, reforms stagnated. In elections in December 1994 the BSP won an absolute majority and formed a government headed by party leader Zhan Videnov, which tried to reestablish subsidies for state-owned enterprises but faced financial losses. In early 1997, when monthly inflation reached about 240 percent, mass protests forced the government to resign.

Zhelev's successor as president, Petar Stoyanov, called a new election, and, after a decisive victory, UDF leader Ivan Kostov formed a pro-market government. It reduced inflation by introducing a currency board (an institution dedicated to reinforcing a fixed exchange rate and to a monetary policy that defends that rate),

sped up privatization, and in early 1997 applied for membership in the North Atlantic Treaty Organization (NATO). In elections in June 2001 Simeon Saxecoburggotski, the former tsar of Bulgaria, led the newly formed National Movement for Simeon II (NDSV) to victory. The new prime minister weathered criticism that he and his ministers lacked political experience, and he continued Bulgaria's program of financial restraint and increased privatization.

In 2002 Stoyanov was replaced as president by Georgi Parvanov, a candidate from a coalition of leftist and nationalist groups backed by the BSP who nevertheless declared his intent to not stray from the goals of membership in NATO and the EU. Parvanov was reelected in October 2006. Bulgaria became a member of NATO in 2004 and a member of the EU in 2007. Meanwhile, Saxecoburggotski's party was defeated in the 2005 legislative elections, and Sergei Stanishev of the BSP became prime minister.

In 2008 Bulgaria's governing institutions received a poor evaluation from the European Commission in its second report on Bulgaria's progress as an EU member. The report concluded that Bulgaria had failed to make reasonable strides in reforming the judiciary, combating corruption, and fighting organized crime. In January 2009, during an extremely cold month, thousands of Bulgarians did not have electricity or heat, and production was halted in major enterprises across the country because of a disruption of natural gas deliveries throughout eastern and southern Europe, which resulted from a gas dispute between Russia and Ukraine. The crisis highlighted the weakness of Stanishev's government, which was already struggling to deal with the effects of the global recession; the government also faced mounting allegations of corruption and of misappropriation of EU funds. In the parliamentary elections in July 2009, the centre-right Citizens for European Development of Bulgaria (Grazhdani za Evropeisko Razvitie Balgariya; GERB), led by former Sofia mayor Boiko Borisov, garnered nearly 40 percent of the votes and secured 116 seats in the 240-seat National Assembly, while the Socialist-led Coalition for Bulgaria claimed only 40 seats. Borisov took office as prime minister on July 27.

In foreign affairs, relations with Russia, Romania, Greece, and Turkey had gradually improved throughout the 1990s, backed by a series of agreements and joint protocols. Internally, in response to prodding by the IMF, EU, and other international agencies, Bulgaria tried to quell corruption and social unrest and to divest itself further of its state-owned enterprises. As with the rest of eastern Europe at the turn of the 21st century, Bulgaria was far along in the uneasy transition from postcommunist regime to full-fledged market economy.

CHAPTER 6

HUNGARY: THE LAND AND ITS PEOPLE

The people of Hungary, a country of central Europe, are unique among the continent's inhabitants in that they speak a language that is not related to any other major European language. Linguistically surrounded by alien nations, Hungarians felt isolated throughout much of their history. This may be the reason why after Christianization they became attached to Latin, which became the language of culture, scholarship, and state administration—and even the language of the Hungarian nobility until 1844.

The flag of Hungary. Encyclopaedia Britannica, Inc.

At the end of World War I, defeated Hungary lost 71 percent of its territory as a result of the Treaty of Trianon (1920). Since then, grappling with the loss of more than two-thirds of their territory and people, Hungarians have looked to a past that was greater than the present as their collective psyche suffered from the so-called "Trianon Syndrome." The syndrome was widespread prior to 1945; it was suppressed during Soviet domination (1945–90); and it reemerged during independence in 1990, when it took on a different form. The modern country appears to be split into two irreconcilable factions: those who are still concerned about Trianon and those who would like to forget it. This split is evident in most aspects of Hungarian political, social, and cultural life.

Landlocked and lying approximately between latitudes 45° and 49° N and longitudes 16° and 23° E, Hungary shares a border to the north with Slovakia, to the northeast with Ukraine, to the east with Romania, to the south with Serbia

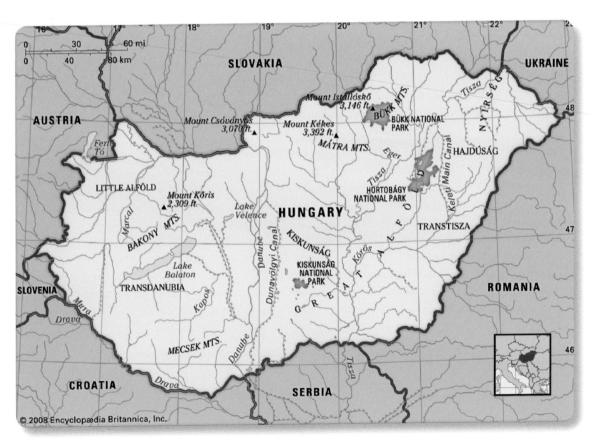

Physical map of Hungary. Encyclopaedia Britannica, Inc.

(specifically, the Vojvodina region) and Croatia, to the southwest with Slovenia, and to the west with Austria.

RELIEF

Dominating the relief are the great lowland expanses that make up the core of Hungary. The Little Alföld (Little Hungarian Plain, or Kisalföld) lies in the northwest, fringed to the west by the easternmost extension of the sub-Alps along the border with Austria and bounded to the north by the Danube. The Little Alföld is separated from the Great Alföld (Great Hungarian Plain, or Nagy Magyar Alföld) by a low mountain system extending across the country from southwest to northeast for a distance of 250 miles (400 km). This system, which forms the backbone of the country, is made up of Transdanubia (Dunántúl) and the Northern Mountains, separated by the Visegrád Gorge of the Danube. Transdanubia is dominated by the Bakony Mountains, with dolomite and limestone plateaus at elevations between 1,300 and 2,300 feet (400 and 700 m) above sea level. Volcanic peaks comprise the Mátra Mountains in the north, reaching an elevation of 3,327 feet (1,014 m) at Mount Kékes, Hungary's highest peak. Regions of hills reaching elevations of 800 to 1,000 feet (250 to 300 m) lie on

AGGTELEK CAVES

The limestone cave system known as the Aggtelek Caves (also called Baradla-Domica Caverns,) is located on the Hungarian-Slovakian border, about 30 miles (50 km) northwest of Miskolc, Hungary, and 40 miles (65 km) southwest of Košice, Slovakia. It is the largest stalactite cave system in Europe, and its stalactite and stalagmite formations are spectacular. The caverns and their surroundings have been designated a national park by both Hungary and Slovakia, and the area was named a UNESCO World Heritage site in 1995.

The caverns were formed in the Cenozoic Era (i.e., within the past 65 million years) in the unevenly uplifted Aggtelek Mountains, which are rich in karstic features. The subterranean streams are fed by 11 sinkholes. There are more than 14 miles (23 km) of charted pathways. The main path for tourists follows the course of the intermittent Acheron River. There are six entrances to the caverns, three in Slovakia (the Devil's Hole and the natural and man-made entrances at Domica) and three in Hungary (the natural entrance at Aggtelek in the highest cliff face in Hungary and the man-made entrances at Jósvafo and Lake Vörös). The narrow corridors of the caverns connect spacious chambers (with names such as the Black Chamber, the Ballroom, the Hall of Tigers, the Concert Hall, the Banquet Hall, the Room of Lace, the Great Chamber, the Room of Ruins, the Heroes' Chamber, the Reményi Ede Room, Rákóczi's Tent Hall, the Hall of Councils, and the Giants' Hall), and the stalactites and stalagmites, with their diverse colours, shapes, and forms, present a remarkable spectacle. It has attracted tourists since the early 1800s.

either side of the mountain backbone, while to the south and west of Lake Balaton is an upland region of more-subdued loess-covered topography.

The Great Alföld covers most of central and southeastern Hungary. Like its northwestern counterpart, it is a basin-like structure filled with fluvial and windblown deposits. Four types of surface may be distinguished: floodplains, composed of river alluvium; alluvial fans, wedge-shaped features deposited at the breaks of slopes where rivers emerge from the mountain rim; alluvial fans overlain by sand dunes; and plains buried under loess, deposits of windblown material derived from the continental interior. These lowlands range in elevation from about 260 to 660 feet (80 to 200 m) above sea level, with the lowest point at 256 feet (78 m), on the southern edge of Szeged, along the Tisza River. In the northeast, bordering Slovakia, is Aggtelek National Park; characterized by karst terrain and featuring hundreds of caves, the area was designated a UNESCO World Heritage site in the late 20th century.

DRAINAGE AND SOILS

Hungary lies within the drainage basin of the Danube, which is the longest river in the country. The Danube and two of its tributaries, the Rába and Dráva rivers, are of Alpine origin, while the Tisza River and its tributaries, which drain much of eastern Hungary, rise in the Carpathian Mountains to the east. The Danube floods twice a year, first in early spring and again in early summer. During these phases, discharge is up to 10 times greater than river levels recorded during the low-water periods of autumn and winter. The Tisza forms a floodplain as it flows through Hungary; large meanders and oxbow lakes mark former channels. At Szolnok, peak discharges 50 times greater than average have been recorded. Devastating floods have occurred on the Danube, the Tisza, and their tributaries. About 2,500 miles (4,000 km) of levees have been built to protect against floods. The relatively dry climate of the central and eastern areas of the Great Alföld has necessitated the construction of large-scale irrigation systems, mostly along the Tisza River.

There are few lakes in Hungary, and most are small. Lake Balaton, however, is the largest freshwater lake in central Europe, covering 231 square miles (598 square km). Neusiedler Lake—called Lake Fertő in Hungary—lies on the Austrian border and was designated a World Heritage site by UNESCO in 2001. Lake Velence lies southeast of Budapest.

Gray-brown podzolic (leached) and brown forest soils predominate in the forest zones, while rich black earth, or chernozem, soil has developed under the forest steppe. Sand dunes and dispersed alkali soils are also characteristic.

CLIMATE

Because of its situation within the Carpathian Basin, Hungary has a moderately dry continental climate. The mean annual temperature is about 50 °F (10 °C). Average temperatures range from 25 to 32 °F (-4 to 0 °C) in January to 64 to 73 °F (18 to 23 °C) in July. Recorded temperature extremes are 109 °F (43 °C) in summer and -29 °F (-34 °C) in winter. In the lowlands, precipitation generally ranges from 20 to 24 inches (500 to 600 mm), rising to 24 to 31 inches (600 to 800 mm) at higher elevations. The central and eastern areas of the Great Alföld are the driest parts of the country, and the southwestern uplands are the wettest. As much as two-thirds of annual precipitation falls during the growing season.

PLANT AND ANIMAL LIFE

Human activities over the ages have largely destroyed the natural vegetation of Hungary. Just about half of the land is regularly cultivated, and about one-sixth is used for nonagricultural purposes. The remainder comprises meadows and rough pasture as well as forest and woodland. No part of the country is of sufficient elevation to support natural coniferous forest. Beech is the climax community at the highest elevations; oak woodland alternating with scrubby grassland are the climax communities at lower elevations in the upland regions.

Deer and wild pigs are abundant in the forests at higher elevations, while rodents, hares, partridge, and pheasant inhabit the lowlands. The once-numerous varieties of marsh waterfowl survive only in nature reserves. There are diverse species of freshwater fish, including pike, bream, and pike perch. Significant water and air pollution occurs in some of the industrial regions of the country.

ETHNIC GROUPS AND LANGUAGES

From its inception in the 10th century, Hungary was a multiethnic country. Major territorial changes made it ethnically homogeneous after World War I, however, and more than nine-tenths of the population is now ethnically Hungarian and speaks Hungarian (Magyar) as the mother tongue. The Hungarian language is classified as a member of the Ugric branch of the Uralic languages; as such, it is most closely related to the Ob-Ugric languages, Khanty and Mansi, which are spoken east of the Ural Mountains. It is also related, though more distantly, to Finnish and Estonian, each of which is (like Hungarian) a national language; to the Sami languages of far northern Scandinavia; and, more distantly still, to the Samoyedic languages of Siberia.

Ethnic Hungarians are a mix of the Finno-Ugric Magyars and various assimilated Turkic, Slavic, and Germanic peoples. A small percentage of the population is made up of ethnic minority groups. The largest of these is the Roma (Gypsies). Other ethnic minorities include Germans, Slovaks, Croats, Romanians, Serbs, Poles, Slovenians, Rusyns, Greeks, and Armenians.

HUNGARIAN LANGUAGE

Hungarian Magyar, a member of the Finno-Ugric group of the Uralic language family, is spoken primarily in Hungary but also in Slovakia, Romania, and the former Yugoslavia, as well as in scattered groups elsewhere in the world. Hungarian belongs to the Ugric branch of Finno-Ugric, along with the Ob-Ugric languages, Mansi and Khanty, spoken in western Siberia.

The language has been written in a modified Latin alphabet since the 13th century CE, and its orthography was stabilized from the 16th century with the introduction of printing. Characteristic of Hungarian orthography are the acute accent (ó) marking long vowels—doubled in the case of long front rounded vowels (ő)—and special representations for sibilant sounds (e.g., sz corresponds to English s, but s corresponds to English sh).

Surrounded by non-Uralic languages, Hungarian has borrowed many words from such sources as Iranian, Turkic, Caucasian, Slavic, Latin, and German. Its phonology and grammar are, however, typically Uralic. Characteristic of its sound system is vowel harmony. Vowels are classed into three groups depending on position of articulation: back vowels (a, á, o, ó, u, ú), front rounded vowels (ö, ő ü, ű), and front unrounded vowels (e, é, i, í). Back vowels and front rounded vowels may not occur together in the same word. Consonant clusters in Hungarian are simple and usually do not occur at the beginning of words. Stress (accent) is always on the first syllable of the word.

Hungarian grammatical categories are usually marked by the use of suffixes; e.g., *ver-et-het-né-lek* "I might cause thee to be beaten" is composed of ver "*beat*" + et "*cause*" + het "may" + *né* (a conditional marker) + *lek* "I thee." In many cases vowels in suffixes shift to match those of the stem in order to maintain vowel harmony (e.g., *ház-ban* "in the house" versus *ember-ben* "in the man").

RELIGION

Hungary claims no official religion and guarantees religious freedom. More than half the people are Roman Catholic, most of them living in the western and northern parts of the country. About one-fifth of the population are Calvinist (concentrated in eastern Hungary). Lutherans constitute the next most significant minority faith, and relatively smaller groups belong to various other Christian denominations (Greek or Byzantine Catholics, Eastern Orthodox, and Unitarians). The Jewish community, which constituted 5 percent of the population before World War II, was decimated by the Holocaust and is now much smaller.

During the communist era, from 1949, Hungary was officially an atheistic state. The Roman Catholic Church struggled with the communist government after it enacted laws diminishing church property and schools. As a result of resistance to these changes, the church was granted broader rights via a 1964 agreement with

ROMA

The Roma (sometimes called Gypsies) are a people originating in northern India but now living worldwide, principally in Europe. Most speak Romany in addition to the local language. It is thought that Roma groups left India in successive migrations, reaching western Europe by the 15th century. In the 20th century they spread to North and South America and Australia. Because of their often nomadic and marginalized lives, population figures are largely guesswork; estimates in the early 21st century range from two to three million. They have often been persecuted and harassed; the Nazis killed about 400,000 Roma in extermination camps. How many Roma retain a nomadic lifestyle is unclear, but those that migrate do so at least seasonally along patterned routes that ignore national boundaries. They pursue occupations compatible with a nomadic life. In the past they were often livestock traders, tinkers, fortune-tellers, and entertainers; today they are often car mechanics, auto-body repairmen, and workers in traveling circuses and amusement parks. Confederations of 10–100 families elect chieftains for life, but their title is not heritable. Women are organized as a group within the confederation and represented by a senior woman. Modern Roma culture faces erosion from urban influences; integrated housing, economic independence, and intermarriage with non-Roma have weakened Roma law.

the Vatican, and in 1972 the Hungarian constitution proclaimed the free exercise of worship and the separation of church and state. Since the fall of communism in 1990, more than 200 religious groups have been officially registered in the country. Nominal membership in a religious denomination, however, does not necessarily mean active participation or even active spiritual belief.

SETTLEMENT PATTERNS

The Great Alföld is the largest region of the country. It is divided into two parts: Kiskunság, the area lying between the Danube and Tisza rivers, and Transtisza (Tiszántúl), the region east of the Tisza. Kiskunság consists primarily of a mosaic of small landscape elements—sand dunes,

Ó-templom, a Baroque church in Kiskunfélegyháza, Hung. Béla Ilovszky/Interfoto MTI, Hungary

The 19th-century Református Nagytemplom (or Great Reformed Church) in Debrecen, Hung. Paul Almasy

loess plains, and floodplains. Kecskemét is the market centre for the region, which is also noted for its isolated farmsteads, known as *tanyák*. Several interesting groups live there, including the people of Kalocsa and the Matyó, who occupy the northern part of the plain around Mezőkövesd and are noted for folk arts that include handmade embroidery and the making of multicoloured apparel.

In the generally homogeneous flat plain of the Transtisza region, only the Nyírség area in the northeast presents any form of topographical contrast. Closely connected with the Nyírség are the Hajdúság and the Hortobágy regions, and all three areas look to Debrecen, the largest city of the plain. The steppe life of earlier times survives in the Hortobágy, where the original Hungarian cattle, horse,

and sheep breeds have been preserved as part of the national heritage. The national park there was designated a UNESCO World Heritage site in 1999.

The Little Alföld, the second major natural region, is situated in the northwest and is traversed by the Danube and Rába rivers and their tributaries. It is more favourably endowed with natural resources than is the Great Alföld; both agriculture and industry are more advanced there. Győr, known for its Baroque architecture, is the region's major city.

The third major region, Transdanubia, embraces all of the country west of the Danube exclusive of the Little Alföld. It is a rolling upland broken by the Bakony and Mecsek ridges. Lake Balaton is a leading resort area. To the south of the lake are the hills of Somogy, Tolna, and Baranya *megyék* (counties), where Pécs, a mining and industrial city, is the economic and cultural centre. Also found in Transdanubia are the Bakony Mountains, whose isolation, densely forested ridges, small closed basins, and medieval fortresses and monasteries have protected the local inhabitants over the course of many stormy centuries. Although modern industrial towns drawing on the bauxite, manganese, and brown coal resources of the area have sprung up, the cultural centre of Transdanubia is the historic city of Veszprém. In the southern part of the region, north and west of Lake Balaton, are health resorts and centres of wine production, notably Keszthely, Hévíz, Badacsony, and Balatonfüred.

Győr, on the banks of the Rába River, in Hungary. Gyorgy Lajos—INTERFOTO MTI

The Northern Mountains, the fourth major geographic region of the country, contains two important industrial areas, the Nógrád and Borsod basins. Agriculture is also important, especially viticulture; notable are the Tokaj (Tokay) and Eger vineyards. Indeed, the region that produces Tokay wines was designated a UNESCO World Heritage site in 2002. Tourism in the Northern Mountains is well-developed, and numerous spas and recreation centres are located there. Miskolc is the main economic centre for the region.

Nearly two-thirds of the population is urban, but, outside of the major cities, the bulk of towns in Hungary have populations of less than 40,000. Until the late 20th century, these were functionally vastly overgrown villages rather than towns.

Urban Hungary is dominated by Budapest, which is several times the size of any of the other major cities. About one-third of Hungary's urban population lives within the Budapest metropolitan area. The major provincial centres are Debrecen, Miskolc, Szeged, Pécs, and Győr, each of which has an economic, cultural, and administrative hinterland that reaches deep into the surrounding countryside along with an expanding industrial capacity. Below the provincial centres in the hierarchy are the traditional market towns, such as Kecskemét, Székesfehérvár, Nyíregyháza, Szombathely, and Szolnok, often with new suburbs extending from their medieval or Baroque town centres.

Also worthy of note are the predominantly industrial towns located close to the mineral resources of the Northern Mountains, which, from small beginnings in the late 19th century, have developed into major industrial centres. They include Tatabánya, Salgótarján, and Ózd. In addition, a number of industrial towns

Veszprém, Hungary, showing the fortress hill with the 11th-century cathedral of St. Michael. ZEFA

were created in the late 20th century on greenfield sites as part of deliberate planning policy. These include the metallurgical centre of Dunaújváros on the Danube and the chemical centre of Kazincbarcika in northeastern Hungary.

The distribution of rural population varies widely from one part of the country to another. For historical reasons connected with resettlement following the Turkish occupation in the 16th century, the villages of the Great Alföld are small in number but large in size. By comparison, rural settlement in Transdanubia and in the Northern Mountains takes the form of many small nucleated and linear

BUDAPEST

As the capital of Hungary, Budapest is the political, administrative, industrial, and commercial centre of the country.

Situated on the Danube River, the city acquired its name in 1873 when the towns of Buda and Óbuda on the river's right bank and the town of Pest on its left bank amalgamated. Although the city's roots date to Roman times and even earlier, modern Budapest is essentially an outgrowth of the 19th-century empire of Austria-Hungary, when Hungary was three times larger than the present country. Hungary's reduction in size following World War I did not prevent Budapest from becoming, after Berlin, the second largest city in central Europe.

Central Budapest, looking north along the Danube River, with the Parliament Building on the east bank. Jean S. Buldain/ Berg & Assoc.

Today, Budapest dominates all aspects of national life. The city is the centre of Hungarian transport and industry. Tens of thousands of commuters converge on Budapest daily, more than half the nation's university students attend school in the city, and about half the country's income from foreign tourism is earned there.

villages. The *tanyák* tend to be concentrated in the Great Alföld. The village of Hollókő, now preserved as a UNESCO World Heritage site, exemplifies the rural settlement typical of Hungary prior to the agricultural changes of the 20th century.

DEMOGRAPHIC TRENDS

Because of major changes in Hungary's borders following World War I, the country's population decreased significantly. Although there were further losses during World War II, Hungary's population recovered slowly, peaking in the late 1970s and early '80s.

Since then, however, Hungary has experienced a negative natural increase rate (meaning the number of deaths has outpaced the number of births). These demographic trends were influenced by the urbanization and modernization process. As modernization spread from urban areas (where people generally have fewer children) into the country-side, so did the declining birth rate. Many Hungarians framed economic decisions as choices between *kocsi* or *kicsi* ("a car or a baby"), and it was often the car that was chosen over the baby.

Life expectancy for women increased consistently from the 1930s, and that for men also increased until the 1970s, when the trend reversed, but both are below those of Hungary's central European neighbours.

Many ethnic Hungarians live in the neighbouring countries of Romania, Slovakia, Ukraine, Serbia, Croatia, Slovenia, and Austria. As a consequence of a net overseas emigration of 1.3 million people before World War I and a continuous, though much smaller, emigration related to major political upheavals in 1918–19, the 1930s, 1944–45, and 1956, large Hungarian communities also live in North America and western Europe. After the collapse of communism and the splintering of Yugoslavia, roughly 100,000 refugees migrated to Hungary from Romania and the former Yugoslav federation. Half of them were ethnic Hungarians.

CHAPTER 7

THE HUNGARIAN ECONOMY

Historically, prior to World War II, Hungary was mostly agrarian. Beginning in 1948, a forced industrialization policy based on the Soviet pattern changed the economic character of the country. A centrally planned economy was introduced, and millions of new jobs were created in industry (notably for women) and, later, in services. This was accomplished largely through a policy of forced accumulation; keeping wages low and the prices of consumer goods (as opposed to staples) high made it possible for more people to be employed, and, because consumer goods were beyond their means, most Hungarians put more of their earnings in savings, which became available for use by the government. In the process, the proportion of the population employed in agriculture declined from more than half to about one-eighth by the 1990s, while the industrial workforce grew to nearly one-third of the economically active population by the late 1980s. Since that time, it has been the service sector that has increased significantly.

Although Soviet-type economic modernization generated rapid growth, it was based on an early 20th-century structural pattern and on outdated technology. The heavy industries of iron, steel, and engineering were given the highest priority, while modern infrastructure, services, and communication were neglected. New technologies and high-tech industries were underdeveloped and further hampered by Western restrictions (the Coordinating Committee for Multilateral Export Controls) on the export of modern technology to the Soviet bloc.

In response to stagnating rates of economic growth, the government introduced the New Economic Mechanism (NEM) in 1968. The NEM implemented market-style reforms to rationalize the behaviour of Hungary's state-owned enterprises, and it also allowed for the emergence of privately owned businesses. By the end of the 1980s, one-third of the gross domestic product (GDP)—nearly three-fifths of services and more than three-fourths of construction—was being generated by private business. The Hungarian economy, however, failed to meet the challenge of the world economic crisis after 1973. The dramatic price increases for oil and modern technology created a large external trade deficit, which led to increasing foreign indebtedness. Growth slowed down and inflation rose, leading to a period of stagflation.

After 1989 Hungary's nascent market and parliamentary systems inherited a crisis-ridden economy with an enormous external debt and noncompetitive export sectors. Hungary turned to the world market and restructured its foreign trade, but market competition, together with a sudden and radical opening of the country and the abolition of state subsidies, led to further economic decline. Agriculture was drastically affected and declined by half. A large portion of the iron, steel, and engineering sectors, especially in northeastern Hungary, collapsed. Industrial output and GDP decreased by 30 percent and 25 percent, respectively. Unemployment, previously nonexistent, rose to 14 percent in the early 1990s but declined after 1994.

By the mid-1990s the economy was again growing, but only moderately. Inflation peaked in 1991 and remained high, at more than 20 percent annually, before dropping to under 10 percent by the early 21st century. As a consequence of unavoidable austerity measures that included the elimination of many welfare institutions, most of the population lost its previous security. In the first several years after the fall of communism, the number of people living below the subsistence level doubled, but it stabilized by the early 21st century. Observers also noted the emergence of a sector of long-term poor, a majority of whom were Roma.

Despite these obstacles, adjustment to the world economy was evident by the turn of the 21st century. Hungary's liberal foreign investment regime attracted more than half of the entire foreign direct investment in central and eastern Europe in the first half of the 1990s. Modernization of telecommunications also began, and new industries (e.g., automobile manufacturing) emerged. Significantly, nearly one million small-scale, mostly family-owned enterprises were established by the early 21st century. State ownership of businesses declined to roughly one-fifth. Another important contributor to economic growth has been a flourishing tourist industry.

AGRICULTURE

Agriculture's role in the Hungarian economy declined steadily in the generations

Harvesting corn near Dunaújváros, central Hungary. Milt and Joan Mann/CameraMann International

following World War II, dropping from half of the GDP in the immediate post-war period to only 4 percent of the GDP by 2005. Nevertheless, agriculture remains important, and Hungary is virtually self-sufficient in food production. The Hungarian climate is favourable for agriculture, and half of the country's land is arable; about one-fifth is covered by woods. About one-tenth of the country's total area is under permanent cultivation. Agriculture accounted for nearly one-fourth of Hungarian exports before the economic transition of the 1990s, during which animal stocks decreased by one-third and agricultural output and exports declined by half.

After the initial period of collectivization (1948–61), Hungarian cooperatives incorporated private farming. Private plots constituted roughly one-eighth of a cooperative's land and produced about one-third of the country's agricultural output. One-fifth of Hungarian farmland belonged to state farms. Since 1990 the land has been reprivatized. Some among the elderly agricultural population have remained in reorganized collective farms; however, private farms are the norm.

Cereals, primarily wheat and corn (maize), are the country's most important crops. Other major crops are sugar beets, potatoes, sunflower seeds, and fruits (notably apples, grapes, and plums). Viticulture, found in the Northern Mountains region, is also significant. Cattle, sheep, pigs, and poultry are raised in Hungary, but, in response to the government's efforts to combat overproduction of animal products, substantial reductions in livestock occurred in the 1990s.

RESOURCES AND POWER

The most important natural endowments of Hungary, particularly in its western

TOKAY WINE

Hungary's famous, usually sweet white wine Tokay (also spelled Tokaji) is made from the Hungarian Furmint grape. The wine derives its name from the Tokaj district of northeastern Hungary. Though some Tokay is dry, the finest version, Tokaji Aszu, is made from late-ripened grapes affected by Botrytis cinerea, a mold that concentrates grape sugars and flavours into honeylike sweetness.

The sweetness of Tokay is traditionally measured by the number of *puttonyos*, or baskets, of sweet grapes used. A three *puttonyos* wine is lightly sweet; five *puttonyos* denotes the highest degree of sweetness. The legendary Tokay Eszencia, a concentrated sweet essence of low alcohol famed for its miraculous restorative properties, is virtually unobtainable today.

The name *tokay* is also applied generically to certain sweet wines of indifferent quality that bear no resemblance to Hungarian Tokay.

and central areas, are its fertile soil and abundant water resources—notably Lake Balaton, a major asset for tourism. Fossil fuel resources are relatively modest. High-quality anthracite (hard coal) is extracted only at Komló, and lignite (brown coal) is mined in the Northern Mountains (notably at Ózd) and in Transdanubia (at Tatabánya). Coal once satisfied half of Hungary's energy requirements; it now represents less than one-third of energy production.

Oil and natural gas were discovered in the late 1930s in Transdanubia and during the decades following World War II at several localities in the Great Alföld, especially near Szeged. Their share of energy production increased from one-third to one-half between 1970 and 2000; however, Hungary is able to meet only a fraction of its oil requirements with domestic resources.

The country's only significant mineral resources are bauxite—of which Hungary has some of the richest deposits in Europe—manganese, in the Bakony Mountains, and the undeveloped copper and zinc resources at Recsk. Extraction of various metal-bearing ores increased significantly in postwar Hungary, but iron ore is no longer mined. Other minerals that are found include mercury, lead, uranium, perlite, molybdenum, diatomite, kaolin, bentonite, zeolite, and dolomite.

MANUFACTURING

As a result of the policy of forced industrialization under the communist government, industry experienced an exceptionally high growth rate until the late 1980s, by which time it constituted about two-fifths of GDP. Mining and metallurgy, as well as the chemical and engineering industries, grew in leaps and bounds as the preferred sectors of Hungary's planned economy. Indeed, half of industrial output was produced by these three sectors. Lacking modern technology and infrastructure, however, Hungarian industry was not prepared to compete in the global economy after the collapse of state socialism. During the first half of the 1990s, industrial employment dropped to one-fourth of the economically active population. Total output declined by nearly one-third, with output in the mining, metallurgy, and engineering industries decreasing by half. During the 1990s, engineering output dropped from nearly one-third to roughly one-fifth of the total.

As industry and the Hungarian economy in general underwent restructuring and modernization during the early 1990s (including the implementation of privatization and the improvement of the quality of goods and services), some industries adapted more successfully to new conditions. Among the industries that regressed least and showed the first signs of growth were the food, tobacco, and wood and paper industries. Of Hungary's traditionally strong sectors, the chemical industry showed the greatest resilience, demonstrating growth again by the mid-1990s after experiencing a large drop in production early in the decade.

Partly through foreign investment, the machine industry (another important component of the economy) also showed signs of improvement by the mid-1990s.

A number of newer industries, including the production and repair of telecommunications equipment and the automobile industry, also showed significant growth.

Between 1950 and 1990, electric power consumption in Hungary increased 10-fold, and by the 1990s more than one-third of industrial output was produced by the energy sector. In the early 21st century, three-fifths of energy consumption was derived from thermal plants burning hydrocarbons (a majority of which were imported). There are several thousand miles of oil and natural gas pipelines. Nuclear power accounted for nearly two-fifths of Hungary's energy production, with plans for further expansion. A small percentage of power generation consisted of hydroelectricity and geothermal alternatives.

FINANCE

Under the Soviet-style, single-tier banking system, the National Bank both issued money and monopolized the financing of the entire Hungarian economy. Beginning in 1987, Hungary moved toward a market-oriented, two-tier system in which the National Bank remained the bank of issue but in which commercial banks were established. Foreign investment was permitted, and "consortium" (partly foreign-owned) banks were formed. In 1990 a stock exchange was established.

In the 1990s, in the postcommunist period, the reform process continued with the founding of private banks, the sale of shares in state-owned banks (though most banks remained state-owned), and the enactment of a law that guaranteed the independence of the National Bank. The currency (forint) also became entirely convertible for business. By the turn of the 21st century, with a dramatic increase in foreign investment and in the number of commercial banks, the Hungarian banking system had been almost completely privatized. In 1986 the state-operated insurance system was split into two separate companies, and by the following decade more than a dozen insurance companies were in operation.

TRADE

Hungary was a charter member of the Comecon (Council for Mutual Economic Assistance; 1949–91). Under its aegis, trade was conducted between the countries of the Soviet bloc on the basis of specialized production, fixed prices, and barter. The Soviet Union was Hungary's most important trading partner, but, in the late 1980s and early '90s, as Hungary became increasingly involved in the global market, less than half of the country's trade remained with Comecon. Unprepared for the competitiveness of global market forces, Hungary accrued a large trade deficit that was covered by foreign loans. In the process the country became heavily indebted and had to use much of its export earnings for repayment.

Nevertheless, by the mid-1990s three-fourths of Hungary's trade was with market economies. Germany became Hungary's most important trading partner, followed by Austria, France, Italy, and the United States. Meanwhile, the proportion of Hungary's imports from the component countries of the former Soviet Union fell from a peak of more than one-fifth in the early 1990s to less than one-tenth at the turn of the 21st century, by which point Hungarian exports to those countries had become negligible. In 1996 Hungary joined the Organisation for Economic Co-operation and Development (OECD), and in 2004 it became a full member of the European Union (EU).

In the early 21st century, machinery and transport equipment were both Hungary's leading import (comprising three-fifths of the total imports) and its leading export (comprising one-half of all exports). In particular, the country's principal trade goods were telecommunications equipment, electrical machinery, power-generating machinery, road vehicles, and office machines and computers.

SERVICES

Throughout the last decade of the 20th century, the service sector's portion of Hungary's GDP rose at an annual average rate of about 0.5 percent. By the early 2000s, services accounted for almost two-thirds of GDP and of the workforce. Tourism played a big role in this development as Hungary became an increasingly popular destination for travelers, especially those from Austria, Croatia, Germany, Montenegro, Romania, Serbia, Slovakia, and Ukraine, most of whom arrived by car. There is also significant tourism via low-cost air carriers from western Europe, as well as from the United States, Canada, and Australia.

LABOUR AND TAXATION

The Soviet-style Central Council of Hungarian Trade Unions was reorganized in 1988 as the National Confederation of Hungarian Trade Unions. It remains the largest trade union in Hungary, with some 40 organizations under its umbrella at the start of the 21st century. It is joined by the Association of Hungarian Free Trade Unions, Democratic Confederation of Free Trade Unions, Forum for the Cooperation of Trade Unions, and Autonomous Trade Union Confederation.

TRANSPORTATION AND TELECOMMUNICATIONS

Railways have long been the centre of Hungary's transportation system. By World War I the country had a modern network that was among the densest in Europe, and it continued to expand regularly until the late 1970s, with electrification beginning in the previous decade. When industrial production declined during the transition to a market economy, rail transport of goods dropped sharply, accompanied by significant cutbacks in government subsidies that contributed to the deterioration of the railway infrastructure. By the end of the 20th century, however, the EU had begun funding rail network improvements, as well as roadway projects.

In the postcommunist era, road haulage has made up an increasing percentage of the overall transport of goods. Buses were once the main form of travel for passenger transportation, but the number of privately owned automobiles grew rapidly after the early 1980s. This growth skyrocketed following the end of the communist regime. Between 1989 and 1996, an additional 1.5 million cars were added to Hungarian roads, the majority of them Western-made. During this same period, the portion of Eastern-made cars declined rapidly.

Road construction and upgrading increased significantly in the early 21st century, with the building of expressways (motorways) radiating out from Budapest toward Vienna, Croatia, Serbia, Romania, and Ukraine.

The Danube River, the country's only important transportation waterway, was historically used for international shipping, via the free port of Csepel. However, as a result of the destruction of bridges in the former Yugoslavia during the intervention by NATO (North Atlantic Treaty Organization) in the Kosovo conflict in 1999, much of the shipping came to a sudden halt. The Hungarian merchant fleet nearly vanished, reduced from about 200 vessels in 1994 to only 1 in 1999.

International air travel passes through airports at Budapest (opened in 1986 and expanded in 1999) and Siófox (opened in 1989). Regional passenger air traffic services Budapest, Nyíregyháza, Debrecen, Szeged, Pécs, Szombathely,

and Győr. Malév Hungarian Airlines, the national carrier, was founded in 1946.

At the start of the 21st century, more than half the population of Hungary were cellular telephone users. Televisions and radios were plentiful, and use of personal computers and the Internet was growing.

CHAPTER 8

HUNGARIAN GOVERNMENT AND SOCIETY

The modern political system in Hungary contained elements of autocracy throughout the 19th and 20th centuries, but in the period between 1867 and 1948 it had a functioning parliament with a multiparty system and a relatively independent judiciary. After the communist takeover in 1948, a Soviet-style political system was introduced, with a leading role for the Communist Party, to which the legislative and executive branches of the government and the legal system were subordinated. In that year, all rival political parties were abolished, and the Hungarian Social Democratic Party was forced to merge with the Communist Party and thus form the Hungarian Workers' Party. After the Revolution of 1956 it was reorganized as the Hungarian Socialist Workers' Party, which survived until the fall of communism in 1989.

In 1989 dramatic political reforms accompanied the economic transformation taking place. After giving up its institutionalized leading role, the Hungarian Socialist Workers' Party abolished itself (with the exception of a small splinter group that continues under its old name) and reshaped itself into the Hungarian Socialist Party. In October 1989 a radical revision of the 1949 constitution, which included some 100 changes, introduced a multiparty parliamentary system of representative democracy, with free elections. The legislative and executive branches of the government were separated, and an independent judicial system was created. The revision established a Constitutional Court, elected by Parliament, which reviews the constitutionality of legislation and may annul laws. It also provides for an ombudsman for the protection of constitutional civil rights and ombudsmen's groups for the protection of national and ethnic minority rights.

The 1989 constitution was amended repeatedly, and a controversial new constitution, pushed through by Prime Minister Viktor Orbán's centre-right government, was promulgated in January 2012. Among other significant recent revisions of Hungarian law was a change in 2010 that allowed nonresidents to attain citizenship if they could prove their Hungarian ancestry and mastery of the Hungarian language.

Supreme legislative power is granted to the unicameral National Assembly, which elects the president of the republic, the Council of Ministers, the president of the Supreme Court, and the chief prosecutor. The main organ of state administration is the Council of Ministers, which is headed by the prime minister. The president, who may serve two five-year terms, is commander in chief of the armed forces but otherwise has limited

Political map of Hungary. Encyclopædia Britannica, Inc.

authority. The right of the people to propose referendums is guaranteed.

LOCAL GOVERNMENT

Hungary is divided administratively into 19 *megyék* (counties) and into cities, towns, and villages. Budapest has a special status as the capital city (*főváros*), headed by a lord mayor (*főpolgármester*) and divided into 22 districts, each headed by its own mayor (*polgármester*). Local representative governments are responsible for protection of the environment, local public transport and utilities, public security, and various economic, social, and cultural activities. Public administration offices, whose heads are appointed by the minister of the interior, supervise the legality of the operations of local governments.

JUSTICE

Justice is administered by the Supreme Court, which provides conceptual guidance for the judicial activity of the Court of the Capital City and the county courts and for the local courts. A chief prosecutor is responsible for protecting the rights of citizens and prosecuting acts violating constitutional order and endangering security. The constitutionality of the laws is overseen by the new Constitutional Court, which began operation in 1990. A constitutional amendment in 1997 called for the addition of regional appellate courts, which came into force in the early 21st century.

POLITICAL PROCESS

Parliamentary elections based on universal suffrage for citizens age 18 and over are held every four years. Under the mixed system of direct and proportional representation, candidates may be elected as part of national and regional party lists or in an individual constituency. In the latter case, candidates must gain an absolute majority in the first round of the elections or runoff elections must be held. Candidates on territorial lists cannot be elected if their party fails to receive at least 5 percent of the national aggregate of votes for the territorial lists.

About 200 political parties were established following the revision of the constitution in 1989, but only six of them became long-term participants in the country's new political life after the first free elections (1990): the Hungarian Democratic Forum, Alliance of Free Democrats, Independent Smallholders' Party, Christian Democratic People's Party, Federation of Young Democrats (Fiatal Demokraták Szövetsége; Fidesz), and Hungarian Socialist Party—the latter being the party of reformed ex-communists. The same six parties were returned to Parliament in 1994, and for the following decade most of them remained represented in the legislature. The hard-core communists reemerged in 1992 as the Workers' Party, while the right-wing Hungarian Justice and Life Party was created in 1993, when it split from the Hungarian Democratic Forum. Fidesz appended Hungarian

FIDESZ

The Federation of Young Democrats–Hungarian Civic Alliance (Hungarian: Fiatal Demokraták Szövetsége–Magyar Polgári Szövetség), commonly known as Fidesz, is a centre-right Hungarian political party. Fidesz (the Federation of Young Democrats) was founded in 1988 as an anticommunist party that promoted the development of a market economy and European integration. Initially, membership was restricted to those age 35 or younger, though this restriction was eliminated in 1993. In 1995 the party appended the name Hungarian Civic Party to its shortened form (altered to Hungarian Civic Alliance in 2003).

Fidesz had its first notable success in 1990, when candidates associated with a coalition of which Fidesz was a member won mayoralties in a number of cities. In elections to the National Assembly that year, Fidesz won 22 seats. In 1997 members of a Christian Democratic group that had dissolved joined Fidesz in the National Assembly, enabling the joint group to form the largest bloc. The following year Fidesz became the single largest party in the National Assembly, winning 148 seats, and formed a coalition government with two other parties; its leader, Viktor Orbán, became prime minister. Orbán's government continued an austerity program, cut taxes and social insurance fees, and pursued Hungary's membership in the European Union. The party was ousted from government following the 2002 elections. After some eight years of Socialist rule, Fidesz, capitalizing on Hungary's ongoing economic problems after the country's economic collapse in 2008, swept back into power in the parliamentary elections of April 2010. By winning more than two-thirds of the seats, Fidesz became the first non-coalition government in the postcommunist history of Hungary.

Civic Party (later changed to Hungarian Civic Alliance) to its name, and between 1998 and 2002 it became the dominant party and formed the government. The Christian Democrats organized the Centre Party alliance in 2002 but failed to make it into the Parliament.

SECURITY

The Hungarian armed forces consist of ground forces, air and air-defense forces, a small navy that patrols the Danube, the border guard, and police. Military service was compulsory for males over the age of 18 until 2004, when Hungary established a voluntary force. (The term of duty varies according to the branch of service but is typically less than one year.) The armed forces are not permitted to cross the state frontiers without the prior consent of Parliament. In the decade between 1989 and 1999, the armed forces declined from 155,000 members to just under 60,000, but, at the same time, they also underwent a process of modernization to prepare Hungary to join the Western military alliance NATO. Membership was finally achieved in March 1999, eight years after the dissolution of the Warsaw Pact, of which Hungary was a member.

HEALTH AND WELFARE

Following World War II, health care improved dramatically under state socialism, with significant increases in the number of physicians and hospital beds in Hungary. By the 1970s, free health care was guaranteed to every citizen. Higher-quality private health care, permitted but limited before the transition period, grew in importance from the early 1990s.

A broad range of social services was provided by the communist government, including child support, extensive maternity leave, and an old-age pension system for which men became eligible at age 60 and women at age 55. This costly welfare system was a heavy burden on the country's finances. At the end of the communist era, Hungary ranked 20th among European countries in terms of per capita GDP, but it was 12th in social spending. Social insurance expenditure, which constituted 4 percent of GDP in 1950, had risen to one-fifth of the GDP by 1990. The Hungarian system had become one of the most expensive in the world, yet there was considerable resistance to efforts to scale it back.

When health insurance was reformed in 1992, it retained its all-encompassing nature and was also made mandatory. At the same time, however, this reform required both employers and employees to contribute to the system's upkeep, as well as to pension plans. The government's move in 2003 to privatize almost half of its health care institutions was rejected in the following year by popular referendum. The private financing of health care slowly increased with the introduction of co-payments for some prescription medications, office visits, and hospital stays.

HOUSING

Housing shortages were constant in Hungary for decades after World War II, despite the million housing units built by the state in urban centres from 1956 to 1985. In the immediate postwar period, Hungary maintained an average of three persons per room, a rate that eventually dropped to one per room by the mid-1990s. Moreover, by the late 1980s, electricity was available for nearly the entire population (it had been in fewer than half of Hungarian homes in 1949, when apartment houses were nationalized), and running water was available for more than three-fourths of homes. The construction of private homes, which had increased in the 1960s and '70s, constituted more than four-fifths of all construction by the mid-1990s, as housing became part of the market economy.

In the 1990s, as the cost of home ownership and rents soared, the housing market became increasingly polarized. The lower class continued to live in

shabby, prefabricated, and often deteriorated apartments, while the upper class
occupied expensive apartments or villas
that approximated Western standards
both in their construction and in their
internal outfitting. High-quality housing
was bought not only by Hungary's nou-
veaux riches but also by many Westerners,
among them a significant number of permanent or seasonal repatriates.

EDUCATION

Ever since the start of obligatory universal education initiated by the Law
of 1868, Hungary followed the German
system of education on all levels. This
included four, then six, and finally eight
years of elementary schooling and—for
a select few, after the first four years of
this basic education—eight years of rigorous gymnasium (*gimnázium*) studies
that prepared the students for entrance
to universities. These universities were
also organized along the German model,
with basic degrees after four or five years,
followed for those in the humanities and
sciences by the doctorate based on a modest dissertation. Those wishing to become
a member of the professorate also had to
go through the process of "habilitation"
(*habilitáció*), which required the defense
of a more significant dissertation based
on primary research.

All this changed after the communist
takeover of Hungary following World
War II. In 1948 schools were nationalized, and the elitist German style of
education was replaced by a Soviet-style
mass education, consisting of eight
years of general school (*általános iskola*)
and four years of secondary education
(*középiskola*). The latter consisted of
college-preparatory high schools that
approximated the upper four years of
the *gimnázium* as well as of the more
numerous and diverse vocational schools
(*technikumok*) that prepared students
for technical colleges or universities but
in most instances simply led directly to
mid-level jobs. This system of education
survived until the 1990s, when the fall of
communism resulted in a partial return to
the traditional educational system. While
much of the Soviet-inspired 8 + 4 system
is still intact, it now competes with the 6
+ 6 and the 4 + 8 systems, wherein the six-
or eight-year *gimnázium* tries to replicate
the intellectually more exclusive pre-
Marxist Hungarian educational system.

During the 1990s the uniformity
of the communist educational system
was further shattered by the introduction of private secondary education.
Nationalized religious schools were
returned to churches and religious institutions, and various new private secular
schools were created. Between the mid-
1980s and mid-1990s, the number of
secondary schools increased from 561 to
887, even though the student-age population had declined from 1.3 million to just
under 1 million.

Mass industrialization obliged women
to take outside jobs, resulting in the creation of an extensive system of preschools

and kindergartens. Attendance was not mandatory, but, given that in many homes both parents worked, most children attended. Up to the mid-1990s, education was free from the kindergarten through the university level and also obligatory from age 6 to 16. At that time a modest tuition was introduced at the state universities and a much steeper one at the increasing number of private schools and institutions of higher learning.

Preparation for higher education became virtually universal by the early 1980s, and by the end of that decade about one-fifth of those between ages 18 and 24 were enrolled in one of Hungary's numerous institutions of higher learning, many of them founded or reorganized after World War II. This growth continued even after the communist regime had ended; in 1990 there were only 70,000 full-time and 100,000 part-time college and university students, but by the first decade of the 21st century the number of full- and part-time students had risen to almost 400,000.

There was a major reorganization of Hungarian higher education in 2000. Prior to then, traditional major institutions of higher learning were Loránd Eötvös University of Budapest, Lajos Kossuth University of Debrecen, Janus Pannonius University of Pécs, Attila József University of Szeged, the Technical University of Budapest, and the Budapest University of Economic Sciences. There were also dozens of specialized schools and colleges throughout the country. In 2000 most of these specialized colleges were combined with older universities or with each other to form new "integrated universities." The result was the birth of the renewed Universities of Debrecen, Pécs, and Szeged; the reorganized Universities of Miskolc and Veszprém; and the newly created St. Stephen University of Gödöllő, University of West Hungary of Sopron, and University of Győr. The main exception to this integration process was in the city of Budapest, where Loránd Eötvös University, Semmelweis Medical University, Technical University, and the University of Economic Sciences and Public Administration (renamed Corvinus University in 2005) remained stand-alone universities.

In the period after the fall of communism, several private and religious universities were established, including the Central European University of Budapest, founded by the Hungarian American philanthropist George Soros as an English-language postgraduate institution where the students are introduced to Sir Karl Popper's idea of an "open society." The best-known religious institutions include Péter Pázmány Catholic University and Gáspár Karoli Reformed University. In addition, some of the specialized colleges of music, fine arts, theatre, and military arts were elevated to university status.

The postcommunist period also saw the restructuring of the university diplomas. Regular degrees remained, but the university doctorate and the Soviet-inspired "candidate" (*kandidátus*)—a research degree offered by the Academy of Sciences—were abolished and replaced by an American-style doctorate. At the same time, the "habilitation" was reintroduced as a prerequisite for university professorships. The science doctorate (*tudományok doktora*),

offered by the Academy of Sciences since 1950 and known as the "great doctorate" (*nagydoktorátus*), remained in force. But, whereas previously it was awarded on the basis of a comprehensive dissertation, it is now given in recognition of major life accomplishments by a very select group of scholars and scientists.

CHAPTER 9

HUNGARIAN CULTURAL LIFE

The cultural milieu of Hungary is a result of the diverse mix of genuine Hungarian peasant culture and the cosmopolitan culture of an influential German and Jewish urban population. Both the coffeehouse (as meeting place for intellectuals) and the music of the Roma (Gypsies) also have had an impact. Cultural life traditionally has been highly political since national culture became the sine qua non of belated nation building from the early 19th century. Theatre, opera, and literature in particular played crucial roles in developing national consciousness. Poets and writers, especially in crisis situations, became national heroes and prophets. Governments also attempted to influence cultural life through subsidy and regulation. During the state socialist era, culture was strictly controlled; party interference was influenced by ideological principles, and mass culture was promoted.

Through much of the 20th century, Hungarian cultural life was characterized by a dichotomy between rural and urban culture and subsequently between "populist" and "urbanist" culture—even though both of the latter were represented by urban-based intellectuals. These intellectuals were divided by their social origins (village versus city) and also by their disagreements about the type of culture that can best serve as the fountainhead of modern Hungarian culture. The populists were suspicious of the urbanists, many of whom were of non-Hungarian origins (mostly German and Jewish), and regarded the village as the depository of true Hungarian culture. The urbanists, on the other hand, viewed the populists as "country bumpkins" with little appreciation of real culture and looked to western European cultural centres as sources for their own version of modern Hungarian culture.

DAILY LIFE AND SOCIAL CUSTOMS

Genuine traditional Hungarian culture survived for a long period in an untouched countryside characterized by rootedness. Peasant dress, food, and entertainment, including folk songs and folk dances—the rituals of weddings and Easter and Christmas holidays—continued until the mid-20th century. The drastic (and in the countryside brutal) modernization of the second half of the 20th century nearly destroyed these customs. They were preserved, however, as folk art and tourist entertainment.

Everyday life changed dramatically, as did the family structure. Families became smaller, and ties with extended families diminished. The culture also became less traditional. Clothing styles began to follow the international pattern, and traditional peasant dress was replaced by blue jeans. Folk songs are still occasionally heard, but in daily life they have been replaced by rock and pop music. Urban culture, especially in the capital city, is highly cosmopolitan and encompasses the tradition of coffeehouse culture. Watching television is a popular pastime, and Hungarians average nearly four hours of TV viewing per day.

Hungary's most traditional cultural element is its cuisine. Hungarian food is very rich, and red meat is frequently used

Paprika peppers hung out to dry in Budapest. © Corbis

as an ingredient. Goulash (*gulyás*), bean soup with smoked meat, and beef stew are national dishes. The most distinctive element of Hungarian cuisine is paprika, a spice made from the pods of chili peppers (*Capsicum annuum*). Paprika is not native to Hungary—having been imported

GOULASH

Goulash (Hungarian: *gulyás*) is a traditional stew of Hungary. The origins of goulash have been traced to the 9th century, to stews eaten by Magyar shepherds. Before setting out with their flocks, they prepared a portable stock of food by slowly cooking cut-up meats with onions and other flavourings until the liquids had been absorbed. The stew was then dried in the sun and packed into bags made of sheep's stomachs. At mealtime, water was added to a portion of the meat to reconstitute it into a soup or stew.

The paprika that is indispensable for flavouring the modern goulash was added to the formulation in the 18th century. The classic "kettle goulash" is prepared by frying cubes of beef or mutton with onions in lard. Garlic, caraway seeds, tomatoes, green peppers, and potatoes complete the stew. *Székely gulyás*, another Hungarian specialty, is a stew of pork and sauerkraut flavoured with tomatoes, onions, caraway seeds, and sour cream.

either from Spain, India by way of the Turks, or the Americas—but it is a fixture on most dining tables in Hungary and an important export. Among Hungary's spicy dishes are *halászlé*, a fish soup, and *lecsó*, made with hot paprika, tomato, and sausage. Homemade spirits, including various fruit brandies (*pálinka*), are popular. Before World War II, Hungary was a wine-drinking country, but beer has become increasingly prevalent. Although Hungarians were not quick to accept foreign cuisines, they appeared in Budapest in the 1990s, a sign both of the growing influence of the outside world and of the presence of increasing numbers of foreigners who have settled in Hungary.

In addition to their observance of the two main religious holidays—Christmas, celebrated as a traditional family festivity, and Easter, characterized by village merrymaking—Hungarians celebrate several national holidays, including March 15 (Revolution of 1848) and August 20 (St. Stephen's Day). After the communist takeover, these traditional national holidays were replaced by April 4 (Liberation Day), May 1 (May Day), and the transformed August 20 (Constitution Day). After 1990 these communist-inspired holidays were replaced once more by the original national holidays, augmented by October 23, which commemorates the Revolution of 1956. All of these holidays are occasions both for solemn remembrance and for popular festivities, including folk dancing, choral singing, and the display of traditional folk arts. The Hungarian national anthem is based on the 1823 poem *Hymnusz* (*Anthem*) by Ferenc Kölcsey; it was set to music by Ferenc Erkel and officially adopted in 1844.

THE ARTS

Traditional folk arts either have disappeared or have become mostly commercialized, and political attempts in the 1930s, '50s, and '70s to preserve them basically failed. National high culture emerged at the turn of the 19th century, with literature taking a central role.

The first Hungarian-language newspaper, *Magyar Hírmondó* ("Hungarian Courier"), appeared in 1780, followed by *Magyar Merkurius* ("Hungarian Mercury") in 1788, *Bétsi Magyar Merkurius* ("Viennese Hungarian Mercury") in 1793, and *Hazai Tudósítások* ("National Informer") in 1806. (The first non-Hungarian-language newspaper published in the country may have been the *Mercurius Hungaricus* [1705–10]. It was created to provide readers outside Hungary with news of the uprising of Ferenc Rákóczi II against the Habsburg rulers.)

Ferenc Kazinczy, an advocate of Enlightenment ideas, founded a movement of language reform and promoted literature through his high standard of literary criticism. In his view, literature was a nation-sustaining or even nation-creating force. This newly born literary language was cultivated by most of the contemporary authors, including Mihály Csokonai Vitéz in his rococo poetry and the brothers Károly Kisfaludy and Sándor Kisfaludy in their early Romantic poetry and plays. Modern Hungarian drama was born in the middle of the 19th century, with József Katona's tragedy *Bánk bán* (1820) and Imre Madách's *Az ember tragédiája* (1861; *The Tragedy of Man*). Among other important 19th- and early-20th-century literary and cultural figures were the poets Mihály Vörösmarty, Sándor Petőfi, János Arany, and Endre Ady; the novelists József Eötvös, Mór Jókai, Kálmán Mikszáth, and Gyula Krúdy; the historians Mihály Horváth, Sándor Szilágyi, and Henrik Marczali; and the sociologist Oszkár Jászi.

During the interwar years, the traditions of these literary pioneers were continued by such poets and novelists as Zsigmond Móricz, Mihály Babits, Dezső Kosztolányi, Lajos Kassák, Frigyes Karinthy, János Kodolányi, Gyula Juhász, Dezső Szabó, Attila József, and Miklós Radnóti and such historians and literary historians as Sándor Domanovszky, Gyula Szekfű, Bálint Hóman, János Horváth, and Antal Szerb. The 1930s were witness to the emergence of the populist-urbanist controversy and the publication of a series of major sociographies about the realities of Hungarian peasant life. They were written by authors such as Gyula Illyés, Géza Féja, Ferenc Erdei, Péter Veres, József Erdélyi, Imre Kovács, and a number of others, who hailed from the countryside and sympathized with the plight of Hungary's rural underclass.

Following World War II, the nationalist and populist tendencies of Hungarian literature and culture were expurgated and replaced by politically inspired manifestations of Socialist Realism. And this applied equally to literature as to writings

IMRE KERTÉSZ

The Hungarian author Imre Kertész (born November 9, 1929, Budapest, Hungary) is best known for his semiautobiographical accounts of the Holocaust. In 2002 he received the Nobel Prize for Literature.

At age 14, Kertész was deported with other Hungarian Jews during World War II to the Auschwitz concentration camp in Nazi-occupied Poland. He was later sent to the Buchenwald camp in Germany, from which he was liberated in May 1945. Returning to Hungary, he worked as a journalist for the newspaper *Világosság* but was dismissed in 1951 following the communist takeover. He refused to submit to the cultural policies imposed by the new regime and turned to translation as a means of supporting himself. Kertész was highly praised as a translator specializing in the works of German-language authors, notably Friedrich Nietzsche, Hugo von Hofmannsthal, Sigmund Freud, Arthur Schnitzler, and Ludwig Wittgenstein.

Kertész was best known for his first and most acclaimed novel, *Sorstalanság* (*Fateless*), which he completed in the mid-1960s but was unable to publish for nearly a decade. When the novel finally appeared in 1975, it received little critical attention but established Kertész as a unique and provocative voice in the dissident subculture within contemporary Hungarian literature. *Sorstalanság* features an adolescent narrator who is arrested and deported to a concentration camp, where he confronts the inexplicable horror of human degradation not with outrage or resistance but with seemingly incomprehensible complacency and detachment. For the narrator the brutal reality of atrocity and evil is reconciled by his inherent and inexorable will to survive—without remorse or a need for retribution. With the fall of communism in Hungary following what was deemed the "quiet revolution" in 1989, Kertész resumed an active literary role. With the publication in 1990 of the first German-language edition of the novel, his literary reputation began to expand in Europe, and the novel was later published in more than 10 languages.

Sorstalanság was the first installment in Kertész's semiautobiographical trilogy reflecting on the Holocaust, and the two other novels—A *kudarc* (1988; "Fiasco") and *Kaddis a meg nem született gyermekért* (1990; *Kaddish for a Child Not Born*)—reintroduced the protagonist of *Sorstalanság*. In 1991 Kertész published *Az angol lobogó* ("The English Flag"), a collection of short stories and other short prose pieces, and he followed that in 1992 with *Gályanapló* ("Galley Diary"), a fictional diary covering the period from 1961 to 1991. Another installment of the diary, from 1991 to 1995, appeared in 1997 as *Valaki más: a változás krónikája* ("I—Another: Chronicle of a Metamorphosis"). His essays and lectures were collected in *A holocaust mint kultúra* (1993; "The Holocaust as Culture"), *A gondolatnyi csend, amig kivégzőoztag újratölt* (1998; "Moments of Silence While the Execution Squad Reloads"), and *A száműzött nyelv* (2001; "The Exiled Language").

in the social sciences such as history. The best of the poets, writers, historians, and social philosophers were silenced, and the rest were forced to toe the party line. In the postwar decades the literary contributions of such urbanists as Tibor Déry,

Sándor Petőfi, István Vas, and István Örkény and such populists or near-populists as Gyula Illyés, László Németh, and László Nagy—some of whom had begun their careers already during the interwar years—were particularly significant, as was the work of the social philosopher István Bibó. The most notable among the writers who emerged after 1956 were András Sütő, Sándor Kányádi, György Konrád, Péter Nádas, Péter Esterházy, and Imre Kertész (who won the Nobel Prize for Literature in 2002). The first two of these were Transylvanians who wrote great literature based on traditional literary models, while the latter four were Budapest urbanites who pursued the diverse paths of avant-garde literature.

Most of the important achievements in Hungarian visual arts and music emerged about the turn of the 20th century. The avant-garde painters Tivadar Csontváry-Kosztka and László Moholy-Nagy elevated Hungarian painting from traditional Romanticism and French-inspired Impressionism to greater international significance through path-breaking stylistic innovations. Hungarian music achieved worldwide renown with the composer Béla Bartók, an exponent of modern Hungarian music that was rooted in archaic folk traditions. Bartók was a central figure of early 20th-century culture who influenced future generations of composers both at home and abroad. Bartók's activities and compositions were paralleled by those of Zoltán Kodály and Ernő Dohnányi. Kodály's contributions went beyond the composition of music to the restructuring of Hungarian music education. His system of music education, the "Kodály method," is now taught throughout the world. The activities of these serious composers were paralleled by the work of such beloved composers of light music and operettas as Jenő

BÉLA BARTÓK

The Hungarian composer, pianist, and ethnomusicologist Béla Bartók (born March 25, 1881, Nagyszentmiklós, Hungary, Austria-Hungary—died September 26, 1945, New York, New York, United States) was an accomplished pianist at an early age. In 1904 he set about researching Hungarian folk music, having discovered that the folk-music repertory generally accepted as Hungarian was in fact largely urban Roma (Gypsy) music. His fieldwork with the composer Zoltán Kodály formed the basis for all later research in the field, and he published major studies of Hungarian, Romanian, and Slovakian folk music. He worked folk themes and rhythms into his own music, achieving a style that was at once nationalistic and deeply personal. He also toured widely as a virtuoso pianist. In 1940 he immigrated to the U.S., where he had great difficulty making a living. His works include the opera *Bluebeard's Castle* (1911), six celebrated string quartets (1908–39), the didactic piano set *Mikrokosmos* (1926–39), *Sonata for Two Pianos and Percussion* (1937), *Concerto for Orchestra* (1943), and three piano concertos (1926, 1931, 1945).

Huszka, Pongrác Kacsóh, Franz (Ferenc) Lehár, and Emeric (Imre) Kálmán.

In addition to composing, many Hungarian musicians have gained international renown as performers. These include the conductors Fritz Reiner, George Szell (György Széll), Eugene (Jenő) Ormándy, Antal Doráti, and Sir Georg Solti, as well as the pianists Franz (Ferenc) Liszt, Annie Fischer, Zoltán Kocsis, and András Schiff.

Since the 1960s, Hungarian motion pictures have attracted significant international interest. In particular, the parabolic films of Miklós Jancsó and István Szabó helped establish the reputation of Hungarian cinema. Nevertheless, most of the films shown in theatres in Hungary today are of American origin.

CULTURAL INSTITUTIONS

Following World War II, high culture that previously had been confined to the upper classes was promoted among the masses. A highly subsidized publishing industry fostered reading: the number of books published increased 10-fold between 1938 and 1988. Reading became a regular habit for about one-third of the population, and a huge network of more than 15,000 public libraries was established. The main national collections are the National Széchényi Library, the Ervin Szabó Library, the libraries of the Hungarian Academy of Sciences and the Hungarian Parliament, and the Central Library of Loránd Eötvös University (all in Budapest), plus the

libraries of the universities of Debrecen, Pécs, and Szeged.

Among the most notable of the thousands of museums and cultural centres are the Hungarian National Museum, the Hungarian National Gallery, the Museum of Fine Arts, and the Museum of Applied Arts (all in Budapest), plus the Christian Museum in Esztergom, the Déri Museum of Debrecen, the Janus Pannonius Museum of Pécs, the Ferenc Móra Museum of Szeged, and the collection of the Benedictine Archabbey of Pannonhalma. Government subsidizing of culture virtually ended with the introduction of a market system in the 1990s. The capital city is also regarded for its architectural legacy from various periods, which led to its being designated a UNESCO World Heritage site.

Teaching and scholarship are both emphasized in Hungary's institutions of higher learning, although, following the Soviet model, scholarly research was de-emphasized in the decades after World War II. During those years, much of the research and the resulting publications moved from the colleges and universities to the several dozen research institutes of the Hungarian Academy of Sciences (established in 1825), as well as to the institutes of various ministries. The academy was at the apex of Hungarian scientific and scholarly life for over four decades following its reorganization in 1949. Beginning in the early 1990s, however, it fell under persistent attack from the new political leadership, which hoped to cleanse it of its allegedly Marxist scientists and scholars, and funding and staffing dropped precipitously. This decline in numbers and funding continued even under the Socialist-Liberal regimes before and after the turn of the century.

Hungary has an international reputation for scholarship, with one of the world's highest per capita rates of Nobel laureates. Because of a lack of funding, however, most of these prizewinners have worked in Germany or the United States. Outstanding Hungarian-born scientists include Theodore von Kármán, Leo Szilárd, Edward Teller, Zoltán Bay, John G. Kemény, and Nobelists Eugene Wigner and Albert Szent-Györgyi. Other Nobel laureates are George de Hevesy, Georg von Békésy, John C. Harsányi, John C. Polányi, and George Oláh.

Some of the top Hungarian social scientists include the psychoanalyst Sándor Ferenczi (a member of Sigmund Freud's inner circle), the social philosophers Karl Mannheim and Michael Polányi, the economist Karl Polányi, and the philosopher and literary critic György Lukács. Hungarian-born mathematicians of international renown include John von Neumann, George Pólya, Gábor Szegő, Pál Turán, and Paul Erdös. Hungarian scholars also have excelled in the disciplines of linguistics, historiography, and literary history.

SPORTS AND RECREATION

Hungary's most popular vacation destinations include Lake Balaton and Lake Velence in Transdanubia, the Danube Bend, and the arty Szentendre Island above Budapest, as well as the Pilis, Mátra, and Bükk mountains in the north of Hungary. Lake Balaton attracts tourists from all over central and eastern Europe. A major attraction for the inhabitants of Budapest is Margit (Margaret) Island, an urban oasis of gardens and swimming pools on the Danube River.

Hungary has a tradition of success in international sporting competition. It has won a number of world championships

KRISZTINA EGERSZEGI

Swimmer Krisztina Egerszegi (born August 16, 1974, Budapest, Hungary) was the youngest athlete ever to win an Olympic gold medal in swimming. She won the 200-metre backstroke at the 1988, 1992, and 1996 Olympic Games, becoming only the second swimmer (after Dawn Fraser) to win an individual event at three Olympiads.

In 1987 Egerszegi competed in her first international event at the European championships in Strasbourg, France, where she finished fifth in the 200-metre backstroke. At age 14 she became the youngest athlete ever to win an Olympic gold medal in swimming when she won the 200-metre backstroke at the 1988 Olympic Games in Seoul, South Korea; Egerszegi also won a silver medal in the 100 metres. In 1991, at age 16, she won both the 100- and 200-metre backstroke at the world championships in Perth, Australia. Also in 1991, she broke world records for both distances at the European championships in Athens.

At the 1992 Olympic Games in Barcelona, Spain, Egerszegi won three gold medals, the most by any woman in individual events. She won the 400-metre individual medley and set Olympic records in both backstroke events. She was named Female World Swimmer of the Year in 1991 and 1992. In 1993 at the European championships in Sheffield, England, she was the first swimmer ever to earn four individual titles in a single European championship, winning the 100- and 200-metre backstroke, the 200-metre butterfly, and the 400-metre individual medley. Egerszegi returned to the Olympic Games in 1996 in Atlanta, Georgia. There she won a gold medal in the 200-metre backstroke and a bronze in the 400-metre individual medley.

and Olympic medals, even before the overpoliticization of sports in Soviet-bloc countries. Football (soccer) is especially popular, and Hungarian athletes also have enjoyed success in fencing, swimming, table tennis, track and field (athletics), rowing, and weight lifting. More recently, tennis and golf have gained in popularity, especially among the upper middle class.

MEDIA AND PUBLISHING

Under communist rule, the Hungarian press—about 30 daily newspapers and 1,500 periodicals—was strictly controlled, yet after the 1960s it became the least restricted within the Soviet bloc. In 1988 press censorship was relaxed and then within the next two years completely eliminated. In the first half of the 1990s, the number of newspapers increased, but their overall circulation declined. As an example, the print run of the country's most popular daily, the *Népszabadság* ("People's Freedom"), declined from 700,000 to about 200,000 at the turn of the

21st century. There was a similar decline in the leading liberal paper, *Magyar Nemzet* ("Hungarian Nation"). The leading weeklies include the *Szabad Föld* ("Free Earth") and *Nők Lapja* ("Women's Journal").

Similar developments took place in book publishing. The change of regime resulted in the birth of several hundred private publishers, but the ending of state subsidies undermined the health of most of the established ones. In the immediate postcommunist period, the number of published books increased by about one-sixth, but the number of copies per book declined by more than two-fifths. Similarly, about half of the public libraries located in smaller settlements were closed down by 1995, and this was accompanied by the reduction of the size of the regular reading public by about one-fourth. Some critics complained that the flood of new books had mass-market appeal but lacked literary or scholarly quality.

After World War II, radio ownership and listening became common. Television appeared only in the late 1950s, but it soon spread throughout the country. By the early 1980s, almost every household had a television. During the communist period there were only two radio stations and two state-run TV channels. In the decade following, however, the number of radio and TV stations—including cable and satellite TV—increased quickly and significantly. There was a precipitous decline in visits to movie houses and theatres. This was accompanied by the rapid spread of programming on recordable media (videotapes, DVDs, CDs), personal computers, and Internet connectivity. Thus, by the 21st century, electronic media occupied a central place in the leisure activities of Hungarians.

CHAPTER 10

HUNGARY: PAST AND PRESENT

I t is generally believed that Hungary came into existence when the Magyars, a Finno-Ugric people, began occupying the middle basin of the Danube River in the late 9th century. According to the "double-conquest" theory of archaeologist Gyula László, however, Hungary's creation can be dated to 670, with the arrival of an earlier wave of conquerors, the Late Avars, whom László classified as the Early Magyars. In either case, in antiquity parts of Hungary's territory had formed the ancient Roman provinces of Pannonia and Dacia. When Rome lost control of Pannonia at the end of the 4th century (Christian tombs from this period in what is now Pécs were designated a World Heritage site by UNESCO in 2000), it was occupied first by Germanic tribes, then by Slavs. The subsequent history of Dacia is unrecorded. The central plains had formed the bases for nomadic immigrant peoples from the steppes north of the Black Sea—Huns, Bulgars, Avars— some of whom extended their domination farther afield. The Avars, who dominated the basin in the 6th through 8th centuries, were crushed about 800 by Charlemagne. According to the double-conquest theory, many of the Late Avars/Early Magyars survived the 9th century to merge with the Magyars who were arriving in the area under the leadership of Árpád.

Charlemagne's successors organized the western half of the area in a chain of Slavic vassal "dukedoms." One of these, Croatia, which extended as far north as the Sava River, made itself fully independent in 869. Another, Moravia, extended as far east as the Gran, or Garam (Hron), River and openly defied its Carolingian overlord. (Later research has suggested that this 9th-century Moravia may have been located on the southern Morava River in present-day northern Serbia.) The Byzantine Empire and Bulgaria exercised loose authority over the south and east of the Carpathian Basin.

THE KINGDOM TO 1526

In 892 the Carolingian emperor, Arnulf, attempting to assert his authority over the Moravian duke Svatopluk, called in the help of the Magyars, whose early homes had been on the upper waters of the Volga and Kama rivers. They were driven, at an uncertain date and by unrecorded causes, southward onto the steppes, where they adopted the life of peripatetic herders. In the 9th century they were based on the lower Don, ranging over the steppes to the west of that river. They then comprised a federation of hordes, or tribes, each under a hereditary chieftain and each composed of a varying number of clans, the members of which shared a real or imagined blood kinship. All clan members were free, but the community included slaves taken in battle or in raids. There were seven Magyar tribes, but other elements were part of the federation, including three tribes of Turkic Khazars (the Kavars). Either because of this fact or perhaps because of a memory of earlier conditions, this federation was known to its neighbours as the On-Ogur (literally "Ten Arrows" or "Ten Tribes").

From the Slavic pronunciation of this term, the name Hungarian is derived, with the initial H added because they were thought by some scholars to be descendants of the Huns.

THE ÁRPÁDS

In 889, attacks by a newly arrived Turkic people called the Pechenegs had driven the Magyars and their confederates to the western extremities of the steppes, where they were living when Arnulf's invitation arrived. The band sent to Arnulf reported back that the plains across the Carpathian Mountains would form a suitable new homeland that could be easily conquered and defended from the rear. Having elected as their chief Árpád, the leader of their most powerful tribe, the Magyars crossed the Carpathians en masse, probably in the spring of 895, and easily subjugated the peoples of the sparsely inhabited central plain. Prior to the conquest, the Magyars lived under a dual kingship that included a sacred ruler with minimal powers called the *kende* and a de facto leader called the *gyula*. At the time of the conquest, Árpád occupied the latter position, and, following the death of the last *kende* in 904, he united the two positions into the office of a duke or prince.

The Magyars destroyed the Moravian state in 906 and in the next year occupied Pannonia, having defeated a German force sent against them. They were then firmly established in the whole centre

ESZTERGOM

The northwestern Hungarian town of Esztergom was the capital and royal residence of the early Árpád princes and kings and successive Hungarian kings until the mid-13th century. Stephen I was born in the town and crowned there in 1000.

This river port on the Danube River (which at that point forms the frontier with Slovakia) lies 25 miles (40 km) northwest of Budapest. Esztergom lies at the western end of the valley cut by the Danube between the Pilis and Börzsöny hills, which divides the Little Alfold (Little Hungarian Plain) from the Great Alfold (Great Hungarian Plain).

The town's archbishopric is the oldest in Hungary, dating from 1001. The town has long been the centre of Roman Catholicism in Hungary, and its archbishops are primate cardinals (since 1991, the archdiocese has been known as Esztergom-Budapest). Esztergom's fortress, last restored in the 18th century, is still largely intact atop Várhegy (Castle Hill). The town's great cathedral (built 1822–60), modeled on St. Peter's in Rome, overlooks the Danube and is the largest church in Hungary, the outside height of the cupola being 348 feet (106 m). It is on the site of St. Stephen's original cathedral (1010). The treasury of the cathedral has a rich collection of medieval goldsmiths' work and a textile collection. The former primate's palace, the Christian Museum, has a rich painting collection. The Castle Museum has relics of the royal palace (10th–12th century, major period of construction).

The town also has many fine Baroque houses. In 1895 a bridge connecting Esztergom with Štúrovo, Slovakia, opened; however, it was destroyed in 1944 and not rebuilt until 2001. After World War II, industries were developed. Manufactures include automobiles, electronics, and optical products.

of the basin, over which their tribes and their associates distributed themselves. Árpád took the central area west of the Danube for his own tribe, on his way to establishing a dynasty. The periphery was guarded by outposts, which were gradually pushed forward, chiefly to the north and the east.

THE CHRISTIAN KINGDOM

During the next half century, the Magyars were chiefly known in Europe for the forays they made across the continent, either as mercenaries in the service of warring princes or in search of booty for themselves—treasure or slaves for domestic use or sale. Terrifying to others, their mode of life was not always profitable. Indeed, their raiding forces suffered a number of severe reverses, culminating in a disastrous defeat at the hands of the German king Otto I in 955 at the Battle of Lechfeld, outside Augsburg (in present-day Germany). By that time the wild blood of the first invaders was thinning out, and new influences, in particular Christianity, had begun to circulate. Both the Eastern and Western churches strove to draw the peoples of east-central Europe into their orbits. The Magyars had established pacific, almost friendly relations with Bavaria. The decisive step was taken by Árpád's great-grandson Géza, who succeeded to the hereditary office of *fejedelem* (duke) sometime before 972 and reestablished its authority over the tribal chiefs. In 973 he sent an embassy to the Holy Roman emperor Otto II at Quedlinburg (Germany), and in 974 he and his family were received into the Western church. In 995 his son, Stephen (István), married Gisella, a Bavarian princess.

Stephen I (reigned 997–1038) carried on his father's work. With the help of heavily armed Bavarian knights, he crushed his rivals for the ducal office. Applying to Pope Sylvester II, Stephen received the insignia of royalty (including the still existent "Holy Crown of Hungary") from the papacy and, according to tradition, was crowned king on Christmas Day, 1000. The event was of immeasurable importance, for not only did Hungary enter the spiritual community of the Western world but it did so without having to recognize the political suzerainty of the Holy Roman Empire. This was possible because Sylvester, who extended papal protection to Hungary, held great sway with the emperor, Otto III, who had once been his pupil. Stephen then effected the conversion of his people to Christianity, establishing a network of 10 archiepiscopal and episcopal sees, which he reinforced with lavishly endowed monastic foundations.

Stephen crushed the surviving disputants of his authority—notably the Kavars—and, furthering his father's work, organized his state on a system that was to remain for many centuries the basis of Hungary's political and social structure. The tribes, as units, disappeared, but the fundamental social stratification was not altered. The descendants in the male line of the old conquerors and elements later equated with them remained a privileged class, answerable in judgment only to the king or his representative and entitled to appear in general assemblage. Their lands—which at this time, since the economy was mainly pastoral, were held by clans or subclans in semi-communal ownership—were inalienable, except for proved delinquency, and free of any obligation. The only duty required by the state of members of this class was that of military service on call. They were allowed to retain their slaves, although Stephen freed his own. All land not held by this class—then more than half the whole—belonged to the crown, which could indeed donate it at will. The non-servile inhabitants of these lands—e.g., descendants of the pre-Magyar population (among them the Late Avars/Early Magyars), manumitted slaves, and invited colonists—were subjects of the crown or of the local landholder.

The whole of this land was divided into counties, each under a royal official called an *ispán* (*comes*)—later *főispán* (*supremus comes*). This official represented the king's authority, administered its unfree population, and collected the taxes that formed the national revenue. Each *ispán* maintained at his fortified headquarters (*castrum* or *vár*) an armed force of freemen. In Stephen's day there were between 40 and 50 such counties.

THE EARLY KINGS

Once Stephen (canonized as St. Stephen in 1083) established his rule, his authority was rarely questioned. He fought few foreign wars and made his long reign a period of peaceful consolidation. But his death in 1038 was followed by many years of discord. His only son, Emeric (Imre), had predeceased him, and the nation rebelled against his designated successor, Peter (the son of Stephen's sister and the doge of Venice), who was expelled in 1041. Peter returned in 1044 with the help of Emperor Henry III. Samuel Aba, the "national" king, who had taken Peter's place, was murdered; however, Peter himself was killed in a pagan rebellion in 1046. He was followed on the throne by Andrew (Endre) I, of a collateral branch of the house of Árpád, who was killed in 1060 while fleeing from a battle lost to his brother, Béla I. After Béla's death there was a further conflict between his sons, Géza and Ladislas (László), and Andrew's son, Salamon.

Peace returned only when, after the short rule of Géza I (1074–77), the throne passed to Ladislas I, who occupied it until 1095. Even then the curse of dynastic jealousy proved to have been exorcised only temporarily. Ladislas's successor, Coloman (Kálmán; 1095–1116), who was the elder son of Géza I, had his own brother, Álmos, and Álmos's infant son, Béla, blinded to secure the throne for his own son Stephen II (1116–31). Béla II (1131–41), the blinded boy, whom his father's friends had brought up in

SAINT STEPHEN'S CROWN

The symbol of Hungarian nationhood, Saint Stephen's Crown, is greatly venerated; without it no Hungarian sovereign was truly accepted by the country's people. It is made from an 11th-century jeweled circlet of Byzantine style, augmented early in the 12th century by the addition of arches and an upper rim composed of alternate pointed and round-topped plaques of enameled gold. Small pendants hang on short chains on both sides and at the back. The cross on the top is crooked because the screw hole in the knob it stands on was set at an angle, suggesting that originally it was not meant to occupy the top of the crown but to go on a sloping surface, possibly the curve of the foremost arch.

The crown was given to a U.S. Army unit by a Hungarian honour guard to keep it from being seized by advancing Soviet troops after World War II. It remained in U.S. guardianship at Fort Knox until it was returned in 1978.

secrecy, and Béla's eldest son, Géza II (1141–62), ruled thereafter unchallenged, but the succession of Géza's son, Stephen III (1162–72), was disputed by two of his uncles, Ladislas II (1162–63) and Stephen IV (1163–65). Happily, the death of Stephen IV exhausted the supply of uncles, and Stephen III's brother, Béla III (1173–96), had no domestic rivals to the throne. However, the short reign of Béla's elder son, Emeric (1196–1204), was spent largely in disputes with his younger brother, Andrew II, who on Emeric's death expelled his infant son, Ladislas III (who died the next year), before beginning his own long reign (1205–35).

CONSOLIDATION AND EXPANSION

These royal disputes caused Hungary much harm. Claimants to the throne often invoked foreign help, for which they paid in political degradation or loss of territory: both Peter and Salamon did homage to the Holy Roman emperor for their thrones; and Aba's war against Peter's protectors cost Hungary its previous territories west of the Leitha River, while the wars of the 12th century cost it areas in the south. The uncertainty delayed political consolidation, and even Christianity did not take root easily; there was a widespread pagan revolt in 1046 and another in 1061.

Yet the political unity of the country and the new faith somehow survived the earlier troubles, and both were firmly established by Ladislas I (1077–95; canonized in 1192 as St. Ladislas), one of Hungary's greatest kings, and by Coloman, who, despite his nefarious power grab, was a competent and enlightened ruler.

Meanwhile, outside factors benefited Hungary. After Austria had grown big at the expense of the imperial authority, most of Hungary's neighbours were states of approximately the same size and strength as itself, and the Hungarians lived with them on terms of mutual tolerance and even friendship. The steppes were quiet: the Cuman (Hungarian: Kun) people, after destroying the Pechenegs there, did not try to go farther, and, after two big raids had been successfully repelled by Ladislas I, they left Hungary in peace. This allowed Hungary to extend its effective frontiers to the Carpathian crest in the north and over Transylvania. Magyar advance guards pushed up the valleys of both areas and were reinforced in the Szepes area and in central Transylvania by imported colonies of Germans (usually called Saxons). In the meantime, colonies of Szeklers (Székely, Szekelyek), a people akin to the Magyars who had preceded them into the central plains, were settled behind Transylvania's eastern passes. The county system was extended to both areas, although with modifications in Transylvania, where the Saxons and Szeklers constituted free communities and the whole was placed under a governor called a *vajda* (*voievod* or *vaivode*). In the south Ladislas I occupied (or reoccupied after an interval) the area between the Sava and Dráva rivers; Coloman assumed the crown of Croatia, which then included Bosnia and northern Dalmatia, although this remained a separate "Land of the Hungarian Crown," over which a governor known as a ban acted as deputy for the king.

In the interior too, natural growth and continued immigration swelled the population, which by 1200 had risen to the then large figure of some two million. The rulers of this big, populous state were now important men. After Ladislas's day, German claims to suzerainty over Hungary ceased. In the 12th century the country intervened in its neighbours' affairs as often as they did in Hungary's. Before becoming Hungary's king, Béla III was an heir to the throne of Byzantine Emperor Manuel I Comnenus. He married a French princess, Margaret Capet, and generated revenues roughly equal to the income of the king of France. He owned half the land of the kingdom outright and held monopolies of coinage, customs, and mining. While the income of the early kings had been mostly in kind, half of Béla's income was cash, coming from royal monopolies and taxes paid by foreign settlers.

SOCIAL AND POLITICAL DEVELOPMENTS

Meanwhile, the pattern of Hungarian society had been changing. The population of the free class, or "nobles" as they were coming to be called, although frequently reinforced by new admissions to its ranks, probably hardly increased in absolute terms and certainly grew far less than the unfree population; from perhaps half the total population in 896, they had been reduced to about one-eighth by 1200. Further, as the economy became agricultural, the old clan lands dwindled until only pockets remained. Where the rest had been and in large parts of the old crown lands, which improvident donations had greatly reduced, the land was held in the form of individual estates. The owner of each of these estates was master of the unfree population on it; the nobles had, to a large extent, become a landed oligarchy. Some individual estates were very large, and their owners had come to constitute a "magnate" class, not yet institutionalized or legally differentiated from their poorer co-nobles but far above them in wealth and influence. Although slavery had practically disappeared, the non-nobles were still a "subject" class. Many of them, including the burghers of the towns (most of which were German foundations) and members of such communities as the Saxons and Szeklers, were protected by special charters and personally free, but even they stood politically outside the magic ring of the *natio Hungarica*—nominally the "Hungarian nation" but in practice just the Hungarian nobility.

As a result of Béla's marriage to the sister of the French king, the Hungarian court became a centre of French knightly culture. Western dress and translations of French tales of chivalry appeared. A royal notary, known to future generations as "Anonymous," wrote the history of the conquest of Hungary. The first known work in the Hungarian language, the ("Funeral Oration"), was part of the otherwise Latin-language Pray Codex written in the early 1190s. Béla also followed a Western model in introducing written documentation of government administrative authority. Moreover, monasteries served as public notaries from the end of the 12th century.

In addition to tents and wooden structures, stone buildings (mostly churches, abbeys, and palaces) appeared in the permanent settlements. The cathedral of Pécs, the Benedictine abbey of Pannonhalma (originally begun in 996; designated a UNESCO World Heritage site in 1996), and the royal palace at Esztergom (where St. Stephen was born about 970) were the first examples of early Gothic architecture.

The Christian Museum, with the dome-topped great cathedral and the fortress of St. Stephen in the background, Esztergom, Hung. ZEFA

Throughout these developments the country had remained an absolutist patrimonial kingship. The king maintained a council of optimates (aristocrats), but his prerogatives were not restricted and his authority remained absolute. A strong king, such as Béla III, could always curb a recalcitrant magnate by simply confiscating his estate. Only the follies and extravagances of the feckless Andrew II evoked a revolt, culminating in 1222 in the issue of the Golden Bull (*Bulla aurea* or *Aranybulla*)—the Hungarian equivalent of England's Magna Carta—to which every Hungarian king thereafter had to swear. Its purpose was twofold: to reaffirm the rights of the smaller nobles of the old and new classes of royal servants (*servientes regis*) against both the crown and the magnates and to defend those of the whole nation against the crown by restricting the powers of the latter in certain fields and legalizing refusal to obey its unlawful commands (the *ius resistendi*). Andrew had done much harm by dissipating the royal revenues through his extravagances and by issuing huge grants of land to his partisans. The royal estate gradually melted away as the *ispáns* and knights became the hereditary owners of the land. Leading aristocratic families—such as the Aba and Csák clans in the north, the Pók and Kán clans in the east and northeast, and the Subich and Köszegi clans in the west and southwest—became the nearly unchallenged rulers of large parts of the country.

Mongol warriors, miniature from Rashīd al-Dīn's History of the World, *1307. Courtesy of the Edinburgh University Library, Scotland*

THE MONGOL INVASION: THE LAST ÁRPÁD KINGS

Andrew's successor, Béla IV (1235–70), began his reign with a series of measures designed to reestablish royal authority, but his work was soon interrupted by the frightful disaster of the Mongol invasion. In the spring of 1241 the Mongols quickly overran the country and, by the time they left it a year later, inflicted ghastly devastation. Only a few fortified places and the impenetrable swamps and forests escaped their ravages. The country lost about half its population, the incidence ranging from 60 percent in the Alföld (100 percent in parts of it) to 20 percent in Transdanubia; only parts of Transylvania and the northwest came off fairly lightly.

Returned from Dalmatia, where he had taken refuge, Béla, whom his country not unjustly dubbed its second founder, reorganized the army, built a chain of fortresses, and called in new settlers to repopulate the country. He paid special attention to the towns. But he was forced to give some of the magnates practically a free hand on their own estates, and a few families rose to near-sovereign local status. Further, one group of immigrants, a body of Cumans who had fled into Hungary before the Mongols, proved so powerful and so turbulent that to ensure their loyalty Béla had to marry his son, Stephen V, to a Cuman princess. The king attempted to counterbalance the power of the magnates by creating his own army, partly from the Cumans. A newly created "conditional" nobility comprising ennobled soldiers and settlers who gained land for military service strengthened the ranks of the lesser nobility. The system of royal estates and judicial power was thereafter transformed in an assembly in which nobles represented their counties.

Stephen died two years after his father's death, after which the country passed to the regency of his widow, the "Cuman woman," whom the Hungarians detested. Her son, who grew up wild and undisciplined, was assassinated and left no legitimate heir, and claims to the throne were made through the female line of the Árpáds. A male heir, Andrew III, was found in Italy, and, although the young man's claim to the throne was impugned, he proved a wise, capable king. With his death in 1301, however, the national dynasty became extinct.

A new Western-style feudal socioeconomic system had emerged in Hungary, but it had yet to take root. During the last third of the 13th century, Hungarian assimilation into Europe was threatened by the ongoing conflicts between various baronial factions. Moreover, Hungary was still the destination of migrating pagan tribes and the focus of barbarian attacks, and it continued to exhibit the features of a country on the borders of Christian feudal Europe.

HUNGARY UNDER FOREIGN KINGS

The extinction of the old native dynasty entitled the nation to choose its successor; but the principle of the blood tie was still generally regarded as determinant, and all the candidates for the throne—Wenceslas of Bohemia, Otto of Bavaria, and Charles Robert of the Angevin house of Naples—based their claims on descent from an Árpád in the female line. But all three claimants were foreigners; one of them and the father of another were actually seated on foreign thrones. From that time until its extinction, the kingship of Hungary was in fact invariably—with two exceptions, one of them disputed—held by a foreigner, nearly always by one occupying simultaneously at least one foreign throne. This could be to the advantage of Hungary when the king used the resources of those thrones in its service, but he could alternatively neglect and exploit Hungary in pursuit of his other interests and use his power to crush national freedoms and institutions. Securing the advantages of foreign rule while escaping its dangers was the abiding dilemma—seldom successfully resolved—of Hungarian history.

THE ANGEVIN KINGS

The problem of foreign kingship did not pose itself at first, as Charles Robert of Anjou (Charles I) had no foreign throne and grew up a true Hungarian. He was still a child when a group of Hungarian nobles crowned him in 1301; however, his claim to the throne was disputed, and the crown went first to Wenceslas of Bohemia, then to Otto of Bavaria, before Charles was recognized as king in 1308, ruling until 1342. He was a capable man who achieved peace after crushing the most rebellious of the regional lords or oligarchs (also known as "kinglets") and winning over the rest. The international situation, with Germany distraught by the power struggle between empire and papacy, the Mongolian Tatars grown passive, and the power of Byzantium in full decay, was again favourable to the states of the "middle zone" of eastern Europe and the Balkans; it is no accident that Poland, Hungary, Bohemia, and Serbia often look on the 14th century as their golden age. Because this situation favoured its neighbours as well as Hungary itself, Charles Robert's attempts at expansion were only moderately successful. In the Balkans he made Bosnia his friend and client but lost Dalmatia to Venice and other territories to Serbia and the newly emerged *voievody* (province) of Walachia. But he drove Czech and Austrian marauders out of the land and on the whole preserved friendly relations with Austria, Bohemia, and Poland.

Charles's son, Louis (Lajos) I (1342–82), the only Hungarian king on whom his country bestowed the appellation "Great," built on his father's foundations. Keeping peace with the West, he repaired his father's losses in the south and surrounded his kingdom with a ring of dependencies over which Hungary presided as *archiregnum* (chief kingdom) in the Balkans, on the lower Danube, and in Galicia. These new dependencies included several *banats* (provinces governed by an appointed *ban*) inhabited by Slavs and the two Vlach provinces of Moldavia and Walachia. In 1370 Louis

Hungary in 1360. Encyclopædia Britannica, Inc.

also ascended the throne of Poland, by virtue of an earlier family compact.

Both Angevin kings (dynastic name derived from Anjou) owed much to the wealth they derived from the gold mines of Transylvania and northern Hungary, some 35 to 40 percent of which went to the king, enabling him to maintain a splendid court. Spared for two generations from serious invasion or civil war, the rest of the country blossomed materially as never before. The population rose to three million, with a total of 49 royal free boroughs, more than 500 smaller towns, and some 26,000 villages. The economy was still mainly rural, but the crafts prospered, trade expanded, and the arts flourished.

The life of the court and the daily life of cities borrowed from western European societies. German settlers and burghers in the cities and the clergy became the main agents of Western culture. The Dominicans built 25 monasteries by the early 14th century and established a theological school in Buda (now part of Budapest). The Franciscans also established monasteries, as did the Cistercians, Premonstratensians, and Paulines. Romanesque style dominated architecture in Hungary until the ascendancy of Gothic design in the late 13th century. Cities built impressive churches, such as the Church of Our Blessed Lady (now better known as the Matthias Church) in Buda. Further testimonies to the spread of western European culture were the palace of Visegrád, the royal castles of Zólyom and Diósgyőr, the miniatures of the Illuminated Chronicle (1360), and the St. George statue in Kolozsvár (1373), as well as the earliest codex predominantly in Hungarian (1370) and the finest example of early Hungarian poetry, *Ómagyar Máriasiralom* (about 1300; "Old Hungarian Lament of the Virgin Mary"). The first universities were established during the 14th century in Pécs and Óbuda, though they were short-lived. Yet, in spite of its advancement, Hungary remained a less-developed borderland of Europe.

The rule of the two Angevin kings was essentially despotic, although enlightened. They introduced elements of feudalism into the political and military system; each lord was responsible for maintaining his own armed contingent (*banderium*). The magnates were held firmly in check, and Louis reaffirmed the rights and privileges of the common nobles. Counties were developing from "royal" into "noble" institutions, each still under a royal official but administered with a wide measure of autonomy by elected representatives of the local nobility. Louis also standardized the tax obligations of the peasants at the figure of one-tenth of their produce (*tithe*) going to the church, another tenth (*nona*) going to the lord, and a house or gate tax (*porta*) going directly to the state.

SIGISMUND OF LUXEMBOURG

The benefits of Louis's rule would have been far greater still had he not wasted much money and many lives on endeavours to secure the throne of Naples for his nephew. His foreign acquisitions served his personal glory more than they did the real interests of his country, the imposing edifice of which largely collapsed when he died. He left as heirs only two daughters. Louis had designated the elder, Maria, to succeed him on both his thrones, but the Poles refused to continue the union. They accepted the younger daughter, Hedvig (Polish: Jadwiga), as queen but married her to Jogaila (Polish: Władysław II Jagiełło) of Lithuania. The Hungarians crowned Maria, whose husband, Sigismund of Luxembourg, became her consort in 1387 and after her death eight years later ruled alone until his own death in 1437.

Under Sigismund, matters took a sharp turn for the worse, although he did much for the arts and commerce and, above all, for the towns. Also, like Andrew II, he promoted Hungarian political institutions by creating the need for them. The principle that the consent of representatives of the privileged classes, assembled in the Diet, was necessary for the grant of any subsidy or additional taxation—and even, later, for any legislation—dates from his reign, being made necessary by his extravagance and arbitrariness. His frequent and prolonged absences from the country increased the importance of the office of the palatine (*comes palatinus, nádor*), which goes back to the reign of Stephen I in the early 11th century. The palatine was appointed by the king with the approval of the nobility (*natio Hungarica*). During Sigismund's long absences from Hungary, the palatine represented the king and also acted as intermediary between him and the people. But these were only palliatives against bitterly felt abuses. The nation hated Sigismund for the cruelty he showed at the outset of his reign to the supporters of a rival. Moreover, Hungarians resented the absenteeism of his later years, when he occupied himself chiefly with imperial and Bohemian affairs (he was elected German king in 1410/11 and Holy Roman emperor in 1433 and became titular king of Bohemia in 1419), neglecting—Hungarians felt—the numerous problems of their country. There was much discontent among the peasants, who were subjected to heavy exactions by the crown and by their masters, the unrest being aggravated by the spread of radical Hussite religious doctrines from Bohemia. Serious revolts occurred in northern Hungary and Transylvania. Above all, there was the growing danger from the Ottoman Turks, who, though they had already taken Bosnia from Louis, could not threaten Hungary proper while Serbia still stood. But in 1389 the power of Serbia was broken at the Battle of Kosovo, and the danger for Hungary became urgent. Sigismund organized a Crusade that was disastrously defeated at the Battle of Nicopolis in 1396. Timur (Tamerlane) gave Europe a respite by his attack on the Turkish rear, but the advance was resumed in 1415. Walachia submitted in 1417; thereafter, Transylvania and southern Hungary suffered repeated raids.

JÁNOS HUNYADI AND
MATTHIAS CORVINUS

The Ottoman sultan Murad II was preparing a grand assault on Hungary when Sigismund died in 1437, leaving as his heir a daughter. She was married to Albert V of Austria, whom the country accepted as Sigismund's successor (as Albert II), but only on condition that he not become Holy Roman emperor or reside abroad without permission of the estates. Albert set about organizing the country's defenses but died in 1439, leaving his widow with an unborn child. To avoid an interregnum and a minority rule, perhaps with a queen, the country elected Władysław III of Poland as king. Within two years of Władysław's death in battle against the Ottoman Turks in 1444, the estates nominally acknowledged Albert's son, Ladislas V (called Ladislas Posthumus), as the king of Hungary. (He was crowned when only a few months old but was not really accepted as the country's ruler until 1453.) Meanwhile, in 1446 the estates elected the great general John (János) Hunyadi as governor (1446–53) and then as captain-in-chief (1453–56) of the country. Hunyadi, who had been repelling the renewed Ottoman attacks, kept up the country's defense under increasing difficulties, constantly thwarted by jealous magnates and harassed by the Czech condottiere Jan Jiškra (Giškra), while Frederick III (first of the house of Habsburg to become emperor) encroached on the western provinces.

Hunyadi died in 1456 after repelling the Turks in defense of Belgrade (Hungarian: Nándorfehérvár), then a Hungarian outpost. Ladislas's maternal uncle, Ulrich II of Cilli, aware of the country's devotion to Hunyadi, had the governor's elder son beheaded and his younger son, Matthias Corvinus (Mátyás Hunyadi), imprisoned in Prague. Ladislas V himself died suddenly a year later. The country was tired of foreign rule and its agents, and on January 24, 1458, a great concourse of nobles acclaimed Matthias king, as Matthias I. Extracted from Prague with some difficulty, he was brought to Buda and crowned amid nationwide rejoicing.

The only national king to reign over all of Hungary after the Árpáds, Matthias has been seen through something of a golden haze by historians. A true Renaissance prince, he was a fine natural soldier, a first-class administrator, an outstanding linguist, a learned astrologer, and an enlightened patron of the arts and learning. His collections of illuminated manuscripts, pictures, statues, and jewels were famous throughout Europe. Artists and scholars were welcomed at his court, which could vie in magnificence with any other on the continent. Sumptuous buildings sprang up in his capital and other centres.

Politically too, he represented the ideas of the Renaissance. He listened to his council, convoked the Diet regularly, and actually enlarged the autonomous powers of the counties. But at heart he was a despot; his real instruments of government were his secretaries, men picked by himself, usually young and often of humble origin. His rule was in the main an efficient and, on balance, a benevolent one. He simplified and improved the administration and, above all, the laws, enforcing justice with an even hand. The debit side of his rule was the increased taxation imposed by him for his administrative innovations, his collections (which cost his subjects vast sums), and, above all, the mercenary standing army, 30,000 strong (largely composed of Hussite mercenaries and known after its commander, "Black John" Haugwitz, as the Black Army), which he kept as part of the royal banderium for use against enemies, at home and abroad.

At first he had much need for such a force; although the Ottoman Turks were quiescent for a decade, there were discontented magnates, and the Czechs and the Austrians were unquiet neighbours. But, after Matthias had crushed, expelled, or bought off these enemies, had built a chain of fortresses along the southern frontier, and had even reestablished a nominal but, in practice, worthless suzerainty over Bosnia, Serbia, Wallachia (Walachia), and Moldavia, he let himself be drawn into an ever-widening circle of campaigns against Bohemia and Austria. In 1469 he made himself master of Moravia, Silesia, and Lusatia, with the title (borne simultaneously by George of Podebrady) of king of Bohemia, and in 1478 he forced Frederick III to cede him Lower Austria and Styria. He argued that his neighbours

were untrustworthy and that he could not organize the great Crusade against the Turks without the resources of the imperial and Bohemian crowns. But his subjects were unconvinced, and in 1470 a party actually conspired to replace him with a Polish prince.

This enterprise collapsed, and Matthias entered on a complex transaction with the new emperor, Maximilian I, under which his illegitimate son John (he had no legitimate issue) was to marry Maximilian's daughter in return for recession of the Austrian provinces and Maximilian's recognition of John. But on May 6, 1490, while on his way to the meeting that should have sealed the bargain, Matthias died suddenly, and the whole enterprise collapsed.

Both Sigismund and Matthias attempted to balance baronial power by strengthening the cities, but they were only partly successful. In contrast with western Europe, urbanization remained moderate, with the development of walled cities lagging behind that of western European counterparts. The number of guilds was limited, and the structure of foreign trade reflected economic backwardness; nearly four-fifths of imports consisted of textiles and about one-eighth of metalware. Exports consisted almost entirely of cattle and wine. The most important aspect of urbanization was the rapid growth of agricultural towns (Hungarian: *mezővárosok*; Latin: *oppidi*). Instead of the approximately 50 families that made up the 20 to 30 portae (taxable units) of the typical village, these oversize peasant settlements had as many as 500 portae. Moreover, the number of these settlements increased from about 300 in the mid-15th century to about 800 in the early 16th century.

THE JAGIELLON KINGS

The magnates, who did not want another heavy-handed king, procured the accession of Vladislas II, king of Bohemia (Ulászló II in Hungarian history), precisely because of his notorious weakness: he was known as King Dobže, or Dobzse (meaning "Good" or, loosely, "OK"), from his habit of accepting with that word every paper laid before him. The emperor Maximilian contented himself with reoccupying his lost provinces and establishing a sort of paternal patronage over Hungary. This was consolidated in 1515 by an agreement under which Vladislas's son, Louis, married Maximilian's granddaughter Mary, while Louis's sister, Anne, married Maximilian's grandson Ferdinand, who was to succeed to Louis's thrones if Louis died without an heir. The agreement was made without the consent of the Hungarian nobility and in violation of the resolution passed by the Diet in 1505 that it would never accept a foreigner as the king of Hungary. The candidate of the "national party" was János Zápolya (Szapolyai), *voievod* of Transylvania.

Meanwhile, the magnates permitted the Black Army to disintegrate (without replacing it) and allowed the country's fortresses to fall into disrepair. Because they had not been paid, some of the Black Army's fragments resorted to banditry and then had to be dispersed by one of Matthias's generals, Pál Kinizsi, in 1494. Vladislas was the magnates' helpless prisoner; he could make no decision without their consent, and his revenues were looted so ruthlessly that he was reduced to selling Matthias's art and book collections. Nearly all of Matthias's reforms were canceled, and the peasants were oppressed grievously. In 1514 there was a peasant uprising that, unlike those that had preceded it, spread nationwide. It was sparked by the call for a Crusade against the Ottomans by the papal legate of eastern Europe, Archbishop Tamás Bakócz. Some 20,000 men gathered near Buda in the spring and, led by a Szekler nobleman, György Dózsa, moved on the southern border. The rebellious, antilandlord sentiment of these "Crusaders" became apparent during their march across the Great Alföld, and Bakócz canceled the campaign. The peasant leaders not only refused to obey this order when it reached them in late May but also confronted and defeated the nobles' army and went on a two-month rampage that came to be known as the Dózsa Rebellion. They burned nobles' manor houses and captured several major towns and cities. By mid-July, however, the peasants had been defeated and Dózsa captured, tortured, and executed. The peasants were condemned to perpetual servitude, and their right to free migration was abolished. The *Tripartitum* legal code (1514), by jurist István Werbőczi, reinforced the power of the aristocracy against both the throne and the peasantry. Although this law was not immediately enforced, it served as the basis for the preservation of serfdom for centuries to come.

When Vladislas died in 1516, his nine-year-old son was proclaimed king as Louis II. The defenses of the kingdom worsened, and in 1521 the new Ottoman sultan, Süleyman I (the Magnificent), demanded tribute from Louis. When the demand was rejected, Süleyman took Belgrade. Suddenly alive to the Turkish danger, the magnates voted to reestablish a standing army, but nothing was done to raise it, because each rival faction tried to put the burden of its upkeep on the others. Appeals for help from abroad met with little response. In 1526 the sultan advanced into Hungary. A general call to arms was proclaimed, but the most important forces—those from Transylvania and Croatia—were late in obeying it. Louis, with a force of 24,000 to 26,000 men, moved down the Danube in August and attacked the Turks at the Battle of Mohács. The Hungarian army, heavily outnumbered, was almost annihilated. Louis himself drowned during his flight. Unable to believe that the pitiful array that had met him was Hungary's national army, the sultan advanced with extreme caution. He occupied Buda on September 10 but returned across the Danube by the end of October, taking with him more than 100,000 captives.

THE PERIOD OF PARTITION

Since the sultan had not meant to remain in Hungary, the disaster of Mohács might have been overcome had the king not perished or had there emerged a strong national leader who could have marshaled the country's resources. As it was, however, there were two claimants to Hungary's throne: John (János Zápolya), who had served as *voievod* of Transylvania, and Ferdinand of Habsburg (later Holy Roman emperor as Ferdinand I). Each had his supporters, and both of them were elected king by rival factions of the Hungarian nobility. This precipitated a civil war, which led to more chaos and weakened the country further. After each of the kings failed to drive out his rival, John appealed for help from Süleyman, who installed him in Buda but at the expense of making him his vassal. This act limited Ferdinand's rule to the western third of the country.

By a secret agreement—the Treaty of Nagyvárad, mediated in 1538 by John's adviser, György Martinuzzi ("Friar George")—Ferdinand was to succeed John upon his death. The agreement was upset when, just before John died, his wife bore a son whom the national party recognized as king. The sultan then decided to act for himself. He recognized the infant as king, but only as his own vassal in Hungary's eastern half, including Transylvania. In 1541 Süleyman occupied Buda and incorporated a great wedge of central and southern Hungary into his own dominions. Thus began Hungary's trisection, which lasted for more than a century and a half. The country's western and northern fringes developed into "Royal Hungary" under Habsburg rule; its eastern half grew into the principality of Transylvania under elected Hungarian princes, who were more or less vassals of the Ottoman sultan, while the central wedge, including the former royal capital of Buda, became "Turkish Hungary" and was integrated into the administrative system of the Ottoman Empire.

The partition of Hungary in 1568.

In 1547 Ferdinand concluded a truce with Süleyman and agreed to pay an annual tribute of 30,000 golden coins in return for recognition of his de facto rule over the territory then held by him. After this the sultan formally declared Transylvania an autonomous principality under his own suzerainty. In 1568 Ferdinand's successor, Maximilian II, was forced to recognize this arrangement. He continued to pay the tribute and accepted the reduction of Royal Hungary to the western fringe of the country, the northwestern mountains, and Croatia. From that time on, the ruling princes of Transylvania followed a policy of semi-independence. They paid tribute to the sultan and occasionally even to the Habsburgs, but they also introduced mercantilist economic policies that generated prosperity. The most successful of these princes were István Báthory (later king of Poland as Stefan Batory) and Gábor Bethlen.

The "age of trisection" was the bleakest in all Hungarian history. Fighting and slave raiding, which went on even in times of nominal peace, reduced the whole south of the country to a wasteland occupied by only a few seminomadic Vlach herdsmen; villages disappeared and fields reverted to swamp and forest. Behind the new frontier, the population was partially preserved to supply the garrisons. The old landholders were replaced by Turkish officials and soldiers whose fiefs, under the timar system, were neither heritable nor even always long-term and who exploited the wretched cultivators to the maximum. Conditions were relatively tolerable only in those districts (*haslar*) managed directly by the Ottoman government. Most of these districts lay along the two banks of the Tisza River, and people flocked into the great *mezővárosok*, or *oppidi* (towns), that are still a feature of the area. There they enjoyed a measure of protection, but the countryside between these towns was abandoned except for scattered huts (*tanyák*) in which the men spent summers scratching a precarious living from the soil.

The Turks left Transylvania relatively unmolested. Martinuzzi devised a constitution based on earlier institutions, consisting, under the prince, of representatives of the three "historic nations": the Hungarians, the Saxons, and the Hungarian-speaking Szeklers. Transylvania was also spared internecine religious strife when, at the Diet of Torda in 1568, the Roman Catholic, Calvinist, Lutheran, and Unitarian churches agreed to coexist on a basis of equal freedom and mutual toleration. The Greek Orthodox faith of the Vlachs (later called Romanians), who constituted the rest of the population, was not made part of this agreement, and it remained only a "tolerated religion." Nor were the Vlachs recognized as one of the "historic nations" of Transylvania.

THE RISE OF TRANSYLVANIA

In the first years after his accession, Ferdinand still hoped to bring the whole kingdom under his rule. He respected its constitution and its institutions and convoked the Diet regularly. But his hopes faded, and, after his succession to the imperial crown in 1558, Royal Hungary became no more than a small outlying annex of his mighty dominions. As it was also an exposed one, without the resources to defend itself, Ferdinand and his successor, Maximilian II, organized a chain of fortresses that stood opposite a similar chain of fortifications organized by Ottomans on their side of the frontier. Many of the larger Habsburg fortresses were garrisoned mostly by German and other Western mercenaries and the smaller ones by Hungarian troops who, not being paid regularly, usually lived off the land. This chain of Habsburg fortresses was complemented by a defensive deployment, the Military Frontier, inhabited by Serb and Vlach refugees from the Balkans and administered from Vienna. The Hungarians complained that they were being ruled and exploited as a subject people by foreigners, while Vienna looked on them as truculent rebels. Matters grew worse when Maximilian was succeeded by the mentally unbalanced Rudolf II, whose advisers hated Hungary and its traditions; and a religious conflict supervened on the constitutional dispute, for in the preceding half century the Reformation had swept over Hungary.

Religious antagonism played an important part when war between the Holy Roman Empire and the Turks broke out again in 1591. In the Fifteen Years' War, imperial troops entered Transylvania, and their commander, George Basta, behaved there (and in northern Hungary) with such insane cruelty toward the Hungarian Protestants that a Transylvanian general, István Bocskay, formerly a Habsburg supporter, revolted. His army of wild freebooters (*hajdúk*) drove out Basta, and in June 1606 Bocskay settled with Rudolf the Peace of Vienna, which left him prince of an enlarged Transylvania and also guaranteed the rights of the Protestants of Royal Hungary. Bocskay then mediated the Peace of Zsitvatorok (November 1606) between the emperor and the sultan, which kept the territorial status quo but relieved the emperor of his tribute to the sultan.

These two treaties ushered in a new era. The balance of power began to shift from the Ottomans toward the Habsburgs. The princes of Transylvania took advantage of this, and the principality entered a half century of prosperity. A scramble for power followed Bocskay's death (1606), but in 1613 the Sublime Porte (the Ottoman government) imposed the election of Gábor Bethlen (1613–29), who proved the most competent of all the Hungarian princes of Transylvania. At home Bethlen's rule was thoroughly despotic; through his monopoly of foreign trade and his development of the principality's internal resources, he almost doubled his revenues, devoting the proceeds partly to the upkeep of a sumptuous court and partly to the maintenance of a standing army. Keeping peace with the Porte, he often intervened against the emperor in the Thirty Years' War (1618–48) and safeguarded the rights of the Protestants in Royal

Hungary. Under the Treaty of Nikolsburg (December 31, 1621), Bethlen gave up the royal title along with the Holy Crown of Hungary. (He had been elected king by the Hungarian estates in the lands under his control in 1620 but declined to accept the crown, even though the Porte approved his election. Being a Protestant, he did not wish to antagonize the Catholic Hungarian magnates.) At the same time, Bethlen retained the title of prince of Transylvania and Hungary. He also gained a big extension of the principality and a duchy in Silesia, besides further guarantees for the Protestants of Royal Hungary.

When Bethlen died suddenly in 1629, his subjects abolished most of his internal reforms, but his successor, György Rákóczi I, maintained the international position of Transylvania, which figured as a sovereign state in the Peace of Westphalia (1648) that ended the Thirty Years' War. Transylvanian support for the Protestants in Royal Hungary, as well as the divisions prevailing among their own members, prevented the Habsburgs from enforcing the Counter-Reformation in Hungary as early and as fully as they did in Austria and Bohemia. Nevertheless, the genius of the cardinal-primate Péter Pázmány won over for Roman Catholicism the majority of the local magnates, who came to form a party attached to the Habsburg cause, which was the more influential because they now formed a separate "table" of the Diet. The nation was thus divided not only between

Transylvania and Royal Hungary but also between the Roman Catholic magnates and their subjects on the one hand and the largely Protestant landowning lower nobility on the other. In religious matters, the Hungarian Catholic magnates and nobles were no more tolerant toward their Protestant fellow countrymen than were the emperor's own German and Czech advisers, although they were not willing to acquiesce in the political centralization championed by the latter.

WAR AND LIBERATION

The Turkish occupation of central Hungary remained a volatile issue, for every Hungarian resented the Habsburgs' policy of leaving the Turks unmolested while pursuing ambitious objectives in the west. This powder keg erupted in 1657 when Prince György Rákóczi II of Transylvania, who had succeeded his father in 1648, allowed the prospect of obtaining the crown of Poland to seduce him into sending across the Carpathians an expeditionary force, which was annihilated by Tatars. The Ottoman grand vizier Köprülü Mehmed Paşa, the architect of the Porte's renaissance, led a force against Transylvania, detached it from the western adjuncts that had been its strength, and installed a new puppet prince. Emperor Leopold sent a force against the Turks; although the Austrian general Raimondo Montecuccoli defeated the Turks at St. Gotthard (Szentgotthárd) on August 1, 1664, the subsequent Peace of Vasvár still recognized all the sultan's gains.

Now even the highest magnates of Royal Hungary plotted to expel the Habsburgs with Turkish and French help, but the Wesselényi Conspiracy was betrayed, and Vienna took its revenge. Nobles were executed or lost their estates, and Protestant pastors were sentenced to be galley slaves. In 1673 the constitution was suspended and Hungary placed under a directorate. A young nobleman, Imre Thököly, earlier had fled to Transylvania, where he was elected leader of the *kuruc* (a term used by the anti-Habsburg forces, probably meaning Crusader) army. He led a revolt that forced Leopold in 1681 to restore the constitution and revoke many of his harshest measures. Thököly's success encouraged the Porte to launch a major campaign against the empire. The sultan sent into Hungary a vast army that in 1683 reached the walls of Vienna itself.

But the tide ebbed as swiftly as it had advanced. Vienna was relieved (partially with Polish help), the Turks were routed, and the imperial general Prince Eugene of Savoy led a series of campaigns in which all of western and central Hungary, including Buda, was cleared of Ottoman control by 1686. Transylvania was liberated in the years following. By the Treaty of Carlowitz (January 1699), the sultan relinquished all of Hungary except the corner between the Maros and Tisza rivers. (This area was ceded in 1718 but kept until 1779 under Austrian administration as the Banat of Temesvár.) The Military Frontier, progressively extended, was kept

THE WESSELÉNYI CONSPIRACY

The Wesselényi Conspiracy is the name given to a group of Hungarians, active about 1664–71, who were organized by Ferenc Wesselényi and who plotted unsuccessfully to overthrow the Habsburg dynasty in Hungary. The efforts of the group resulted in the establishment of an absolutist, repressive regime in Hungary.

When the Habsburg emperor Leopold I (reigned 1658–1705) ceded a large portion of Hungarian land to the Ottoman Turks (1664; Treaty of Vasvár), he provoked the opposition of many previously pro-Habsburg Hungarian Roman Catholic magnates, including the palatine administrator Ferenc Wesselényi; the bán (governor) of Croatia, Péter Zrínyi; the chief justice of Hungary, Ferenc Nádasdy; and Ferenc Rákóczi. They formed a conspiracy to free Hungary from Habsburg rule and secretly negotiated for assistance from France and Turkey.

Finally in 1670 Zrínyi received some encouragement from the sultan and prepared to march into Styria. Rákóczi, believing rumours that a formal alliance had been concluded, also assembled his forces and arrested Count Rüdiger von Starhemberg, the imperial commander in the northern Hungarian city of Tokay. The Turks' chief interpreter, however, had revealed the plot to Habsburg officials in Vienna. Imperial troops rescued Starhemberg and easily dispersed the rebels. Several leaders were tried for high treason by an Austrian court, and Zrínyi, Nádasdy, and two others were executed (April 30, 1671). Wesselényi had earlier died of natural causes, and Rákóczi was fined.

Special commissions, set up throughout Habsburg Hungary, arrested about 2,000 nobles, accused them of participating in the conspiracy, and confiscated their estates. In addition, Leopold's advisers concluded that, by conspiring against the regime, the Hungarian nation had forfeited its special rights and privileges and had become subject to the emperor's absolute rule.

under a similar regime, and Transylvania was organized as a separate principality.

HABSBURG RULE, 1699–1918

The emperor, not Hungary, was the victor, for the retreating Turks and the advancing armies of the so-called liberators ravaged the country. In 1687 Leopold reconfirmed the constitution subject to Hungary's acceptance of his dynasty in the male line and to the abolition of the *ius resistendi* (right to resist) conceded under the Golden Bull of 1222, but the government that followed was in fact another cruel Vienna-centred dictatorship. In 1703 this provoked another rebellion, led by Francis (Ferenc) Rákóczi II (Thököly's stepson).

HABSBURG RULE TO 1867

After eight years of indecisive and fruitless fighting between the *kuruc* and the

Habsburg armies, peace was established by the Treaty of Szatmár (April 1711). On paper, this did little more than confirm what had been agreed in 1687, but the new king, Charles III (Emperor Charles VI), genuinely wanted peace with Hungary, and the worst abuses were now ended.

CHARLES III AND MARIA THERESA

Charles's chief concern was to secure the acceptance in Hungary of the Pragmatic Sanction, the imperial decree by which his daughter Maria Theresa was to inherit his dominions. After the Diet accepted the Pragmatic Sanction in 1723, Charles convoked the body only once more and Maria Theresa, after her coronation in 1740, only twice—each time to ask for money. Her rule, like her father's, was essentially autocratic. She was severe toward the Protestants, and she allowed her advisers to exclude Hungary from the subsidized industrialization that was bringing wealth to other parts of her dominion. Internal tariff barriers were introduced between the hereditary provinces and Hungary. Imports to Hungary from outside the empire were hindered by high tariffs, but customs for "imports" from Austria and Bohemia were very low. Hungary's exports were all but banned to non-Habsburg lands, and only those agricultural and raw materials that were required in the western part of the monarchy received preferential treatment. Hungary became more dependent on, and subordinate to, Austria than before.

Agriculture received some incentives, but the road to industrialization was blocked. Lacking modern credit, entrepreneurial attitude, and strong urban markets, Hungary, unlike Austria and Bohemia, was prevented from entering the preindustrial age.

Maria Theresa's rule was not unduly harsh, even toward the Protestants. Toward the magnates, on whom she lavished many favours, it was positively benign, and she respected the most cherished liberty of the lesser nobles: their exemption from taxation. Exhausted by so many wars and rebellions, the country asked for nothing more, contenting itself with the blessing that her rule brought it an uninterrupted peace that enabled the population to grow once again and the material ravages to be repaired. But a lethargy descended on the country. Political life sank to the parish-pump level, and the towns stagnated. The peasants, into whose conditions the queen introduced some improvements (notably the Urbarial Patent in 1767, which attempted to standardize peasant holdings and obligations), followed their masters in aspiring to nothing more than as much material comfort as could be obtained with a minimum of effort. The national language itself was becoming little more than a peasant dialect, since the language of public administration and the Diet was Latin and of business life was German; like the language, the national spirit seemed near moribund.

JOSEPH II AND LEOPOLD II

The nation was shocked out of its lethargy by the accession of Maria Theresa's son Joseph II on her death in 1780. Evading the obligation of a king on coronation to swear allegiance to the constitution, by not submitting himself to coronation at all (he had the Holy Crown conveyed to Vienna), Joseph drew Hungary into the Habsburg realm. The counties were transformed into local branches of the state service, taking all their orders from above. German was made the language of government and all education above the elementary level. (A secularized school system had been introduced in 1777.) The land was surveyed in preparation for taxing all estates equally. The position of the peasants was improved, which pleased them but not their lords. When Joseph fell mortally sick, the country was on the brink of open revolt. On his deathbed he retracted his administrative reforms, but his successor, Leopold II (1790–92), was obliged to restore the ancient constitution and to swear to treat Hungary as a wholly independent kingdom, to be ruled only in accordance with its own laws and customs.

FRANCIS I: THE REFORM GENERATION

When Leopold died with tragic suddenness in 1792, his young son, Francis, delivered a coronation oath that went through the motions of conforming, but soon afterward he returned to the old ways. The Diet was convoked simply to supply money and, after 1811, did not convene for 14 years. Social reaction accompanied this political absolutism, and the stranglehold on economic development was not relaxed.

For many years the Diet, composed either of magnates who identified their interests with those of the court or of landowners who had prospered during the Napoleonic Wars, was as nonprogressive as Francis himself. In wider circles the spirit of the age had given birth to a great cultural revival that was now bringing forth its first literary fruits. The new national pride that it at once embodied and enhanced was demanding fulfillment of Leopold's promises and an end to the veiled but oppressive dictatorship of Vienna. A great reform movement was set in motion by István, Count Széchenyi, the primary advocate of Hungary's social, economic, and political modernization, who boldly proclaimed that the ancient privileges of the nobility were no bastion but a prison. He argued that the servile state of the peasants was humanly degrading and a source of weakness for the nation and also that the system of forced field labour, as well as the nobles' exemption from taxation, was economically harmful even to its supposed beneficiaries. Financial stringency had forced Francis to reconvoke the Diet in 1825 and to convoke it regularly thereafter.

Doctrines like these were taken up by a whole "reform generation," the most prominent figures of which—besides Széchenyi himself—were the legal expert Ferenc Deák, who subsequently became the primary architect of the Austro-Hungarian Compromise of 1867; József, Baron Eötvös, leader of a small group of moderates that opposed breaking with the ruling dynasty; and, above all, the more radical Lajos Kossuth, who largely changed the current of the reform movement by his insistence that social and economic reform could be fully realized only after the achievement of political independence. After Francis had been followed on the throne in 1835 by the luckless Ferdinand—in practice by the government of the two principal ministers, Klemens, prince von Metternich, and Anton, count von Kolowrat—Vienna was driven increasingly into a defensive position. It was forced to make repeated concessions, especially with respect to the replacement of Latin and German by Magyar as the language of the Diet, administration, and education—a demand pressed with especial insistence by many of the reformers.

THE NATIONALITIES

The substitution of Magyar for Latin and German raised a new and painful issue. The population of Hungary, even excluding Croatia, had never been purely Magyar, but the pre-Magyar inhabitants of the plains and the newcomers to them (outside the towns) had quickly become Magyarized; and, while this was not true of the peripheral areas, their populations were relatively sparse. By the end of the 15th century, the Slovaks and Ruthenes of the north, the Germans of the free boroughs, Szepes (Zips), and Transylvania, and the Vlachs, or Romanians, of the country's eastern region numbered hardly more than 20 to 25 percent of the total. The Magyar majority included almost the entire politically active noble class, the non-Magyar recruits to which assimilated most readily. The surviving non-Magyar peasants had neither the wish nor the ability to question the Magyar character of the state, which for its part was uninterested in what languages were spoken by the politically disregarded, unfree populace.

Between 1500 and 1800, however, the ethnic composition of the country changed. The most purely Magyar areas were heavily depopulated during the Turkish wars. These losses were accompanied by mass immigrations of Serbs, Croats, and Romanians from the Balkans and later by the introduction by the Austrian government of large numbers of German and other Western colonists. By 1720 the Magyars numbered only some 35 percent of the total population. By 1780 the figure had risen to nearly 40 percent, but the periphery, although it contained islands of Magyar population, was still largely non-Magyar. Moreover, as a result of this ethnic colonization, the population of Hungary grew to nearly 10 million by the end of the 18th century, almost trebling the country's population of some 3.5 million in 1720.

In this environment the ideas of the French Revolution and of nationalism, one of its major consequences, took hold. Hungarians and most of the other ethnic groups discovered their own national identities. From the late 18th century, poetry, drama, fiction, and literary criticism combined to elevate the Hungarian vernacular to the standard of a literary language, partly in response to the forced Germanization by the Habsburgs but even more as part of an international trend that was particularly strong in central Europe. Institutions such as the National Library, the National Theatre, and the Hungarian Academy of Sciences—all organized during this period—were also part of the linguistic-cultural movement that soon took the form of self-conscious chauvinism and then became an organized political movement.

REVOLUTION, REACTION, AND "COMPROMISE"

The Hungarian reformers' opportunity came in the spring of 1848. Inspired by the Revolution of 1848 in Paris, a popular upheaval caused the breakdown of central authority in Vienna. On March 15—a date celebrated in Hungary ever since—a bloodless revolution led by young intellectuals, including the poet Sándor Petőfi, abolished censorship in Pest (later part of Budapest) and formulated a series of demands. Seizing the moment, Kossuth prodded the Diet to rush through a body of laws. The March Laws (also known as the April Laws) enacted important internal reforms, such as the generalizing of taxes, the abolition of villein status and the transfer of villein holdings to their cultivators, and the reorganization of the lower table of Parliament on a representative basis. They also provided for the restoration of the territorial integrity of the lands of the Hungarian crown (subject, in the case of Transylvania, to the agreement of its Diet) and the appointment of a "responsible independent Hungarian Ministry," which was headed by a progressive magnate, Lajos, Count Batthyány, and included Kossuth, Széchenyi, Deák, and Eötvös. But the new government had enemies: the conservatives resented the land reform, and the centralists (i.e., those who advocated a Vienna-dominated empire) regarded the independent ministry as dangerous to the integrity of the monarchy. They found allies among the disaffected nationalities, notably the Serbs and Romanians, and in the Croats, whose *ban*, Josip Jelačić, refused to recognize the authority of Buda and Pest.

Tension between Vienna and Buda-Pest mounted steadily, and in September, when the rest of the monarchy had been reduced, Jelačić, on Vienna's orders, invaded Hungary. Batthyány and other ministers resigned, leaving Kossuth in charge. An improvised national army drove Jelačić out of the country, but in December Ferdinand (whose coronation oath bound him to observe the March Laws) was made to abdicate in favour of his young nephew, Francis (Franz) Joseph. The invasion was now renewed. A panmonarchic constitution abolished the March Laws, in reply to which a rump Diet, inspired by Kossuth, proclaimed the full independence of Hungary and the deposition of the Habsburg dynasty (April 14, 1849). The Hungarian forces, led by a young soldier of genius, Artúr Görgey, held their own until the Austrian court appealed for help to the Russian tsar, who sent an army across the Carpathians. Bitter fighting went on for some weeks more, led by György Klapka and other generals, but the odds were too heavy. On August 12, Kossuth fled the country, transferring his authority to Görgey, who the next day surrendered at Világos to the Russian commander.

Savage reprisals followed, and the country was again subjected to an absolutist and extortionate rule exercised from Vienna through a foreign bureaucracy. This "Bach regime" (named for Alexander Bach, Austrian minister of the interior) was maintained, unrelaxed in principle although with some alterations in practice, until Austria's defeat in Italy in 1859 forced Francis Joseph to begin his retreat from absolutism. The followers of the exiled Kossuth were irreconcilable, but many inside Hungary rallied behind Deák. He held that the March Laws were legally valid and that Hungary's right to complete internal independence was inalienable but that under the Pragmatic Sanction, which he accepted, foreign affairs and defense were subjects common to the two halves of the monarchy and that a mechanism could be devised for handling these affairs constitutionally. A Diet convoked in 1861 was dissolved after a few weeks because the gap between the Hungarians' views and those of Francis Joseph and his centralist ministry in Vienna was still too wide to be bridged. Absolutism was reimposed, but the pressure of international and internal economic difficulties gradually drove Francis Joseph to further concessions. In July 1865 he dismissed his centralist ministry; in December a new Diet was convoked and the negotiations reopened. Interrupted by the outbreak of the Seven Weeks' War, they were resumed after Austria's defeat by Prussia in 1866 had further convinced both parties of the necessity of agreement.

THE DUAL MONARCHY, 1867–1918

A new Transylvanian Diet had already approved reunion with Hungary. Austria-Hungary was formed in February 1867 through a constitutional agreement known as the Compromise (German: Ausgleich; Hungarian: Kiegyezés). Francis Joseph admitted the validity of the March Laws on the condition that conduct of common (i.e., overlapping) affairs would be revised. He appointed a responsible Hungarian ministry under Gyula (Julius), Count Andrássy, who—strangely enough—had been involved in the Revolution of 1848 and afterwards was hanged in effigy. A committee of the Diet then elaborated a law that, while laying down Hungary's full internal independence, provided for common ministries for foreign affairs and defense, each under a joint minister. A third common minister was in charge of the finance for these portfolios. The respective quotas to be paid for these services by each half of the monarchy were reconsidered every 10 years, as were commercial and customs agreements. At first the two countries formed a customs union. On June 8, 1867, Francis Joseph was crowned king of Hungary, and on July 28 he gave his assent to the law.

Francis Joseph had stipulated that the settlement should include a revised Hungaro-Croatian agreement and provisions guaranteeing adequate rights for the non-Magyars of Hungary. The Croatian settlement, known as the Nagodba (1868), left Croatia, including Slavonia, as part of the Hungarian crown, under a ban appointed on the proposal of the Hungarian prime minister. Croatia was to enjoy full internal autonomy, but certain matters were designated as common to Croatia and Hungary. When these were under discussion, Croatian deputies attended the central Parliament, in which they could speak in Croatian, the sole language of internal official usage in Croatia.

The Nationalities Law (1868) guaranteed that all citizens of Hungary, whatever their nationality, constituted politically "a single nation, the indivisible, unitary Hungarian nation," and there could be no differentiation between them except in respect of the official

usage of the current languages and then only insofar as necessitated by practical considerations. The language of the central administrative and judicial services and of the country's only university was Hungarian, but there were to be adequate provisions for the use of non-Hungarian languages on lower levels. The consolidation was completed by the incorporation of the Military Frontier (in stages lasting several years) and of Transylvania, the latter process involving the abolition of the old "Three Nations," except that the Saxon "university" (territorial autonomy) was allowed to survive as a purely cultural institution.

HUNGARY UNDER DUALISM

The Austro-Hungarian Compromise of 1867 restored territorial integrity to Hungary and gave it more real internal independence than it had enjoyed since 1526; the monarch's powers in internal affairs were strictly limited. In the conduct of foreign affairs or defense, however, Hungary still formed only part of the monarchy, and its interests in these fields had to be coordinated with those of its other components. But Hungary had a large voice in the monarchy's policy in these fields and enjoyed the great advantage—which weighed heavily with soberer men, including Deák, when negotiating the Compromise—that the resources of the great power of which it formed a part stood behind the country. To some, however, the price still seemed too high, and the parliamentary life of Hungary from 1867 to 1918 was dominated by the conflict between the supporters and the opponents of the Compromise. The latter ranged from complete separatists to those who accepted the Compromise in theory but wanted details of it altered.

The supporters of the Compromise, then known as the Deák Party, held office first but soon got into such financial and personal difficulties that complete chaos threatened. It was averted when in 1875 Kálmán Tisza, the leader of the moderate nationalist Left Centre, merged his party with the remnants of the Deákists on a program that amounted to putting his party's main demands into cold storage until the political and financial situation was stabilized. This new Liberal Party then held office for nearly 30 years. During these years the Compromise stood intact, but there was mounting friction with Vienna over the army, which the Hungarians regarded, with some reason, as imbued with a spirit hostile to themselves; over the economic provisions of the Compromise; and over the question of Hungarian participation in control of the National Bank. An army question in 1889 marked something of a turning point, after which relations between the supporters of the Compromise, behind whom stood the crown, and its nationalist opponents were permanently strained.

The tension reached a climax in 1903, when the obstruction of the "national opposition" made parliamentary government practically impossible. The prime minister, István, Count Tisza (Kálmán Tisza's son), dissolved Parliament. Elections in January 1905 gave a coalition of national parties a parliamentary majority, but Francis Joseph refused to entrust the government to them on the basis of their program, which included national concessions over the army. A period of nonparliamentary government followed until April 1906, when the coalition leaders, under threat of an extension of the suffrage if they proved recalcitrant, gave the king a secret undertaking that, if appointed, they would not press the essentials of their program. On this basis he appointed a coalition government, but under a Liberal, Sándor Wekerle. With their hands thus tied, the coalition made a wretched showing. Tisza reorganized the Liberal Party as the Party of National Work, and in the elections of 1910 this party secured a large majority. After Károly, Count Khuen-Héderváry (1910–12), and László Lukács (1912–13), Tisza himself again became prime minister, and Francis Joseph ceased to press his demand for effective franchise reform, to which Tisza was inexorably opposed— more for national than for social reasons. (He was afraid that in case of universal manhood suffrage the national minorities would join hands with the political radicals and end Magyar control over the state.)

SOCIAL AND ECONOMIC DEVELOPMENTS

Hungary underwent much change after 1867. The achievements of the Deákist and Liberal governments included the assimilation of the former outlying areas of Transylvania and the Military Frontier, a reform of the relations between the central government and the counties, and a general reorganization of the administration. The judicial system was modernized. Relations between the state and the churches were, after a long struggle, restated in 1894–95 on terms satisfactory to the liberal philosophy of the day. This completed the full emancipation of Hungary's large Jewish population, who had already gone through the basic emancipation process in 1868, based on a law prepared by Baron Eötvös. In 1868 Eötvös also carried through an admirable elementary education act, and much headway was made in raising the educational and cultural level of the country. After long difficulties the national finances were put in order and the public debt reduced.

There was considerable economic progress in many fields. Agriculture remained the mainstay of the economy. The medium and small landowners had been hard-hit by the land reform of 1848, but the survivors were helped by the

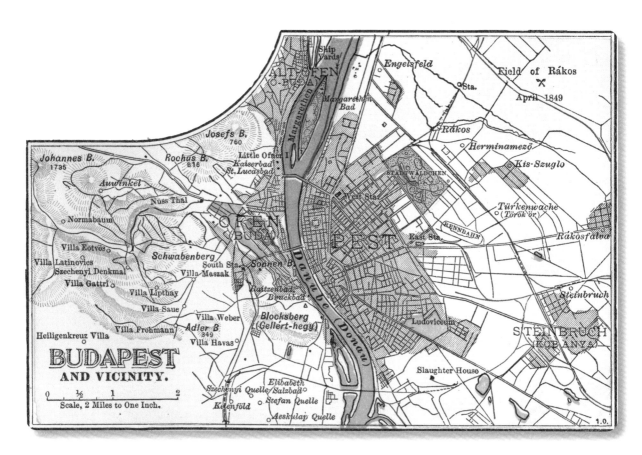

Map of Budapest (c. 1900), from the 10th edition of Encyclopædia Britannica.

high agricultural prices and the secure Austrian market. Afterward, the general European agricultural depression plunged even the big landowners into difficulties, but these diminished near the end of the century when prices rose again, while the quality and quantity of production improved. Many branches of industry failed to survive the customs union with Austria, but agriculture prospered, and later, as domestic capital accumulated, a process of industrialization, helped by state legislation, set in and expanded rapidly after 1890. As late as 1910, agriculture was still the most important branch of the economy, and more than two-thirds of the population still derived its livelihood from the soil, while about one-sixth did so from industry and mining.

Urbanization proceeded apace. The growth of Budapest—formed in 1872–73 through the merger of Buda, Pest, and Óbuda—was meteoric. Its population during the age of dualism rose from 270,000 to nearly 1 million. Not counting Zagreb in Croatia, five other cities in the Hungarian realm (Szeged, Szabadka [Subotica], Debrecen, Pozsony, and Temesvár) had populations between 75,000 and 120,000, and a dozen more cities totaled about 50,000 inhabitants. The urban population for the country as a whole doubled from 2 million to about 4 million. Communications were largely modernized, particularly through a Budapest-centred complex railroad system.

For all this, Hungary was still a relatively poor country. The continued extremely rapid growth of the population—from about 15 million in 1869 to more than 20 million in 1910 (with the population of Croatia gaining along the same lines)—had far outstripped that of the means of production. The growth of industry was still too slow to absorb the surplus rural population, and, in spite of a high emigration rate, which in the years before World War I averaged 100,000 annually, acute rural congestion had developed. While 35 percent of the land was held in 4,000 large estates, there were about two million small, or dwarf, holdings, and a further 1.7 million persons (wage earners) were totally landless. A large proportion of these rural workers were forced to live in conditions of extreme misery and near starvation. The living standards and conditions of the industrial workers, especially the unskilled, were also very low.

Emigration was viewed by many as a welcome safety valve, but some Magyars regretted that it had significantly reduced their presence in the multinational Kingdom of Hungary. As best as can be ascertained from the often conflicting Hungarian and American statistics, in the period between 1880 and 1914, about 1,800,000 Hungarian citizens emigrated to the United States. Of the U.S.-bound migrants, more than one-third (650,000–700,000) were Magyars, while the rest included Rusyns, Slovaks, Germans, Romanians, Croats, and other South Slavs. Significantly smaller numbers emigrated to western Europe and elsewhere.

The political structure was not modern. The unreformed franchise excluded the masses from political influence, and even the vocational organization that they were able to achieve was primitive. The industrial and financial development had been largely the work of Jews (who also played a large part in the professions) or of Magyarized Germans. Its own quasi-alien character and its small numbers prevented the Hungarian middle class from developing into a positive factor in the political life, which continued to be dominated by a landowning class whose social and political ideas failed to move with the times.

The "nationalities problem" remained intractable. After 1868 Hungarian political philosophy insisted more strongly than ever that the Hungarian state must be Magyar in spirit, in its institutions, and, as far as possible, in its language. Suggestions to the contrary, or appeals to the Nationalities Law, met with derision or abuse. In spite of the law, the use of minority languages was banished almost entirely from administration and even justice. While the autonomy of the church schools was hardly attacked until the 20th century, most denominations saw to it that all secondary education in their schools, with trivial exceptions, was in Hungarian. The Magyar language was also overrepresented in the primary schools, as it was in practically all instruction in the state schools founded from 1870 onward. For example—discounting Croatia, which had its own educational system—in 1912 there were 13,453 Hungarian-language elementary schools, compared with 2,233 schools that instructed in Romanian, 447 in German, 377 in Slovak, 270 in Serbian, 59 in Ruthenian, 12 in Italian, and 10 in various other languages.

By the end of the century, the state apparatus was entirely Hungarian in language, as were business and social life above the lowest levels. The proportion of the population with Hungarian as its mother tongue rose from 46.6 percent in 1880 to 51.4 percent in 1900. The Magyarization of the towns had proceeded at an astounding rate. Nearly all middle-class Jews and Germans and many middle-class Slovaks and Ruthenes had been Magyarized.

Most of the Magyarization, however, had been in the centre of Hungary and among the middle classes, and much of it was the direct result of urbanization and industrialization. It had hardly touched the rural populations of the periphery, and the linguistic frontiers had hardly shifted from the line on which they had been stabilized in the 18th century. In these areas, moreover, a hard core of national feeling had survived. This had weakened during the first decades after the Compromise but was reviving again at the beginning of the 20th century. This was especially so among the Romanians and was being encouraged from across the frontiers of Romania and Serbia and (in the case of the Slovaks) from Bohemia. Hungaro-Croatian relations too deteriorated, after a period of quiescence, when the Serbian government began propagating a theory of South Slav (Yugoslav) unity designed

Before the outbreak of World War I, Austria-Hungary was a vast and powerful empire. After its defeat in the war, it was divided into a number of smaller countries. Encyclopaedia Britannica, Inc.

to detach the Croats from the monarchy.

Many of these developments threatened the very basis of the Compromise, and to this another uncertainty was added. Francis Joseph could be trusted to support and accept the policies of any Hungarian government that on its side maintained the Compromise loyally; but he was an old man, and his heir presumptive, Archduke Francis Ferdinand, was notoriously hostile to the Hungarian regime. In touch with many of its opponents, the archduke was credited with designs of overthrowing the Compromise to the benefit not of its traditional opponents, the Hungarian Independents, but of its enemies in the opposite camps, especially the nationalities.

WORLD WAR I

The assassination of Archduke Francis Ferdinand on June 28, 1914, removed this danger and plunged Austria-Hungary into World War I. For the first two years of the war, Tisza upheld the internal system

ARCHDUKE FRANCIS FERDINAND

Francis Ferdinand (German: Franz Ferdinand; born December 18, 1863, Graz, Austria—died June 28, 1914, Sarajevo, Bosnia and Herzegovina) was an Austrian archduke whose assassination was the immediate cause of World War I. He was the eldest son of the archduke Charles Louis, who was the brother of the emperor Francis Joseph. The death of the heir apparent, the archduke Rudolf, in 1889, made Francis Ferdinand next in succession to the Austro-Hungarian throne after his father, who died in 1896. But because of Francis Ferdinand's ill health in the 1890s, his younger brother Otto was regarded as more likely to succeed, a possibility that deeply embittered Francis Ferdinand. His desire to marry Sophie, countess von Chotek, a lady-in-waiting, brought him into sharp conflict with the emperor and the court. Only after renouncing his future children's rights to the throne was the morganatic marriage allowed in 1900.

In foreign affairs he tried, without endangering the alliance with Germany, to restore Austro-Russian understanding. At home he thought of political reforms that would have strengthened the position of the crown and weakened that of the Magyars against the other nationalities in Hungary. His plans were based on the realization that any nationalistic policy pursued by one section of the population would endanger the multinational Habsburg empire. His relationship with Francis Joseph was exacerbated by his continuous pressure on the emperor, who in his later years left affairs to take care of themselves but sharply resented any interference with his prerogative. From 1906 onward Francis Ferdinand's influence in military matters grew, and in 1913 he became inspector general of the army.

In June 1914 he and his wife were assassinated by the Serb nationalist Gavrilo Princip at Sarajevo; a month later World War I began with Austria's declaration of war against Serbia.

and held the country to its international course and, when Francis Joseph died, persuaded the new king, Charles IV (Austrian Emperor Charles I), to accept coronation (December 1916), thus binding himself to uphold the integrity and the constitution of Hungary. Charles, however, insisted on electoral reform, and Tisza resigned (May 1917).

While short-lived minority governments struggled with increasing difficulties, a threefold agitation grew: of Hungarian nationalists, against a war into which, they maintained, Hungary had been drawn in the interest of Germany and Austria; of the political left, growing daily more radical under the stimuli of privation and the Russian Revolution of 1917; and of the nationalities, encouraged by the favour that their kinsfolk were finding with the Triple Entente. The country began to listen to Mihály, Count Károlyi, leader of a faction of the Independence Party, who proclaimed that a program of independence from Austria, repudiation of the alliance with Germany, and peace with the Entente, combined with social and internal political reform and concessions to the nationalities, would safeguard Hungary against all dangers at once.

Hungary's submergence in the long, devastating war included the mobilization of 3.8 million men, the death of 661,000, and the exhaustion of the Hungarian economy. Agricultural output declined by half during the last years of the war, and the currency lost more than half of its value. In the autumn of 1918, Hungary was on the brink of economic collapse.

REVOLUTION, COUNTERREVOLUTION, AND THE REGENCY, 1918–45

On October 31, 1918, when the defeat of the monarchy was imminent, Charles appointed Károlyi prime minister at the head of an improvised administration based on a left-wing National Council. After the monarchy had signed an armistice on November 3 and Charles had "renounced participation" in public affairs on the 13th, the National Council dissolved Parliament on the 16th and proclaimed Hungary an independent republic, with Károlyi as provisional president. The separation from Austria was popular, but all Károlyi's supposed friends disappointed him, and all his premises proved mistaken. Serb, Czech, and Romanian troops installed themselves in two-thirds of the helpless country, and, in the confusion, orderly

social reform was impossible. The government steadily moved leftward, and on March 21, 1919, Károlyi's government was replaced by a Soviet republic controlled by Béla Kun, who had promised Hungary Russian support against the Romanians. The help never arrived, and Kun's doctrinaire Bolshevism, resting on the "Red Terror," antagonized almost the entire population. On August 1 the Hungarian Soviet Republic fell, and Kun and his associates fled Budapest; three days later Romanian troops entered the city.

Shadow counterrevolutionary governments had already formed themselves in Szeged (then occupied by French troops) and Vienna and pressed the Allies to entrust them with the new government. The Allies insisted on the formation of a provisional regime including democratic elements that would be required to hold elections on a wide, secret suffrage. The Romanians were, with difficulty, induced to retire across the Tisza River, and a government, under the presidency of Károly Huszár, was formed in November 1919. Elections (for a single house) were held in January 1920.

The new Parliament declared null and void all measures enacted by the Károlyi and Kun regimes as well as the legislation embodying the Compromise of 1867. The institution of the monarchy was thus restored, but its permanent reinstatement was predicated on the resolution of the differences between the nation and the dynasty, an issue that divided Hungarians. In the interim, Admiral Miklós Horthy, who had organized the counterrevolutionary armed forces, was elected regent as provisional head of state (March 1, 1920). The Huszár government then resigned, and on March 15 a coalition government, composed of the two main parties in the Parliament (the Christian National Union and the Smallholders), took office under Sándor Simonyi-Semadam.

THE REGENCY, 1920–45

The Allies had long had their peace terms for Hungary ready but had been unwilling to present them to an earlier regime. It was, thus, the Simonyi-Semadam government that was forced to sign the Treaty of Trianon (June 4, 1920). The Allies not only assumed without question that the country's non-Hungarian populations wished to leave Hungary but also allowed the successor states, especially Czechoslovakia and Romania, to annex large areas of ethnic Hungarian population.

The final result was to leave Hungary with only 35,893 of the 125,641 square miles (92,962 of the 325,408 square km) that had constituted the lands of the Hungarian crown. Romania, Czechoslovakia, and Yugoslavia took large fragments, while others went to Austria and even Poland and Italy. Of the population of 20,866,447 (1910 census), Hungary was left with 7,615,117. Romania received 5,257,467; Yugoslavia, 4,131,249; Czechoslovakia, 3,517,568; and Austria, 291,618. Of the 10,050,575 persons for whom Hungarian was the mother tongue, no fewer than

3,219,579 were allotted to the successor states: 1,704,851 to Romania, 1,063,020 to Czechoslovakia, 547,735 to Yugoslavia, and 26,183 to Austria. While the homes of some of these—e.g., the Szeklers—had been in the remotest corners of historic Hungary, many were living immediately across the new frontiers.

In addition, the treaty required Hungary to pay in reparations an unspecified sum, which was to be "the first charge upon all its assets and revenues," and limited its armed forces to 35,000, to be used exclusively for the maintenance of internal order and frontier defense.

Conditions in Hungary in 1920 were exceedingly difficult in every respect. The prolonged war, the Bolshevik regime (before which mobile capital had fled headlong), and the rapacious Romanian occupation had exhausted its resources, and the economy had been further disrupted by the new frontiers, which cut factories off from both their accustomed supply sources and their markets. Industrial unemployment had reached unprecedented heights, and the surviving national resources were being strained to support nearly 400,000 refugees from the successor states.

Both industrial and agrarian workers were embittered by the failure of their revolutionary hopes. Even more dangerous were the armies of the "new poor," not only the homeless refugees but also a large part of the middle classes in general, reduced to penury by the galloping inflation. They formed a radical army, one of the right that ascribed their misery precisely to the revolutions, on which they put the blame for all Hungary's misfortunes. Feelings ran particularly high against the Jews, who had played a disproportionately large part in both revolutions, especially Kun's, but the resentment extended also to the Social Democrats and even to Liberal democracy.

"White terrorists" wreaked indiscriminate vengeance on persons whom they associated with the revolutions. Huszár's government itself had turned so sharply on the Social Democrats and the trade unions that the former withdrew their representatives from the government and boycotted the elections, in protest against the widespread killings, arrests, and internments. (Modern calculations have put the number of those executed to somewhere between 1,000 and 2,000.) Communists, radical democrats, Jewish intellectuals, and assorted academics emigrated in large numbers, among them such renowned personalities as scientists Theodore von Kármán and Leo Szilárd, social philosophers Michael Polányi and Karl Mannheim, economist Karl Polányi, sociologist Oszkár Jászi, philosopher György Lukács, film directors Sir Alexander Korda and László Vajda, and artists László Moholy-Nagy and Béni Ferenczy.

The government of Pál, Count Teleki, who succeeded Simonyi-Semadam in July 1920, blunted the edge of the agrarian unrest with a modest reform—promised, indeed, only as a first installment—that took 1.7 million acres (7.5 percent of the total area of the country) from the biggest estates for distribution in smallholdings. But it had hardly touched any other social problem when in March 1921 the legitimist question was raised in acute form by King Charles's sudden return to Hungary. He was ordered to withdraw by the Allies with the willing compliance of the right-wing radicals, toward whom Horthy was then leaning. The government, several of whose members were legitimists, resigned, and the succession was assumed by the conservative István, Count Bethlen, who had been waiting behind the scenes. Bethlen devised a formula that, while not legally excluding the king's return (under Entente pressure, Parliament had voted a law dethroning the Habsburgs, but even Hungary's own antilegitimists never took it as morally binding), excluded it in practice. In return for this, the Smallholders' Party agreed with the antilegitimists among the Christian nationalists to form a new Party of Unity under Bethlen's leadership.

In March 1922 Bethlen persuaded Parliament to accept as still legally in force the franchise enacted in 1918, which reduced the number of voters and reintroduced open voting in rural districts. As a result of this law, 2.4 million of Hungary's 8 million citizens (about 29 percent of the population) had the right to vote. This proportion compared favourably with those of France, Switzerland, and Yugoslavia but less favourably with those of Austria, England, and the Scandinavian countries. Conducted under this law, the elections in May 1922 gave the Party of Unity a large majority.

Meanwhile, a second attempt by King Charles (in October 1921) to recover his throne failed, and the legitimist question lost its acuteness with Charles's death in 1922. In December 1921 Bethlen concluded a secret pact with the Social Democrats, under which the latter promised to abstain from political agitation and to support the government's foreign policy in return for the end of persecution, the release of political prisoners, and the restoration of the sequestrated trade union funds. The peasant leaders were persuaded to accept the indefinite postponement of further land reform. The "White Terror" was liquidated quietly but effectively, chiefly by finding government employment for the right-wing radical leaders.

Bethlen's domestic program was made possible by his cautious international policy. Almost all Hungarians were passionately convinced of the injustice of the Treaty of Trianon, the redress of which was the all-dominant motive of Hungary's foreign policy throughout the interwar period and the key to the hostile relations between Hungary and those states that had chiefly profited by it. Bethlen was as revisionist at heart as any of his countrymen, but he was convinced that Hungary could not act effectively in this field until it had acquired friends abroad and had achieved political and economic consolidation at home. This depended

on financial reconstruction. To achieve this, he applied for Hungary's admission to the League of Nations, which was granted (not without difficulty) in September 1922. In March 1924, in return for an agreement to carry out loyally the obligations of the treaty, he obtained a League loan, which had almost magical effects. Inflation stopped immediately. The League loan was followed by a flood of private lending, and the expatriated domestic capital returned. With this help, Hungary enjoyed some years of prosperity, during which agriculture revived and industrialization made progress.

Abroad, Bethlen's only other important move was the conclusion in 1927 of a treaty of friendship with Italy. At home his regime, which was conservative but not tyrannical, rested on what came to be called Hungary's conservative-liberal forces, to the exclusion of extremism from left or right.

FINANCIAL CRISIS: THE RISE OF RIGHT RADICALISM

Bethlen's command of Parliament was complete and unshaken by the disastrous fall in world wheat prices in 1929. In June 1931 he had just held elections that returned his party with its usual large majority when a world financial crisis supervened on the economic one to shatter the foundations of his structure. Foreign creditors called in their money, and Hungary, its trade balance annihilated by the collapse of the wheat market, could not meet their demands and had to apply for help from the League of Nations, which imposed a regime of rigid orthodox deflation. Industrial unemployment soared again, the agricultural population was rendered almost literally penniless, and the government services had to carry through large-scale dismissals and salary reductions in the interests of a balanced budget. Consequently, in the early 1930s, many persons with university degrees were scurrying around for jobs as bellhops and street cleaners.

In August Bethlen resigned. His successor, Gyula, Count Károlyi, was unable to cope with the situation. Political agitation mounted, and on October 1, 1932, Horthy appointed as prime minister the leader of the right-wing radicals, Gyula Gömbös.

At home Gömbös found the financial forces, international and domestic, as invincible as had his predecessors. Previously a violent anti-Semite, he had to recant his views on this point and was unable to carry through any other points of his fascist program, particularly as Horthy at first refused to allow him to hold elections. Neither was he able to realize his foreign political ideal of an "Axis" composed of Hungary, Italy, and Germany, since his two proposed partners were then at loggerheads over Austria. Gömbös, one of whose first acts had been to dash to Rome and breathe new life into Hungary's friendship with Italy, now found himself drawn into the "Rome Triangle" (Italy, Austria, and Hungary) that was directed precisely against Germany. Finally, Adolf Hitler upset another of Gömbös's calculations by telling him that, while Germany would help Hungary against Czechoslovakia, it would not do so against Romania or Yugoslavia.

Nevertheless, by the time of Gömbös's premature death in October 1936, he had managed to achieve at least some of his goals. Shortly before Gömbös died, Horthy had at last allowed him to hold elections, which had brought into Parliament a strong right-wing radical contingent from which it could never thereafter free itself. Abroad, when Benito Mussolini became subordinate to Hitler, Hungary found itself in a sort of Axis camp after all, membership of which might help it at least to accomplish partial revision of the Treaty of Trianon. On the other hand, if Germany chose to apply economic or political pressure, Hungary would be defenseless but for such shadow help as Italy could offer.

This threat already loomed large, and thenceforward it became inextricably involved with Hungary's own internal politics, by reason of the ideological character of the Nazi regime and in particular its anti-Semitism. Anti-Semitism at that stage was running high in Hungary itself, and those infected by it—not just the right-wing radicals of various brands but other members of the middle classes as well—welcomed Germany's support for their own ideas while making light of its dangers. They even argued, not without reason, that the danger lay in affronting Germany, which could easily crush unarmed little Hungary but would not wish to attack a friend and ideological partner. Many of them (as well as most army officers) further believed that, should Hitler's policies lead to war, Germany would emerge the victor; Hungary's salvation thus lay in joining forces with Germany.

On the other side, a curious shadow front emerged, composed of all elements antagonistic to Nazism—not only Hungary's Jews but also the legitimists, the traditionalist conservative-liberals, and the Social Democrats. Many of these people were not convinced that Germany was invincible and held that, if war came, only disaster could follow for Hungary if it became too closely involved with Germany. Even they, however, were unwilling to draw the ultimate conclusion that Hungary should abandon all its revisionist claims and join hands with the Little Entente, which for its part indicated that it would accept nothing short of total renunciation. It was of the highest importance that by this time Horthy had shed his earlier right-wing radical leanings and sympathized with this shadow front.

To succeed Gömbös, Horthy appointed Kálmán Darányi, who was more of a conservative than a right-wing radical. His appointment was ill-received in Germany, which grew even more hostile the next year, when Darányi's foreign minister, Kálmán Kánya, obtained the tacit consent of the Little Entente for

Hungary to rearm, although Hungary was still sadly short of armaments, for which, again, Germany was its only source of supply. On a visit to Berlin, Darányi and Kánya smoothed over the difficulties; but, when Darányi tried to placate the extremists at home, Horthy replaced him (in May 1938) with Béla Imrédy, who introduced a largely token "Jewish Law" (May 29, 1938) but nevertheless pinned his hopes on the West.

When the crisis of the Munich Agreement broke in September 1938, Imrédy and Kánya, while presenting Hungary's claims on Czechoslovakia, limited those claims to what they hoped would be acceptable to the Western powers, whose endorsement they made every effort to obtain. Ignored by the West, the Hungarian leaders had to turn to Germany and Italy after all, which, under the "First Vienna Award" of November 2, gave Hungary the fringe of southern Slovakia inhabited by ethnic Hungarians. Imrédy, disillusioned with the West, dismissed Kánya for the pro-Axis István, Count Csáky, and sought to recover Hitler's favour by introducing a more far-reaching Jewish Law (May 2, 1939). Imrédy's enemies secured his resignation in February 1939 by unearthing documents purporting to show a Jewish strain in his own ancestry. Pál, Count Teleki, who succeeded him, was sympathetic to the West, but Hungary's recovery of Carpatho-Ruthenia (March 1939) with Hitler's sanction and approval made it difficult for him to pursue a pro-Western policy.

WAR AND RENEWED DEFEAT

When Germany attacked Poland (September 1, 1939), Hungary refused to allow German troops to cross Hungarian territory but permitted remnants of the Polish army, fleeing civilians, and Polish Jews to enter the country. In the first months of World War II, none of the belligerents wanted the war to extend to southeastern Europe, so Teleki and Horthy were able to keep Hungary at peace. After the Soviet Union had occupied Bessarabia in June 1940, the Hungarian leaders compelled a reluctant Germany (but a willing Italy) to cede to Hungary northern Transylvania under the "Second Vienna Award" (August 30). They then allowed German troops to cross Hungarian territory into southern Romania and in November signed the Tripartite Pact.

The next step was more fatal still. In his search for insurance, Teleki concluded with the like-minded government of Yugoslavia a treaty (December 12, 1940) unluckily characterized as one of "Eternal Friendship." On March 26, 1941, that Yugoslav government was overthrown by a pro-Western regime. Hitler prepared to invade Yugoslavia and called on Hungary to help. Caught in an unanticipated situation, Hungary refused to join in the attack but again allowed German troops to cross its territory. Great Britain threatened to declare war, and Teleki, blaming himself for the development of a situation that it had been his life's aim to avoid, committed suicide on April 2.

His successor, László Bárdossy, waited until Croatia had declared its independence (April 10) and then, arguing that Yugoslavia had already disintegrated, occupied the ex-Hungarian areas of Yugoslavia.

Although he was not a fascist, Bárdossy believed that the Axis powers would win the war and that Hungary's salvation lay in placating them. Otherwise, so he believed, Romania (now pro-Axis) would persuade Hitler to reverse the Second Vienna Award. Accordingly, when Germany attacked the Soviet Union (June 22, 1939), Bárdossy sent a token force to assist in what everyone expected to be a brief operation. The strength of the Soviet resistance upset the calculation, and in January 1942 the Germans forced Hungary to mobilize practically all its available manpower and send it to the Soviet Union. Meanwhile, amid a flurry of declarations of war in December 1941 and after the Japanese attack on Pearl Harbor provoked the United States to formally enter the war, Britain (by this point allied with the Soviet Union) declared war on Hungary, which in turn declared war on the United States. Further, Britain recognized the Czechoslovak government-in-exile and withdrew recognition of the First Vienna Award, while the Soviet Union recognized Czechoslovakia's 1937 frontiers.

Many Hungarians by then agreed with Bárdossy that Hungary's only course was to fight on until the Axis won the war—the more so because all Hungarians except those of the extreme left regarded

Bolshevism as the embodiment of evil. Horthy, however, while sharing this view, still believed in a Western victory and thought it possible for Hungary, while continuing the struggle in the East, to regain the favour of the West. In March 1942 he replaced Bárdossy with Miklós Kállay, who shared these hopes. For two years Kállay conducted a remarkable balancing act—protecting Hungary's Jews and allowing the left (except for the communists) almost untrammeled freedom while putting out innumerable feelers to the Western Allies, to whom he actually promised to surrender unconditionally when their troops reached Hungary's frontiers. Meanwhile, in January 1943 the Hungarian expeditionary force suffered a crushing defeat at Voronezh in western Russia that cost it much of its manpower and nearly all its equipment.

But the Western forces did not approach the Danube valley, and, as the Soviet army neared the Carpathians, Hitler, from whom few of Kállay's activities were hidden, decided that he could not leave his vital communications at the mercy of an untrustworthy regime. In March 1944 he offered Horthy the choice between full cooperation under German supervision or undisguised German occupation with the treatment accorded to an enemy. On March 19, while Horthy was visiting Hitler in Klessheim, Germany, the Germans began the occupation of Hungary, leaving Horthy no choice but to appoint a collaborationist government under the openly Germanophile Döme Sztójay.

For a while the Germans did much as they wished—they suppressed parties and organizations of potential opponents and arrested their leaders. With the cooperation of Hungarian authorities, Jews were compelled to wear a yellow star, robbed of their property, and incarcerated in ghettos as in other Nazi-occupied areas. Except for the Jews in the capital and those in the forced-labour camps of the Hungarian army—whose turn would come later—Hungarian Jews were deported to the gas chambers of German extermination camps. In spite of the efforts of representatives of some neutral countries—such as Raoul Wallenberg of Sweden, the papal nuncio, and diplomats from Switzerland, Portugal, and even Spain—which saved tens of thousands of lives, some 550,000 of Hungary's 800,000 Jews (as defined by "racial" legislation) perished during the war. At the same time, with the help of sympathetic citizens who risked their own lives, about 250,000 Hungarian Jews survived.

In the summer of 1944, the pressure relaxed; and in August, after Romania's surrender to the Allies, Horthy appointed a new government under the loyal general Géza Lakatos and again extended peace feelers. A "preliminary armistice" was concluded in Moscow, but, when on October 15 Horthy announced this on the radio, he was abducted by the Germans, who forced him to recant and to abdicate. The Germans put Ferenc Szálasi, the leader of the right-wing extremist Arrow Cross Party, in charge. By then, however, Soviet troops were far inside the country.

The Germans and their Hungarian allies were driven back slowly, while numerous refugees fled with them. The last armed forces crossed the Austrian frontier in April 1945.

The occupying Red Army wreaked havoc in the country. Hundreds of thousands of rapes were committed. A similar number of civilians were abducted; accused of various political crimes—such as alleged Nazi affiliation, fighting against Soviet forces, spying for the West, or being involved in sabotage activities—they were convicted and deported for 10 to 25 years to the Soviet Gulag. Others were simply taken off the streets to perform a "little work" (*malenky robot*) and were sent, without trial, for three to five years to the slave labour camps scattered throughout the Soviet Union. Still others became prisoners of war who, in violation of the Geneva Conventions, were reclassified by the tens of thousands as "war criminals" and kept for years as forced labourers in the Gulag.

Hungary's defeat was sealed in a new peace treaty, signed in Paris on February 10, 1947, which restored the Trianon frontiers, with a rectification in favour of Czechoslovakia and the Soviet Union. It imposed on Hungary a reparations bill of $300 million and limited its armed forces. The implementation of the treaty's provisions was to be supervised by a Soviet occupation force, a large contingent of which remained in the country until June 1991.

HUNGARY IN THE SOVIET ORBIT

As in 1920, a new regime recognized the defeat of its predecessor. As early as December 1944, a makeshift Provisional National Assembly had accepted a government list and program presented to it by communist agents following in the wake of the Soviet armies. Beginning cautiously, the communists announced that the new Hungary was to rest on "all its democratic elements." The government contained only two communists; its other members were representatives of four noncommunist left-wing parties—the Smallholders, the Social Democrats, the National Peasants, and the Progressive Bourgeoisie—and four men associated with the Horthy regime, including two generals who had been in Moscow in connection with the armistice talks. The program provided for the expropriation of the large estates and the nationalization of the banks and heavy industry; but it promised guarantees of democratic rights and liberties, respect for private property, and encouragement of private initiative in trade and small industry.

THE COMMUNIST REGIME

The full political takeover proceeded systematically, although not according to any timetable, because the communists, misjudging feeling in the country, allowed the first elections (November 1945) to be relatively free. Only the parties of the coalition were allowed to contest them; but the adherents of the proscribed parties voted for the Smallholders, who received an absolute majority. The head of the Soviet mission, however, insisted that the coalition must be maintained; a Smallholder was allowed to be prime minister, but the Ministry of the Interior, with the control of the police, was given to the communists. Pressure and intimidation were then applied to the Smallholders to expel their more-courageous members as "fascists," and in the next manipulated election (August 1947) the Smallholders polled only 15 percent of the votes cast.

POLITICAL DEVELOPMENTS

The communists had meanwhile forced the Social Democrats to form a "workers' bloc" with them. Although the pressure was considerable, the bloc still polled only 45 percent of the votes (other parties were allowed to participate this time). The communists then forced the Social Democrats to join them in a single Workers' Party, from which recalcitrants were expelled.

In the next election, in May 1949, voting was open, and the voters were presented with a single list, on which candidates identified as Smallholders and National Peasants were actually crypto-communists. In late summer a new constitution was enacted, which was a copy of the constitution of the Soviet Union. It was promulgated on August 20—Hungary's traditional St. Stephen's Day—specifically with the goal of transforming that national holiday connected with Hungary's Christianization into the politically inspired Constitution Day. With this constitution, Hungary—a republic since February 1, 1946—became a "people's republic." Although its president (Zoltán Tildy) and for a while its prime ministers (Ferenc Nagy, then Lajos Dinnyés) were Smallholders, all real power rested with the Hungarian Workers' [communist] Party, controlled by its first secretary, Mátyás Rákosi.

Finally, the party's "Muscovite" wing turned on its "national" wing. The leader of this latter group, László Rajk, was executed on questionable charges in October 1949, and his chief adherents were similarly executed or imprisoned. Meanwhile, hundreds were executed or imprisoned as war criminals, many of them for no offense other than loyalty to the Horthy regime. Many thousands more were interned. The State Security Department, replaced in 1948 by the State Security Authority, was omnipotent. The judiciary, civil service, and army were purged, and party orthodoxy became the criterion for positions in them. The trade unions were made into mere executants of party orders.

Those who were distrusted were collected, convicted, and sent to various internment camps, the most notorious of which was the camp at Recsk in north-central Hungary, which functioned in great secrecy between 1950 and 1953. In May–June 1951, about 12,700 upper- and

JÓZSEF MINDSZENTY

The Roman Catholic clergyman József Mindszenty (born József Pehm, March 29, 1892, Csehimindszent, near Szombathely, Austria-Hungary [now in Hungary])—died May 6, 1975, Vienna, Austria) personified uncompromising opposition to fascism and communism in Hungary for more than five decades of the 20th century. Politically active from the time of his ordination as a priest in 1915, Mindszenty was arrested as an enemy of totalitarian governments twice in 1919 and again in 1944, the year in which he was consecrated bishop of Veszprém. In 1945 he was appointed primate of Hungary and archbishop of Esztergom, and in 1946 he was made a cardinal.

His refusal to permit the Roman Catholic schools of Hungary to be secularized prompted the communist government to arrest him in 1948 and convict him in 1949 on charges of treason. Sentenced to life imprisonment, he was set free during the uprising of 1956 and, when the communist government regained control, he sought asylum in the U.S. embassy in Budapest. He spent 15 years in voluntary confinement there, rejected requests from the Vatican to leave Hungary, and relented only in 1971, at the entreaty of the U.S. president Richard M. Nixon. As the guest of the Vatican and, after 1971, in Vienna, he criticized the pope's attempts to deal with Hungary's communist regime and in 1974 was retired from his posts as archbishop and primate. His *Memoirs* were published in 1974. Mindszenty was originally buried in Austria, but in 1991, after the fall of Hungary's communist government, he was reburied in the Basilica in Esztergom, Hungary.

upper-middle-class people were driven out of their apartments in Budapest and deported to small peasant villages on the Great Alföld or to scattered labour camps on the mud flats of Hortobágy in the vicinity of Debrecen.

After the dissolution of the parties, the chief ideological opposition to the communist regime came from the churches; but their estates were expropriated, making it impossible for them to maintain their schools, and in 1948 the entire educational system was nationalized. The Calvinist and Lutheran churches accepted financial arrangements imposed by the state. The head of the Roman Catholic Church, József

Cardinal Mindszenty, who refused to follow their example, was arrested on transparent charges in December 1948 and condemned to life imprisonment. The monastic orders were dissolved. Thereafter, the Roman Catholic Church accepted financial terms similar to those offered to other churches, and eventually the bishops, with visible repugnance, took the oath of loyalty to the state.

ECONOMIC DEVELOPMENTS

The communists' economic program, like their political program, could not be realized immediately, because in 1945 Hungary was in a state of economic chaos worse even than that of 1918. This time the country had been a theatre of war. Many cities were in ruins, and communications were wrecked; the retreating Germans had destroyed the bridges between Buda and Pest and had taken with them all they could of the country's portable wealth. The Soviet armies lived off the land, and the Soviet Union took its share of reparations in kind, placing its own values on the objects seized. It also took over former German assets in Hungary, including Jewish property confiscated during the Nazi occupation.

A three-year plan introduced in August 1947 was devoted chiefly to the repair of immediate damage. This was declared completed, ahead of schedule, in December 1949. By then the communists were in full political control, and measures nationalizing banking, most industry, and most internal and all foreign trade had been enacted. Hungary joined other Soviet-bloc countries in founding Comecon (Council for Mutual Economic Assistance) in 1949. The land outside the big estates was not touched at first, but in 1948 Rákosi announced a policy of collectivization of agriculture. Three forms were envisaged: state farms and two types of cooperative. Peasants were forced by various pressures into the cooperatives, the character of which approached ever more closely that of the state farms.

The three-year plan was succeeded by a five-year plan, the aim of which was to turn Hungary into a predominantly industrial country, with an emphasis on heavy industry. Huge sums were devoted to the construction of foundries and factories, many of them planned with little regard for Hungary's real resources and less still for its needs. In fact, the plan was concerned with the needs of the Soviet Union, for which Hungary was to serve as a workshop. Hungary's newly discovered deposits of uranium went straight out of the country. Industrial production rose steeply, but the standard of living did not; the production of consumer goods was throttled and that of agriculture stagnated.

THE REVOLUTION OF 1956

Rákosi—who in 1952 came to preside over the government as well as the party—was, under Moscow's direction, all-powerful until the death of Stalin in 1953, when a period of fluctuation began. In July 1953 Rákosi was deposed from the prime ministership in favour of Imre Nagy—a "Muscovite" but a Hungarian in his attitudes and not unpopular in the country. Nagy promised a new course—an end to the forced development of heavy industry, more consumer goods, no more forcing of peasants into the collectives, the release of political prisoners, and the closing of internment camps. He introduced some of these reforms, but Moscow hesitated to support him. In the spring of 1955, Nagy was dismissed from office and expelled from the party.

Rákosi was reinstated, and he put the country back on its previous course. He was dismissed again in July 1956, this time from all his offices and in disgrace. The new Soviet leader, Nikita S. Khrushchev, had sacrificed Rákosi as a gesture to the Yugoslavian leader Josip Broz Tito, whom Rákosi had offended personally and whom the Soviet leadership wished to placate. The new leader, Ernő Gerő, Rákosi's deputy, was almost as detested as Rákosi himself. Gerő promptly announced that there would be no concessions on matters of principle to Nagy and his group.

The relaxation of pressure under Nagy (though transitory), Khrushchev's "secret speech" denouncing Stalin's cult of personality—delivered at the 20th Congress of the Communist Party of the Soviet Union in February 1956—and the Polish challenge to the Soviet Union in the spring and summer of 1956 emboldened Hungarians. On October 23, students in Budapest staged a great procession, which was to end with the presentation of a petition asking for redress of the nation's grievances. People flocked into the streets to join them. Gerő answered with an unwise and truculent speech, and police fired into the crowds. The shots turned a peaceful demonstration into a revolutionary one. The army joined the revolutionaries, and army depots and munitions factories handed out arms. Outside Budapest, local councils sprang up in every centre. The peasants reoccupied their confiscated fields. The communist bureaucracy melted away. Prison doors were opened. The members of the State Security Authority fled if they could. A cheering crowd escorted Cardinal Mindszenty back to the primate's palace.

In kaleidoscopic political changes, Nagy resumed power on October 25 but then was driven from one concession to the next. On November 3 he found himself at the head of a new and genuine coalition government representing the reconstituted Hungarian Socialist Workers' Party and the revived Smallholders' Party, Social Democratic Party, and Petőfi [former National Peasant] Party.

The Soviet troops had withdrawn, and Nagy was negotiating for their complete evacuation from Hungary. On November 1 he announced Hungary's withdrawal from the Warsaw Pact (to which it had adhered since 1955) and asked the United Nations to recognize his country as a neutral state, under the joint protection of the great powers. Soviet officials were uncertain whether to act or to let matters take their course, for fear of Western intervention. But the growing pressures for intervention from China and neighbouring Romania, Czechoslovakia, and eventually even Yugoslavia; the danger posed by Nagy's gravitation out of the Soviet bloc; Israeli, British, and French involvement in the Suez Crisis; and an increasing realization that the United States would not risk a global confrontation over Hungary emboldened the Soviet leadership to act. Their tanks, which had halted just across the frontier, began to return, reinforced by other units. On November 4 the Soviet forces entered Budapest and began liquidating the revolution. Nagy took refuge in the Yugoslav embassy and Cardinal Mindszenty in the U.S. legation. Gen. Pál Maléter, the Nagy government's minister of defense, who had been invited by the Soviet commanders to negotiate, was taken captive and eventually executed.

In the early morning of the same day, János Kádár—who had defected from the Nagy government and left Budapest on November 1—broadcast a radio speech wherein he declared the illegitimacy of the Nagy government and proclaimed the formation of the new Soviet-supported "Hungarian revolutionary workers' and peasants' government." It consisted entirely of communists, who now congregated under the flag of the Hungarian Socialist Workers' Party that had replaced the discredited Hungarian Workers' Party. The new government was headed by Kádár as prime minister and Ferenc Münnich as his second in command. Kádár promised that once the "counterrevolution" was suppressed and order was restored, he would negotiate for the withdrawal of the Soviet garrison (although the denunciation of the Warsaw Pact was retracted). Having been imprisoned himself by Rákosi's Stalinist regime, he now dissociated himself from the "Rákosi-Gerő clique" and promised substantial internal reforms.

Most Hungarians, however, were skeptical of these promises, and fighting continued. But the odds were too heavy in favour of the Soviets, and the major hostilities were over within a fortnight, although sporadic encounters continued into January 1957. The workers continued their struggle by proclaiming a general strike and other forms of peaceful resistance. It took many weeks before they were brought to heel and many more months before some semblance of normality returned to the country. The price in human lives was great. According to the calculations of historians, the Hungarians suffered about 20,000 casualties, among them some 2,500 deaths, while the Soviet losses consisted of about 1,250 wounded and more than 650 dead.

Meanwhile, Nagy, who had left his place of refuge under safe conduct, had been abducted and taken to Romania. After a secret trial, he and Maléter and a few close associates were executed in 1958. Many lesser figures were seized and transported to the Soviet Union, some never to return, and 200,000 refugees escaped to the West (about 38,000 of whom emigrated to North America in 1956–57). Thus, a substantial proportion of Hungary's young and educated classes was lost to the country, including several top noncommunist political leaders and intellectuals, as well as Gen. Béla K. Király, the commander of the Hungarian National Guard organized during the revolution. Material damage was also very heavy, especially in Budapest.

THE KÁDÁR REGIME

In the first uncertain weeks of his regime, Kádár made many promises. Workers' councils were to be given a large amount of control in the factories and mines. Compulsory deliveries of farm produce were to be abolished, and no compulsion, direct or indirect, was to be put on the peasants to enter the collectives. The five-year plan was to be revised to permit more production of consumer goods. The exchange rate of the ruble and forint was to be adjusted and the uranium contract revised. For a time there was even talk of a coalition government.

The larger hopes were dashed after representatives of the Soviet Union, East Germany, Czechoslovakia, Romania, and Bulgaria conferred with those of Hungary in Budapest in January 1957. A new program was soon issued stating that Hungary was a dictatorship of the proletariat, which in foreign policy relied on the Soviet Union and the Soviet bloc. Further, it was asserted that the Soviet garrison was in Hungary to protect the country from imperialist aggression. Internal reforms were again promised, however, and foreign trade agreements were to be based on complete equality and mutual advantage.

Subsequently, Kádár was at great pains to give the Soviet Union no cause for uneasiness over Hungary's loyalty. When any international issue arose, he invariably supported Moscow's policy with meticulous orthodoxy, even sending a contingent into Czechoslovakia in 1968 to help crush the "Prague Spring." At home he ignored some of his promises and honoured others only superficially. The peasants were so greatly pressured to enter cooperatives that within a few years practically no private farms survived. The workers' councils were dissolved, but

trade unions were later granted rights to query decisions by management. Parliament remained a rubber stamp, and a Patriotic People's Front (PPF), on which noncommunists were represented, was a mere facade.

The bloody retributions in 1957–59 resulted in the execution of "counterrevolutionaries" (among them Prime Minister Imre Nagy and several of his associates) and the imprisonment of thousands of others. Yet by the 1960s, conditions had changed for the better. Between 1960 and 1963, by way of two separate amnesty decrees, most of those imprisoned for "counterrevolutionary activities" or for the misuse of their party positions during the "years of the personality cult" (i.e., the Rákosi regime) were pardoned and released. At this time the United Nations (UN) ended its debate on the "case of Hungary" and by June 1963 helped to remove the moral stigma from the Kádár regime by the formal acceptance of its credentials at the UN.

Almost simultaneously, Kádár enunciated the principle that "he who is not against us is with us," which meant ordinary people could go about their business without fear of molestation or even much surveillance and could speak, read, and even write with reasonable freedom. Technical competence replaced party orthodoxy as a criterion for attaining posts of responsibility. More scope was allowed to private small-scale enterprise in trade and industry, and the New Economic Mechanism (NEM), initiated in 1968, introduced the profit motive into state-directed enterprises. Agricultural cooperatives were allowed to produce industrial goods for their own use or to sell on demand, while the private plots of their members supplied a large proportion of fruits and vegetables for the rest of the population.

Contacts with the West were encouraged. A modus vivendi was found with the Vatican and with Protestant churches. The standard of living began to rise substantially. Tourism developed as a significant industry. In addition to a huge influx of foreign visitors—many of them from western Europe, the United States, and Canada—an increasing number of Hungarians traveled abroad. This was especially true after the introduction (January 1, 1988) of "global passports," which removed restrictions on travel. Income from tourism increased dramatically, yet the net balance was less in Hungary's favour than would be expected, because Hungarians going to the West spent most of their official hard currency quotas on purchases of consumer goods, owing to shortages and skyrocketing prices at home.

The two decades of the NEM, which went beyond the liberalization that took place in the Soviet Union itself, were only partially successful. Productivity failed to rise according to expectations. Government regulations persisted in many areas, and the economy remained geared to the Soviet-led Comecon. A burdensome system of subventions aimed at keeping down the prices of basic necessities and services and at promoting the production of state-preferred goods made realistic cost accounting impossible. The price rise of petroleum and other industrial raw materials on the world market in the early 1970s also aggravated the situation. The gap grew between the price of energy, sophisticated industrial hardware, and raw materials, on the one hand, and the price of agricultural products, a main item in Hungary's foreign trade, on the other. Also burdensome was Hungary's growing indebtedness, which began in 1970 and climaxed in the mid-1990s. By the end of the Kádár regime, the nation's gross foreign debt to the West had passed the $18 billion mark.

Political opposition to reform, including Soviet and Comecon criticism of the NEM, all but brought it to a halt in 1973–78. Administrative interventions by state agencies and party and trade union organizations caused a return to the methods of the centralized command economy under the pretext of protecting the relative earnings of industrial workers compared with those in agriculture or of taxing only "unearned" profits of successful enterprises. Rezső Nyers, the architect of the NEM, was demoted in 1974, only to be brought back to the Politburo in May 1988, at a time of deepening political and economic crisis. By the end of the 1970s, reformers had again prevailed over their opponents. New measures included cuts in the central bureaucracy, encouragement of small firms and private enterprises, revisions of the price and wage system to reflect more closely conditions on the world market and costs of production, and the creation of a commercial banking system.

REFORMS OF THE LATE 1980S

Hungary's efforts to introduce market reforms into the country's socialist economy extended to the international arena. Already a member of the General Agreement on Tariffs and Trade (GATT), Hungary was admitted to the International Monetary Fund (IMF) in 1982 and received assistance from the World Bank. Hungary was the first among members of Comecon to enter into agreement with the European Economic Community (later succeeded by the European Union).

ECONOMIC REFORMS

While the Soviet Union remained Hungary's most important trading partner and the source of its energy supply, Hungary had to turn to the West for technological assistance and capital investment in the process of modernizing the economy. Trade relations with the West, in which Austria and West Germany played particularly important roles, were crucial at a time when barely half of Hungary's foreign trade involved members of Comecon. Foreign trade constituted a larger proportion of Hungary's gross national product (GNP) than that of any other Comecon country.

Efforts to adjust Hungary's economy to the world market were handicapped by the adverse effects of the energy crisis of the 1970s and the de facto reversal of

the NEM in the same decade. Although agricultural production continued to advance, in part because of favourable international market conditions, the rest of the economy deteriorated. This process was further aggravated by misallocation of funds, reluctance to abandon costly projects such as the Danube hydroelectric power plant, and participation in joint projects of Comecon. There was also unwillingness to drastically reduce subsidies to inefficient enterprises and for many basic necessities and services, which were kept at an artificially low price level. As a result, Hungary's hard currency indebtedness by the end of the 1980s was the highest per capita indebtedness of any country in eastern Europe. Inflationary pressures began to build up, and real wages and living standards declined.

The appointment of Károly Grósz as prime minister in mid-1987 led to a program of severe belt-tightening; a harsh, hastily prepared income tax law aimed at cutting consumption; anticipated unemployment in some segments of the economy; and steep rises in consumer prices, transportation costs, and basic services such as gas, electricity, telephone, water, and rents. Minor changes in the party leadership, still controlled by Kádár, and the reshuffling of the government—including the establishment of the first Ministry of the Environment in eastern Europe—eased acceptance of unpopular measures introduced to stabilize the collapsing economy. But, as a consequence of these growing economic difficulties,

Kádár's prestige—which had peaked in the late 1970s and early '80s and made him the most popular communist leader within the Soviet bloc—plummeted.

POLITICAL REFORMS

By the late 1980s, growing numbers of Hungarians had concluded that years of misgovernment could not be erased by economic reforms alone. The process of de-Stalinization reinforced the desire to reexamine the political premises of Grósz's program, which seemed to imply that to keep their hard-won personal freedoms Hungarians should pay with economic misery and further social polarization. By the time the annual inflation rate reached 17 percent, public pressure compelled the party conference in May 1988 to replace Kádár with Grósz and also to replace several of Kádár's supporters within the Politburo and the Central Committee. In November 1988 a young economist, Miklós Németh, became the prime minister, and in June 1989 a quadrumvirate composed of Imre Pozsgay, Grósz, Németh, and Nyers—chaired by the latter—temporarily took over the direction of a deeply split party. In October the party congress announced the dissolution of the Hungarian Socialist Workers' Party and its transformation into the Hungarian Socialist Party. A splinter group of conservatives, under the leadership of Gyula Thürmer, saved a small fraction of the old party under its original name and continued allegiance to its communist policies.

Meanwhile, informal associations, clubs, and debating circles such as the Hungarian Democratic Forum, the Federation of Young Democrats (Fiatal Demokraták Szövetsége; Fidesz), the Network of Free Initiatives, and the Bajcsy-Zsilinszky Society proliferated and served as points of departure for new political parties. The Democratic Union of Scientific Workers, supported by a substantial portion of academic and clerical employees of scholarly institutions, was the first independent professional association to challenge the communist-controlled National Council of Trade Unions and to establish contact with the Polish union Solidarity, as well as with organized labour in the West. Filmmakers, writers, and journalists rediscovered their right of free speech, publishers printed manuscripts that had been kept locked up for decades, new periodicals appeared, and the press, radio, and television threw over taboos that had prevailed for more than 40 years.

The 950th anniversary of the death of King St. Stephen I, who led the Christianization of Hungary, was celebrated with medieval pomp in August 1988. It was commemorated in the presence of the primate of Poland, József Cardinal Glemp, representing Pope John Paul II. This began the transformation of Constitution Day—introduced four decades earlier under Rákosi—back into the original St. Stephen's Day.

Major achievements were made in the areas of religious freedom and state-church relationship through the Law on

Freedom of Conscience and Religion, passed in January 1990. Full diplomatic relations with the Vatican were reestablished in March 1990, and Pope John Paul II made an official visit to Hungary in August 1991. In 1988 the Boy Scouts (viewed as a conspicuously Christian organization in Hungary) was resuscitated, in 1989 the law that had disbanded Christian religious orders in 1950 was repealed, and in 1990 the state began to return to the Catholic and Protestant churches some of their former prestigious educational institutions. The World Jewish Congress held its executive session in Budapest in 1987, and in June 1990 the Hungarian Christian-Jewish Council was established to promote interaction among religious denominations.

The fate of the Hungarian minorities in the neighbouring countries of Czechoslovakia, Romania, and Yugoslavia, as well as, after 1945, in Subcarpathian Ruthenia (now known as Carpatho-Ukraine), had been a concern of every Hungarian government in the period between Hungary's dismemberment after World War I and the rise of communist domination following World War II. Territorial revisionism had been a cornerstone of interwar Hungarian foreign policy, and concern for the minorities remained alive among a significant portion of the Hungarians both at home and abroad even after World War II. But this concern did not apply to the communist Hungarian government, which forbade even mentioning this question during the three decades following World War

II. The fate of the minorities, however, became an increasingly acute issue after Nicolae Ceaușescu's rise to power in Romania and his brutal anti-Hungarian domestic policy in Transylvania.

The Kádár regime tried to avoid this question so as not to offend fraternal communist governments within the Soviet bloc, but the ascension of human rights in international politics during the 1970s made it increasingly difficult to do so. By the late 1980s, conditions had reached a point where Hungarian party and government leaders were obliged to join the worldwide public protests against the repression of Hungarians in the surrounding states. They were particularly incensed by Romania's policy of reapportionment and relocation of the rural population, which, if fully implemented, would have destroyed a large number of ethnic Hungarian settlements and in effect would have advanced the cause of the policy of mass assimilation. By granting asylum to refugees from Transylvania (not only Hungarians but also Romanians and Germans) at a moment of economic insecurity, by tolerating if not encouraging a sharp media campaign and mass demonstrations in front of the Romanian embassy in Budapest, and by submitting formal complaints to international organizations after an unsuccessful meeting between Grósz and Ceaușescu in August 1988, the Hungarian government indicated its determination to take an active interest in the fate of Hungarian minorities in neighbouring countries. This policy in defense of human rights, combined with renewed openings toward Austria, establishment of trade relations with South Korea, and resumption of diplomatic relations with Israel (severed since the Arab-Israeli war of 1967), was taken as a sign of a more independent foreign policy, as were the efforts at strengthening Hungary's ties with western Europe.

All the while, Hungarian American organizations were very active—in advance of the Hungarian government—in trying to turn the attention of world leaders to the plight of the Hungarian minorities in the surrounding states, especially in Ceauşescu's Romania. Their incessant agitation aggravated and embarrassed the Hungarian government, which soon addressed the issue of Hungarian minorities.

Nevertheless, by the late 1980s this issue created a breach in the leadership of the Hungarian Socialist Workers' (communist) Party, with some of the reform communists demanding greater attention to the plight of the Hungarian minorities. Some also asked for a reassessment of the Hungarian Revolution of 1956, which for more than three decades had simply been referred to as an "imperialist-inspired counterrevolution." The first major figure to label that revolution a "popular uprising" (not a "counterrevolution") was Imre Pozsgay, who, though a member of the Politburo, was already moving away from strict Marxist ideology. He joined forces with a most unlikely partner, Archduke Otto von Habsburg, the oldest son of the last king of Hungary, to sponsor the

Pan-European Picnic of August 19, 1989, when hundreds of East Germans who were visiting Hungary breached the formerly unbreachable Iron Curtain and fled to Austria. Within three weeks the Hungarian government had opened the long-closed western border and permitted tens of thousands of East German refugees to cross into Austria on their way to West Germany. This government-approved mass exodus—combined with interviews broadcast by Hungarian television with Alexander Dubček and Ota Šik, leaders of the Czechoslovak reform movement, and with the exiled king Michael of Romania—led to formal protests by the governments in East Berlin, Prague, and Bucharest, but this did not alter the course of events.

The changes on the domestic scene were no less dramatic. They extended to the constitutional framework built since the communist takeover. Guidelines for a new constitution, drafted by the government and approved by both the party and the National Assembly, did not mention the "leading role of the Party," spelled out by the constitution of 1949. The draft of the new constitution sanctioned a multiparty system that had already been accepted in principle by the party leadership. The new constitution—which transformed the communist-inspired "People's Republic" into the "Republic of Hungary" and which was promulgated on October 23, 1989, the 33rd anniversary of the Revolution of 1956—was based on the principle of the separation of legislative, executive, and judicial powers and also included guarantees of individual and civil rights. Many additional changes followed that year, including the creation of the post of president (to be elected by Parliament) in place of the Presidential Council and the establishment of a Constitutional Court to examine the constitutionality of existing laws, decrees, and regulations and to nullify all laws found to violate the words and spirit of the constitution. The National Assembly, which theretofore had served only as a rubber stamp for party and governmental decisions, also underwent significant changes. In its autumn 1988 session, it rejected the government's budget and then gradually transformed itself into an independent legislature that came to be solely responsible for all legislation.

Important new legislation included amendments to the law of assembly, which granted the holding of indoor meetings without special permission. It also featured a new enterprise law, which allowed the private ownership of businesses with up to 500 employees, permitted foreigners to own up to 100 percent of an enterprise, and allowed mixed (i.e., joint state and private) ownership of property. Also indicative of the new reforms, the government consulted with independent organizations and spokesmen of the opposition in the course of preparing the new laws.

Alternative independent parties and organizations continued to grow in the late 1980s. The first and most prominent among the new parties was the Hungarian Democratic Forum, followed by Fidesz and the Alliance of Free Democrats. Soon several of the traditional political parties that had been destroyed or emasculated by the communists in the late 1940s also emerged, including the Independent Smallholders' Party, the Social Democratic Party, the National Peasant Party (under the new name of Hungarian People's Party), the Christian Democratic People's Party, and finally the ex-communist Hungarian Socialist Party. Their emergence was accompanied by the rise of several partylike interest groups, such as the Historical Justice Committee, the Independent Legal Forum, the Opposition Roundtable, and the Bajcsy-Zsilinszky Society. Some of these parties leaned toward socialism, others moved more in the direction of liberalism, still others positioned themselves as agrarian peasant parties, and there were also those that combined Christian Socialism with a big dose of traditionalism.

POSTCOMMUNIST HUNGARY

After it had become evident that the existing communist regime was doomed, the transitional government headed by Németh (November 1988–May 1990) began a systematic dialogue with the opposition. This took the form of a National Roundtable (March–September 1989), wherein the methods of a peaceful transition were discussed by the representatives of the government and the major opposition parties. As a result,

Parliament passed a new election law, which introduced a system of proportional representation for a unicameral National Assembly to consist of 386 members. Of these 386 parliamentarians, 176 were to represent individual electoral districts, while the remaining 210 seats were to be allocated on the basis of voting for regional and national lists of candidates.

POLITICAL DEVELOPMENTS

The elections for the newly constituted National Assembly were duly held in two rounds in March and April 1990, resulting in a major victory for a right-centre Hungarian Democratic Forum-led coalition that included the Smallholders and the Christian Democrats and which took nearly three-fifths of the seats in Parliament. The opposition was represented by the Alliance of Free Democrats, which captured one-fourth of the seats, and the Hungarian Socialist Party and Fidesz, each of which garnered fewer than one-tenth of the seats. Because these three parties stood for three distinct ideologies, they were unable to create a united front, which put them at a considerable disadvantage.

The dominant figure in the right-centre coalition was József Antall, who served as postcommunist Hungary's first prime minister until his death on December 12, 1993. A "liberal" leader, though mostly in the 19th-century sense of the word, Antall favoured an egalitarian and tolerant society. But he also wanted an ordered society with respect for law and national traditions and with concern for the Hungarian minorities in neighbouring states.

Many Hungarians believed Antall made a major mistake when he failed to sweep entrenched communists from the Hungarian bureaucracy, government agencies, and security forces. Initially, these former communists kept a low profile, but many carried out the privatization of state enterprises in a way that lined their own pockets. The former "party aristocracy" became the new "moneyed aristocracy," some of whom began to move back into the country's political leadership as well (a pattern that was detectable in virtually all of the former Soviet-bloc countries).

As a consequence of the difficulties it faced and the problems it failed to tackle, the ruling coalition's popularity waned after four years in power, and, in elections in 1994, the ex-communist Socialist Party captured 54 percent of the seats in Parliament. In spite of their absolute majority, the Socialists decided to form a coalition with the Alliance of Free Democrats, thus gaining control of nearly three-fourths of the seats in Parliament. This left-centre coalition was led by Gyula Horn, communist Hungary's last foreign minister, who in that capacity had been at least partially responsible for the policies that led to Hungary's reorientation to the West and the tearing down of the Iron Curtain. As prime minister, he pursued many of the policies initiated by Antall, including the privatization of the economy and the move toward membership in the North Atlantic Treaty Organization (NATO) and the European Union (EU). At the same time, he undid many of the Hungarian Democratic Forum's cultural policies that had been designed to take Hungary in the direction of traditional patriotism.

The alternation of left-centre and right-centre governments continued in the 1998 elections with the victory of a right-centre alliance consisting of the Fidesz–Hungarian Civic Party, the Smallholders, and the much-reduced Hungarian Democratic Forum, which together controlled slightly more than 55 percent of parliamentary seats. The leader of this coalition, Viktor Orbán, moved to strengthen the position of prime minister. He also oversaw the ascendance to NATO membership in 1999.

Orbán's greater attention to national issues, including the fate of the Hungarian minorities in the surrounding states, was frowned upon by the Socialist-led opposition. This created an ever-widening chasm between the right-centre and left-centre in Hungarian politics that carried into the 21st century.

In 2002 the tables turned again, after a divisive election with a wide turnout (nearly three-fourths of those eligible voted) brought the Socialist–Free Democrats coalition back to power. The new prime minister, Peter Medgyessy, guided Hungary to membership in the EU in 2004 but also became the first

postcommunist premier to resign, after losing the confidence of his party. He was succeeded in late 2004 by Ferenc Gyurcsány, a onetime party bureaucrat who made a fortune in the free-for-all business activities in the 1990s, including profiteering from the privatization of Hungarian state assets. In elections in 2006, the Gyurcsány-led Socialist–Free Democrats coalition became the first government to win consecutive terms since the end of the communist era.

ECONOMIC AND SOCIAL CHANGE

Even though there were major differences in the ideological motivations of the various postcommunist political parties and governments, they all agreed on the main goals to be achieved. These included the privatization of state-owned assets, the creation of a politically and culturally pluralistic society, and the attainment of membership in the Western community of nations by joining NATO and the EU.

Reforms under the Antall regime left no sector of the economy untouched, as the reintroduction of the market economy demanded a whole new economic and institutional infrastructure. Despite fits and starts, the first postcommunist government liberalized trade, deregulated most prices, and introduced and executed a wide-ranging privatization policy. Within two years of attaining power, it relaunched the Budapest Stock Exchange and a largely independent Central Bank and initiated the most-liberal foreign investment policy among the states of the former Soviet bloc. Moreover, despite the massive dislocation this approach caused, the government also introduced a bankruptcy policy that wrung out many of the inefficient state enterprises from the economy.

Hungarian privatization policy differed from its counterparts in other countries in east-central Europe. The Hungarian government sold off companies on a trade-sale basis rather than adopting the coupon privatization of the Czech Republic, Russia, or, to a lesser extent, Poland. While the government was criticized for selling out the "family silver" to offshore investors, limits were set on foreign participation in the key strategic sectors of energy and telecommunications. This Hungarian approach to privatization was comparatively slower than those of other former communist countries, but it resulted in company-level restructuring that was absent from privatization plans implemented elsewhere.

Ironically, the same government that paved the way for a relatively strong institutional infrastructure for the emerging market economy was simultaneously weak in implementing a stable macroeconomic policy. Hungary suffered from a high debt burden and "twin deficits"—fiscal deficits and current account deficits. In the mid-1990s the International Monetary Fund and other international institutions held the country in low esteem. Lajos Bokros, finance minister for Horn, attempted a turnaround with an austerity package (since known as the Bokros package) that called for the dismantling of the last vestiges of Hungary's expensive cradle-to-grave socialist policies. He devalued the currency, reduced social benefits, and accelerated the sale of key sectors of the Hungarian economy—such as electricity and gas—to foreign investors. While international financiers cheered these reforms, Bokros himself was widely reviled in the Hungarian press.

These economic reforms brought stability but were not without social costs, including the corruption that characterized the privatization process. State assets were secretly funneled into the companies of political apparatchiks, many of whom were never brought to justice. In consequence of this rapid privatization, property relationships during the 1990s changed significantly. In 1989 about four-fifths of the gross domestic product (GDP) was still produced by state enterprises, but by the end of the 1990s this share had been reduced to less than one-third. The bulk of the private investors were domestic, but significant foreign investment was made by Germans, Americans, Austrians, the Dutch, and the French. Privatization in the agricultural sector was rapid, with more than four-fifths of all agricultural land having moved into private hands by the end of the 20th century—even though a significant portion was not cultivated.

The postcommunist transformation brought about other unforeseen difficulties for Hungary, including the collapse of the country's traditional eastern markets (Comecon) and the protectionist agricultural policy of the EU. Low-quality Hungarian goods and produce that had previously supplied the uncritical markets of the Soviet bloc now had to compete in the open market. The gradual reorientation of Hungarian foreign trade to the West required painful readjustments and led to trade deficits. By 1997 about three-fifths of trade was with the EU. The difficulties stemming from the transformation resulted in a radical and increasing decline in the country's GDP as the millennium approached. Double-digit inflation was another bugbear, peaking at 35 percent in 1991 and riding a roller coaster until the end of the century. Inflation affected wages and pensions as well as employment levels, all of which showed losses in the immediate postcommunist period. Some of this unemployment was because of the collapse of the Soviet-bloc markets and the liquidation of many inefficient industrial plants and mines that had been kept in operation by the communist regime through state subsidies simply to hold down unemployment.

The introduction of the free market also resulted in the radical polarization of Hungarian society. The relatively egalitarian society of the communist years had relinquished its place to economic inequality and an increasingly class-structured society, in which the average income of the upper one-tenth of the Hungarian population was many times that of the lowest tenth. By the mid-1990s the living standards of perhaps one-third of the population had declined to below subsistence level. The collapse of the old regime also resulted in the collapse of the cradle-to-grave social welfare system, which had been the hallmark of the communist state. Although of moderate to questionable quality, the existence of that system had supplied a measure of security to the population. All of these changes in the Hungarian way of life were accompanied by the growth of corruption, the rapid spread of narcotics among the young, and a huge jump in the crime rate (between 1985 and 1997 the number of reported crimes increased from 165,000 to 514,000). As a result, beginning even in the early 1990s, a growing number of people began to think with a degree of nostalgia about the world they had left behind. According to surveys conducted in 1991, 1994, and 1995, respectively 40 percent, 51 percent, and 54 percent of the population believed that the "new system [was] worse than the old one."

Nevertheless, at the turn of the 21st century, many saw the country's changing nature in a very positive light. In addition to joining NATO and the EU, Hungary had been instrumental in 1999 in reviving the Visegrád Forum of Cooperation, first established in 1991 by the leaders of Hungary (József Antall), Poland (Lech Wałesa), and Czechoslovakia (Václav Havel). Having lapsed in 1994 because of a lack of interest by the Czech political leadership, the Visegrád Forum was revived with the inclusion of both halves of former Czechoslovakia—the Czech Republic and Slovakia. Even more dramatic was Hungary's integration into the transatlantic world, underscored by the growing cooperation between Hungary and the United States.

In contrast, the rift between Hungary and Romania deepened. Ethnic disturbances in Romania had continued even after the fall of the Ceaușescu regime, and in February 1990 Hungary renounced their 1979 bilateral agreement, which made it impossible for Hungarians in Romania to hold dual citizenship. The continued mistreatment of the Hungarian minorities—particularly in Romania and Slovakia, but also in Serbia and Carpatho-Ukraine—was a lingering issue in the relationship between Hungary and the so-called "successor states." The situation for the Hungarian minorities was significantly better in Austria, Croatia, and Slovenia.

In 2000 Hungary celebrated the millennium of its establishment by St. Stephen I as a Christian kingdom in the heart of Europe. (The state was actually founded prior to the year 1000, at the time of the Árpáds' conquest of the Carpathian Basin.) As Hungary began its second millennium as a Christian state, its infrastructure had been rebuilt, its automobile stock increased, its roadways improved, its telephone system modernized, and its businesses updated. Accompanying the inflow of foreign capital and the arrival of major American, European, and Japanese corporations, important native corporations flourished. Shortages that used to characterize communist society had disappeared—albeit

at the expense of emphasizing the growing difference between the haves and the have-nots. At the beginning of the 21st century, political conditions had stabilized, and the Hungarian economy had become one of the most competitive in east-central Europe. Assessing Hungary's transformation at the end of the 1990s, the London-based *Financial Times* reported, "Hungary's economy is now able to flourish untouched by political developments...to which no government can do substantial harm."

Sadly, this projection did not turn out to be quite correct. The Socialist-Liberal coalition government elected in 2002 introduced social-spending programs that created significant problems for the Hungarian economy. By 2006 Hungary had recorded the worst fiscal deficits of any country in the EU, forcing the Gyurcsány government to introduce austerity measures reminiscent of the Bokros package of 1995. The crisis atmosphere that resulted first boiled over in September 2006, with Gyurcsány's secret speech to the Hungarian Socialist Party, in which he acknowledged that "we did not actually do anything for four years....Instead, we lied morning, noon, and night." The ensuing confrontation between the Gyurcsány-led governing coalition (Hungarian Socialist Party and Alliance of Free Democrats) and the Orbán-led opposition (Fidesz) reached a symbolic flash point on October 23, 2006, the 50th anniversary of the Revolution of 1956. While Gyurcsány held a small official commemoration in front of the

Parliament Building, an Orbán-led mass meeting on the streets around Hotel Astoria was interrupted by conflict between the police and demonstrators.

The Gyurcsány government's austerity policies—largely undertaken in an attempt to hit the economic benchmarks required for inclusion in the euro currency zone—took further aim at the country's health care system, introducing legislation in 2007 that restructured hospitals and allowed for private investment in a new system of health insurance funds. While the increasingly unpopular government was successful in reducing the deficit, in the autumn of 2008 the already shrinking Hungarian economy was rocked by an international financial crisis, and the government received a rescue package of $26 billion from the EU, the IMF, and the World Bank. Earlier in the year, more than 80 percent of the electorate had approved a Fidesz-initiated referendum to abolish fees for doctor and hospital visits and university tuition that had been enacted by the government. In March 2009 Gyurcsány, still reeling from this defeat and unable to stem the downward-spiraling economy, announced that he would resign from office. In April he was replaced as prime minister by the economics minister, Gordon Bajnai.

In parliamentary elections in April 2010, Fidesz crushed the Hungarian Socialist Party, capturing more than two-thirds of the seats to become the first non-coalition government in the history of postcommunist Hungary and paving the way for Orbán to again become prime minister. As significant as Fidesz's win and the Socialists' poor showing was the ascendance of the right-wing Jobbik party, which won only 12 fewer seats than the Socialist Party. Although it had been a notable presence on the Hungarian political scene for only a short time, Jobbik was well known for its anti-Roma and anti-Semitic posturing.

In early October 2010 a reservoir burst at an aluminum plant in Ajka, releasing a torrent of toxic red sludge (waste product from the aluminum-making process) that inundated large tracts of southwestern Hungary, killing 10 people and injuring more than 100. Quick action by the Hungarian government averted a much larger environmental disaster, however, as emergency crews were able to dilute much of the spill's strongly alkaline content before it contaminated the Danube.

Fidesz used its parliamentary majority throughout 2010 and 2011 to enact a series of sweeping legislative measures that culminated in the adoption of a new constitution on January 1, 2012. Conservative moral and religious themes figured prominently in the new constitution, which had a Christian emphasis, defined marriage as the union of a man and a woman, and declared that a fetus was entitled to legal protection from the moment of conception. Protests against the new constitution ensued in Hungary, and harsh foreign criticism of it included a report by the Council of Europe that raised concerns about judicial reforms that curtailed the independence of Hungarian courts. Foreign objections also played a major role in prompting the Orbán government to scale back a proposed media law that would have given Fidesz a great deal of direct control over the press.

The debt crisis that gripped the euro zone was a drag on Hungary's finances, and all three major ratings agencies had cut the country's credit rating to junk status by early 2012. Concern within the European Union over the Hungarian government's debt management and what some saw as the regressive nature of Hungary's new constitution threatened continued EU and IMF financial and economic support for Hungary. Compliance with European law was seen as an essential precondition to the delivery of loan payments to Hungary, and investors and EU officials alike called for revisions to the constitution.

In the meantime, a crisis in the office of the president consumed domestic politics. In January 2012 Hungarian Web sites reported that Pres. Pál Schmitt had plagiarized significant portions of his 1992 doctoral dissertation. A subsequent investigation by the university that had conferred the degree revealed that Schmitt had copied extensively from a pair of sources, and he was stripped of his degree. In a blow to the prestige of both Orbán and Fidesz, Schmitt resigned from the largely ceremonial post in April 2012. The next month, however, János Áder, a cofounder of Fidesz, won the presidency in an election that was boycotted by the Socialists.

CHAPTER 11

ROMANIA: THE LAND AND ITS PEOPLE

Romania is bounded by Ukraine to the north, Moldova to the northeast, the Black Sea to the southeast, Bulgaria to the south, Serbia to the southwest, and Hungary to the west. There is a certain symmetry in the physical structure of Romania. The country forms a complex geographic unit centred on the Transylvanian Basin, around which the peaks of the Carpathian Mountains and their associated subranges and structural platforms form a series of crescents. Beyond this zone, the extensive plains of the south and east of the

The flag of Romania. Encyclopaedia Britannica, Inc.

country, their potential increased by the Danube River and its tributaries, form a fertile outer crescent extending to the frontiers. There is great diversity in the topography, geology, climate, hydrology, flora, and fauna, and for millennia this natural environment has borne the imprint of a human population.

Romania comprises a number of geographic regions, some of which correspond roughly to the historic regions whose names they share. In the southern part of the country, following the general contours of the former principality of the same name, Walachia (Wallachia) stretches south from the Southern Carpathians (Transylvanian Alps) to the Bulgarian border and is divided by the Olt River. In the southeast, situated between the lower Danube and the Black Sea, is the historic and geographic region of Dobruja, which also encompasses part of Bulgaria. The geographic region of Moldavia, comprising only part of the former principality of Moldavia (the remainder of which constitutes the

Physical map of Romania. Encyclopaedia Britannica, Inc.

country of Moldova), stretches from the Eastern Carpathian Mountains to the Prut River on the Ukrainian border. In western Romania, the historic Banat region is bounded on the north by the Mureș River and reaches west and south into Hungary and Serbia. Finally, bounded on the north and east by the Eastern Carpathians, on the south by the Southern Carpathians, and on the west by the Bihor Mountains is the geographic region of Transylvania, which is roughly contiguous with the borders of the former principality of Transylvania and in most schemes includes the Banat.

RELIEF

The relief of Romania is dominated by the Carpathian Mountains, which can be divided into the Eastern Carpathians, the Southern Carpathians, and the Western Carpathians. The Eastern Carpathians extend from the Ukrainian frontier to the Prahova River valley and reach their maximum elevation in the Rodna Mountains, with Pietrosu rising to 7,556 feet (2,303 m). They are made up of a series of parallel crests that are oriented in a more or less north-south direction. Within these mountains is a central core that is made up of hard, crystalline rocks and has a bold and rugged relief. Rivers have cut narrow gorges here (known as *cheile*)—including the Bistriței and Bicazului gorges—which offer some magnificent scenery. This portion of the Carpathians is bounded on the eastern side by a zone of softer flysch. For some 250 miles (400 km) on

the western fringe, the volcanic ranges Oaș and Harghita, with a concentration of volcanic necks and cones, some with craters still preserved, lend character to the landscape. St. Ana Lake—the only crater lake in Romania—is also found there. The volcanic crescent provides rich mineral resources (notably copper, lead, and zinc) as well as the mineral-water springs on which are founded several health resorts. The Carpathian range proper is made up in large part of easily weathered limestones and conglomerates, which again provide some striking scenery. The Maramureș, Giurgiu, Ciuc, and Bârsei depressions further break up the mountainous relief.

The Southern Carpathians, or Transylvanian Alps, lie between the Prahova River valley on the east and the Timiș and Cerna river valleys to the west. They are composed mainly of hard crystalline and volcanic rocks, which give the region the massive character that differentiates it from the other divisions of the Carpathians. The highest points in Romania are reached in the peaks of Mounts Moldoveanu (8,346 feet [2,544 m]) and Negoiu (8,317 feet [2,535 m]), both in the Făgăraș Mountains, which, together with the Bucegi, Parâng, and Retezat-Godeanu massifs, form the major subdivision of the region. The latter contains Retezat National Park, Romania's first established (1935) national park, which covers about 94,000 acres (38,000 ha), offers spectacular mountain scenery, and provides an important refuge for the chamois (*Rupicapra rupicapra*) and other animals. Ancient erosion platforms, another distinguishing feature of the area, have been utilized as pastures since the dawn of European history. Communication is possible through the high passes of Bran, Novaci-Şugag, and Vâlcan, at elevations up to 7,400 feet (2,260 m), but the scenic Olt, Jiu, and Danube river valleys carry the main roads and railways through the mountains. At the Iron Gate gorge, on the Danube, a joint navigation and power project by Romania and the former federation of Yugoslavia harnessed the fast-flowing waters of the gorge. In addition to greatly improving navigation facilities, the project created two power stations, which are jointly administered by Romania and Serbia. Finally, as in the Eastern Carpathians, there are important lowland depressions within the mountains (notably Brezoi, Haţeg, and Petroşani), and agriculture and industry are concentrated in them.

The Western Carpathians extend for about 220 miles (350 km) between the Danube and Someş rivers. Unlike the other divisions of the Carpathians, they do not form a continuous range but rather a cluster of massifs around a north-south axis. Separating the massifs is a series of deeply penetrating structural depressions. Historically, these depressions

Kazan Gorge, cut by the Danube River, on the border of Serbia (left) *and Romania* (right). Thomas M. Poulsen

have functioned as easily defended "gates," as is reflected in their names: the Iron Gate of Transylvania (at Bistra); the Eastern Gate, or Poarta Orientală (at Timiş-Cerna); and, most famous, the Iron Gate on the Danube.

Among the massifs themselves, the Banat and Poiana Ruscăi mountains contain a rich variety of mineral resources and are the site of two of the country's three largest metallurgical complexes, at Reşiţa and Hunedoara. The marble of Ruschiţa is well known. To the north lie the Apuseni Mountains, centred on the Bihor Massif, from which emerge finger-like protrusions of lower relief. On the east the Bihor Mountains merge into the

IRON GATE

The Iron Gate (Romanian: Portile de Fier, Serbo-Croatian: Gvozdena Vrata) is the last gorge of the Đerdap gorge system on the Danube River, dividing the Carpathian and Balkan mountains and forming part of the boundary between Serbia and Romania. It is about 2 miles (3 km) long and 530 feet (162 m) wide, with towering rock cliffs that make it one of the most dramatic natural wonders of Europe. Near the town of Sip a large rock reef (called Perigrada) obstructed nearly the whole width of the river until the construction of the Sip Canal in 1896. A joint development project of Romania and Yugoslavia on the Danube River (including a dam and hydroelectric power plant) was completed in 1972, providing equal amounts of energy to each country and quadrupling the annual tonnage of shipping. The name Iron Gate is commonly applied to the whole 90-mile- (145-kilometre-) long gorge system.

limestone tableland of Cetățile Ponorului, where the erosive action of water along joints in the rocks has created a fine example of the rugged karst type of scenery. To the west lie the parallel mountain ranges of Zărand, Codru-Moma, and Pădurea Craiului; to the south, along the Mureș River, the Metaliferi and Trascău mountains contain a great variety of metallic and other ores, with traces of ancient Roman mine workings still visible. The Western Carpathians generally are less forested than other parts of the range, and human settlement reaches to the highest elevations.

The great arc of the Carpathians is accompanied by an outer fringe of rolling terrain known as the Subcarpathians and extending from the Moldova River in the north to the Motru River in the southwest. It is from 2 to 19 miles (3 to 31 km) wide and reaches elevations ranging between 1,300 and 3,300 feet (400 and 1,000 m). The topography and the milder climate of this region favour vegetation (including such Mediterranean elements as the edible chestnut) and aid agriculture; the region specializes in cereals and fruits, and its wines—notably those of Odobești and the Călugărească Valley—are known throughout Europe. The area is densely populated, and there are serious problems of economic development in remoter areas where there is little scope for further agricultural expansion.

Tablelands are another important element in the physical geography of Romania. The tableland of the Transylvanian Basin is the largest in the country and has an average elevation of 1,150 feet (350 m). In the east, between the outer fringe of the Subcarpathians and the Prut River, lies the Moldavian Plateau, with an average elevation of 1,600 to 2,000 feet (500 to 600 m). The Dobruja (Dobrodgea) tableland, an ancient, eroded rock mass in the southeast, has an average elevation of 820 feet (250 m) and reaches a maximum elevation of 1,532 feet (467 m) in the Pricopan Hills.

Plains cover about one-third of Romania, reaching their fullest development in the south and west. Their economic importance has increased greatly since the early 19th century. In the southern part of Romania is the Walachian Plain, which can be divided into the Romanian Plain to the east of the Olt River and the Oltenian Plateau to the west. The whole region is covered by deposits of loess, on which rich black chernozem soils have developed, providing a strong base for agriculture. The Danube floodplain is important economically, and along the entire stretch of the river, from Calafat in the west to Galaţi in the east, former marshlands have been diked and drained to increase food production. Willow and poplar woods border the river, which is important for fishing but much more so for commerce. River port towns—including Drobeta–Turnu Severin, Turnu Măgurele, Giurgiu, Brăila, Galaţi, and Tulcea—complement the rural settlements.

On the northern edge of the Dobruja region, adjoining the Moldavian Plateau, the great swampy triangle of the Danube delta is a unique physiographic region covering some 2,000 square miles (5,180 square km), of which the majority is in Romania. The delta occupies the site of an ancient bay, which in prehistoric times became wholly or partially isolated from the sea by the Letea sandbanks. The delta, which was designated a UNESCO World Heritage site in 1991, contributes about half of Romania's fish production from home waters, with fishing off the Danube mouth contributing to the majority of the catch of sturgeon (banned since 2006) and Danube herring. It also is home to hundreds of species of birds, some of which are rare. For this reason the delta region is of great interest not only to a growing number of tourists but also to scientists and conservationists. Two dozen or more settlements are scattered over the region, but many are exposed to serious flood risks. Sulina and Tulcea are the major ports.

Romania lies in an active earthquake zone at the junction of three tectonic plates. Devastating earthquakes in both 1940 and 1977 caused considerable damage and loss of life in Romania.

DRAINAGE

The rivers of Romania are virtually all tributary to the Danube, which forms the southern frontier from Moldova Nouă to Călăraşi. Nearly two-fifths of the total Danubian discharge into the Black Sea is in fact provided by Romanian rivers. The final discharge takes place through three arms—the Chilia (two-thirds of the flow), Sfântu Gheorghe (one-fourth), and Sulina (the remainder)—that add to the scenic attraction of the delta region. The most significant of the Romanian tributary rivers are the Prut, Mureş, Olt, Siret, Ialomiţa, and Someş. The rivers have considerable hydroelectric potential, although there are great seasonal fluctuations in the discharge and few natural lakes to regulate the flow. The total surface-water potential of the tributary rivers is dwarfed by the volume discharged at the Danube mouth, which is more than five times as large. Subsoil waters have been estimated at an annual volume of some 250 billion cubic feet (700 million cubic metres).

The total theoretical hydroelectric potential of Romania—given optimum technological conditions—is tremendous, but for technical and economic reasons only a fraction of this potential can be developed. Geographically, the hydroelectric reserves of Romania are concentrated along the Danube and in the valleys of rivers emerging from the mountain core of the country. Other hydrographic resources include more than 2,500 lakes, ranging from the glacial lakes of the mountains to those of the plains and the marshes of the Danube delta region. The main effort since the 1940s, however, has been on the Argeş, Bistriţa, Lotru, Olt, Mare, Sebeş, and Someş rivers, as well as on the Danube at the Iron Gate.

SOILS

Romania has generally fertile soils. About one-fifth of the country is covered with chernozem—humus-rich black soils. These and reddish brown forest soils are found on the plains to the south and east of the Carpathians, as well as in the Banat. Gray-brown podzolic (leached) soils are found at higher elevations. A broad expanse of alluvial soils covers the Danube floodplain. Ill-advised cultivation methods during the communist period and profligate use of pesticides and industrial pollution after 1990 resulted in a legacy of significant soil erosion.

CLIMATE

Romania's location in the southeastern portion of the European continent gives it a climate that is transitional between temperate regions and the harsher extremes of the continental interior. In the centre and west of the country, humid Atlantic climatic characteristics prevail; in the southeast the continental influences of the Russian Plain (East European Plain) make themselves felt; and in the extreme southeast there are even milder sub-Mediterranean influences. This overall pattern is substantially modified by the relief, however, and there are many examples of climatic zones induced by changes in elevation.

The average annual temperature is in the low 50s F (about 11 °C) in the south and in the 40s F (about 8 °C) in the north, although, as noted, there is much variation according to elevation and related factors. Extreme temperatures range from about 112 °F (45 °C) in the Bărăgan region to –37 °F (–38 °C) in the Braşov Depression.

Average annual rainfall amounts to about 25 inches (640 mm), but in the Carpathians it reaches about 55 inches

(1,400 mm), and in the Dobruja it is only about 16 inches (400 mm). Many regions are subject to periodic drought and flooding. Since the early 1990s Romania's northern regions have been affected by severe rainfall and flooding. In 1998 and 1999 an unprecedented amount of rain fell in the Retezat Mountains, resulting in landslides, flooding, and widespread destruction and loss of lives. On the other hand, the southern areas of the country have suffered drought and high temperatures since the 1990s. These conditions have been exacerbated by injudicious agricultural practices.

Humid winds from the northwest are most common, but often the drier winds from the northeast are strongest. A hot southwesterly wind, the *austru*, blows over western Romania, particularly in summer. In winter, cold and dense air masses encircle the eastern portions of the country, with the cold northeasterly known as the *crivăț* blowing in from the Russian Plain, and oceanic air masses from the Azores, in the west, bring rain and mitigate the severity of the cold.

Romania enjoys four seasons, though there is a rapid transition from winter to summer. Autumn is frequently longer, with dry warm weather from September to late November.

PLANT AND ANIMAL LIFE

Forests, which cover about one-fourth of Romania's area, are an important component of the vegetation cover, particularly in the mountains. Up to about 2,600 feet (800 m), oaks predominate, followed by beeches between 2,600 and 4,600 feet (800 and 1,400 m) and conifers between 4,600 and 5,900 feet (1,400 and 1,800 m). At the highest levels, Alpine and sub-Alpine pastures are found. In the tableland and plains regions, the natural vegetation has to a large degree been obliterated by centuries of human settlement and agriculture.

The rich and varied animal life includes some rare species, notably the chamois and eagle, which are found on the Alpine heights of the Carpathians. Forest animals include the brown bear, red deer, wolf, fox, wild pig, lynx, and marten and various songbirds. The lower course of the Danube, particularly the delta, is rich in animal and fish life. The delta is also home to hundreds of species of birds, including pelicans, swans, wild geese, ibis, and flamingos, which are protected by law (as are wild pigs and lynx). It also serves as a seasonal stop for migratory birds. Some rare species of birds found in the delta and the neighbouring Dobruja region are Dalmatian pelicans, pygmy cormorants, spoonbills, red-breasted and white-fronted geese, and whooper swans.

ETHNIC GROUPS

Historical and archaeological evidence and linguistic survivals confirm that the area of present-day Romania had a fully developed society of Dacian tribes long before the Roman armies crossed the Danube into what became the province of Dacia. Therefore, though Roman influence was profound and created a civilization that managed to maintain its identity during the great folk migrations that followed the collapse of the empire, some Romanians are quick to identify their country's origins in the intermixing of the indigenous Dacian people and the Roman settlers.

About nine-tenths of the country's people are ethnically Romanian. There are also many ethnic Hungarians, who largely reside in Transylvania, in the northwestern area of the country. A small percentage of Romanian citizens identify themselves as Roma (Gypsies), and ethnic Germans make up an even tinier amount of the populace. In 1930 there were about 342,000 Germans living in Romania (about 4 percent of the population). Following World War II, tens of thousands of ethnic Germans were deported to the Soviet Union, and others emigrated as opportunities presented themselves, generally to the Federal Republic of Germany (West Germany). After the Romanian revolution of 1989, there was another mass exodus of ethnic Germans to Germany; at the onset of the 21st century, Germans made up less than 1 percent of the population.

Similarly, Romania's Jewish population significantly decreased during and after World War II. The events of the Holocaust and opportunities to emigrate to other parts of the world reduced the Jewish population from about 750,000 in 1930 to 43,000 in 1966. A mass exodus

to Israel ensued after the revolution, leaving an even smaller Jewish community behind.

LANGUAGES

Romanian, a Romance language, is the official language of the country. Four principal dialects may be distinguished, but it is the Daco-Romanian dialect, the basis of the standard language, that is spoken by nine-tenths of the Romanian populace in several regional variants.

The vocabulary of Romanian is based on that of Latin, but because of Romania's isolation, loanwords from non-Romance languages are frequent. Most common are Slavic words, but borrowings from Turkish, Hungarian, and Albanian also occur.

Hungarian is the only other language of Romania that is spoken by more than a million people. Smaller numbers speak Romany, German, Turkish, Serbian, and other languages.

RELIGION

Under communist rule, religion was officially viewed as a personal matter, and relatively few restrictions were placed upon it (compared with those imposed by other communist regimes), although the government made efforts to undermine religious teachings and faith in favour of science and empiricism. When the communists came to power in 1948, they continued the monarchy's practice of requiring all churches to be registered with the state (under its Department of Cults), which retained administrative and financial control, thus becoming the ultimate authority on matters of religion. Despite these incursions, Romanians remained devout. After the 1989 revolution, Romanians were free to practice their religions.

About nine-tenths of Romanians are adherents of the Romanian Orthodox Church, headed by a patriarch in Bucharest. Roman Catholicism is the primary religion of ethnic Hungarians and Swabian Germans. The Eastern rite (Uniate) church is prominent in Transylvania. In 1948 it was forcibly united with the Romanian Orthodox Church by the communist regime, but its independence was restored after 1989. Protestantism, both Lutheran and Calvinist, is practiced by some ethnic Hungarians and Germans. Other Protestant churches that are represented in Romania include the Presbyterian Evangelical Church and the Unitarian church. In 1950, Baptists, Seventh-day Adventists, and Pentecostals were forced to form the Federation of Protestant Cults, but they too had their independence restored after 1989. There is a small Jewish community, and Islam is practiced in the Dobruja and along the Black Sea coast by ethnic Tatars and Turks. The Roma have traditionally blended Romanian Orthodoxy with their own spiritual traditions. Since 1989 some Roma also have been attracted to the Pentecostal and Evangelical denominations of Protestantism.

Church of St. Michael, Cluj-Napoca, Romania. Art Resource, New York

SETTLEMENT PATTERNS

The natural environment of Romania long has offered favourable conditions for human settlement. The accessibility of the region to the movements of peoples across the Eurasian landmass has predisposed the region to absorb cultural influences from many countries and peoples, and this too is reflected in the contemporary patterns of Romanian life.

About one-third of Romania's population lives within the regions of Transylvania and Dobruja, with the remainder in Walachia and Moldavia. During the medieval period the principalities of Walachia and Moldavia, which united in 1859 to form the state of Romania, were independent feudal states, with mountain crests marking a political frontier. Initially, the core areas of these states were centred in the foothills of the

BUCHAREST

The economic, administrative, and cultural centre of Romania is its capital, Bucharest (Romanian: Bucuresti). It lies in the middle of the Romanian plain, on the banks of the Dâmbovița, a small northern tributary of the Danube.

Although archaeological excavations have revealed evidence of settlements dating back to the Neolithic Period, the first written appearance of the name Bucuresti dates from 1459, when it was recorded in a signed document of Vlad III (the Impaler), the ruler of Walachia. Vlad III built the fortress of Bucharest—the first of many fortifications—with the aim of holding back the Turks who were threatening the existence of the Walachian state.

The modern city is characterized by a number of squares from which streets and boulevards radiate. The two chief streets, running roughly parallel through the centre of the city, are Calea Victoriei and Bulevardul Magheru. Bulevardul Unirii, formerly called, under communism, the "Boulevard of the Victory of Socialism," was vastly expanded in the 1980s under the dictator Nicolae Ceausescu and was bordered by such buildings as the palatial marble House of the People (Casa Poporului, now the Palace of the Parliament). About 25,000 acres (10,000 hectares) of old Bucharest were razed to make room for the new palace and grand boulevard.

Republic Square—with the palace hall and the historical Crețulescu Church (1722)—is one of the most beautiful squares of the city. It is linked to Revolution Square (formerly Palace Square), which is surrounded by an imposing group of administrative, political, and cultural buildings including the Romanian Athenaeum, notable for its columned facade, and the former royal palace (now the National Art Museum).

The city has a large number of churches, usually small, in Byzantine style. In addition to the Curtea Veche (Old Court) church (1559), the church of the former Antim Monastery (1715) and Stavropoleos church (1724) are of considerable architectural interest.

Carpathians; only later, as the Romanian lands on the plains were gradually consolidated, were the major settlements transferred from the mountains, first to Târgoviște and Suceava and later to Bucharest and Iași. The Roma community is divided between those who have assimilated into Romanian culture and those who follow a traditional nomadic lifestyle. The period of Ottoman rule left an ethnic legacy of Turk and Tatar settlements along the lower Danube.

Szeklers, a Hungarian-speaking people, began settling in southeastern Transylvania after 900 CE. The Saxon Germans from the Rhineland areas were encouraged by the Hungarians to settle along the Carpathian arc in the 12th and 13th centuries. They built fortified villages and churches (many of which were designated UNESCO World Heritage sites in 1993) to defend Transylvania against invading Tatars and Turks. The Roma appeared in what is now Romania in the 14th century, having migrated in stages from northern India, only to be enslaved until the mid-19th century. In the early 18th century, Austria-Hungary's Habsburg rulers encouraged Germans to settle in the Banat, which had been ravaged under Ottoman domination. The Habsburgs hoped that these Germans would help to fortify the region against invasion, revive destroyed farmland, and promote Roman Catholicism in eastern Europe. As enticements, the German settlers were offered land, supplies, and livestock and were exempt from paying taxes. Although only some of the emigrants were from Swabia, in southwestern Germany, the Hungarians referred to all the newly arrived Germans as Swabians. Throughout the 18th century, communities of Serbs, Croats, Bulgarians, and Romanians also settled in the plains of the Banat. Jews from Poland and Russia arrived during the first half of the 19th century.

Romania's urban settlements were situated at points of commercial or strategic significance, and the great majority of present-day towns are either on or in the immediate neighbourhood of the ruins of ancient settlements, whether fortress or market towns. The oldest towns were founded on the Black Sea shores, and urban development spread only later to the plains and then to the mountains. It was common for settlements at opposite ends of the main trans-Carpathian routes to acquire urban status. In fact, the turbulent history of the country favoured some of these early settlements, which grew into modern towns and cities. The ancient commercial trade between these old market towns lends support to the view that the mountains have served as much as a link as they have as a barrier in the country's development. During the Middle Ages many "Ungureni"—Romanians from the inner side of the mountains under Hungarian rule—came to settle on the outer side with its greater agricultural potential. In the many lowland areas scattered among the mountains there has been a long continuity of settlement, as may be seen in very old place-names and distinct regional consciousness.

A dispersed type of rural settlement is generally found in the foothill, tableland, and upland regions. The scattered village proper is found at the highest elevations and reflects the rugged terrain and pastoral economic life. The population maintains many traditional features in architecture, dress, and social customs, and the old market centres, or *nedei*, are still important. Small plots and dwellings are carved out of the forests and on the upland pastures wherever physical conditions permit. Where the relief is less difficult, the villages are slightly more concentrated, although individual dwellings still tend to be scattered among agricultural plots. Mining, livestock raising, and agriculture are the main economic activities, the latter characterized by terrace cultivation on the mountain slopes, a legacy of Roman times. The Subcarpathian region, with hills and valleys covered by plowed fields, vineyards, orchards, and pastures and dotted with

Cobbled alley in the old section of Sibiu, Romania. William Gelman/Black Star

dwelling places, typically has this type of settlement. More-familiar concentrated villages, marked by uniform clustering of buildings, are found in the plains, particularly those given over to cereal cultivation.

A belt of towns has grown up on the margins of the Subcarpathian region, and these often parallel another outer fringe of towns commanding the main trans-Carpathian passes. Examples of such "double towns" include Suceava and Bistrița, Făgăraș and Câmpulung, Sibiu and Râmnicu Vâlcea, Alba Iulia and Arad, and Cluj Napoca and Oradea. In contrast to Transylvania, which experienced considerable urban development during the Dacian and Roman periods, Moldavia did not begin to develop towns until the Middle Ages, when the old Moldavian capitals of Iași and Suceava had close commercial connections with the towns of Transylvania and derived benefit from trade passing between the Baltic and Black Sea ports.

Ethnic Romanians traditionally inhabited the countryside, while the cities were home to minorities: Hungarians, Germans, Jews, Greeks, and Armenians. This pattern began to change in the 19th century with the start of industrialization, and ethnic Romanians have become the majority in the larger cities.

DEMOGRAPHIC TRENDS

The substantial changes in the social composition of the population that took place in Romania as a result of increasing industrialization and urbanization were reflected in the rise of the working-class population. Similarly, the collectivization of agriculture transformed the rural population. Since World War II there has been a sharp rise in the proportion of the population that has received some kind of higher education. Differing rates of economic development in different parts of Romania have produced a movement toward towns and cities, largely for daily and seasonal work, so that less than half of the population lives in rural areas. The communist government sought to reduce migration across county boundaries by trying to ensure that each area had its share of development and that the benefits of modernization were spread throughout the country. They were only partially successful, and sharp regional contrasts persist.

The population density of the country as a whole has doubled since 1900, though it is still lower than most central European states. The overall density figures, however, conceal considerable regional variation. Population densities are naturally highest in the towns, with the plains (up to elevations of some 700 feet [200 m]) having the next highest density, especially in areas with intensive agriculture or a traditionally high birth rate (e.g., northern Moldavia and the "contact" zone with the Subcarpathians); areas at elevations of 700 to 2,000 feet (200 to 600 m), rich in mineral resources, orchards, vineyards, and pastures, support the lowest densities.

Since the 1990s the population of Romania itself has declined. Several factors have contributed to this downturn. Primarily, abortions and birth control were restricted under communist rule; after the revolution the restrictions were lifted, causing a plunge in the birth rate. Secondarily, a sharp decline in the standard of living and in the quality and availability of public health and medical facilities has leveled off life expectancy. The number of stillbirths and infant deaths, which had fallen significantly from the early 1970s to the early '80s, rose in the late '80s and remained high through the early 2000s. The proportion of the population under age 14, which was about one-third in the 1980s, had dropped to less than one-fifth by the early 21st century. These statistics have caused concern regarding the deterioration of Romania's population. The lifting of emigration restrictions also resulted in a loss of population, especially among minorities and particularly ethnic Germans. Moreover, many Romanians, especially young adults, emigrated from Romania after 1989, searching for economic opportunities in western Europe and North America.

CHAPTER 12

THE ROMANIAN ECONOMY

Romania's modern economic development dates to the opening of maritime trade routes to western Europe in the early 19th century. After independence in 1878, exploitation of the cereal lands, forests, and oil fields was complemented by a policy of encouraging industry, but, in spite of considerable success, Romania still had a predominantly agrarian economy at the end of World War II. The communist regime concentrated on the expansion of industry, with priority given to the heavy industries of metallurgy, chemical manufacture, and engineering. Industrialization was assisted by a flood of cheap labour from rural areas, where collectivization and discriminatory price-fixing meant that farmers not only lost their own holdings but secured only modest returns as farmworkers. It also benefited from close economic integration with the Soviet Union, which secured markets for manufactured goods while supplying raw materials and fuels at relatively low cost.

Socialist development transformed the economy. Industry's contribution to national income rose from 35.2 percent in 1938 to 68.3 percent in 1986. Unemployment was avoided despite a substantial growth of population, and services were able to expand to meet demand. The transport system was modernized, and increasing numbers of families took vacations on the Black Sea coast and at mountain resorts. Nevertheless, incomes remained low and living conditions poor (with high housing densities and low welfare standards). Much of industry was inefficient, with overmanned factories achieving only low productivity and producing goods of inferior quality that could be sold only within the communist bloc (or in world markets at low prices that did not always reflect the actual costs of production). After large development loans were secured from Western creditors in the 1960s and '70s, dependence on foreign capital was minimized by the settlement of all foreign debts during the 1980s. This left many sectors of industry starved of investment in new technology, and the persistence of a primitive command structure left people with little capacity to innovate and take initiatives. Moreover, serious pollution problems arose, especially in the chemical industry.

The postcommunist government faced a difficult transition toward a market economy. It approached privatization cautiously, since few Romanians had significant capital to invest and many state-owned enterprises were not attractive to foreign investors. Despite expectations that the replacement of markets lost through the collapse of the Soviet Union would lead to a revival in production and that restructuring would then proceed gradually, the shift to a market economy was at best intermittent and slow. Throughout the 1990s the government had to support a large number of unemployed workers, and it was left with an antiquated industrial base. Nevertheless, many small retail and tourism-related businesses were created.

By the end of the 1990s, a mixed economy had evolved in Romania, and a trend toward a full-fledged market economy was clearly visible. Important

sectors of heavy industry, mining, transport, and communications, however, remained under government control and were relatively immune to market forces. High unemployment and inflation rates led to an overall decline in the standard of living.

Despite an initial outpouring of foreign aid following the revolution in 1989, ongoing aid and investment was discouraged by confusing and inconsistent investment and tax laws and the widespread perception of corruption. It was not until 1997 that laws were changed to attract foreign investment to stimulate the economy. In 2001 the Romanian Agency for Foreign Investment was established. By the early 2000s the leading sources of foreign investment came from the Netherlands, Austria, France, Germany, Italy, and the United States. Also during this period, gross domestic product (GDP) rose, and inflation rates had dropped to the single digits by mid-decade.

Under the constitution, private property rights and a market economy are guaranteed. Natural resources are public property, but they can be leased. Thousands of state-owned enterprises (apart from utilities) were privatized under a program of the National Privatization Agency.

AGRICULTURE, FORESTRY, AND FISHING

Agriculture has traditionally been the backbone of the Romanian economy; some three-fifths of the land is devoted

Hoeing potatoes near Cugir, in the foothills of the Transylvanian Alps of Romania. William Gelman/Black Star

to cultivation (including vineyards, orchards, and vegetable gardens). A radical land reform, begun in 1921 and completed in 1948, redistributed farmland from large owners to peasant farmers, but the restructuring of the economy after the communist takeover included the compulsory collectivization of agriculture, carried out between 1949 and 1962. Since 1989, state farms have been retained as large units of up to about 120 acres (50 hectares) with shareholders, but collective farms have been broken up into individual holdings—although in some areas they have been replaced by loose cooperative associations. Romania faced major problems following the breakup of these collective farms and the resulting uncertainty of ownership. These small individual plots became devoted to the subsistence crops traditionally cultivated by peasants. Despite a bountiful cereal crop in 1995, there was an overall downward trend in

agriculture in the 1990s, as the endemic lack of capital investment and limited technologies continued to hinder the agricultural sector. Moreover, irrigation systems that had been installed during the communist era, especially on the southern and western plains, fell into disrepair by 2000. Restoration efforts have been under way with aid from the World Bank since 2003.

The climate and relief of the extensive Romanian plains are most favourable to the development of cereal crops, although these also are found in the Subcarpathians and in the Transylvanian Basin, where they occupy a high proportion of the total arable land. Wheat and corn (maize) are most important, followed by barley, rye, and oats. Two-row barley is cultivated in the Brașov, Cluj, and Mureș areas, where it is used for brewing. The tendency is for the acreage of cereals to fall as yields increase and industrial crops require more land.

Vegetables and legumes—peas, beans, and lentils—are planted on relatively small plots. Peas are the predominant crop; maturing in time for an early harvest, they allow a second crop, usually fodder plants, to be grown on the same ground. Vegetable cultivation is particularly marked around the city of Bucharest, with specialization in the production of early potatoes, tomatoes, onions, cabbages, and green peppers. Similar gardening areas are found around Timișoara, Arad, Craiova, Galați, Brăila, and other cities. The most important potato-growing areas are the Brașov,

Sibiu, Harghita, and Mureș districts. Other related crops include sugar beets; sunflower seeds, mostly on the Danube, Tisa, and Jijia plains; hemp; flax; rape; soybeans; and tobacco.

Romania can be counted among the main wine-producing countries of Europe. It specializes in the production of high-quality wines, using modern methods; with the growth of the tourist trade, its wines are becoming known to, and appreciated by, a larger international public. Large quantities are exported annually. The best-known vineyards are at Odobești, Panciu, and Nicorești, though there are a half-dozen or more other major centres. Both white and red wines have won various international awards.

At an elevation between 1,000 and 1,600 feet (300 and 500 m), orchards are found on almost all the hillsides on the fringe of the Carpathians. There is specialization in fruits with a high economic yield. Orchards have solved problems of soil erosion on many unstable hillsides.

Livestock raising has a very long history in Romania. Sheep can be raised wherever grass is available, whether in the Alpine pastures or the Danube plain and valley. About half the cattle are raised for beef, which is an important export. In the 1990s the livestock sector experienced many of the same declines that crop cultivation did; however, by the early 2000s the trend reversed, and beef exports increased. Dairy products are also an important component of Romanian agriculture, as are wool, eggs, and honey.

Romanian forests traditionally yielded sawn timber, but since the 1990s the emphasis has been placed on finished products. The country's timber is used primarily for building materials, fibreboard, and furniture manufacturing. Reeds from the Danube delta produce cellulose, which is used to make hardboard.

The rivers of Romania, its lakes—especially the group around Lake Razelm—and its Black Sea coastal region support a well-developed fishing industry. During communist rule, ocean fishing in foreign waters was developed rapidly to supplement the domestic catch and to increase the export of meat. Since the 1990s, demand for fish has fallen, largely because of the reduction in fleet and resources and the increase in the price of fish relative to other animal protein products. The largest quantity of fish comes from the Danube River, and most of the annual catch is consumed fresh. In the mid-1980s Romania's leader, Nicolae Ceaușescu, attempted to transform the Danube delta into a region of grain fields. Local residents were forced out as dikes were built to pump water out of the delta, and the grounds were flattened and planted with wheat and rice. Thousands of marine plants and animals were killed. After the revolution, the Romanian government created the Danube Delta Biosphere Reserve in 1991 to oversee the restoration of the delta. Among the fish found in the Danube delta are carp, sheat fish, pike, and zander, along with fish that migrate from the Black Sea, such as the Danube mackerel and the sturgeon, which produces caviar, Romania's most valuable fish product. In 2006, however, Romania issued a 10-year ban on commercial sturgeon fishing, citing concerns about the decline in sturgeon populations. Canneries are located at Tulcea, Constanța, and Galați. Trout farms are scattered throughout the country, though water pollution has endangered many of them. Mackerel, anchovy, and plaice can be caught on the Black Sea shore.

RESOURCES AND POWER

Romania has an unusually rich and well-balanced mix of natural resources. Hydrocarbons are found across two-thirds of the country, and the petroleum industry dates to the 19th century. Oil deposits are found in the flysch formations that run in a band along the outer rim of the Carpathians and through the Subcarpathians. Deposits in the plains, notably near the town of Videle, have been tapped since World War II. The areas around Bacău and Ploiesti have long been famous for their oil-refining industry, and they have been joined by production from Pitești. Some oil also was discovered in the Romanian sector of the Black Sea in 1981. Romania had large reserves of natural gas, found mainly in Transylvania, where large deposits of methane gas and salt were first exploited for a chemical industry in the 1930s. These reserves, however, have been depleted.

A large lignite field in the Motru valley, in the southwestern part of the country, supplies two of Romania's largest power stations, located in Rovinari and Turceni. One of the greatest problems facing Romania after World War II, when the Soviet Union demanded the delivery of Romanian petroleum as war reparations, was the very limited development of power stations based on other fuels. Nevertheless, under a plan spanning the years 1951–60 and supplemented by later plans, a remarkable rise in power output took place. The foundation for this increase was a series of large power projects, each having a capacity of 200,000 to 1,000,000 kilowatts. Both thermal and hydroelectric plants were built (though the largest capacities were installed in the Motru valley lignite field). Romania's multiple river systems, coupled with the Danube, give the country considerable hydroelectric potential. At least three-fifths of electricity is generated at the Iron Gate. Two nuclear reactors were launched with Canadian assistance at Cernavodă, on the lower Danube, the first in the mid-1990s, followed by another reactor in the early 2000s.

The largest coal reserves are those of bituminous coal (soft coal); half of Romania's bulk coal production comes from the Jiu Valley alone. Reserves of poorer-quality lignite increasingly are being tapped to meet energy requirements. Except for the Baraolt-Vârghiș Basin, which lies within the Carpathians, most of these deposits are found along the fringe of the mountain areas. There are concentrations in Moldavia, Transylvania around the city of Cluj, the

Coal-based manufacture behind a medieval castle-museum in Hunedoara, west-central Romania.
Earl Dibble/Photo Researchers

Jiu Valley, and on the Danube floodplain. Anthracite (hard coal) is found in the Banat and Walachia regions. Mining is especially central to life in the Jiu Valley, where it is the only significant industry, and the frequent threat of widespread layoffs has long been answered by protests and strikes that have erupted into violent confrontations.

A wide variety of metals are found in Romania. Major iron deposits are located in southeastern and southwestern Transylvania, the Banat, and the Dobruja. Manganese is mined in northern Transylvania near the headwaters of the Bistrița River and in the Banat. Chrome and nickel deposits are found near the Iron Gate along the Danube. Copper, lead, and zinc exist in the Maramureș near the headwaters of the Bistrița River and in the Apuseni Mountains, where silver and gold deposits and molybdenum are also found. Important bauxite mines are located southeast of Oradea. Minerals including sulphur, graphite, and mica are also found in limited quantities.

Moreover, there are large salt deposits near Slanic, Tirgu Ocna, and Ocna Mures.

MANUFACTURING

After World War II Romanian manufacturing underwent a radical structural change. Three branches became much more important: engineering and metalworking accounted for 25.8 percent of all industrial production in 1990, compared with 13.3 percent in 1950, while electricity and fuels increased their share from 13.2 to 19 percent and chemicals from 3.1 to 9.6 percent. Two other branches, metallurgy and building materials, showed a slight relative advance. The main relative declines were in wood processing and paper, textiles and clothing, and food processing.

Development in the manufacturing sector in Romania following the 1989 revolution was discouraging and remained so throughout the 1990s. Because the heavy industry that the communist government had invested in had not received the required maintenance and modernization during the austerity of the 1980s, it became inefficient and uncompetitive. Furthermore, the manufacturing labour force became increasingly angered by the inflated salaries awarded to communist officials and the conduct of a largely naive and corrupt management class that was unfamiliar with international business practices. For all of these reasons, Romanian manufacturing struggled as it attempted to compete in the world market.

In the years following the revolution, the conflict between the former managers of heavy industry, who opposed transition to a market economy, and labourers, who sought reform, was at the heart of political developments in Romania. Administrations rose and fell based on their plans for the manufacturing, mining, metallurgy, and energy sectors and workers' responses to them.

At the beginning of the 21st century, much heavy industry was standing idle or operating well below capacity. Light industry, on the other hand, proved to be a hopeful prospect, attracting some foreign joint-venture investment. The machine-building and metal-processing industry remains the main branch of the industrial economy, accounting for about one-fifth of bulk industrial production. It provides a good index of the changing priorities in the Romanian economy: before World War II it accounted for only 10 percent of the total, being exceeded in importance by food processing and even by the textile and ready-made clothing industry. Contemporary centres of production are Bucharest, Braşov, Ploieşti, Cluj-Napoca, Craiova, Arad, Reşiţa, and many others, with a considerable degree of regional specialization. There has been a strong tendency to concentrate on such modern branches as the electronics industry, as well as to widen and diversify the range of production. Beginning in the 1990s, foreign electronic manufacturers opened facilities in Romania, attracted by low labour costs and the proximity to western European markets.

The Romanian iron industry has particularly strong connections with Galați, as well as with Călărași, Hunedoara, and Reșița (the last having a record of activity extending back to the 18th century). Smaller units exist at Brăila, Câmpia Turzii (near Turda), Iași, Oțelul Roșu, Roman, and Târgoviște. The nonferrous metallurgical industry, which also dates from the Dacian-Roman period, is largely concentrated in the southwest and west, with copper, gold, and silver production still active, especially in the Apuseni Mountains. Aluminum production is a more recent development; alumina factories at Oradea and Tulcea supply the aluminum reduction complex at Slatina in the Olt district.

In contrast to metallurgy (which relies on imports of ore and coke to supplement the modest domestic resources), the wood products industry is readily supplied with domestic timber. A chain of modern wood industrialization combines turns out a range of products, including furniture and chipboard, which have done well in foreign markets. The building materials industry also utilizes a wide range of resources across the country; cement manufacture represents an important subbranch. The main centres are at Turda, Medgidia, Bicaz, Fieni, and Târgu Jiu.

The long-established textile industry has also undergone steady development since its radical overhaul in the 1930s.

The closely connected ready-made clothing industry has undergone considerable expansion, with heavy investment in new plants. Silkworm production retains a modest importance despite the introduction of synthetic fibres.

The food industry—formerly the foundation of the economy—has been all but eclipsed by the rapid development of other branches. It has, nevertheless, continued to grow in absolute terms, and processing plants are distributed throughout the country.

FINANCE

The initial euphoria after the 1989 revolution subsided during the 1990s as foreign investment declined. The financial stability of Romania was threatened at various times during this period by severe inflation. In an attempt to lower the inflation rate, the Romanian currency, the leu, was revaluated in 2005. The National Bank of Romania, founded in 1880, implements the monetary policy of the Ministry of Finance, managing budgetary cash resources and issuing currency. The Bucharest Stock Exchange opened in 1995, and by 1999 hundreds of companies were being traded. By 1998 there were dozens of banks in Romania, including foreign, domestic, and jointly owned institutions.

TRADE

The modernization of the Romanian economy during the communist period resulted in a considerable upsurge in its foreign trade and commercial contacts, which involved more than 100 countries. Romania was the first member of Comecon (Council for Mutual Economic Assistance) to negotiate independently with the European Economic Community (later succeeded by the European Union [EU]), signing a trade agreement in 1980. The country also took part in numerous international fairs and exhibitions. Since the disbanding in 1991 of Comecon, great attention has been paid to broadening trade with less-developed countries as well as with industrialized Western countries. In the decade following the revolution, however, the Romanian government failed to implement many of the macroeconomic reforms that other eastern European countries with transitional economies had undertaken. Nevertheless, in 1993 the United States reinstated most-favoured-nation trading status with Romania, which had been suspended in 1988.

By the beginning of the 21st century, traditional Romanian exports such as textiles and clothing accounted for more than one-fifth of exports, followed by metals, electrical equipment, oil, and non-electrical machinery. Significant imports included textiles, machinery and electrical equipment, chemical products, oil, and foodstuffs. Total foreign trade has increased since the 1990s, but exports have not kept pace with imports, resulting in a persistent deficit in balance of payments. By the mid-2000s, Romania

was actively pursuing membership in the EU, which required that the country adopt measures to establish a free market economy and curb corruption and smuggling. Romania was admitted to the EU in 2007. Romania's main trading partners are Italy, Germany, Russia, France, and Turkey.

SERVICES

About one-tenth of Romania's labour force works in the service industry. Tourism has the potential to become a significant source of income for the country. The unstable economy, ethnic tension, and widespread reports of deprivation and shortages caused a precipitous decline in tourism in the early 1990s. Most visitors were from neighbouring countries such as the Balkan states and Turkey. Efforts to improve accommodations, especially in the large cities, and a generally favourable exchange rate helped to restore tourism, and from the late 1990s to the early 2000s the number of foreign visitors doubled.

Tourist attractions range from winter sports in the mountains to summer seaside activities in the resort belt fringing the Black Sea, with health spas receiving special emphasis, including those that have been built on the salt lakes of Transylvania, most notably in the towns of Ocna Sibiului and Sovata. The historic town of Sighişoara is a popular tourist draw. The towns of Năvodari, Mamaia, and Eforie were erected after World War II, while the older settlements of Mangalia

SIGHIŞOARA

The central Romanian town of Sighisoara is located in the historic region of Transylvania, 40 miles (65 km) northeast of Sibiu city and 110 miles (175 km) northwest of Bucharest. The town circles a hill, on the summit of which stands a citadel with a ring of walls, nine extant towers (including the "Tower of the Clock"), and a number of medieval churches.

Settlement of the area dates from the Bronze Age and, later, the era of Roman Dacia, but the town itself originated in the 12th century when it was colonized by Saxon Germans. In the 14th century they secured its designation as a free city, enabling it to become an important centre of trade by the second half of the 16th century. Much of the lower town had to be rebuilt after being ravaged by fire in 1676. The historic centre of the town was inscribed on UNESCO's World Heritage List in 1999.

Tower of the Clock, Sighişoara, Romania. © Alexandru Paler

and Techirghiol have undergone extensive redevelopment. Lakes—among which Lakes Taşaul, Siutghiol, Agigea, Techirghiol, and Mangalia are the most significant—further enhance the attractions of the region. Several of them contain deposits of mud and sulfurous hot springs believed to have therapeutic properties.

The Danube delta too has become increasingly popular, because of the growing worldwide interest in ecology and conservation. Special features of interest to tourists include the mountain lakes and underground cave systems of the Carpathians and the fine churches and monasteries, with frescoes dating from the 14th to the 16th century, that are found in northern Moldavia. More generally, the folk costumes and the ancient folklore of Romanians, notably in the Carpathian Mountains, provide a reminder of the country's long traditions.

LABOUR AND TAXATION

Although high unemployment resulted from the collapse of communism, in the 1990s, as the number of people who migrated increased, a labour deficit arose in certain sectors of the economy, such as construction, agriculture, tourism, mechanical processing, and the clothing industry.

Women represent slightly more than two-fifths of Romania's labour force and generally work in retail, education, and health care. Child labour has been a problem in Romania, especially among Roma girls, with children generally working in agriculture, construction, and domestic service. Various child labour elimination laws were passed at the beginning of the 21st century; however, the problem still exists.

Among the hopeful signs that emerged in the 1990s was the growth of vigorous and independent labour unions as well as chambers of commerce and other nongovernmental organizations. Besides the Central Union of Consumer and Credit Cooperatives, a union of producers and credit institutions dating from the communist era, organizations appropriate to a private economy are emerging.

Romania has a wage tax, a corporate income tax, and a public finance tax. A value-added tax (VAT), a capital tax, and a global income tax also were implemented in the 1990s to attract foreign investment. A flat income tax at the corporate and individual level was introduced in 2004.

TRANSPORTATION AND TELECOMMUNICATIONS

Romania is located at a crossroads of European transport. Railways provide the main method of transportation for both freight and passengers in the country. There are good local rail connections with the main lines, including the two that cross the Danube, at Cernavodă (linking Bucharest with the Black Sea port of Constanța) and Giurgiu (connecting Romania with Bulgaria). Since the 1930s, diesel locomotives have been in service, and about one-third of the major lines have been electrified. Most of Romania's system of national roads has been brought up to modern standards.

The main lines of communication tend to focus on Bucharest and include many scenic routes. The country has maritime connections with many countries, and the port of Constanța, which has undergone major expansion, plays a large role in the national economy. Finally, the Danube River, supplemented since 1984 by the Danube–Black Sea Canal from Cernavodă to Constanța, is a major transportation route between the Black Sea, the Middle East, and western Europe. The principal ports on the Danube are Drobeta-Turnu Severin, Calafat, Turnu Măgurle, Giurgiu, Calaraşi, Cernavodă, Brăila, Galaţi, Tulcea, and Sulina. Bucharest also is the main centre for air transportation. In addition to local travel, international traffic has grown in significance, and there are international airports in Constanţa, Cluj-Napoca, Arad, Timişoara, and Sibiu. The great majority of flights by the Romanian national airline TAROM (derived from Transporturile Aeriene Române) are to Europe, North Africa, and the Middle East.

Romania's telecommunications sector was privatized in 2003. Within five years, the fixed-line market expanded substantially, and there was an increase in Internet availability. About four-fifths of Romanians have cellular phone subscriptions, up from about one-tenth in 2000.

CHAPTER 13

ROMANIAN GOVERNMENT AND SOCIETY

Following the collapse of communism in 1989, a constituent assembly drafted a constitution that was approved by the Romanian parliament on November 21, 1991, and by referendum on December 8, 1991. This document established a bicameral parliament consisting of a Chamber of Deputies and a Senate. Members of both houses are elected to four-year terms from each of the country's administrative counties under a system of proportional representation: the number of seats allotted to each county is determined by the number of votes cast within the county, and the seats are divided among political parties according to their share of the vote.

The president, who serves a five-year term, is elected directly by a popular vote. As commander of Romania's armed forces and chairman of the Supreme Defense Council, the president has the power to declare martial law or national emergencies. Laws are approved by the majority vote of the members present in each chamber. In most cases, presidential decrees must be subsequently submitted for parliamentary approval and countersigned by the prime minister, who serves as the head of government. The president also nominates (but cannot remove) the prime minister, who, along with the cabinet, is responsible for implementing the domestic and foreign policy of the state.

LOCAL GOVERNMENT AND JUSTICE

Romania is divided into 41 *județ* (counties) and the city of Bucharest. The central government appoints a prefect for

Political map of Romania. Encyclopaedia Britannica, Inc.

each county who acts as the local representative for the national government. Mayors and community councils are directly elected by citizens.

The judicial system is headed by a Supreme Court of Justice, whose members are appointed by the president for six-year terms. Other elements include county courts, local courts (whose decisions may be appealed to county courts), and military courts.

POLITICAL PROCESS

There is universal suffrage for all citizens age 18 and over. Before the 1989 revolution, the Communist Party of Romania was enshrined as the only legal political

CORRUPTION AND POLITICAL REFORM

In July 2010 the EU published a report critical of the faltering struggle against corruption. Both the EU and the U.S. ambassador, Mark Gitenstein, expressed concern about the record of the judiciary. Romania was one of only two members of the EU whose justice system continued to be closely monitored by the pan-European entity. The only sign of political renewal in a year of sharp polarization was the announcement in October by Foreign Minister Teodor Baconschi of his intention to set up a new political formation based on Christian Democratic principles.

party and the leading force in Romanian society. The 1991 constitution replaced single-party rule with a democratic and pluralist system, but former communists have maintained prominence in politics through the formation of such parties as the Social Democratic Party (Partidul Social Democrat; PSD). Parties dating from before World War II have been revived, notably the National Liberal Party (Partidul Naţional Liberal; PNL) and the National Peasant Party (Partidul Naţional Ţărănesc; PNT), which with smaller anticommunist parties formed the Democratic Convention of Romania (Convenţia Democrată Română; CDR). The Democratic Liberal Party (Partidul Democrat-Liberal; PDL) emerged as a new centrist party in the early 21st century. There are also parties representing environmentalists, Romanian nationalists, Romania's Hungarian minority, and the Roma.

SECURITY

The Romanian police force is organized nationally under the Ministry of Administration and Interior. There is a national police force, a national gendarmerie (the military branch of the national police), and a border police force. Serious crimes are prosecuted by the Ministry of Justice.

Beginning in 1989, Romania sought to become part of the North Atlantic Treaty Organization (NATO). In January 1994 it became the first eastern European country to join NATO's Partnership for Peace program, but there was widespread disappointment in 1999 when Romania was denied NATO membership. Five years later, Romania, which occupies a strategic location on the Black Sea, was admitted to NATO. In preparation for membership, Romania was required to sign friendship treaties with its neighbours.

HEALTH AND WELFARE

During communist rule, medical care was provided free by the state, and public funds were allotted also to pensions and health resorts for children and workers. The quality of medical service improved with the training of more doctors and the construction of hospitals in the main towns and as a result of the new drugs that became available from the country's growing pharmaceutical industry. Since the early 1970s, life expectancy for Romanians has increased slightly; however, it is still lower than most other countries in central and eastern Europe, with the exception of most of the countries of the former Soviet Union. Medical services suffered from the austerity program of the 1980s, when priority was given to the repayment of foreign debts. The number of doctors and dentists per capita, which had risen rapidly from 1970 to 1985, failed to keep pace with the growth of population. Ancillary staff actually decreased between 1985 and 1990. Medical treatment for the elderly was also restricted during the latter years of the Ceaușescu era.

Severe inflation, the difficulties of an economy in transition, and the government's concomitant lack of resources to address the impoverished national health service greatly affected the health care system during the 1990s. The practice of giving underweight babies microtransfusions of unscreened blood resulted in large numbers of them testing positive for HIV (human immunodeficiency virus), which causes AIDS (acquired immune deficiency syndrome). By the beginning of the 21st century, the transmission of the virus from mother to child was the main cause of the spread of the virus. This period also marked changes in the provision of health care, as private medical and pharmaceutical practices started to slowly emerge, though the majority of hospitals are still state-owned.

Under communist rule, in order to keep up population growth, abortion and contraception were made illegal, and large numbers of unwanted children were placed in orphanages. The appalling conditions in these orphanages attracted the attention of many international charities and adoption agencies; however, Romania's lack of resources coupled with unclear policies and inconsistent legislation delayed a solution to the problem of Romanian orphans and street children. Since the 1990s the conditions have generally improved in Romania's state-run orphanages (of which there were more than 200 in the early 21st century). Moreover, in 2004, as a way to end corruption in the system, the Romanian government passed a child welfare law prohibiting international adoption of Romanian orphans.

HOUSING AND EDUCATION

Since 1991 a significant number of new homes have been constructed throughout the country. Much of the housing boom was propelled by the emergence of a real estate market and an accumulation of wealth due to a free market economy. Most of the income was spent on single family homes in the suburbs of Bucharest and on second homes and villas in rural areas. Typical housing for peasants in rural villages is a one- or two-room hut built of locally available materials: wood, stone, wattle, or mud with stucco covering.

Throughout the communist period, education in Romania was strictly controlled by the state and reflected the country's official socialist ideology. Following the revolution, private education was permitted, but it was largely restricted to higher education. Under the Ministry of Education, schooling is generally compulsory through age 16, and more than nine-tenths of the population is literate.

Higher education is provided by universities, polytechnical schools, vocational schools, and other institutes. University study traditionally lasts four to six years, depending on the particular discipline, and is modeled on the French system, with large lecture halls. Criticism of this system and interest in more student-teacher interaction attracted some students to the various private universities that were established after 1989. Nevertheless, most students attend state-run universities. The major Romanian universities are the University of Bucharest (1864), the Technical University of Iași (1937), and the Technical University of Cluj-Napoca (1948). The largest technical university in Romania is the Polytechnic University of Bucharest, founded in 1818 as the National School of Bridges, Roads, and Mines. Other polytechnic universities are found in the cities of Brașov, Craiova, Oradea, Suceava, and Timișoara. There are also public schools that cater to national minorities. The Babeș-Bolyai University (1956), in Cluj-Napoca, is a multicultural university, offering courses in Romanian, Hungarian, German, and Romany.

CHAPTER 14

ROMANIAN CULTURAL LIFE

Each geographic region in Romania has its own culture, which reflects and is the product of regional history. Transylvania and the Banat were ruled for many centuries by Austria and Hungary, and their architecture reflects Romanesque, Gothic, and Baroque styles. Moldavia, in eastern Romania, has a culture that reflects its proximity to Ukraine and Russia, though traces of Tatar and other Central Asian influences have been identified in its folk art. The loggia, an open-air porch that evolved in the Mediterranean, was first incorporated into homes in Romania in Walachia. The region also traditionally absorbed influences from the Byzantine Empire and the Islamic Middle East. The Hungarian, German, and Roma minorities, who are scattered throughout the country, maintain their own traditions, which are reflected in their folk arts, cuisine, and dress.

DAILY LIFE AND SOCIAL CUSTOMS

Romanians' lives are generally guided by the religious traditions to which they adhere. Thus, ethnic Romanians who follow the practices of Eastern Orthodoxy participate in elaborate customs and ceremonies during Holy Week and at Easter. The Hungarian and German minorities, who generally belong to the Roman Catholic and Protestant churches, put a greater emphasis on the celebration of Christmas. The Hungarian and German communities also have traditional folk dress for both men and women that distinguishes them from ethnic Romanians and that is worn on special occasions.

Romanians in traditional folk costumes pose in front of a sign announcing the 2008 NATO summit in Bucharest. Native Romanian garb varies from one county to another. Dimitar Dilkoff/AFP/ Getty Images

Among the ethnic Romanians, the folk costume has been tenaciously retained in the rural areas, and virtually every county has its own variant of colour and style. Silk, the weaving of which was long the occupation of peasant women in the south and southwest, has lent much to the beauty of local folk costumes, especially the richly embroidered blouses and head scarves.

Romanian cuisine owes much to Turkish and Greek cooking. Soups with meat, vegetables, and noodles, thick cabbage soup, pork stew with lots of garlic and onions, and stuffed cabbage leaves are all staple fare. Desserts include *placinta* (turnovers), *saraille* (an almond-flavoured cake covered in syrup), and *baclava* (a pastry made of thin layers of dough filled with nuts and topped with honey syrup). Moldavian wines and local beers are popular, and the potent *palinca* (a plum brandy) is usually served before dinner.

Romanian national holidays include the New Year (January 1 and 2), the Monday following Orthodox Easter, May 1, National Day (the day of Romanian unification with Transylvania, celebrated December 1), and Christmas Day. Mărțișor, on March 1, is the traditional celebration of the beginning of spring in Romania, when men offer women charms or other decorative objects tied with red and white ribbons, which are traditionally worn throughout the month.

THE ARTS

Romanian culture offers a variety of forms of folk art that have survived years of outside interference and domination. Wood carvings, brightly ornamented costumes, skillfully woven carpets, pottery, and other elements of traditional Romanian culture remain popular and, with the growth of tourism, have become known internationally. Folk art is characterized by abstract or geometric designs and stylized representations of plants and animals. In embroidery and textiles, designs and colour schemes can be associated with particular regions of the country. Special folk arts of Romania include the decoration of highly ornamental Easter eggs and painting on glass, which sometimes includes religious icons.

Music remains an especially vibrant medium of expression in Romania. Major instruments are the *cobza* (a stringed instrument resembling a lute), the *tambal* (a hammered dulcimer), and the *flaut* (flute), which is the most common folk instrument. Other musical instruments played in Romania are the alphorn, bagpipes, a pear-shaped lute, and *nai* (panpipes). Energetic Roma songs are closely associated with this area of eastern Europe, and folksinging and dance festivals are popular throughout the country. Folk music includes dance music, laments known as *doinas* (which are unique to Romania), ballads, and pastoral music. Folk melodies are preserved in the music of modern Romanian composers such as Georges Enesco.

By the beginning of the second half of the 19th century, Romanian artists who were attracting international attention included poets Mihail Eminescu and Tudor Arghezi, storyteller Ion Creanga, painter Nicolae Grigorescu, and playwright Ion Luca Caragiale.

During and after World War II, many leading Romanian artists and intellectuals emigrated to elsewhere in Europe and to North America to escape oppression. Among them were playwright Eugène Ionesco; poet, essayist, and commentator Andrei Codrescu; philosopher Emil Cioran; writer and film director Petru Popescu; sculptor Constantin Brancusi; and historian of religion Mircea Eliade. Tristan Tzara, a Romanian-born French poet and essayist, is known as a founder of Dada and wrote many of the first Dada texts.

Eminescu was the driving force behind a school of poetry that influenced Romanian writers in the 19th and 20th centuries. Ionesco, who gained fame while working in France, inaugurated the Theatre of the Absurd with his one-act "anti-play," *The Bald Soprano*, which features his recurrent themes of self-estrangement and the difficulty of

TRISTAN TZARA

The Romanian-born French poet and essayist Tristan Tzara (born Samuel Rosenstock, 1896, Moinesti, Romania—died December 1963, Paris, France) is known mainly as the founder of Dada, a nihilistic revolutionary movement in the arts, the purpose of which was the demolition of all the values of modern civilization. The Dadaist movement originated in Zürich during World War I, with the participation of the artists Jean Arp, Francis Picabia, and Marcel Duchamp. Tzara wrote the first Dada texts—*La Première Aventure céleste de Monsieur Antipyrine* (1916; "The First Heavenly Adventure of Mr. Antipyrine") and *Vingtcinq poèmes* (1918; "Twenty-Five Poems")— and the movement's manifestos, *Sept Manifestes Dada* (1924; "Seven Dada Manifestos"). In Paris he engaged in tumultuous activities with André Breton, Philippe Soupault, and Louis Aragon to shock the public and to disintegrate the structures of language.

In about 1930, weary of nihilism and destruction, Tzara joined his friends in the more constructive activities of Surrealism. He devoted much time to the reconciliation of Surrealism and Marxism and joined the Communist Party in 1936 and the French Resistance movement during World War II. These political commitments brought him closer to his fellowmen, and he gradually matured into a lyrical poet. His poems revealed the anguish of his soul, caught between revolt and wonderment at the daily tragedy of the human condition. His mature works started with *L'Homme approximatif* (1931; "The Approximate Man") and continued with *Parler seul* (1950; "Speaking Alone") and *La Face intérieure* (1953; "The Inner Face"). In these, the anarchically scrambled words of Dada were replaced with a difficult but humanized language.

communication. Many literary works were based on Romanian ballads and folklore. Perhaps the best-known of these revolved around the vampire myth captured in the Bram Stoker novel *Dracula* (1897) and several later films on the subject. The character Count Dracula was based on Prince Vlad III (Vlad Țepeș ["the Impaler"]), who was the ruler of Walachia and built the fortress of Bucharest in the 13th century.

Romanian filmmaking dates to the turn of the 20th century, and the country's first feature film, *Independence of Romania*, was made in 1912. The National Cinematographic Office was set up in the 1930s. Following World War II and the nationalization of the industry, three large studios were constructed (one for making feature films, one for documentaries, and another for animation), and in the following decades Romania produced many films. Several prominent Romanian directors, including Liviu Ciulei, Lucian Pintilie, and Andrei Serban, moved effortlessly between film and theatre. The expense involved in film production and the limited amount of government support after 1989, however, significantly reduced Romania's film output in the 1990s.

But in the early 21st century, filmmaking in Romania underwent a resurgence. Foreign productions began to make use of the extensive facilities developed at Castle Film Studios near Bucharest, and, following the international success of director Cristi Puiu's *The Death of Mr. Lazarescu* (2005), critics began trumpeting the "Romanian New Wave" in filmmaking. Other films by Romanian directors that were widely praised include Cătălin Mitulescu's *The Way I Spent the End of the World* (2006), Corneliu Porumboiu's *12:08 East of Bucharest* (2006), and Cristian Mungiu's *4 Months, 3 Weeks and 2 Days* (2007).

In the early years of the communist period, strident Socialist Realism was mandated for all the arts in Romania. By 1965 communist authorities had lifted certain restrictions, but no work that unabashedly criticized the regime was allowed; those who wished to enjoy full honours and privileges of citizenship rendered homage to the communist state and its leaders.

Romanian architecture stagnated during the communist period; its most famous structures were stale reproductions of the Soviet style referred to as "wedding cake," or Stalinist Gothic. The best-known of these were the Casa Scînteii ("House of the Free Press," constructed 1952–57) and the Palatul Parlamentului ("Palace of Parliament," 1984–89), longtime communist ruler Nicolae Ceaușescu's creation and one of the largest buildings in the world, requiring the clearing of large areas of downtown Bucharest.

By adopting the Soviet style, the Romanian government turned its back on two quite distinctive native Romanian architectural traditions. The first was a national style associated with the late 19th- and early 20th-century architects Ion Mincu and brothers Grigore Cerchez and Cristofi Cerchez, who modernized the 17th-century Brâncoveanu style, with its characteristic floral motifs and stone sculptures. The second tradition was that of interwar modernism, which flourished particularly in Bucharest and drew attention to the accomplishments of such architects as George Matei Cantacuzino, Horia Creanga, and Marcel Jancu. Buildings in this style include the Library of the Romanian Academy and the former Ministry of Foreign Affairs in Bucharest, along with the Hotel Bellona in Eforie.

Following the revolution of 1989, the Romanian state made no demands on its artists, but the confusion of the past and the difficulties of transition turned the attention of many intellectuals and artists away from the humanities and fine arts and toward history, journalism, economics, and political science.

CULTURAL INSTITUTIONS

The Romanian Ministry of Culture is responsible for the support and encouragement of cultural life and cultural institutions throughout the country. In the early years of the communist period, Romania's cultural institutions were generously supported by the government as it sought to gain prestige and to maintain control of the arts. Later, however, when the Ceauşescu government focused on retiring the country's international debt, such support diminished considerably. Following the 1989 revolution and the overall decline in the standard of living, Romanians had less discretionary income to spend on cultural activities. Moreover, with only limited government support, the performing arts struggled to find sources of funding in the private sector.

Bucharest is the cultural capital of Romania and is home to numerous theatres, of which the largest is the National Theatre. The city holds an annual theatre festival. Music is central to Bucharest's cultural life; the city is home to an opera house as well as the George Enescu Philharmonia and the Romanian National Orchestra. Notable museums in Bucharest include the National Museum of Art of Romania (badly damaged by a fire in the 1989 revolution but since reopened), the National History Museum of Romania, the Grigore Antipa National Natural History Museum (named for Romania's most illustrious naturalist), the Romanian Peasant Museum, and the open-air National Village Museum, which has assembled examples of peasant homes and other traditional buildings from throughout the country. Other large Romanian cities have their own regional history museums. The Brukental Museum in Sibiu (1817) houses the personal art collection and library of Baron Samuel von Brukental. The Museum of Natural History and Archaeology in Constanţa has an important collection of Greek and Roman artifacts from the ancient city of Tomis (7th century BCE). In addition to subsidizing cultural institutions, the Romanian government awards scholarships and other grants to artists, composers, and writers.

Bucharest is home to the three largest libraries in the country: the National Library of Romania, the Central University Library of the University of Bucharest (damaged during the revolution but since restored), and the Library of the Romanian Academy. The Romanian Academy (founded in 1866 as the Romanian Literary Society) is renowned for preserving the Romanian language and culture and is responsible for coordinating the work of research institutes. The Academy's seat is in Bucharest, but it also has branches in Iaşi, Cluj, and Timişoara.

SPORTS AND RECREATION

The traditional Romanian sport is *oina*, which is played with a bat and a leather ball and resembles baseball. Football (soccer), however, is by far the country's most popular sport, and all the big cities have stadiums and teams in the national professional league. The Romanian national team periodically has enjoyed international success, especially in the 1990s, when it was led by Georghe Hagi, one of

NADIA COMĂNECI

The Romanian gymnast Nadia Comaneci (born November 12, 1961, Gheorghe Gheorghiu-Dej, Romania) was the first gymnast to be awarded a perfect score of 10 in an Olympic gymnastic event. Comaneci was discovered by Bela Karolyi, later the Romanian gymnastics coach, when she was six years old. She first competed in the national junior championships in 1969, placing 13th, and she won the competition in 1970. Her first international competition was in 1972 in a pre-Olympic junior meet for the communist-bloc countries in which she won three gold medals, and in 1973 and 1974 she was all-around junior champion. In her first international competition as a senior in 1975, she bested the Russian Lyudmila Turishcheva, the five-time European champion, winning four gold medals and one silver. She won the American Cup in New York City in 1976, becoming the first woman to perform a backward double salto as a dismount from the uneven parallel bars.

Nadia Comăneci performs her gymnastics floor exercise during the 1976 Summer Olympic Games in Montreal. Getty Images

At the 1976 Olympic Games in Montreal, Comaneci received seven perfect scores and won the gold medals for the balance beam, the uneven bars, and the all-around individual competition. She won a silver medal as a member of her team and a bronze medal for the floor exercises. After the 1976 Games, she was named a Hero of Socialist Labour by her country. The song used to accompany her floor exercises was retitled "Nadia's Theme (The Young and the Restless)" and became an international hit, earning a Grammy Award in 1977. She finished a disappointing fourth in the world championships in 1978, however, and was out of competition during most of 1979 with an infected hand. At the 1980 Olympic Games in Moscow, she won gold medals for the beam and the floor exercises (tying for first in the latter event with Nelli Kim of the U.S.S.R.). She won a silver medal as a member of her team and tied with Maxi Gnauck of East Germany for second place in the all-around individual competition. She retired from competition in 1984.

Comaneci defected to the United States in 1989; she became a U.S. citizen in 2001. In 1996 she married American gymnast Bart Conner, with whom she works to promote gymnastics. She published an autobiography, *Nadia* (1981), and a book on mentoring, *Letters to a Young Gymnast* (2003).

the era's finest European players. In general, Romanians participate in sports and recreation through membership in clubs, the most popular being dedicated to cycling, football, handball, tennis, rugby, and martial arts. Basketball, volleyball, handball, and skating are also popular.

Romania's first Olympic appearance was at the 1924 Winter Games in Chamonix, France, and it was the only Warsaw Pact country to attend the boycotted 1984 Los Angeles Games. Romanian women have excelled in gymnastics, most notably Nadia Comăneci, who earned six medals at the 1976 Montreal Games. Among the country's other legendary athletes are Iolanda Balas, who dominated the women's high jump during the late 1950s and '60s, and tennis player Ilie Nastase.

Romania's busiest sporting and recreational regions are in the Carpathian Mountains and along the Black Sea coast. In summer, mountain areas attract rock climbers and hikers, and in winter they draw skiers and snowboarders. On the coast, the Danube delta attracts bird-watchers, and beaches are crowded during warm weather.

MEDIA AND PUBLISHING

Following the revolution, there was a rapid expansion of media representing a variety of regional and political interests. The economic decline of the 1990s caused many publications to cease production.

Among Romania's leading newspapers are *Libertatea* ("Freedom") and *Jurnalul Național* ("National Journal"), both of which are published in Bucharest. *Monitorul Oficial* ("Official Monitor") is the government newspaper. In-depth coverage of political news can be found in *Evenimentul Zilei* ("Events of the Day"). *Adevărul* ("The Truth") replaced the former Communist Party paper in 1990. Numerous privately owned publishing houses emerged after 1990, but many became relatively inactive during the economic downturn, issuing only an occasional title. Publishing rebounded in the early 21st century but only to about one-fifth of its former level.

The Romanian Press Agency, known by its foreign acronym Rompres, is the country's official news service. Privately owned Media Fax was launched in 1991. There are also foreign news agencies that are based in Bucharest. Since the 1990s, state-run Romanian Radio and Television has faced competition from dozens of private radio and television channels. One of the most successful television outlets is PRO-TV, which airs international programs.

On the whole, Romanian media has received widespread criticism for being overly influenced by the government, and, indeed, there have been occasional incidents of politically motivated prosecution of journalists. The constitution upholds freedom of expression but prohibits defamation of the country and the government.

CHAPTER 15

ROMANIA: PAST AND PRESENT

The Carpathian-Danube region in which the Romanian ethnic community evolved was settled about 2000 BCE by migratory Indo-Europeans who intermingled with native Neolithic (New Stone Age) peoples to form the Thracians. When Ionians and Dorians settled on the western shore of the Black Sea in the 7th century BCE, the Thracians' descendants came into contact with the Greek world.

ANTIQUITY

The Greek historian Herodotus, writing in the 5th century BCE, called the Thracian people of the Black Sea region Getae (Getians). Together with kindred tribes, known later to the Romans as Dacians, who lived in the mountains north of the Danubian Plain and in the Transylvanian Basin, the Getae developed a distinct society and culture by the second half of the 4th century BCE.

THE DACIANS

The expansion of Rome into the Balkan Peninsula in the 3rd and 2nd centuries BCE decisively affected the evolution of the Geto-Dacians. To oppose the Roman advance, they revived their old tribal union under the leadership of Burebista (reigned 82–44 BCE). From its centre in the southern Carpathians, this union stretched from the Black Sea to the Adriatic and from the Balkan Mountains to Bohemia. It posed such a threat to Rome's ascendancy in the peninsula that Julius Caesar was preparing to undertake a major campaign against the Geto-Dacians when he was assassinated in 44 BCE. In the same year, Burebista was also assassinated, by disgruntled tribal chiefs who opposed his centralizing rule. His imposing tribal union disappeared with him.

The final showdown between Rome and the Geto-Dacians came at the beginning of the 2nd century CE. By that time the Geto-Dacians had reconstituted a powerful state that, under their resourceful ruler, Decebalus, threatened Rome's Danubian frontier. Geto-Dacian civilization was at its height, but its flourishing economy, prosperous cities, and bustling trade throughout southeastern Europe posed as great a challenge as its army to Rome's ambitions in the region. To end the danger, the emperor Trajan mounted two campaigns between 101 and 106 CE to force Decebalus into submission. The Romans triumphed, and, with his state in ruin, Decebalus committed suicide.

For more than a century and a half the Transylvanian Basin and the plain to the south constituted the Roman province of Dacia. Officials, soldiers, and merchants from all over the Roman world settled alongside the native Dacians. Although the population was ethnically diverse, Roman administration, numerous cities, and the Latin language brought about intense Romanization and rapid integration into the empire. Dacia, in turn, supplied the empire with grain and precious metals.

The constant pressure of migratory peoples on the long, exposed boundaries of Dacia led the emperor Aurelian to withdraw the Roman army and administration in 271–275. The upper classes and many urban dwellers followed, but the majority of the population, who lived in the countryside and were engaged in agriculture, stayed behind. Once again, the Danube became the frontier of the empire, although written and archaeological evidence points to continued

TRAJAN'S COLUMN

In 106–113 CE the Roman emperor Trajan erected a monument in the ruins of Trajan's Forum in Rome that survives intact and is known as Trajan's Column. A marble column of the Roman Doric order, it measures 125 feet (38 m) high together with the pedestal, or base, within which there is a chamber that served as Trajan's tomb. Originally the column stood in the middle of a courtyard surrounded by galleries from which one could view at various levels the spiral band (over 800 feet [240 m] long and about 4 feet [1.2 m] wide) covered with low-relief sculpture that forms a continuous narrative of the emperor's two campaigns in Dacia. A spiral staircase is contained within the shaft's interior, which measures 12 feet 2 inches (3.7 m) in diameter. At first a bronze eagle had been placed on top of the column and then after Trajan's death a bronze statue of the deceased emperor, which was replaced in 1588 by a statue of St. Peter.

trade and to the maintenance of military bases on the north bank of the river until the 6th century. In addition, during this period there was an intensified propagation of Christianity, which had been only sporadically present in old Dacia.

The fate of the Romanized, or Daco-Roman, population north of the Danube after Aurelian's withdrawal has been a subject of great controversy. Many scholars, especially Hungarians, argue that Romanization in Dacia was, in fact, modest and that the later Romanian population living north of the Carpathians was not native to the region but migrated there from south of the Danube. Other scholars, including the majority of Romanians, insist that a substantial Romanized population maintained itself continuously in old Dacia and that the ethnogenesis of the Romanian people occurred precisely there. The account that follows expands upon the latter interpretation.

THE SLAVS

For nearly eight centuries after the withdrawal of the Roman administration and army, Dacia was overrun by a series of migratory peoples. The earliest of them—the Visigoths (275–376), the Huns (end of the 4th century to 454), and the Germanic Gepidae (454–567)—had little impact on the Daco-Roman population. But the Avars' defeat of the Gepidae in 567 opened the way for a massive advance of Slavs into Dacia. Together with the Avars, the Slavs then broke through the Danube frontier of the Byzantine Empire in 602 and occupied much of the Balkan Peninsula. Now, for the first time since Trajan's conquest, Dacia was cut off from the Roman (Byzantine) world.

The Slavs achieved political and social preeminence in Dacia in the 8th century, but even then they were undergoing assimilation by the more numerous Daco-Romans. Their position was enhanced in the 9th century when the rulers of the first Bulgarian empire extended their control over Dacia following Charlemagne's crushing defeat of the Avars in 791–796. Local Slav chiefs apparently entered into a vassal relationship with the Bulgarian tsars, who, after the conversion of Boris I to Christianity in 864, served as religious and cultural intermediaries between Dacia and the Byzantine Empire.

ROMANIANS AND HUNGARIANS

The ethnogenesis of the Romanian people was probably completed by the 10th century. The first stage, the Romanization of the Geto-Dacians, had now been followed by the second, the assimilation of the Slavs by the Daco-Romans.

Between the 10th and 14th centuries new political formations emerged in the Carpathian-Danube region. The Hungarians, who had settled in Pannonia at the end of the 9th century and who entered Dacia in the 10th century, overwhelmed the Slavic-Romanian duchies, or voivodates, that they encountered there.

In the 11th century they made the territory north of the Carpathians, which was to become known as Transylvania, a part of the Hungarian kingdom. To the south a number of small voivodates coalesced by 1330 into the independent Romanian principality of Walachia, and to the east a second principality, Moldavia, achieved independence in 1359.

THE MIDDLE AGES

Between the 14th and 18th centuries the Romanian principalities of Moldavia and Walachia evolved as part of the Eastern Orthodox religious and cultural world: their ecclesiastical allegiance was to the patriarchate of Constantinople; their princes emulated the Byzantine emperors and drew their written law from Byzantine codes; their economy was agrarian and their society rural; and their art and literature followed Eastern religious and didactic patterns. Yet the Romanians also possessed qualities that set them apart from their neighbours and drew them westward: they spoke a language derived from Latin, and they recognized the Romans as their ancestors.

BETWEEN TURKEY AND AUSTRIA

Nearly four centuries of Ottoman Turkish domination between the 15th and 19th centuries reinforced the Romanians' attachment to the East. Hardly had the principalities achieved independence than they were forced to confront the relentless advance of Ottoman armies into southeastern Europe. By recognizing the suzerainty of the sultan and by paying him annual tribute, the Romanians avoided direct incorporation into the Ottoman Empire. The Romanians thus preserved their political institutions, laws, and social structure, and they avoided a massive settlement of Muslims onto the land.

The autonomy of the principalities was not seriously compromised until the beginning of the 18th century. The princes carried on their own foreign policy (although such action violated their formal vassal status), and they even joined anti-Turkish coalitions in order to throw off Ottoman domination. The reign of Michael the Brave of Walachia (1593–1601) marked the high point of Romanian autonomy. In order to help drive the Ottomans out of Europe, Michael adhered to the Holy League of European powers and the papacy; he thus regained full independence and even united Moldavia and Transylvania under his rule. But the breakup of the coalition ended his brief success, for the Romanians were too outnumbered to stand alone against the Ottomans.

The heaviest burden of Ottoman suzerainty was not political but economic. The tribute rose steadily, and demands for goods of all kinds—grain, sheep, and lumber, supplied at less than market value—knew no bounds. The Ottomans prized wheat especially, and by the end of the 16th century Constantinople had become dependent on supplies from the principalities.

MICHAEL, PRINCE OF WALACHIA

The Romanian national hero Michael, prince of Walachia, was also called Michael the Brave (Romanian: Mihai Viteazul; born Mihai Basarab, 1558—died August 19, 1601, Torda, Walachia). He briefly united much of the future national patrimony under his rule.

Acceding to the princely throne of Walachia in 1593, Michael submitted in May 1595 to the suzerainty of the prince of Transylvania, Sigismund Báthory, in order to secure support against Ottoman rule. He routed the Turks at Calugareni (August 1595) and Giurgiu (October 1595). In 1598 he took an oath of fealty to the Habsburg emperor, Rudolf II, and also concluded a peace with the Turks. The following year he attacked his new Transylvanian suzerain, Andreas Báthory, and defeated him at Selimbar (October 1599). Having now proclaimed himself prince of Transylvania, Michael next conquered Moldavia (May 1600) and assumed the title of "prince of Ungro-Walachia, Transylvania, and Moldavia." In September of that year, however, the troops of Emperor Rudolf divested him of Transylvania, while Polish forces wrested Moldavia from his control the following month. Reconciled to the emperor in 1601, he helped suppress a rebellion of Magyar nobles at Goraslau (August 1601) but was killed shortly thereafter on the order of the imperial general Giorgio Basta. During the 19th century, Michael acquired the reputation among Romanian nationalists as the pioneer of national unity.

Ottoman domination reached its height in the 18th century during what is generally known as the Phanariot regime. The Romanian principalities were now vital military bulwarks of the empire, as Russia and the Habsburg monarchy pressed relentlessly against its frontiers, and Ottoman officials decided to replace native princes with members of Greek or Hellenized families from the Phanar district of Constantinople who had amply demonstrated their loyalty to the sultan. As a consequence, the autonomy of the principalities was drastically curtailed, and the payment of tribute and the delivery of supplies rose precipitously. Greek influence in the church and in cultural life expanded, despite opposition from native boyars (nobles) and churchmen.

Yet many of the Phanariot princes were capable and farsighted rulers: as prince of Walachia in 1746 and of Moldavia in 1749, Constantin Mavrocordat abolished serfdom, and Alexandru Ipsilanti of Walachia (reigned 1774–82) initiated extensive administrative and legal reforms. Alexandru's enlightened reign, moreover, coincided with subtle shifts in economic and social life and with the emergence of new spiritual and intellectual aspirations that pointed to the West and to reform.

SOCIETY IN WALACHIA AND MOLDAVIA

The political system in the principalities resembled an oligarchy rather than an absolute monarchy. The prince was indeed the central figure and exercised broad executive, legislative, and judicial powers. Yet his authority was not unlimited, for he depended on the boyars and the clergy for crucial material and moral support. The boyars sat in the highest councils of state and assisted the prince in governing and dispensing justice. The higher clergy shared these civil responsibilities, since a separation of church and state was still an alien idea. Nevertheless, despite the involvement of boyars and clergy in political life, representative institutions failed to develop—perhaps primarily because of the lack of cohesiveness among the boyars. Although they were able to impose a so-called boyar regime on the princes in the 17th century, they were unable to secure their predominance by a strong institutional base.

Society in the two principalities was rural. It was highly stratified, and social mobility was strictly limited. The great boyars, few in number, monopolized political and economic power, but the lesser boyars and myriad other groups enjoyed numerous privileges, especially exemptions from taxation. The mass of peasants bore the main burdens of society and received little from it in return. Merchants and artisans, organized in guilds in order to restrict competition and to ensure profits, lent urban life its particular air, but they found no place in the prince's councils. Nor did they exercise self-government, because cities were the property of the crown.

The economies of the principalities rested upon agriculture. The estates of boyars and monasteries formed the superstructure of agricultural production, but the peasants, who worked the land in traditional ways, supplied the draft animals and tools and made fundamental decisions about what to raise and how. By the beginning of the 18th century, the majority of peasants had sunk to the level of serfs.

ROMANIANS IN TRANSYLVANIA

Outside the principalities lay Transylvania, whose government and economy were dominated in the countryside by the Calvinist and Roman Catholic Hungarian nobility and in the cities by the Lutheran German-speaking Saxon upper class. A large Romanian population lived there also, but Romanians were excluded from public affairs and privileges because they were overwhelmingly peasant and Orthodox. Their fortunes improved when Transylvania was brought under the Habsburg crown at the end of the 17th century. In order to strengthen the Roman Catholic Church as a unifying force, Austrian officials and Jesuit missionaries persuaded a portion of the Romanian Orthodox clergy to accept a union with Rome in 1697–1700. In return for recognizing the pope as head of the Christian church and accepting a few minor changes in doctrine, Romanian clerics were promised a political and economic status equal to that of Roman Catholic priests.

Although the advantages promised the new Eastern rite Catholic, or Uniate, clergy by the union fell short of expectations, they did allow a vigorous, public-spirited Romanian intellectual elite to form under the guidance of Bishop Ion Inochentie Micu-Klein (in office 1729–51). In the second half of the 18th century, Micu-Klein's disciples strove to achieve recognition of the Romanians as a constituent nation of Transylvania. They also elaborated a modern, ethnic idea of nationhood based on the theory of Roman origins and the continuous presence of the Daco-Romans in Dacia since Trajan's conquest. It was to serve as the ideology of the Romanian national movement in the 19th century.

NATION BUILDING

Between the end of the 18th century and World War I, the Romanians turned away from the East and toward the West. Commercial exchanges and foreign investment expanded, and the penetration of Western ideas and institutions obliged Romanian politicians and intellectuals to consider new models of development.

THE GROWING ROLE OF RUSSIA

The immediate objective of Romanian boyars—the traditional leaders of society—was independence. In the last quarter of the 18th century, success seemed near, as Russia, in the Treaty of Küçük Kaynarca (1774), gained the right to protect the Orthodox Christians of the Ottoman Empire. As a result, Russian influence in the principalities increased; but the boyars were reluctant simply to exchange Ottoman for Russian domination, and they were dismayed by Russia's annexation of the Moldavian region of Bessarabia in 1812.

The international crisis caused by the War of Greek Independence had important repercussions in Moldavia and Walachia. Because all Greeks were now suspect, the Ottomans abolished the Phanariot regime and restored the native Romanian princes. Another consequence was Russian dominance in the principalities. The Treaty of Adrianople (Treaty of Edirne) of 1829, which ended another Russo-Turkish war, established a virtual Russian protectorate over the principalities and reduced Ottoman suzerainty to a few legal formalities. Paradoxically, the treaty also raised a challenge to Russian hegemony by abolishing the Ottomans' commercial monopoly and opening the principalities to the international market.

The Russian protectorate, despite a promising beginning—notably the promulgation of constitutions, which brought unaccustomed order to government administration—increased Romanian resentment of Russia. Liberal, Western-educated boyars demanded political reform and an end to foreign domination, which kept authoritarian princes in power. Many of these boyars and other intellectuals formed the vanguard of the revolutionaries of 1848. Responding enthusiastically to the overthrow of conservative regimes in Paris and Vienna, they drafted liberal constitutions and proclaimed their intention to form governments that would be responsive to the economic and social needs of the common people. But they lacked a mass following and an organization, and they relied too heavily on the power of ideas to bring about social change. In Moldavia the prince quickly put down their agitation for reform, but in Walachia more-radical "forty-eighters" established a provisional government to carry out reform and prevent foreign intervention. Despite desperate efforts, they failed to gain support from France and Great Britain, and in September 1848 a Russian army occupied Bucharest and dispersed the provisional government.

INDEPENDENCE

In the 1850s forty-eighters led the struggle for the union of Moldavia and Walachia, which they regarded as an essential preliminary to independence. This time they had the support of the western European Great Powers. The victory of the European allies over Russia in the Crimean War brought an end to that country's domination of the principalities and placed them under the collective tutelage of the West. The powers stopped short of recognizing the union of the principalities or their independence, but the Romanians themselves settled the matter of union by electing the same man, Alexandru Cuza, as prince in both Moldavia and Walachia in 1859.

The reign of Cuza, a forty-eighter, was a crucial stage in the achievement of independent statehood. He brought about the administrative union of the principalities in 1861 and initiated an ambitious program of political and social reform, which culminated in 1864 in an extension of the franchise, the enactment of land reform, and the promulgation of a new constitution that assured the prince's predominance in government. He also promulgated legislation that diminished the role of the Orthodox clergy in civil affairs, thereby contributing to the secularization of Romanian society. By initiating these changes on his own authority before seeking permission from his nominal suzerain, the Ottoman sultan, Cuza asserted the de facto independence of Romania, as the united principalities were now known. But his authoritarian methods made many enemies, and these foes united in 1866 to force his abdication.

The reign of Cuza's successor, Charles of Hohenzollern-Sigmaringen (prince, 1866–81; King Carol I, 1881–1914), coincided with new achievements in nation building: a constitution, based in large part on Western models, was promulgated in 1866; political groupings coalesced into two major political parties, the Liberal and the Conservative, which were the primary engines of political life until World War I; and formal independence was achieved through participation in the Russo-Turkish War of 1877–78. In order to enhance his country's and his own prestige, Carol obtained the Great Powers' formal recognition of Romania as a kingdom in 1881.

During Carol's reign the main features of the Romanian parliamentary system were defined. The king himself was the key figure in both domestic and foreign policy. A relatively small political class shared power with him, and a narrow franchise excluded the mass of the population from direct participation in political life. Yet freedom of the press and of association were generally respected, and this allowed the opposition ample scope to air its views.

Carol's main objective in foreign policy (shared by the majority of Liberal and Conservative leaders) was to make Romania a regional power and an indispensable ally of the Great Powers in maintaining international stability, thereby guaranteeing his kingdom's security and vital interests. To this end Carol and a small number of ministers made Romania a member of the Triple Alliance in 1883. The primary attraction was Germany, whose military and economic power they admired and hoped to use as protection against Russia. But the majority of Romanians were sympathetic to France, and for this reason the treaty was kept secret. Also, Romania's adherence to the Triple Alliance was under constant strain because of friction with Germany's partner, Austria-Hungary.

The united Romanian principalities after 1859. Encyclopaedia Britannica, Inc.

By 1900 the primary issue in dispute between Romania and Austria-Hungary had become the Hungarian government's policy of assimilating the Romanians of Transylvania. To achieve this goal, Budapest restricted the use of the Romanian language in education and public affairs and diminished the autonomy of the Orthodox and Uniate churches—the principal Romanian cultural bulwarks. The Hungarians also rejected Romanian demands for collective political rights as a nationality, while the Romanians resisted integration into a Hungarian national state. Compromise proved impossible, for both sides were convinced that ethnic survival itself was at stake.

ROMANIAN SOCIETY: BETWEEN TRADITION AND MODERNITY

The traditional structures of Romanian society remained largely intact during this period. The great majority of people continued to live in the countryside. The large landowners, although small in number, exercised enormous political and economic power through the Conservative Party. The peasantry formed the broad base of the rural population. At the top was a narrow stratum of well-off peasants, whose relatively comfortable circumstances contrasted sharply with the condition of the landless and other poor at the bottom of the scale; in between lay the bulk of peasants, who lived out precarious existences. In the cities a middle class of industrialists, bankers, and professionals rose to political and economic prominence and, through the Liberal Party, challenged the great landowners for leadership of the nation.

Agriculture remained the foundation of the national economy and provided the majority of the population with its livelihood. Agricultural production grew but, because of obsolete methods and tools, at a lower rate than the increase in land brought under cultivation. By the end of the century both landlords and peasants had become dependent on the raising of grain, especially wheat, for export and had thus exposed themselves to the vagaries of the international market. In 1907 harsh working and living conditions led to a massive peasant uprising; the deaths of many peasants gave a powerful impetus to reform, but change came slowly.

Other branches of the economy were experiencing more significant changes. Beginning in the 1880s, industry, which benefited from government protection and foreign capital, supplied an increasing quantity of consumer goods. Yet by 1914 it still lacked such crucial elements of a modern industrial base as metallurgy. Foreign trade expanded, especially with Germany and Austria-Hungary, and was characteristic of underdevelopment in consisting of exports of agricultural products and raw materials and imports of manufactured goods. Accompanying this accelerated economic growth were the reorganization of financial structures—notably the foundation of large private banks and of the National Bank of Romania in 1880 as the coordinator of financial policy—and a major expansion of the railroad and highway networks.

Romanian intellectuals observed with mixed feelings the course of development that their country had taken since the early decades of the 19th century. Titu Maiorescu, the leading literary critic of the second half of the 19th century, spoke for the influential Conservative group Junimea (Youth) when he criticized the Romanians' sharp "deviation" from an agrarian past and ascribed to it the "contradictions" of contemporary Romanian society. Constantin Stere, the chief theorist of Romanian populism, argued at the turn of the century that Romania could become a prosperous, modern state by following the "laws" of development specific to agrarian societies. But others, such as the Liberal economist Petre Aurelian, who promoted industrialization, insisted that Romania must follow the Western model to become strong and secure.

GREATER ROMANIA

World War I proved decisive in the development of modern Romania. In 1916 the country entered the war on the Allied side in return for French and British promises of territory (in particular Transylvania) and a steady supply of war matériel through Russia. But the war went badly, and by the end of the year the Romanian army and government had been driven back into Moldavia. The Russian Revolution cut Romania off from all Allied assistance and forced it to conclude a separate peace with the Central Powers in May 1918. Upon the Central Powers' collapse later that year, Romania reentered the war in time to gain a victor's place at the Paris Peace Conference. But victory had come at the cost of enormous human and material destruction.

As a result of the war, Greater Romania—the expanded nation-state encompassing the majority of Romanians—came into being. Through the acquisition of Transylvania and the Banat from Hungary, Bukovina from Austria, and Bessarabia from Russia, the country's territory was doubled. Romania's population also doubled to more than 16 million—and it now included substantial minorities,

Greater Romania after World War I. Encyclopaedia Britannica, Inc.

particularly Hungarians in Transylvania and Jews in Bessarabia, which raised the non-Romanian population to almost 30 percent of the total.

The majority of Hungarians chose to stay in Transylvania rather than emigrate to Hungary, so that in 1930 they formed 31 percent of the population of the province. Nonetheless, they strove to preserve their ethnic and cultural distinctiveness and resisted integration into Greater Romanian society. The Romanian government—and Romanians generally—remained wary of Hungarian irredentism, the centre of which, they were certain, was Budapest, and they rejected demands from the Hungarians in Transylvania for political autonomy. The German-speaking Saxons, 7.7 percent of the population of Transylvania in 1930, were also anxious to maintain their ethnic separateness in the face of Romanian nation building, and, to a certain extent, they succeeded at the local level. The Jewish community, 4.2 percent of the country's population in 1930, was subject to discrimination, as anti-Semitism had adherents in all social classes—although acts of violence were rare until the outbreak of World War II.

FROM DEMOCRACY TO DICTATORSHIP

The fundamental political issue in interwar Romania was the struggle between parliamentary government and authoritarianism. In the 1920s the prospects for democracy seemed bright, for the two strongest parties supported representative institutions. The Liberal Party, the dominant political force of the decade, sponsored a revision of the constitution in 1923 that protected middle-class political and economic values. The National Peasant Party was headed by the recognized pillar of Romanian democracy, Iuliu Maniu. Its overwhelming victory in the elections of 1928, the freest in Romanian history until the 1990s, was the high point of Romanian democracy.

Two events boded ill for the future of democracy: the accession of Carol II to the throne in 1930 and the world economic depression. The new king had a disdain for democracy and intended to make himself the "decisive force" in national affairs. He was aided by the collapse of agricultural prices and widespread unemployment, which undermined confidence in democratic government and encouraged many to seek salvation in extremist politics. Some joined the Iron Guard, the most successful political movement on the far right, which propounded a mixture of nationalism, Orthodox spirituality, and anti-Semitism. Few Romanians were attracted to the Romanian Communist Party; outlawed in 1924, it carried on a precarious existence because of its subordination to the Soviet Communist Party, its antinationalist stance, and its neglect of peasant interests. Carol's solution to the country's problems was to proclaim a royal dictatorship in 1938 and to dissolve all political parties.

In foreign policy the primary objective of all interwar Romanian governments was to protect the frontiers of Greater Romania. Eager advocates of the principle of collective security and staunch defenders of the international system constructed by the treaties of Paris, they helped to form regional alliances (notably the Little Entente in 1921 and the Balkan Entente in 1934) and adhered to international peace and disarmament conventions. But they saw in France and Britain the chief guarantors of the postwar international order.

The foundations of this foreign policy were gradually undermined in the 1930s. Faith in France and Britain was shaken by the indifference of these two countries to the economic plight of Romania during

IRON GUARD

The Romanian fascist organization known as the Iron Guard (Romanian: Garda de Fier) constituted a major social and political force between 1930 and 1941. In 1927 Corneliu Zelea Codreanu founded the Legion of the Archangel Michael, which later became known as the Legion or Legionary Movement; it was committed to the "Christian and racial" renovation of Romania and fed on anti-Semitism and mystical nationalism. Codreanu established the Iron Guard, a military wing of the Legion, in 1930, and its name became the one commonly applied by outsiders to the movement as a whole. The Legion was dissolved by government fiat in December 1933, but it reappeared as Totul Pentru Tara (All for the Fatherland) and flourished, with some support from King Carol II. Suppressed again after King Carol proclaimed a personal dictatorship (1938), it was revived when the king abdicated (1940). Guardists served in Gen. Ion Antonescu's cabinets (1940–41), but the group was discredited by its failures to provide an efficient administration and to mobilize mass support for Antonescu's dictatorship. In January 1941 Antonescu used the army to crush the Guard, thereby ending its significant role in Romanian political life.

the Great Depression and by their failure to counteract Germany's repeated violations of the Treaty of Versailles. Relations with the Soviet Union continued to be strained over Bessarabia, and even the resumption of diplomatic relations in 1934 did not relieve Romanian politicians of the fear of attack. They looked to Germany for protection, but to no avail. The German-Soviet Nonaggression Pact of August 23, 1939, and the defeat of France in June 1940 deprived Romania of Great Power support. Between June and September 1940 the Soviet Union took Bessarabia and northern Bukovina, Hungary took northern Transylvania, and Bulgaria took the southern Dobruja. King Carol's dictatorship could not survive the catastrophe, and he was forced to abdicate on September 6.

SHIFTS IN SOCIETY AND ECONOMY

Romanian society and economy between the wars offered striking contrasts between persistent underdevelopment and burgeoning, if uneven, industrialization and urbanization. Massive land reforms, undertaken in 1918–21, transferred 15 million acres (6 million ha) from large landowners to smallholders, thus reinforcing peasant agriculture. Geared to the raising of grain for export, it was inefficient in organization and primitive in technology and could not keep up with overpopulation and crushing debt. Meanwhile, industry registered impressive increases in steel, coal, and oil production. By 1939 almost all domestic needs for food, textiles, and chemicals could be met by domestic producers, but Romanian industry could not yet provide all the technology and machines necessary for its own continued growth.

The state expanded its role as a coordinator of the economy, thanks mainly to the Liberals, who were eager to build a strong economy and thereby consolidate the new nation-state. Convinced that the era of classical economic liberalism had passed, the Liberals were committed to a directed economy based on systematic organization and well-defined goals. They focused their attention on industry as the most certain way of bringing Romania into the modern world and provided favoured industries with numerous advantages, including direct financing. The Liberals were also economic nationalists who were anxious to avoid economic subordination to foreigners. But they were also realists: knowing that domestic capital was inadequate for their purposes, they cultivated good relations with the Western powers, which controlled international commerce and financial markets.

The structure of Romanian society continued to follow prewar patterns. The population grew steadily, owing to a high birth rate in rural areas, but the mortality rate, especially among children, also remained high. The majority of the population continued to live in the countryside and to depend on agriculture as their primary source of income. Social differentiation, one of the consequences of growing capitalist relations, sharpened the distinction between well-off peasants and the majority of smallholders, who

lived on the edge of poverty. The great landowners as a class had disappeared with the postwar land reforms, and their place was taken by a gentry that was largely middle-class in outlook. Romanian society as a whole was becoming more urban, as the number and size of cities increased and their role in the national economy expanded. Bucharest, by far the largest city, occupied a special place as the capital and as the industrial, financial, and cultural centre of the country. It was from here that the middle class, which had now come into its own, exercised its immense economic and political power.

Among social theorists and politicians, the prewar debate over national identity and over models of development intensified with the creation of Greater Romania. The "Europeanists," such as the literary critic Eugen Lovinescu, saw no alternative to the Western model, since Europe intellectually was drawing closer together. On the opposite side were the "traditionalists"—for example, the journalist and theologian Nichifor Crainic—who insisted that the country remain true to its Eastern Orthodox spiritual heritage. In between stood the economist Virgil Madgearu, who advocated a "third way" of development, neither capitalist nor collectivist but rooted in small-scale peasant agriculture.

WORLD WAR II

Theories of development became academic during World War II. In September 1940 General Ion Antonescu forced Carol

II to abdicate, and Antonescu and the Iron Guard established an authoritarian "National Legionary State." Never a member of the Guard, Antonescu nonetheless intended to use its popularity to rally support for the new regime. Yet, despite their shared contempt for democratic institutions, these new partners were incompatible. Antonescu stood for order, while the Guard shunned economic and social planning. Mutual hostility culminated in open war in January 1941. Antonescu, supported by the army, was victorious and destroyed the Guard as a significant political force. For the next three and a half years he ruled the country as a military dictator.

Antonescu based his foreign policy on an alliance with Germany, which he was certain would win the war. In June 1941 he (and the majority of Romanians) joined enthusiastically in the German invasion of the Soviet Union in order to gain back Bessarabia and northern Bukovina and to end the Soviet threat once and for all. But Antonescu showed little restraint in committing Romanian manpower and resources to the German war effort, for he expected thereby to recover northern Transylvania. The consequences proved disastrous, and after the Battle of Stalingrad he lost hope that Germany would win the war.

The main concern of both Antonescu and the democratic opposition, led by Iuliu Maniu, was to avoid being overrun by the Red Army. But complex negotiations between Maniu and the Western Allies in 1944, which were intended

Romania after World War II. Encyclopaedia Britannica, Inc.

to allow Romania to surrender to the West, obliged the Romanians instead to deal directly with the Soviet Union. As Antonescu clung desperately to the German alliance, Maniu and King Michael, who had succeeded his father, Carol II, took the initiative in overthrowing the dictatorship on August 23 and in establishing a new government committed to the Allied war effort against Germany. The occupation of Bucharest by the Red Army a week later marked the beginning of a new era in Romanian history.

COMMUNIST ROMANIA

During the three years after the overthrow of Antonescu, a struggle for power took place between the democratic parties, which held fast to the Western political tradition, and the Communist Party, which was committed to the Soviet model. The communists, though they had few supporters, came to power in the spring of 1945 because the Soviet Union had intervened forcefully on their behalf.

THE SEIZURE OF POWER

The decisive factor in settling the struggle for the country's leadership was the Soviet leader Joseph Stalin's approval of a seizure of power. He gave this approval during a visit to Moscow in January 1945 by Gheorghe Gheorghiu-Dej, the leader of the so-called "native" faction of the party (composed mainly of ethnic Romanians), and Ana Pauker, who headed the "Muscovites" (those who had spent their careers mainly in the Soviet Union and were not ethnic Romanians). Extraordinary pressure by Soviet authorities forced King Michael to appoint a procommunist government led by the "fellow traveler" Petru Groza on March 6.

Between the installation of the Groza government and the parliamentary elections in November 1946, the Communist Party used its control of the security apparatus and other key government agencies to suppress the opposition. The democratic forces were led by Maniu, the

FELLOW TRAVELER

The Russian term *poputchik* ("fellow traveler") was originally used to denote a writer in the Soviet Union who was not against the Russian Revolution of 1917 but who did not actively support it as a propagandist. The term was used in this sense by Leon Trotsky in *Literature and the Revolution* (1925) and was not meant to be pejorative. Implicit in the designation was the recognition of the artist's need for intellectual freedom and his dependence on links with the cultural traditions of the past. Fellow travelers were given official sanction in the early Soviet regime; they were regarded somewhat as experts who were filling the literary gap until the eventual emergence of a true proletarian art—one by and for the proletariat that would be free of all bourgeois influence. In the 1920s some of the most gifted and popular Soviet writers, such as Osip Mandelshtam, Leonid Leonov, Boris Pilnyak, Isaak Babel, Ilya Ehrenburg, and members of the Serapion Brothers were fellow travelers. The period during which they dominated the literary scene is now regarded as the brilliant flowering of Soviet literature. They were bitterly opposed, however, by champions of a new proletarian art, and by the end of the decade the term came to be practically synonymous with counter-revolutionary.

Outside the Soviet Union the term *fellow traveler* was widely used in the Cold War era of the 1950s, especially in the United States, as a political label to refer to any person who, while not thought to be an actual "card-carrying" member of the Communist Party, was in sympathy with its aims and supported its doctrines.

National Peasant Party leader. Maniu had the king as an ally, but he despaired of success without vigorous intervention by the American and British governments. These indeed protested the communists' tactics, but, when they officially recognized the Groza government in February 1946 in return for the promise of early elections, they gave up any remaining leverage they might have had. The communists postponed the elections because they lacked adequate support among the population and needed more time to cripple the opposition. When elections finally took place on November 19, 1946, the official tally gave about 80 percent of the vote to the communists and their allies, but strong evidence indicates that the results were falsified in order to hide a substantial victory by the National Peasants.

The year 1947 was the final year of modern Romania: liberal political and economic structures and individualist mentalities nurtured during the preceding century gave way to a collectivist model of development and an alien ideology. With the signing of a peace treaty in February 1947 that ratified the terms of the 1944 armistice and returned northern Transylvania to Romania, Western influence in the country came to an end. The Communist Party proceeded to eliminate the remaining opposition in a campaign that culminated in show trials and the condemnation of Maniu and other democratic leaders to long prison terms. The final act was the forced abdication

of King Michael and the proclamation of the Romanian People's Republic on December 30, 1947. The communists were now able to accelerate the Sovietization of public life, which was to result in an isolation from the West far more complete than that which the Romanians had experienced at the height of Ottoman domination.

IMPOSITION OF THE SOVIET MODEL

From 1948 to about 1960, communist leaders laid the foundations of a totalitarian regime. They provided themselves with a formal political structure in 1948 by adopting a Soviet-style constitution that reserved ultimate authority for the party. Governmental institutions served merely as the machinery to carry out party decisions. The party also established the Securitate, the centrepiece of a vast security network. It dissolved private organizations of all kinds and severely curtailed the ability of churches to perform their spiritual and educational tasks. In their place, and mainly in order to mobilize public opinion, it created mass organizations in every sphere of activity. A further step in the consolidation of power was the purge of Pauker and the Muscovites by Gheorghiu-Dej in 1952.

In reordering the Romanian economy, the party adopted Stalinist principles: rigid central planning and direction, as well as emphasis on heavy industry at the expense of consumer goods. It also undertook the forcible collectivization of agriculture, a campaign completed in 1962.

In cultural and intellectual life, the communists expected Romanian artists and writers to subordinate their creativity to party directives and to contribute works that were relevant to contemporary society. A particular aspect of Romanian cultural life in the 1950s was Sovietization, or Russification. Soviet accomplishments in all fields were held up as models to be emulated, and a massive effort was undertaken to make Russian the second language for Romanians. This campaign, however, failed to wean the Romanians from their Western sympathies and instead intensified their traditional Russophobia.

The Soviet Union formalized its domination of Romanian affairs through various devices: Comecon (Council for Mutual Economic Assistance), created in 1949 to coordinate economic activity within the Soviet bloc; the Warsaw Treaty Organization (or Warsaw Pact), formed in 1955 to counteract the Western allies' North Atlantic Treaty Organization (NATO); and Soviet "advisers" throughout the Romanian party and government. Integration into the Soviet sphere was evident in Romania's unstinting support of Soviet foreign policy.

NATIONAL COMMUNISM

The decade of the 1960s brought a period of relaxation at home and defiance of the Soviet Union in international relations.

Although no genuine political liberalization took place and there was no retreat from the fundamentals of the Stalinist economic model, the intrusiveness of the regime in individual lives was curtailed. The availability of consumer goods and housing improved, and such social services as health care, education, and pensions—all positive accomplishments of the communist regime—became more generous. Change was especially evident in cultural and intellectual life, as scholars were permitted to broaden the scope of their research, and writers dealt with subjects that previously had been forbidden. A notable innovation was the flourishing of cultural exchanges with the United States and Europe, which signaled the resumption of old ties with the West and an end to Russification.

The source of this relaxation lay in the emergence of Romanian national communism, which was accompanied and in part stimulated by growing friction with the Soviet Union. Strains in the relations between Gheorghiu-Dej and Soviet party leaders came to the surface in the late 1950s. Gheorghiu-Dej feared that the de-Stalinization campaign launched by the new Soviet leader, Nikita Khrushchev, might force him from power, since he had been (and continued to be) one of the most rigid of Stalinists. But he also objected to Khrushchev's insistence that Romania abandon its headlong drive to industrialize and, instead, accept the more modest role of supplier of agricultural products and raw materials to the designated "industrial powers" of

Comecon. Tension between the two leaders culminated in a so-called "declaration of independence" by the Romanian Communist Party in 1964.

After Gheorghiu-Dej's death in 1965, his successor as head of the party, Nicolae Ceaușescu, redoubled efforts to lessen the country's dependence on the Soviet Union. Ceaușescu sought to expand economic relations with the West and skillfully played on the widespread anti-Soviet sentiments of the population in order to mobilize support for the Romanian party. The high point of his "independent" foreign policy was his denunciation of the Soviet-led invasion of Czechoslovakia in 1968.

The reaction of Soviet leaders to Romania's "independence" was relatively benign. Ceaușescu's challenges—even his refusal to allow Warsaw Pact maneuvers on Romanian territory and his stubborn opposition to the economic division of labour within Comecon—did not seem to them dangerous enough to require military intervention. They calculated, correctly, that Ceaușescu knew the limits of defiance. Especially reassuring for them was Ceaușescu's contempt for Western institutions and values, his maintenance of the party's monopoly of power, and his continued membership in the Warsaw Pact.

In domestic affairs, Ceaușescu brought the period of relaxation to an end with his July Theses of 1971, in which he demanded a return to rigid ideological orthodoxy and reasserted the leading role of the party. In the nearly two decades of "neo-Stalinism" that followed, the Communist Party intensified its control of mass organizations and intruded more deeply than ever before into the daily lives of citizens. Ceaușescu promoted a cult of personality that was unprecedented in Romanian history and that served as the foundation of a dictatorship which knew no limits. To prevent the emergence of other power centres, he continually rotated officials in both the party and the government and relied increasingly on members of his family (notably his wife, Elena) to fill key positions. In an effort to pay off the large foreign debt that his government had accumulated through mismanaged industrial ventures in the 1970s, Ceaușescu in 1982 ordered the export of much of the country's agricultural and industrial production. The resulting extreme shortages of food, fuel, energy, medicines, and other basic necessities drastically lowered living standards and intensified unrest.

His adherence to the Stalinist economic model had disastrous consequences: both industry and agriculture fell into disarray, and the standard of living steadily deteriorated. In foreign affairs, the West withdrew the financial credits and commercial advantages that it had earlier granted to Romania as a reward for its independence, and, in order to keep the economy afloat, Ceaușescu was obliged to turn once again to the Soviet Union. This act was doubly painful for him, because it not only increased his dependence on an old antagonist but also occurred at a time when its new leader, Mikhail Gorbachev, was promoting reform—a course utterly abhorrent to Ceauşescu.

Among Ceauşescu's grandiose and impractical schemes was a plan to bulldoze thousands of Romania's villages and move their residents into so-called agrotechnical centres. As economic and political conditions deteriorated, the position of Romania's minorities became increasingly precarious. The regime sought to weaken community solidarity among the Hungarians of Transylvania by curtailing education and publication in their own language and by promoting the immigration of Romanians into cities with large Hungarian populations. The Hungarians feared especially an extension to their rural communities of Ceauşescu's "village systematization" campaign, which had as its primary objective the destruction of the peasantry as a distinct social class and had already caused the leveling of numerous Romanian villages. The Saxon and the Jewish communities, on the other hand, ceased to be significant political problems for the regime. Both had suffered heavy losses as a result of World War II, and afterward their numbers steadily declined through emigration—the Saxons to West Germany and the Jews to Israel.

COLLAPSE OF COMMUNISM

By the late 1980s, Ceauşescu had transformed Romania into a police state. Institutions and organizations, even the Communist Party itself, had been eviscerated and had become mere instruments for carrying out his will. The Securitate had become the chief prop of his rule. Physical hardship and moral despair overwhelmed the society. Yet the Ceauşescu dictatorship, which had come to seem unassailable, was overthrown in the course of a single week in December 1989.

THE REVOLUTION OF 1989

The uprising that led to Ceauşescu's downfall began with minor incidents in the Transylvanian city of Timişoara starting on December 16. The following day Ceauşescu ordered his security forces to fire on antigovernment demonstrators there. The demonstrations spread to Bucharest, and on December 22 the Romanian army defected to the demonstrators. That same day Ceauşescu and his wife fled the capital in a helicopter but were captured and taken into custody by the armed forces. On December 25 the couple were hurriedly tried and convicted by a special military tribunal on charges of mass murder and other crimes. No formal dissolution of the Communist Party took place: it simply melted away.

The Romanian "revolution" of 1989 appears to have been a combination of spontaneous uprising by the general populace and conspiracy against Ceauşescu organized by reform communists and disaffected elements of the Securitate and army. A loose coalition of groups opposed to Ceauşescu quickly formed the National Salvation Front (NSF) to lead the country through the transition from communism to democracy; but, by the spring of 1990, fundamental differences had arisen within this group over the direction and pace of change. Those who favoured the removal of all former communists from positions of authority and the rapid introduction of a free-market economy left the NSF. Those who remained—the majority of them former communists—transformed the NSF into a political party that showed little enthusiasm for Western economic practices.

In elections held in May 1990, the NSF won handily, owing in part to its control of the media and in part to the failure of the opposition to mount an effective campaign. The opposition consisted of reconstituted National Peasant and Liberal parties, but these were led by returned émigrés whose programs harked back to the interwar period and seemed foreign to the mass of voters. To counter their anticommunist appeal, the NSF raised the spectre of unemployment and inflation, which they claimed would run rampant in Romania if the opposition came to power; they also promised to protect the social benefits put in place during the communist era.

The NSF assumed formal direction of the country with the inauguration of its head, Ion Iliescu, as president on June 20, 1990. An advocate of state direction of the economy before 1989, Iliescu, as president, remained wary of private enterprise and the move toward a free market.

Disagreement over the pace of economic reform caused the NSF itself to break apart, and Iliescu's supporters formed the Democratic National Salvation Front (DNSF). The party maintained its political dominance, as evidenced by its successes in parliamentary and presidential elections held in September and October 1992, in which Iliescu was reelected and his party emerged as the largest in parliament. A loose coalition of opposition parties, the Democratic Convention, also made a significant showing.

NEW CONSTITUTION

The approval by referendum of a new constitution on December 8, 1991, setting up a democratic republic, had given promise of political stability. Nonetheless, grave problems beset the new government. Particularly troublesome was a resurgence of nationalism, which exacerbated relations between Romanians and Hungarians in Transylvania and encouraged the rise of ultranationalist organizations. But the most intractable problem of all remained the economy. The loss of markets following the collapse in 1991 of Comecon (whose members received the bulk of Romania's exports) and an inability to find new markets in western Europe had catastrophic consequences for an economy already undermined by several decades of mismanagement and inefficiency under Ceaușescu.

Little progress was made between 1991 and 1996 in solving the pressing economic problems left over from the Ceauşescu era. The elections of 1992 brought no significant political change, and the country continued to be governed by Iliescu and former communists. In a sense, they governed by default, because in the 1940s and early 1950s the noncommunist political class had been destroyed or forced into exile. Yet democracy prevailed as party politics returned to something like the give-and-take of the interwar years, and a variety of opinions could be expressed in a diverse newspaper press and even on television and radio, where government influence was strong.

Iliescu pursued closer relations with western Europe, and in November 1992 his government introduced the economic reforms, including price liberalization, recommended by the World Bank and the International Monetary Fund to bring Romania in line with other emerging market economies. The result was soaring inflation (reaching about 300 percent) and rising unemployment. Deteriorating living conditions, mounting corruption, and the inability of the DNSF—renamed the Party of Social Democracy in Romania (Partidul Democraţiei Sociale din România; PDSR) in 1993—to revive the economy and ensure essential social services led to widespread unrest and strikes. In 1996 Iliescu lost the presidency to Emil Constantinescu, the leader of the Democratic Convention of Romania (Convenţia Democrată din România; CDR), whose party had

formed a centre-right coalition with the Social Democratic Union (Uniunea Social Democrată; USD) and the Hungarian Democratic Union of Romania (Uniunea Democrată a Maghiarilor din România; UDMR). In 1997 the former monarch Michael, whom the communists had forced to abdicate in 1947, returned to Romania after 50 years in exile.

Prime Minister Victor Ciorbea quickly sought to restructure and privatize the economy, and the new government had some success in alleviating tensions between Romanians and Hungarians. However, continued economic recession—the economy contracted by more than 15 percent between 1996 and 2000—and corruption led to a collapse of support for the CDR. As a result, Iliescu was returned to power in the elections of 2000. The following year, the ruling PDSR was reorganized as the Social Democratic Party (Partidul Social Democrat; PSD). In 2004 it was ousted from power by another centre-right coalition of parties, including the Democratic Party (Partidul Democrat; PD), whose Traian Băsescu was elected president.

In the first years of the 21st century, gross domestic product (GDP) began showing positive growth, inflation fell, and privatization was accelerated. In March 2004 Romania entered the North Atlantic Treaty Organization (NATO), and in January 2007 it joined the European Union (EU).

In the spring of 2007 the Romanian parliament voted to impeach President

Băsescu, but the result of a subsequent referendum allowed him to remain in office. Parliamentary elections in 2008 resulted in a near tie between the leftist PSD and the Democratic Liberal Party (Partidul Democrat-Liberal; PDL), Băsescu's new centrist party; the two parties formed a centre-left coalition government that December. This government lasted only until October 2009, when the PSD left the coalition in protest over the dismissal of a PSD member from a ministerial post. With a caretaker government still in place, no clear winner emerged in the country's presidential election in November 2009. In a runoff election held the following month, Băsescu won the vote by less than a percentage point, prompting runner-up Mircea Geoană of the PSD to contest the results in court. Romania's Constitutional Court subsequently ruled in favour of Băsescu, who took office in December. The president asked Emil Boc, who had been heading the caretaker government, to continue serving as prime minister, this time at the helm of a new coalition government comprising the PDL and the Democratic Alliance of Hungarians in Romania.

Discontent with the government simmered throughout 2010, as Boc implemented a series of austerity measures that were required as a condition of a €20 billion ($26 billion) loan that was granted in 2009 by the EU, the International Monetary Fund (IMF), and the World Bank. Sales tax was increased to 24 percent, and the salaries of public workers were cut by one-fourth. As the euro zone struggled with an ongoing public debt crisis, Romania's economy continued to falter, and in February 2011 the EU and the IMF granted the government an additional €5 billion ($6.8 billion) line of credit. In return the government pledged to accelerate privatization plans for state-owned enterprises. However, a scheme to partially privatize emergency health care services proved to be the tipping point for many Romanians. In January 2012 Raed Arafat, a popular health minister, resigned over the matter, and violent street protests left more than 50 people injured. Arafat was ultimately reinstated in his position, but by that time the demonstrations had begun to focus on wider issues related to the government's austerity program, its perceived corruption, and its apparent disconnect from the Romanian people. As protests continued in the streets of Bucharest, Adrian Nastase, a former prime minister (2000–04), was sentenced to two years in prison for misusing campaign funds. After almost a month of civil unrest, the Romanian government collapsed. On February 6, 2012, Boc resigned as prime minister, and Băsescu appointed Justice Minister Cătălin Predoiu interim prime minister. Later that day Băsescu nominated intelligence chief Mihai Răzvan Ungureanu to succeed Boc, and Ungureanu began talks with coalition leaders about the composition of his cabinet and the formation of a new government.

Ungureanu continued the budget-cutting policies of his predecessor, and protesters returned to the streets with renewed intensity. Opposition lawmakers headed by Victor Ponta of the Social-Liberal Union (Uniunea Social Liberală; USL) brought down the two-month-old government in a vote of no confidence on April 27, 2012. Ponta, who became prime minister the following month, acted quickly to solidify his power, prompting criticism from EU officials when he stripped Romania's Constitutional Court of its oversight function and orchestrated the impeachment of his political rival, Băsescu. As in 2007, Băsescu was subject to a referendum on his presidency, but the vote, held on July 29, 2012, fell short of the 50 percent participation rate required to validate the result.

CHAPTER 16

THE CZECH REPUBLIC: THE LAND AND ITS PEOPLE

The Czech Republic comprises the historical provinces of Bohemia and Moravia along with the southern tip of Silesia, collectively often called the Czech Lands. Despite its landlocked location, there were brief periods in the Middle Ages during which Bohemia had access to the Baltic and Adriatic seacoasts.

A region of rolling hills and mountains, Bohemia is dominated by the national capital, Prague. Set on the Vltava River, this picturesque city of bridges and spires is the unique work

Flag of the Czech Republic. Encyclopaedia Britannica, Inc.

of generations of artists brought in by the rulers of Bohemia. Brno, Moravia's largest city, was the site of Gregor Mendel's groundbreaking genetic experiments in the 19th century and the birthplace of contemporary novelist Milan Kundera. Moravians are as proud of their vineyards and wine as Bohemians are of their breweries and the Pilsner beer that originated in the town of Plzeň (Pilsen). The country is bordered by Poland to the north and northeast, Slovakia to the east, Austria to the south, and Germany to the west and northwest.

RELIEF

The Bohemian Massif occupies the major portion of the Czech Republic. It consists of a large, roughly ovoid elevated basin (the Bohemian Plateau) encircled by mountains divided into six major groups. In the southwest are the Šumava Mountains, which include the Bohemian Forest (Böhmerwald). In the west are the Berounka River highlands. In the northwest, the Ore Mountains (Czech: Krušné hory; German: Erzgebirge) form the frontier with Germany. The point at

Czech Republic. Encyclopaedia Britannica, Inc.

which the Elbe (Labe) River breaches this range is the lowest in the country, with an elevation of 384 feet (117 m). The so-called Sudeten system of mountains (a name never applied in the Czech language) in the northeast forms most of the border with Poland west of the city of Ostrava. The highest point in the Czech Republic, Mount Sněžka, with an elevation of 5,256 feet (1,602 m), is found in the major segment of this system, the Giant Mountains (Czech: Krkonoše; German: Riesengebirge). Farther to the east is the Oder (Odra) River lowland, a small fringe along the Polish border. Finally, southeast of the Bohemian Plateau are the Bohemian-Moravian Highlands, which include the spectacular Moravian Karst.

In the east the Outer Carpathian Depressions, known to geographers as the Moravian-Silesian Beskids, include the valleys of the upper Oder and Morava rivers and the headstreams of the Dyje. Along the Czech-Slovak border rise the Little Carpathian (Bílé Karpaty) and Javorníky ranges, the westernmost of the Western Carpathian Mountains that dominate Slovakia.

DRAINAGE AND SOILS

The Czech Republic lies in the headwater area of the central European watershed. The Elbe River rises near the Czech-Polish border and sweeps southwestward across Bohemia, receiving the Jizera, Vltava, and Ohře rivers before flowing northward into Germany. The Vltava is navigable from Prague to Mělník, where

it empties into the Elbe. From that point onward river traffic can travel all the way to Hamburg. The Morava River, flowing south toward the Danube (Dunaj) River, drains most of Moravia in the east. The Oder River rises in the northeastern Czech Republic and flows northward into Poland. There also are many smaller rivers of little economic importance. Larger rivers such as the Vltava are sources of hydroelectric power. The country is rich in mineral springs, and groundwater reserves are extensively used.

The soil profile of the Czech Republic consists of some rich, black chernozems and good-quality brown soils in the drier and lower areas. Podzols are found in the wet districts, and stony mountain soils are typical at high elevations. Alluvial soils occur in the river basins, and heavy clay soils are found in the eastern ridges.

CLIMATE

The Czech climate is mixed. Continental influences are marked by large fluctuations in both temperature and precipitation, while moderating oceanic influences diminish from west to east. In general, temperatures decrease with increasing elevation but are relatively uniform across the lower portions of the country. The mean annual temperature at Cheb in the extreme west is 45 F (7 °C) and rises to only 48 °F (9 °C) at Brno in southern Moravia. High temperatures can exceed 90 °F (32 °C) in Prague during July, and low temperatures may drop as low as 0 °F (-17 °C) in Cheb during

February. The growing season is about 200 days in the south but less than half that in the mountains.

Annual precipitation ranges from 18 inches (450 mm) in the central Bohemian basins to more than 60 inches (1,500 mm) on windward slopes of the Krkonoše Mountains of the north. Maximum precipitation falls during July, while the minimum occurs in February. There are no recognizable climatic zones but rather a succession of small and varied districts; climate thus follows the topography in contributing to the diversity of the natural environment.

PLANT AND ANIMAL LIFE

Although large areas of the original forest cover have been cleared for cultivation and for timber, woodlands remain a characteristic feature of the Czech landscape. Oak, beech, and spruce dominate the forest zones in ascending order of elevation. In the highest reaches can be found taiga and tundra vegetation characteristic of more-northerly or more-elevated regions elsewhere in Europe. The timberline runs at about 4,500 feet (1,400 m) above sea level. At these higher elevations, as in the Giant Mountains, the tree cover below the timberline consists of little more than dwarf pine. The Alpine zone supports grasses and low-growing bushes.

The country's wildlife is extensive and varied. Large mammals include bears, wolves, lynx, and wildcats (*Felis sylvestris*). Smaller mammals, such as marmots, otters, martens, and minks, also inhabit the forests and wetlands. Game birds, especially pheasants, partridges, wild geese, and ducks, are common. Rarer species, such as eagles, vultures, ospreys, storks, eagle owls, bustards, and capercaillies, generally are protected.

The preservation of the natural heritage is an important goal of the Czech government. Rare or endangered species such as the mouflon (a mountain sheep) are bred in game reserves, and nature reserves have been created to preserve especially important landscapes, notably the Šumava Forest, Moravian Karst, and Jizera Mountains. Tourists are given controlled access to the reserve areas. Krkonoše National Park, established in 1963, protects glacial landscapes and Alpine vegetation as well as some relict boreal-Arctic species, such as the Alpine shrew (*Sorex alpinus*); despite these preservation efforts, however, the park has been extensively developed as a ski resort.

ETHNIC GROUPS

Czechs make up roughly nine-tenths of the population. The Moravians consider themselves to be a distinct group within this majority. A small Slovak minority remains from the Czechoslovakian federal period. An even smaller Polish population exists in northeastern Moravia, and some Germans still live in northwestern Bohemia. Roma (Gypsies) constitute a still smaller but distinct minority, having resisted assimilation for the most part.

LANGUAGES

Czech is the official state language and as a literary language dates to the late 13th century. The majority of the population speaks Czech as their first language. Czech and Slovak are mutually intelligible languages belonging to the West Slavic language group, which uses the Latin (Roman) rather than the Cyrillic alphabet. Among the other languages spoken by minorities in the Czech Republic are Romani, German, and Polish.

RELIGION

During the communist era, no official statistics were kept on religion, though the activities of churches were financed by the government following the nationalization of all church property by 1949. Atheism was the official policy of the communist government, and the churches' role was largely restricted to religious rites. Religious freedom was restored in 1989, however, and by the early 21st century more than three-fifths of Czechs

EVANGELICAL CHURCH OF CZECH BRETHREN

The religious denomination known as the Evangelical Church of Czech Brethren (also called the Evangelical Church of Bohemian Brethren; Czech: Českobratrská Církev Evangelická) was organized in 1918 by uniting the Lutheran and Reformed churches in Bohemia and Moravia (now Czech Republic). Subsequently, other smaller Czech Protestant groups merged into this church. Its roots go back to the 16th-century Protestant Reformation and to the 15th-century Hussite movement in Bohemia, which was made up of the followers of the reformer Jan Hus. His followers were crushed in 1434, but the movement persisted underground. During the 16th-century Reformation, the Hussites emerged again and flourished for a brief period, but in 1547 they were again suppressed. Lutheran and Reformed groups also made progress in the country until the Czech Protestants' unsuccessful revolt against the Habsburgs in 1618, following which thousands of them fled the country and many of their leaders were executed. Protestants in Bohemia did not regain religious rights until 1781 when Joseph II, the Holy Roman emperor, issued his Edict of Toleration.

The new country of Czechoslovakia was created in 1918 by merging Bohemia, Moravia, Slovakia, and Ruthenia. The Evangelical Church of Czech Brethren quickly became the leading Protestant church in the nation. It was a leader in the fields of theological education and social work. The church and the nation again suffered severely during World War II under Nazi rule. When the Communists gained control of the government in 1948, the Evangelical Church of Czech Brethren tried to work with them, but the church suffered severe repression under the government from 1969 until the fall of the Communist regime in 1989–90.

claimed a religious affiliation. A visit to Czechoslovakia by Pope John Paul II in April 1990 celebrated the resurgence of Roman Catholicism, which counts about two-fifths of the population as adherents. There are also Eastern Orthodox congregations and various small Protestant sects, of which the Evangelical Church of Czech Brethren is one of the most important. A significant number of Czechs are members of the national Czech church, which was founded in 1920 and took the name Czechoslovak Hussite Church in 1972. Almost one-third of the population claims no religious affiliation.

SETTLEMENT PATTERNS

Industrialization and urbanization have changed the face of the Czech traditional regions, although Bohemia and, to a lesser extent, Moravia are still recognizable entities, reflecting different national and cultural heritages. Southern Bohemia and southeastern Moravia preserve local traditions of cuisine, and residents wear folk costumes on special occasions. Traditional wooden architecture is a distinctive feature of some rural areas.

Population density in the Czech Republic is high; in general, communities are only a few miles apart. A notable exception are some frontier areas—the low densities of which reflect the induced emigration of minorities, such as the three million Sudeten Germans who were expelled after World War II. Rural settlements are characteristically compact, but in the mountainous regions, colonized during the 13th and 14th centuries, villages straggling along narrow valleys are common. The collectivization of farmland that took place in the decades following World War II resulted in a pattern of large, regularly shaped fields, replacing the centuries-old division of land into small, irregular, privately owned plots.

Urbanization in the Czech Republic is not particularly high for an industrialized country, with about three-fourths of the population being urban. Even the smallest urban centres, however, usually contain some manufacturing industry. Prague, the national capital, has historically occupied a predominant role. Brno is the chief industrial and cultural city of Moravia. Other large cities include Ostrava, the leading coal-mining and steel centre, and Plzeň, with old, established engineering and brewing industries.

New towns were founded both before and after World War II. Notable among prewar settlements is the Moravian valley town of Zlín, founded in 1923. The towns of Havířov, in the Ostrava region, and Ostrov, near Karlovy Vary in the west, were built since World War II.

DEMOGRAPHIC TRENDS

During the 19th and early 20th centuries, population growth was mitigated by emigration to the urban centres of Austria-Hungary and overseas, especially to the United States. In general, the outstanding feature of the years of federation was stable population growth.

PRAGUE

The capital of the Czech Republic is Prague (Czech: Praha). Lying at the heart of Europe, it is one of the continent's finest cities and the major Czech economic and cultural centre. The city has a rich architectural heritage that reflects both the uncertain currents of history in Bohemia and an urban life extending back more than 1,000 years.

The physical attractions and landmarks of Prague are many. Among the finest is the Charles Bridge (Karlův most), which stands astride the Vltava River. The winding course of the Vltava, with its succession of bridges and changing vistas, contrasts with the ever-present backdrop of the great castle of Hradčany (Prague Castle), which dominates the left-bank region of the city from behind massive walls set high on a hill. The narrow streets and little taverns and restaurants of the older quarters contrast with the broad sweep of Wenceslas Square and modern parks and housing developments, while the great 18th-century Baroque palaces have their own elegance and splendour. Seen from the surrounding hills, the many church towers make up a unique perspective, giving Prague its description as the "city of a hundred spires." This architectural harmony was enhanced by post-1945 planning, which preserved the ancient core of the city as a major monument and carefully supervised all modern building. In 1992 the historic city centre was added to UNESCO's World Heritage List.

Prague is famous for its cultural life. Wolfgang Amadeus Mozart lived there, and his *Prague Symphony* and *Don Giovanni* were first performed in the city. In addition, the lyric music of the great Czech composers Bedřich Smetana, Antonín Dvořák, and Leoš Janáček is commemorated each year in a spring music festival. The U kalicha ("At the Chalice") beer parlour, which is still popular with local residents and tourists alike, provided the setting for the humorously anti-authoritarian activities of Schweik, immortalized by the novelist Jaroslav Hašek in *The Good Soldier Schweik*. The writings of Franz Kafka, dwelling in a different way on the dilemmas and predicaments of modern life, also seem indissolubly linked with life in this city.

This rather slow rate of growth was attributable in part to changes in lifestyle associated with urbanization and with the increased employment of women outside the home. Since the mid-1990s, however, the population of the Czech Republic has been declining. Moreover, by the early 21st century a decrease in the birth rate and increase in the average life span resulted in a generally older Czech population.

CHAPTER 17

THE CZECH ECONOMY

With the so-called Velvet Revolution of 1989, Czechoslovakia freed itself of communist control and set out to adapt its command economy to the free market. The government introduced a program based on policies of price liberalization, the opening of markets to foreign trade and investment, internal convertibility of the country's currency, privatization of state-owned enterprises, and tax reform. While the Czech Republic and Slovakia both were successors to the federal state, long-standing inequities in economic development gave the Czechs a decided advantage over the Slovaks. Rigid economic compartmentalization under Comecon (Council on Mutual Economic Assistance) made Slovakia, with its mineral resources and hydroelectric potential, a major producer of armaments for the former communist countries of eastern Europe. The economy of the Czech Republic, on the other hand, was relatively diversified and stable, reflecting both a more amenable geography and the historic predominance of Czechs in the federal administration.

Once the political breach appeared inevitable, Czechs and Slovaks faced the unprecedented challenges of dividing Czechoslovakia's economy and assets. The historical imbalance in government assets between the two and the problems it posed for fair apportionment were particularly pronounced in the case of military installations and equipment, of which the Czech Republic held the great majority. The bulk of Slovakia's military-industrial component, by contrast, consisted of its armament manufacture, which declined precipitously with the collapse of its communist markets.

Based on its inherent advantages—a well-educated and skilled labour force, proximity to western Europe, and a low level of foreign debt—the Czech Republic experienced fairly low unemployment and respectable economic performance during its first years as a separate entity. The new government, headed by Pres. Václav Havel and Prime Minister Václav Klaus (Czechoslovakia's former finance minister and a principal architect of post-communist economic policy), pledged to continue along the path of economic reform, with the goal of large-scale privatization as a priority. Privatization was achieved by means of a voucher system through which Czech citizens purchased shares in state-owned enterprises. Restructuring of the country's antiquated and inefficient manufacturing sector, however, lagged behind. Nevertheless, the Czech Republic's success in keeping down unemployment and inflation while maintaining steady growth resulted in its being singled out as one of the greatest economic successes of postcommunist eastern Europe. In addition, large influxes of visitors fostered the rapid development of the tourism industry and service sector, which provided new employment that helped limit some of the usual hardships of economic restructuring.

Within a few years, however, it became obvious that the Czech economy was not as healthy as had been believed. The government's failure to proceed with restructuring of key sectors of the economy and to create transparent financial market regulations began to take a toll. Poor management and corruption in the banking industry (much of which had remained largely state controlled) resulted in the failure of eight banks in 1996. In addition, many Czechs who had turned over their privatization vouchers to unregulated private investment funds—in exchange for promises of substantial returns—lost their investments when these dubious funds began to go bankrupt. In 1997 the government responded to the economic crisis by instituting a package of austerity measures and introducing a floating exchange rate, which resulted in a significant depreciation of the koruna, the state currency.

Despite these economic measures and the establishment of a new securities commission, in the late 1990s the Czech Republic fell into a recession, marked by declines in gross domestic product (GDP) and wages, a growing foreign-trade deficit, and rising unemployment. In the opening years of the 21st century, the economy rebounded, faltered briefly, and then rebounded again; and though the country's public finance deficit grew precipitously, many positive economic indicators surpassed the high levels of the mid-1990s, as the Czech economy became among the fastest-growing in the European Union (EU), which the Czech Republic joined in 2004.

For the most part, Czechs enjoy a standard of living higher than other former communist countries in eastern

Europe. However, employment rates and, consequently, standards of living vary by region. For example, Prague, with its thriving international tourist trade, has had a negligible unemployment rate of less than 1 percent at the same time that some rural regions were experiencing rates as much as 20 times higher. Nationally, by the mid-2000s less than one-tenth of the workforce was unemployed. This remained true even during the economic downturn that buffeted the euro-zone countries beginning in 2008.

AGRICULTURE AND FORESTRY

Czech agriculture is among the most advanced in eastern Europe, with better than average yields. The country does not suffer from a shortage of agricultural land, but its land is used far less efficiently than that in western Europe. With the end of communism, land that had been confiscated after World War II to form large state-controlled farms was gradually restored to its previous owners. Although members of smaller collective farms were entitled to withdraw their land from the collective, small land holders did not necessarily receive their own land back; instead, they often were allotted a plot of comparable worth at another location. The agricultural market is now wholly liberalized, with about one-fourth of farmland cultivated by individuals, one-third by cooperatives, and about two-fifths by corporations.

Wheat, sugar beets, barley, rye, oats, and potatoes are the most important crops. Pigs, cattle, sheep, and poultry are the dominant livestock. High-quality hops used by the country's breweries are cultivated in Bohemia. Moravia, particularly southern Moravia, is a grape-growing region and is the centre of the Czech Republic's wine industry, though vineyards are also found elsewhere.

Reforestation efforts of the early 1980s were offset by the effects of acid rain, which prompted cutting beyond the projected rate. By 1989 nearly three-fifths of the republic's forests had been destroyed or seriously damaged. Since then, renewed reforestation efforts have been more effective with deciduous trees than with conifers, resulting in little overall change in the total forest area, which occupies about one-third of the country.

RESOURCES AND POWER

Although reserves are limited, the Czech Republic produces significant quantities of bituminous, anthracite, and brown coal. Most of the bituminous coal is derived from the Ostrava-Karviná coalfield in the northeast, although it is also mined near Kladno in the Plzeň basin, as well as near Trutnov and Brno. A high proportion of the bituminous coal is of coking quality. Production of brown coal increased rapidly up to the mid-20th century and remained fairly static until the 1990s, when production declined as the industry faced restructuring and privatization. The main areas of brown-coal mining are in the extreme west around Chomutov, Most, Teplice, and Sokolov. Brown coal

Coal excavation at a surface mine in the Czech Republic. One of the country's primary fuel sources, coal is an important yet limited natural resource in the region. Bloomberg/Getty Images

is used in thermal power stations, as fuel in the home, and as raw material in the chemical industry. Small quantities of petroleum and natural gas are produced near Hodonín on the Slovak border. Pipelines import Russian oil and natural gas, the latter supplementing existing coal gas supplies. The completion in the late 1990s of an oil pipeline that transports oil from the port of Trieste, Italy, allowed the Czech Republic to be less reliant on Russian oil sources. Nuclear power plants located in Dukovany and Temelín, as well as nuclear power from Slovakia, have reduced the country's dependence on coal only slightly; about three-fourths of the Czech Republic's electricity is derived from fossil fuels.

The Czech Republic has limited deposits of metallic ores. Lead and zinc ores are mined near Kutná Hora and Příbram in Bohemia and in the Hrubý Jeseník Mountains in the northeast. Uranium is mined near Příbram and around Hamr in northern Bohemia. There is a significant gold deposit at Mokrsko, in central Bohemia, south of Prague. The Ore Mountains of Bohemia yield small quantities of tin. Other mineral resources include graphite near České Budějovice and kaolin near Plzeň and Karlovy Vary.

MANUFACTURING

Although much of the industry in the Czech Republic in the early 1990s could be characterized as obsolete by western European standards, some sectors, notably the automobile and electronics industries, are now modern and efficient. Engineering is the largest branch of industry. Also very important are food processing and brewing, as well as the chemical, rubber, cement, textile, footwear, and glass industries. The Czech iron and steel industries have traditionally been among the largest in eastern Europe but rely mainly on imported ores (especially from Ukraine). Steel production is centred on the plants of the Ostrava area (in Moravia), with lesser amounts produced at Kladno, Plzeň, and Chomutov (all in Bohemia). The heavy manufacturing sector produces automobiles, trucks, tractors, buses, airplanes, motorcycles, and diesel and electric locomotives and rail and tram cars.

The major Czech car manufacturer remains Škoda, eastern Europe's oldest car manufacturer, whose main plant is located in Mladá Boleslav. Taken over in the early 1990s by the German company Volkswagen and thoroughly modernized, Škoda became the Czech Republic's biggest export earner in the early 2000s, accounting for about one-tenth of the country's overall exports and becoming a source of national pride.

FINANCE

On the day of partition, the Czech National Bank and its Slovak counterpart replaced the federal monobank, the State Bank of Czechoslovakia. Initially, however, the federal monetary system remained essentially intact, with each country identifying its currency by applying stamps to it. The rapid economic divergence of the two republics, however, ended this arrangement after only one month, and separate currencies were inaugurated.

The National Bank oversees all financial institutions in the country. Numerous commercial and joint-venture banks, providing a full range of financial services, came into being after democratization. Improper lending practices and embezzlement contributed to the failure of the Kreditni bank, the sixth largest in the nation, in 1996 and sparked a major crisis in the banking industry that put a serious strain on the state's financial resources. Moreover, continued instability in the banking sector at the end of the 20th century spurred the government to hasten preparations for fuller privatization of the largest banks.

Since the demise of the command economy, numerous joint ventures have taken place between foreign and Czech firms, and there has been significant foreign direct investment in the country. German banks, firms, and individuals were the first to become leading investors, but investment also has come from the United States, the Netherlands, Switzerland, France, and Austria. The largest proportion of it was made in the communications, transportation and transportation equipment, and consumer goods industries.

TRADE

Czechoslovakia was one of the largest foreign traders in eastern Europe and a member of Comecon until the organization disbanded in 1991. Czech trade patterns shifted during the early 1990s in response to the changes occurring both within the country and throughout eastern Europe. By 2000, four years before the Czech Republic joined the EU, its exports to former Comecon members had declined to about one-fourth of total exports. In the early 21st century, Germany ranked as the chief destination for exports as well as the main source of imports. Other important trading partners included Slovakia and Austria. Machinery and transportation equipment made up the largest share of both exports and imports.

SERVICES

Prior to 1989 the Czech tourism industry catered largely to visitors from other eastern European countries. Following the demise of the Soviet bloc, an increasing proportion of tourists came from western Europe and the United States. Among the principal attractions are historic Prague, numerous spas and mineral springs, winter resorts, and various cultural festivals. Earnings from tourism increased dramatically throughout the 1990s, contributing significantly to the country's revenues and playing a major role in the development of the service sector, which by the first years of the 21st century accounted for more than half of the country's GDP and employed more than half of all Czech workers.

The Czech Republic has a wealth of cultural and historic sites that have been designated by UNESCO as World Heritage sites. Among them are the historic centres of Český Krumlov, Prague,

ČESKÝ KRUMLOV

The historically well-preserved Czech city of Český Krumlov (German: Krumau or Krumau an der Moldau) is located in the South Bohemia region of the southwestern Czech Republic. Situated roughly 15 miles (25 km) southwest of the larger city of České Budějovice, it lies on the Vltava River. The first part of the city's name, Český, means "Czech," and the second part, Krumlov, was derived from a German description of the tight bends in the river there.

continued from page 239

The town grew up around a Gothic castle, built on the cliffs above the Vltava by Bohemian nobles in the mid-13th century. In the succeeding centuries, aristocratic occupants, including members of the house of Schwarzenberg, expanded the castle, incorporating Renaissance and Baroque elements and ultimately creating one of the largest castle complexes in central Europe. The medieval character of central Ceský Krumlov has been preserved, and it was inscribed on UNESCO's World Heritage List in 1992. From the Middle Ages to the mid-20th century, the city was populated by a mixture of Czechs and Germans. After the creation of Czechoslovakia in 1918, the Czechoslovak government rejected the German form of the city's name in favour of the present Czech version, and after World War II the government expelled the German-speaking population. Today tourism is a major economic activity; in addition to hundreds of historic buildings, attractions include local museums, art galleries, theatres, and festivals.

and Telč (all inscribed in 1992), the Holašovice Historical Village Reservation (1998), Litomyšl Castle (1999), and the Jewish Quarter and St. Procopius's Basilica in Třebíč (2003).

LABOUR AND TAXATION

Under the communist regime, trade union activity was very restricted. Nevertheless, a general labour strike in November 1989 was one of the catalysts of the Velvet Revolution. The leading trade organization to arise in the postcommunist era was the Czech-Moravian Confederation of Trade Unions (Českomoravská Konfederace Odborových Svazů), which held its first congress meeting in 1994.

Czechs pay a flat personal income tax. The corporate tax rate is less than half of what it was in 1992, the final year of federation. The country also employs a value-added tax (VAT), with reduced rates for services related to the provision of water and heating, as well as for food, medication, newspapers, and books.

TRANSPORTATION AND TELECOMMUNICATIONS

Owing to terrain, settlement patterns, former federal policies, and geographic orientation toward western Europe, the Czech Republic possesses a more extensive transportation system than that of Slovakia. Rail lines serve all regions of the country, link the republic with its neighbours, and connect Prague with most major European cities. Urban light-rail serves the major metropolitan areas. Most freight moves along mainline routes, but shorter routes between the larger towns accommodate considerable passenger traffic. However, there has been a steady decline in both passenger and freight operations, in spite of the fact that the railways were modernized at the end of the 20th century. An extensive network of paved roads criss-crosses the Bohemian Plateau, while a superhighway links Prague, Brno, and Bratislava.

The Elbe and the Vltava are the principal navigable rivers in the Czech Republic, with Děčín and Prague as their chief ports, respectively. The Oder provides access to the Baltic Sea via the Polish port of Szczecin. Prague is a major international air terminus; foreign flights also arrive in Brno, Ostrava, and Karlovy Vary.

Per capita personal computer availability is greater in the Czech Republic than it is in the rest of central Europe but still lags far behind western European standards. On the other hand, per capita cell phone availability in the country is equal to or greater than that in most western European countries.

CHAPTER 18

CZECH GOVERNMENT AND SOCIETY

On December 16, 1992, the Czech National Council adopted a new constitution establishing the Czech Republic as a parliamentary democracy. This document reflects the Western liberal tradition of political thought and incorporates many of the principles codified in the Charter of Fundamental Rights and Freedoms, which was adopted by the former Czechoslovak Federal Assembly in January 1991. The constitution provides for a bicameral Parliament consisting of a Chamber of Deputies (elected on a proportional basis for four-year terms) and a Senate (elected on a district basis for six-year terms).

Executive power is shared by the prime minister and the president. Elected by a joint session of Parliament to a five-year term, the president, who is also the head of state, appoints a prime minister, who heads the government and advises the president on the appointment of other members of the government.

LOCAL GOVERNMENT

The Czech Republic was formerly divided into 77 *okresy* (districts). These units are still recognized, but in 2000 the country reestablished 13 *kraje* (regions) and one *hlavní mesto* (city) that reflect administrative divisions in place from 1948 to 1960. Local governments have the power to raise local taxes and are responsible for roads, utilities, public health, and schools.

Political map of the Czech Republic. Encyclopædia Britannica, Inc.

JUSTICE

The Czech Republic's judicial system consists of the Constitutional Court, the Supreme Administrative Court, and the Supreme Court as well as high, regional, and district courts. Military courts are under the jurisdiction of the department of defense. During the 1990s, the Czech government took steps to modify its legal system (based on pre-1918 Austrian criminal code) to meet standards set by the Organization for Security and Co-operation in Europe.

POLITICAL PROCESS

The electoral system is one of universal direct suffrage. There are several prominent political parties, including the Civic Democratic Party, the Christian and Democratic Union–Czech People's Party, the Czech Social Democratic Party, the Green Party, and the Communist Party of Bohemia and Moravia. Some parties that enjoyed significant support in the late 20th and early 21st centuries, such as the Freedom Union and the Civic Democratic Alliance, have lost importance or disbanded.

SECURITY

The withdrawal of Soviet troops from Czechoslovakia in mid-1991 coincided with the disbanding of the Warsaw Pact. At partition, apportioning military resources was one of the major tasks of the new Czech and Slovak defense ministries. Two-thirds of the matériel went to the Czech military, which includes ground and air forces and frontier guards. The Czech Republic, along with Poland and Hungary, became a member of NATO in 1999. At the end of 2004, the military had transformed itself from an organization dependent on conscription to an all-volunteer force.

HEALTH AND WELFARE

To restructure the health care system inherited from the communist era, the Czech Republic sought to end state control of health services, create a system that would include privately administered facilities, and introduce a funding structure to underwrite the system. By 1994 privatization had been accomplished and the number of privately administered health care facilities had increased tremendously. Poor economic and organizational handling of the restructuring, however, resulted in spiraling health care costs that initially proved difficult to address. Despite the increased cost of health care, however, Czechs benefited from greater access to advanced medical technologies and procedures and enjoy a level of health care that compares favourably with that of other EU countries. The overall level of social subsidies during the postcommunist era declined, although the government attempted to keep something of the social safety net intact.

HOUSING

Beginning in the late 1980s, the shortage of housing in the Czech Republic was a severe problem that was not adequately addressed until the start of the 21st century, when the housing situation, for the most part, stabilized. Although about half of existing housing was constructed between 1950 and 1990—much of it prefabricated high-rise urban apartment buildings known as *paneláks*, referring to the panel blocks used in construction— the general condition of Czech housing is relatively good in comparison with many other countries of the former Soviet bloc. The growth of building societies within the Czech banking sector has played an important role in the increase in home construction and ownership.

EDUCATION

Children aged 3 to 6 may attend state kindergartens. Compulsory education lasts 10 years, from age 6 to 16. Most students 15 to 18 years of age continue their education either at a general secondary school, which prepares them for college or university studies, a vocational school, or a technical school. Since 1990 many

CHARLES UNIVERSITY

The Czech Republic's oldest university is Charles University (Czech: Universita Karlova). Located in Prague, it is also known as the University of Prague. The state-controlled institution of higher learning was founded in 1348 by the Holy Roman emperor Charles IV, from whom it takes its name. It was the first university in central Europe. Among its buildings, scattered throughout Prague, is the Carolinum, one of the oldest existing university buildings in the world.

An early rector of the university, elected in 1409, was the Bohemian religious reformer Jan Hus. During the 17th century, the Jesuits renamed the institution Charles-Ferdinand University after the Holy Roman emperor Ferdinand II, who placed the university under their control, but in the late 18th century, a period of Jesuit suppression, it became a state institution. In 1882 it was divided into separate Czech and German institutions, each called Charles-Ferdinand. When the university was reopened after World War II (1945), the German university was abolished.

Charles University comprises faculties of mathematics and physics, natural science, general medicine, pediatrics, humanities, law, journalism, and education. Also attached are the Astronomical Institute and the Institute of Teacher Education.

private and religious schools have been established.

Enrollment in colleges and universities in the Czech Republic is low in comparison with other European countries, such as Poland, Austria, and Germany, which all have university enrollments at least twice as high. The leading institutions of higher education, providing four to five years of intensive study, have long-standing traditions. Charles University (founded 1348) and the Czech Technical University (founded 1707), both in Prague, are among the oldest universities in central Europe. Brno has two universities, and Olomouc has one. Since 1990 a number of teachers' colleges have been redesignated as universities. Research work is carried out at universities and at special research institutions affiliated with the Academy of Sciences of the Czech Republic.

CHAPTER 19

CZECH CULTURAL LIFE

The territory of the Czech Republic traditionally has been between the German and Slav lands, and Czech cultural traditions are a mixture of both. Influences from farther afield also have been strong. Visually the most striking influences are Italian—in Renaissance and Baroque architecture, for instance—while literature, music, the visual arts, and popular culture also are indebted to a variety of external influences. Most of the Western cultural influences on the Czech Lands have passed through a German filter, and for this reason Czech traditions in popular culture are marked by a strong sense of national identity.

DAILY LIFE AND SOCIAL CUSTOMS

The seven public, or bank, holidays in the Czech Republic are New Year's Day (January 1; also the Day of Recovery of the Independent Czech State), Liberation Day (May 8), the Day of Slavonic Apostles Cyril and Methodius (July 5), Jan Hus Day (July 6), the Day of Czech Statehood (September 28), Independence Day (October 28), and the Day of Students' Fight for Freedom and Democracy (November 17; also St. Wenceslas Day). In addition, most Czechs, including atheists, celebrate Christian holidays, including Easter and Christmas, which remain the oldest public holidays and were recognized even during the communist period. The main celebration of the Christmas holiday is on Christmas Eve, when part of the family decorates the Christmas tree while the remainder prepares the Christmas meal, traditionally consisting of fish, preferably carp, purchased live from huge wooden tubs, erected in all Czech cities during the Christmas week along with tents selling Christmas trees.

Staples of the Czech diet include potato and sauerkraut soups (*bramborová polévka* and *zelná polévka*, respectively), main dishes made of chicken and pork, bread and potato dumplings (*houskové knedlíky* and *bramborové knedlíky*), and, for dessert, fruit-filled dumplings, apple strudel, and honey cake. Bohemia has a brewing tradition that dates to the early 19th century, and Czechs are among the world's most avid beer drinkers. Wine, produced locally in Moravia, is also popular.

LITERATURE

Czech literature can claim a remote ancestry in the vernacular writing connected with the mission sent to Moravia in 863 CE by the Byzantine emperor Michael III. As Christianity reached the Slavs of Bohemia from the west under the political aegis of the Frankish empire, Prince Rostislav, the ruler of Great Moravia (reigned 846–870), sought help from the east. The mission was led by an experienced scholar and diplomat, Cyril (originally named Constantine), and his brother Methodius. The brothers translated the greater part of the Bible and the essential liturgical texts into what must have been a Slavonic literary language of Cyril's devising, based on the Macedonian-Slavonic vernacular of his native Salonika but enriched from other sources, notably Greek and the Slavonic of Moravia.

The most noteworthy literary monuments of this language (now known as Old Church Slavonic) are the *Lives* of the two brothers, which were almost certainly written before 900 (though they are preserved only in later copies). Other Old Church Slavonic texts, however, can be assigned to the Czech era, notably the *Legends* about Wenceslas I (Václav), prince of Bohemia (ruled 921–929), and his grandmother, Saint Ludmila, probably from the 10th century. The Old Church Slavonic language, used for a while along with Latin, fell out of use after 1097, when the last Slavonic monastery in Bohemia was taken over by Benedictine monks.

Writing in the Czech language emerged in the late 13th century, establishing a generally continuous tradition of vernacular literature. Chivalrous romances and chronicles, legends of the saints, love lyrics, satires, translations of the Bible, and religious prose were written in the 14th and 15th centuries. The main repository, however, of highly developed literary Czech was the Kralice Bible, a comprehensive translation of the Bible published between 1579 and 1593 by the Unitas Fratrum (Bohemian Brethren, or Moravian Brethren) scholars and named for the small Moravian town where it was printed. It was mainly thanks to this single book that the Czech literary language was preserved during its suppression for two centuries until it was resuscitated during the national revival. During the Counter-Reformation there was a serious decline in the social and administrative use of Czech, though the Baroque period brought fresh impulses to popular poetry and influenced both Roman Catholic and non-Catholic writers. There was a renewed flowering of Czech literature during the 19th century (commonly referred to as the Czech National Revival) that started as a widespread cultural enterprise, manifested in translations, schools, poetry, newspapers, theatre, novels, and operas. Later, the movement took on distinctly political overtones.

For the Czechs to become full-fledged members of the 19th-century community of European nations, their history had to be constructed and their language rediscovered, reconstructed, and codified. Josef Dobrovský, a Jesuit priest and scholar who wrote in German, published an outstanding systematic grammar of the Czech language. František Palacký, a historian turned politician, published the first volume of an ambitious history of the Czech nation in German in 1836. After 1848 Palacký continued his history in the Czech language only, though volumes published thereafter appeared in both Czech and German.

Meanwhile, the Romantic literary movement of western Europe began to affect the emerging Czech literature. The Czech Romantic school of poetry, dating from the early 19th century, is best represented by Karel Hynek Mácha and Karel Jaromír Erben. In Bohemia the Romantic movement gave way in the 1840s to a more descriptive and pragmatic approach to literature. Božena Němcová's novel *Babička* (1855; *The Grandmother*, also translated as *Granny*) became a lasting favourite with Czech readers, while the journalist and poet Karel Havlíček Borovský tried to acquaint the Czechs with some of the stark facts of political life. Jan Neruda, in his poetry and short stories, domesticated literary sophistication within a familiar Prague framework. Toward the end of the 19th century, the historical novels of Alois Jirásek began to claim a wide readership, while poetry moved through Parnassian, Symbolist, and Decadent phases.

The making, and breaking, of the Czechoslovak state between the two world wars was reflected in its literature. Jaroslav Hašek's sequence of novels *Osudy dobrého vojáka Švejka za světové války* (1921–23; *The Good Soldier Schweik*) made a mockery of authority, especially that of the former Austro-Hungarian army. Karel Čapek wrote popular plays, novels, and travel books, many of which have been translated into English. Vítězslav Nezval, František Halas, Vladimír Holan, Josef Hora, and Nobel Prize winner Jaroslav Seifert were among other writers whose poetry came to prominence during the first half of the 20th century. As World War II and German-imposed censorship closed in, poetry became even more

KAREL ČAPEK

Czech novelist, short-story writer, playwright, and essayist Karel Čapek (born January 9, 1890, Malé Svatonovice, Bohemia, Austria-Hungary [now in Czech Republic]—died December 25, 1938, Prague, Czechoslovakia) is remembered for his many accomplishments in a variety of literary forms and as the inventor of the word *robot*. The son of a country doctor, Čapek suffered all his life from a spinal disease, and writing seemed a compensation. He studied philosophy in Prague, Berlin, and Paris and in 1917 settled in Prague as a writer and journalist. From 1907 until well into the 1920s, much of his work was written with his brother Josef, a painter, who illustrated several of Karel's books.

Almost all of Čapek's literary works are inquiries into philosophical ideas. The early short stories—in *Zářivé hlubiny* (with Josef, 1916; "The Luminous Depths"), *Krakonošova zahrada* (with Josef, 1918; "The Garden of Krakonoš"), and *Trapné povídky* (1921; in *Money and Other Stories,* 1929)—are mainly concerned with human efforts to break out of the narrow circle of destiny and grasp ultimate values. Another series of works presents Čapek's "black utopias," showing how scientific discoveries and technological progress tempt humankind into titanic rebellions. Thus, in the play *R.U.R.: Rossum's Universal Robots* (published 1920, performed 1921), a scientist discovers the secret of creating humanlike machines that are more precise and reliable than human beings. Years later the machines dominate the human race and threaten it with extinction, though at the last moment it is saved. For this play Čapek invented the word "robot," deriving it from the Czech word for forced labour.

Other works, following the pattern of R.U.R., include the novel *Továrna na absolutno* (1922; *The Absolute at Large*); *Krakatit* (1924; *An Atomic Phantasy*); and *Válka s mloky* (1936; T*he War with the Newts*).

In another vein, Čapek's comic fantasy *Ze života hmyzu* (with Josef, 1921; *The Insect Play*) satirizes human greed, complacency, and selfishness, emphasizing the relativity of human values and the need to come to terms with life. His faith in democracy made him support his friend Tomáš Masaryk and write a biography of him.

The problem of identity and the mystery of people's underlying motivations are the theme of Čapek's most mature work, a trilogy of novels that together present three aspects of knowledge. *Hordubal* (1933) contrasts an inarticulate person's awareness of the causes of his actions with the world's incomprehension; *Povětroň* (1934; *Meteor*) illustrates the subjective causes of objective judgments; and *Obyčejný život* (1934; *An Ordinary Life*) explores the complex layers of personality underlying the "self" an "ordinary" man thinks himself to be.

The growing threat posed by Nazi Germany to Czechoslovakia's independent existence in the mid-1930s prompted Čapek to write several works intended to warn and mobilize his countrymen. The realistic novel *Prvni parta* (1937; *The First Rescue Party*) stressed the need for solidarity. In his last plays the appeal became more direct. *Bílá nemoc* (1937; *Power and Glory*) presented the tragedy of the noble pacifist; and *Matka* (1938; *The Mother*) vindicated armed resistance to barbaric invasion.

popular than in peacetime; the brief life and work of Jiří Orten is an outstanding example of his tragic generation.

Before the destruction of Czech Jewry by the Nazis and the expulsion of the German minority at the end of the war, Bohemia and Moravia had a strong German literary tradition. About the mid-19th century, Adalbert Stifter's descriptions of nature and the common people inspired local followers in the borderland between Bavaria and Bohemia. During the first half of the 20th century, the German-Jewish group of writers in Prague—Franz Kafka, Franz Werfel, Rainer Maria Rilke, and Max Brod—achieved international recognition.

Among the postwar generation of writers, Bohumil Hrabal became well-known for his haunting short stories. While Hrabal remained largely apolitical, after 1948 the majority of Czech writers became enthusiastic members of the Communist Party. Communism had strong domestic roots and thrived as an ideology among intellectuals as well as organized workers, as communist propagandists successfully integrated strong doses of anti-German hatred with pan-Slavic solidarity and socialist visions of utopia.

The Stalinist purges of the 1950s and the uprisings of 1956, however, discredited the party and gave birth to a reform movement. Before and after 1968 and the invasion of Czechoslovakia by Warsaw Pact forces, Czech writers were at the forefront of the communist reform movement. They paid a high price for their political commitment: a number of writers, including Milan Kundera and Josef Škvorecký, were forced to live and work abroad. Ludvík Vaculík and Ivan Klíma, writers of the same generation and of similar convictions, were among those whose novels were circulated in Prague as underground publications. Since 1989, Czech writers have continued to have a major political influence, perhaps most obviously exemplified by the fact that Czechs elected a prominent dissident playwright, Václav Havel, as their first postcommunist president.

THEATRE

The beginnings of modern theatrical tradition are usually connected with the Prague National Theatre, which was completed in 1881 and funded entirely by small private donations. In the 1930s the "liberated theatre" movement—made popular by two comic actors, Jiří Voskovec and Jan Werich, and the musician Jaroslav Ježek—launched a new genre of political satire. Czech stage designers such as František Tröster, Frantisek Muzika, and Josef Svoboda achieved worldwide recognition. Havel's best known and most translated plays are *Zahradní slavnost* (1963; *The Garden Party*) and *Vyrozumění* (1965; *The Memorandum*).

MUSIC

During the 18th century, Bohemia produced a number of musicians and composers who greatly influenced musical styles throughout Europe. Composer Johann Stamitz, the founder of the Mannheim school of symphonists, made key contributions to the development of Classical symphonic form and had a profound influence on Mozart. The Benda family of musicians and composers was also highly influential, as was Josef Myslivecek, whose operas and symphonies were much admired in Italy, where he was known as "il divino Boemo" ("the divine Bohemian"), as well as in his homeland.

During the 19th century, operatic and symphonic music retained its high

BEDŘICH SMETANA

The first truly important Bohemian nationalist composer, Bedřich Smetana (born March 2, 1824, Leitomischl, Bohemia, Austrian Empire [now Litomyšl, Czech Republic]—died May 12, 1884, Prague), composed operas and symphonic poems and founded the Czech national school of music. Smetana studied music under his father, an amateur violinist. He early took up piano under a professional teacher and performed in public at the age of six. He continued his studies and later became music teacher to the family of Leopold, Count von Thun. Encouraged by Franz Liszt he opened a piano school in Prague in 1848 and the next year married the pianist Katerina Kolářová. In 1856 he wrote his first symphonic poems and in the same year was appointed conductor of the philharmonic society of Gothenburg (Sweden), where he remained until 1861. He then returned to Prague, where he played the leading part in the establishment of the national opera house.

Smetana's first opera, *Braniboři v Čechách* (*The Brandenburgers in Bohemia*), was produced in Prague in 1866. This was followed by the production on May 30, 1866, of his second opera, *Prodaná nevěsta* (*The Bartered Bride*), which later established Smetana's reputation as a distinctively Czech composer. His later operas were less successful. *Dalibor*, written under the influence of Wagner, was performed in 1868. *Libuše*, named after a legendary figure in the history of Prague and intended to celebrate the projected coronation (which never took place) of the emperor Francis Joseph as king of Bohemia, was not produced until 1881.

In 1874 Smetana's health began to deteriorate as a result of syphilis. Greatly concerned, he resigned his conductorship of the Prague Opera. He became totally deaf in late 1874, but between that year and 1879 he wrote the cycle of six symphonic poems bearing the collective title *Má vlast* (*My Country*), which includes *Vltava* (*The Moldau*), *Z českých luhů a hájů* (*From Bohemia's Meadows and Forests*), and *Vyšehrad* (the name of a fortress in Prague). From this period also came the string quartet to which he gave the title *Z mého života* (*From My Life*), considered among his finest works; *Hubička* (*The Kiss*), successfully produced in 1876; *Čertova stěna* (*The Devil's Wall*), performed in 1882; and a number of piano solos, including many polkas. Following attacks of depression and symptoms of mental instability, Smetana entered an asylum at Prague and died there.

place in Czech cultural life. Bedřich Smetana was the first composer to inject a noticeable element of Czech nationalism into his work, most notably in his opera *Prodaná nevěsta* (*The Bartered Bride*) and his cycle of symphonic poems *Má vlast* (*My Country*). Antonín Dvořák, Leoš Janáček, and Bohuslav Martinů, each of whom drew heavily on folk music for inspiration, achieved international fame, and their works often are played at the annual spring music festival held in Prague. Under the batons of distinguished conductors such as Václav Talich, Karel Ančerl, and Václav Neumann, the Czech Philharmonic has developed into one of the world's leading orchestras.

Since World War II, Czech musicians have gained notice on the European jazz circuit, and jazz-rock keyboardist Jan Hamr (Jan Hammer) won international acclaim for his television and motion picture sound tracks. Traditional folk music continues to have wide appeal among Czechs.

FILM

Under communism, the medium of film was valued as a propaganda tool, and the state-supported Czechoslovak motion picture industry produced an average of 30 feature films annually. With the withdrawal of state sponsorship during the 1990s, fewer than 20 films appeared each year. Despite the limitations imposed by a small market, Czech films and film directors have made their mark internationally, especially since the 1960s. Many Czech films are conceived on a small scale, with a sharp focus on the everyday, common life of the people. Among the best known are those of the Czech New Wave period (1962–68), including Miloš Forman's *Lásky jedné plavolvlásky* (1965; *Loves of a Blonde*) and Jiří Menzel's *Closely Watched Trains* (1967), which won an Academy Award. Jan Svěrák's *Kolya* (1997) also received international attention, as did Menzel's *I Served the King of England* (2006). There is a strong Czech tradition in producing animated films, with the work of Jiří Trnka and Jan Švankmajer being perhaps the most revered.

FINE, APPLIED, AND FOLK ARTS

The architecture of the Czech Republic is rich and varied. Prague is especially noted for its wealth of building styles. Among Prague's architectural treasures are the Romanesque Church of St. George, which dates from the 10th century, and the twin-spired St. Vitus's Cathedral, representative of the Gothic style. The city contains many fine Baroque structures, with the Valdštejn and Clam-Gallas palaces and the Antonín Dvořák Museum being some of the most magnificent examples. The Bedřich Smetana Museum is exemplary of the Classical style, and the National Theatre and the National Museum are the principal examples of the Neoclassical style. Notable buildings of

Historic and architecturally compelling astronomical clock on the town hall tower, destroyed during World War II and rebuilt in 1953, in Olomouc, Czech Republic. Flip Schulke/ Black Star

art, such as the happy marriage between Jaroslav Hašek's texts and Josef Lada's illustrations. Since the 19th century, Czech painters and graphic artists have on the whole followed the broad European movements, but realism generally prevails. One of the best-known painters of the 19th century was Josef Mánes. In the late 19th and early 20th centuries, Paris-based illustrator Alphonse (Alfons) Mucha captured the elusive fin de siècle mood in his paintings and posters, which gained him world renown. During the 20th century, Czech painters such

Egg decorated for Easter using the folk art technique known as pysanky, *in Czechoslovakia, 20th century.* Encyclopædia Britannica, Inc.

the 20th century include those designed in the Cubist style; the first such building now houses the Museum of Czech Cubism.

The Czechs have a strong tradition in the graphic arts. This includes many forms of caricature: Josef Čapek, the brother of the writer Karel Čapek, is remembered for a series of drawings entitled *The Dictator's Boots*, from the time when Adolf Hitler was ascending to power. Much of Czech graphic art derives its inspiration from popular, narrative

as František Kubka, Emil Filla, Toyen (Marie Cermínová), Jindrich Štyrský, and Josef Šíma were much influenced by Cubism and Surrealism. Painters active

ALPHONSE MUCHA

The Art Nouveau illustrator and painter Alphonse Mucha (born Alfons Maria Mucha, July 24, 1860, Ivančice, Moravia, Austrian Empire [now in Czech Republic]—died July 14, 1939, Prague, Czechoslovakia) was noted for his posters of idealized female figures. After receiving his early education in Brno, Moravia, and working for a theatre scene-painting firm in Vienna, Mucha studied art in Prague, Munich, and Paris in the 1880s. He first became prominent as the principal advertiser of the actress Sarah Bernhardt in Paris. He designed the posters for several theatrical productions featuring Bernhardt, beginning with *Gismonda* (1894), and he designed sets and costumes for her as well. Mucha designed many other posters and magazine illustrations, becoming one of the foremost designers in the Art Nouveau style. His supple, fluent draftsmanship is used to great effect in his posters featuring women. His fascination with the sensuous aspects of female beauty—luxuriantly flowing strands of hair, heavy-lidded eyes, and full-lipped mouths—as well as his presentation of the female image as ornamental, reveal the influence of the English Pre-Raphaelite aesthetic on Mucha, particularly the work of Dante Gabriel Rossetti. The sensuous bravura of the draftsmanship, particularly the use of twining, whiplash lines, imparts a strange refinement to his female figures.

Between 1903 and 1922 Mucha made four trips to the United States, where he attracted the patronage of Charles Richard Crane, a Chicago industrialist and Slavophile, who subsidized Mucha's series of 20 large historical paintings illustrating the "Epic of the Slavic People" (1912–30). After 1922 Mucha lived in Czechoslovakia, and he donated his "Slavic Epic" paintings to the city of Prague.

during the latter part of the 20th century included Jan Zrzavý, Mikuláš Medek, Jiří Tichý, and Jiří Kolář.

In the applied arts, manufactured glass ornaments, traditional northern Bohemian costume jewelry, and toys are probably the best-known objects. Popular art has been preserved most often in useful ceramic and wood objects; embroideries and traditional costumes have come to be of less importance.

CULTURAL INSTITUTIONS

The Czech Republic's impressive network of public libraries dates back to the 19th century. The largest library is the National Library in Prague, created in 1958 by the merger of several older libraries. Other major collections are in the National Museum Library, also in Prague and founded in 1818, and the State Scientific Library in Brno.

Of the republic's many museums, three in Prague are especially noteworthy: the National Museum (founded 1818), the National Gallery (1796; whose collection is exhibited in several locations), and the Museum of Decorative Arts (1885), the latter housing one of the world's largest collections of glass. The Prague Zoological Garden is known for

Przewalski's horse, the last of a wild horse subspecies.

SPORTS AND RECREATION

Czechs enjoy a variety of outdoor activities, including golf, canoeing, cycling, and hiking, as well as winter sports such as cross-country skiing, snowboarding, and ice hockey. The Czech Republic's ice hockey team distinguished itself throughout the 1990s, winning the world championships in 1996 and 1999 and taking the gold medal at the 1998 Olympics in Nagano, Japan. Two of the players who starred on that gold-medal-winning team also enjoyed great success in the National Hockey League: goaltender Dominik Hašek and prolific scorer Jaromir Jagr. The former Czechoslovakia also produced world-class football (soccer) teams and finished second in the World Cup competition in 1934 and 1962. Jaroslav Drobny, Jan Kodeš, Martina Navratilova, Ivan Lendl, and Hana Mandlikova head an impressive list of Czechs who have experienced international success in tennis.

The Czech Republic made its Olympic debut at the 1996 Summer Games in Atlanta, though Czech athletes (representing Bohemia and later Czechoslovakia) had begun participating in 1900. Indeed, early Czech Olympic heroes include long-distance runner Emil Zátopek, "the bouncing Czech," who won three gold medals at the Helsinki Games in 1952, and gymnast Vera Cáslavská, the winner of many Olympic gold medals and world championships in the 1960s. More recently, Jan Železný, who won gold medals in the javelin in 1992, 1996, and 2000, is arguably the most accomplished athlete in that sport's history.

MEDIA AND PUBLISHING

All publishers and news media were, until the political changes in late 1989, subject to censorship through the government's Office for Press and Information. The government owned all telephone, telegraph, television, and radio systems, and news was disseminated by the official Czechoslovak News Agency. In the postcommunist years, with the abolition of censorship, the introduction of a free-market economy, and the advent of the Internet, dissemination of information changed radically. During the 1990s many new newspaper and book publishers came into existence, although, owing to unstable economic conditions, many of these enterprises were fairly short lived. Widely read daily newspapers include *Mladá fronta Dnes* ("Youth Front Today"), *Právo* ("Right"), and *Hospodářské noviny* ("Economic News"), all published in Prague.

State control of radio and television broadcasting ended in 1991. The Czech Republic has several nationwide radio networks that broadcast news and cultural programs as well as a number of local radio stations. The nation has two state-run television networks. Independent commercial stations also operate, among them Nova Television and Prima Television.

CHAPTER 20

SLOVAKIA: THE LAND AND ITS PEOPLE

Slovakia is a landlocked country of central Europe that is bordered by Poland to the north, Hungary to the south, Austria to the west, and the Czech Republic to the northwest. It is roughly coextensive with the historic region of Slovakia, the easternmost of the two territories that from 1918 to 1992 constituted Czechoslovakia. The short history of independent Slovakia is one of a desire to move from mere autonomy within the Czechoslovak federation to sovereignty—a history

The flag of Slovakia. Encyclopaedia Britannica, Inc.

of resistance to being called "the nation after the hyphen." Although World War II thwarted the Slovaks' first vote for independence in 1939, sovereignty was finally realized on January 1, 1993, slightly more than three years after the Velvet Revolution—the collapse of the communist regime that had controlled Czechoslovakia since 1948.

RELIEF

The Western Carpathian Mountains dominate the topography of Slovakia. They consist of a system of three regions of east-west-trending ranges—Outer, Central, and Inner—separated by valleys and intermontane basins. Two large lowland areas north of the Hungarian border, the Little Alfold (called the Podunajská, or Danubian, Lowland in Slovakia) in the southwest and the Eastern Slovakian Lowland in the east, constitute the Slovakian portion of the Inner Carpathian Depressions region.

The Outer Western Carpathians to the north extend into the eastern Czech Republic and southern Poland and contain the Little Carpathian (Slovak: Malé Karpaty), Javorníky, and Beskid mountains. Located roughly in the middle

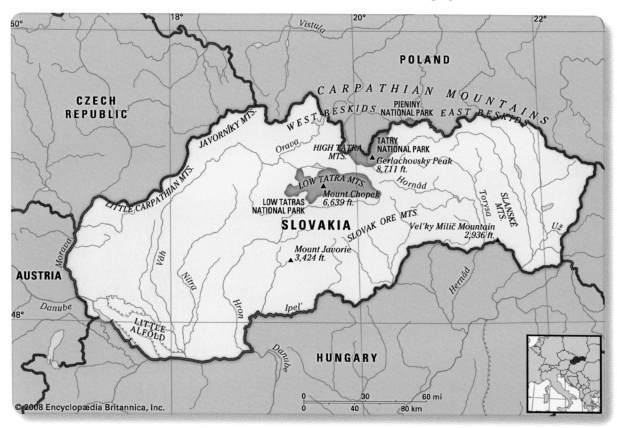

Physical map of Slovakia. Encyclopædia Britannica, Inc.

of the country, the Central Western Carpathians include Slovakia's highest ranges: the High Tatra (Vysoké Tatry) Mountains, containing the highest point in the republic, Gerlachovský Peak, at 8,711 feet (2,655 m); and, to the south of them, the Low Tatra (Nízke Tatry) Mountains, which reach elevations of about 6,500 feet (2,000 m). Farther to the south are the Inner Western Carpathian Mountains, which extend into Hungary and contain the economically important Slovak Ore (Slovenské Rudohorie) Mountains.

DRAINAGE

Slovakia drains predominantly southward into the Danube (Dunaj) River system. The Danube and another major river, the Morava, form the republic's southwestern border. The principal rivers draining the mountains include the Váh, Hron, Hornád, and Bodrog, all flowing south, and the Poprad, draining northward. Flows vary seasonally from the torrents of spring snowmelt to late-summer lows. Mountain lakes and mineral and thermal springs are numerous.

SOILS

Slovakia contains a striking variety of soil types. The country's richest soils, the black chernozems, occur in the southwest, although the alluvial deposit known as Great Rye Island occupies the core of the Slovakian Danube basin. The upper reaches of the southern river valleys are covered with brown forest soils, while podzols dominate the central and northern areas of middle elevation. Stony mountain soils cover the highest regions.

CLIMATE

Slovakia's easterly position gives it a more continental climate than that of the Czech Republic. Its mountainous terrain is another determining factor. The mean annual temperature drops to about 25 °F (-4 °C) in the High Tatras and rises to just above 50 °F (10 °C) in the Danubian lowlands. Average July temperatures exceed 68 °F (20 °C) in the Danubian lowlands, and average January temperatures can be as low as 23 °F (-5 °C) in mountain basins. The growing season is about 200 days in the south and less than half of that in the mountains. Annual precipitation ranges from about 22 inches (570 mm) in the Danubian plains to more than 43 inches (1,100 mm) in windward mountain valleys. Maximum precipitation falls in July, while the minimum is in January. Snow remains on the higher peaks into the summer months.

PLANT AND ANIMAL LIFE

Although Slovakia is a small country, its varied topography supports a wide variety of vegetation. Agriculture and timber cutting have diminished the republic's original forest cover, but approximately two-fifths of its area is still forested. Forestland is most extensive in the mountainous districts. The forests in the western Beskid Mountains on the Czech-Slovak border and those in central Slovakia near Žiar nad Hronom are among the most endangered. The major forest types include the oak-grove assemblages of the Podunajská Lowland, the beech forests of the lower elevations of the Carpathians, and the spruce forests of the middle and upper slopes. The highest elevations support taiga and tundra vegetation. The timberline runs at about 5,000 feet (1,500 m). At these upper elevations, particularly in the Tatras, the tree cover below the timberline consists largely of dwarf pine. At about 7,500 feet (2,300 m), alpine grasses and low-growing shrubs give way to lichens.

Slovakia's wildlife is abundant and diverse; the Tatry (High Tatras) National Park shelters an exceptional collection of wild animals, including bears, wolves, lynx, wildcats, marmots, otters, martens, and minks. Hunting is prohibited in the parks, and some animals, such as the chamois, are protected nationwide. The forests and lowland areas support numerous game birds, such as partridges, pheasants, wild geese, and ducks. Raptors, storks, and other large birds are protected.

ETHNIC GROUPS

More than four-fifths of Slovakia's population are ethnic Slovaks. Hungarians, concentrated in the southern border districts, form the largest minority, making up about one-tenth of the republic's population. Small numbers of Czechs, Germans, and Poles live throughout the country, while Ruthenians (Rusyns) are concentrated in the east and northeast. There is a sizable and relatively mobile population of Roma (Gypsies), who live mainly in the eastern part of the country.

LANGUAGES

Although the majority of the population identifies Slovak as its mother tongue, a law that came into effect on January 1, 1996, establishing Slovak as the country's official language was controversial primarily because of its impact on Slovakia's Hungarian minority. Widespread fluency in Czech is a legacy of the period of federation. As members of the West Slavic language group, Slovak and Czech are closely related and mutually intelligible; both use the Roman rather than the Cyrillic alphabet. In addition to Hungarian, Polish, German, Ukrainian, Rusyn (related to Ukrainian), and Romany are among the other languages spoken in Slovakia. Croatian speakers, living in a small number of villages in western Slovakia, make up a tiny linguistic minority.

RELIGION

Four decades of official atheism ended with the collapse of communist control in 1989, and the widespread persistence

SLOVAK LANGUAGE

The Slovak language (Slovak: Slovenčina) is the official language of Slovakia. It is a West Slavic language closely related to Czech, Polish, and the Sorbian languages of eastern Germany. Slovak is written in the Roman (Latin) alphabet. Although there are traces of the Slovak language in Latin documents of the 11th–15th century and in the Czech of the 14th–16th century, the earliest-known attempts to increase the use of written Slovak came in the 17th and 18th centuries, when Roman Catholics centred at the University of Trnava tried to introduce Slovak for use in their hymnal and other church books. The language did not become accepted as a literary language, however, until a group led by the Protestant Ľudovít Štúr (1815–56) began to write in the central Slovak dialects. The language of these writings, as modified and codified by Martin Hattala in his grammar of 1852, rapidly gained approval and was accepted as standard.

There are three major Slovak dialect groups: Eastern, Central, and Western. The Western dialects of Slovak shade into the Moravian dialects of the Czech language. Except for perhaps the extreme Eastern Slovak dialects and the Bohemian Czech dialect, all dialects of Slovak and Czech are mutually comprehensible, for there are no sharp linguistic frontiers.

of religious affiliation quickly manifested itself in both the sectarian and political spheres. The majority of Slovaks are Roman Catholic, but Protestant churches, particularly the Evangelical Church of the Augsburg Confession (Lutheran) and the Reformed Christian Church (Calvinist), claim a significant minority of adherents. Greek Catholics and Eastern Orthodox Christians are found in Ruthenian districts. More than one-tenth of the population professes no religious belief.

SETTLEMENT PATTERNS

Largely because of its rugged terrain, Slovakia has a relatively low density of settlement. Rural settlements with up to several hundred inhabitants tend to prevail except in the more heavily urbanized southwest. Highland villages, many of them dating from the Middle Ages, conform to linear ridges and valleys. Historically, Turkish invasions from the south, lasting up to the 18th century, forced much of the population to resettle farther north. Dispersed settlement occurs along the Czech border and in the central mountains, reflecting the later colonization of the 17th and 18th centuries. The introduction of mining in central Slovakia led to the foundation of independent mining towns such as Banská Bystrica, Banská Štiavnica, Kremnica, and others. The most concentrated population is found in the Podunajská Lowland. Collectivization of farmland

BRATISLAVA

Archaeological evidence suggests prehistoric habitation of the site on which Bratislava now stands. The area was later fortified and settled by the Celts and Romans, and finally, in the 8th century, was inhabited by the Slavs. The community developed as a trade centre and was granted the rights of a free royal town in 1291. The first university in what was then Hungary, the Istropolitana Academy, was founded there in 1467. Bratislava served as the Hungarian capital from 1526 until 1784, when most of the middle Danube basin was in the hands of the Turks, and the Hungarian parliament continued to meet there until 1848. The Habsburg rulers were crowned kings of Hungary in the city's Gothic Cathedral of St. Martin.

The city is dominated by its enormous castle, which stands on a plateau 300 feet (100 m) above the Danube. The castle was the residence of the Austrian royal family until it was destroyed by fire in 1811; it has since been largely restored. In 1741 Empress Maria Theresa of Austria fled to Bratislava when Vienna was threatened by French and Bavarian troops. The so-called Peace of Pressburg (1805) was signed by Napoleon and the Austrian emperor Francis II, after the Battle of Austerlitz, in the city's Baroque Archbishop's Palace. Following World War I, Bratislava was made the capital of Slovakia in the first Czechoslovakian Republic, and it remained the capital when Slovakia emerged as an independent nation in 1993.

The modern city of Bratislava is a cultural centre and the seat of Comenius University (1919; successor to the medieval Istropolitana Academy), the Slovak Academy of Sciences (1953), several specialized schools and technical institutes, the Slovak National Theatre, and the Slovak National Gallery and Museum. An important road and rail junction and river port, Bratislava has diversified industries producing textiles, chemicals, and metal and electrical goods.

under Czechoslovakia's communist regime supplanted the ancient small-scale pattern of land use with a giant agricultural grid. Reprivatization of farmland following the Velvet Revolution of 1989 effected a gradual reconfiguration of the arable landscape.

The capital of Slovakia is Bratislava (German: Pressburg; Hungarian: Pozsony). It lies in the extreme southwestern part of the country, along the Danube where that river has cut a gorge in the Little Carpathian Mountains near the meeting point of the frontiers of Slovakia, Austria, and Hungary. Vienna is 35 miles (56 km) west.

Industrialization programs during and following World War II increased urbanization in Slovakia. More than half of Slovakia's population lives in urban areas. In addition to Bratislava, regional centres include Nitra, Banská Bystrica, Žilina, Košice, and Prešov. Partizánske and Nová Dubnica, both in the west, are examples of new towns founded, respectively, just before and after World War II.

DEMOGRAPHIC TRENDS

Historically, emigration to Hungary (especially Budapest) and other more urbanized areas of Europe, as well as to the United States, kept Slovakia's growth rate low. Well over half a million Slovaks emigrated to the United States prior to 1914. During communist rule, emigration virtually stopped, but industrialization policies were responsible for significant internal migration. Slovakia's birth rate fell by more than half during the second half of the 20th century.

CHAPTER 21

THE SLOVAK ECONOMY

The brevity of the fanfare that greeted the rebirth of Slovakia in 1993 was largely an acknowledgement of economic reality. Slovak political autonomy was a popular idea, but many Slovaks viewed the pursuit of it outside the relative security of a Czechoslovak federation as potentially disastrous. Others argued that the conversion to a market economy in a federated Czechoslovakia would favour the Czech region. Geographic and historical conditions, including the central planning of the communist era, had left Slovakia more rural and less economically diversified than its Czech neighbour, which had roughly twice Slovakia's population. Indeed, the process of privatization undertaken after the fall of the communist regime in 1989 had proceeded much more slowly in Slovakia than in the Czech Republic.

The apportionment of government assets posed another vexing challenge at the time of separation. Primary among these were the former Czechoslovak military facilities. Although Slovakia had in the last years of the Czechoslovak federation accounted for as much as two-thirds of the federation's armament production, this industry was in severe decline. The majority of army bases, aircraft, and associated equipment remained on Czech soil, where the frontiers with western Europe had been more heavily protected.

The complexities of partition aside, both the Czech and Slovak economies felt the drag of economic downturns in the early 1990s. Acceleration of the privatization program was viewed as the most promising means of increasing foreign investment. In January 1995, however, Prime Minister

Vladimír Mečiar's government canceled the privatization by voucher of a number of state-owned enterprises, effectively suspending the privatization program. The cancellation was declared unconstitutional, and in July the government instituted a program called the National Property Fund, whereby citizens would receive bonds that could be redeemed for shares in privatized industries. Despite the erratic pace of privatization, by the turn of the 21st century it was estimated that more than three-fourths of Slovakia's gross domestic product (GDP) was generated by the private sector.

Initially, the engineers of the political separation of Czechoslovakia had assumed that the nascent economies of the two independent republics could share, for a limited period, the existing monetary system. Such an arrangement quickly came to be perceived as untenable: Czechs foresaw a contagious inflation in Slovakia, and Slovaks feared economic "shock therapy" by the Czechs. The short-lived plan that finally emerged—in an atmosphere rife with rumour, denial, false starts, and delays—prescribed a stepped transition in which each republic would recall a portion of its Czechoslovak currency supply for stamping with a country mark, and then newly printed bills would gradually replace the stamped ones. The agreement established an initial exchange rate of 1 to 1 for the new currencies, known as koruny, but the Slovak koruna soon became less valuable than the Czech koruna. Following its entry into the European Union (EU) in 2004, however, Slovakia became the first of the two countries to replace its currency with the euro, which it adopted in 2009.

Although Slovakia started the process of transforming its economy in less-favourable circumstances than the Czech Republic, on average Slovakia achieved greater economic growth and lower inflation rates than its Czech counterpart. Slovakia's macroeconomic performance positioned it as one of the most successful of the former Eastern-bloc countries. A key feature of growth was the burgeoning service sector, which provided employment to about half the labour force. Nevertheless, during the 1990s unemployment remained rather high, and inflation inched upward. Foreign debt continued to increase at a rapid pace, and the country's budget and current account deficits widened. However, by 2004, when Slovakia joined the EU, the economy had expanded, inflation had fallen substantially, the current account deficit had shrunk, and foreign investment in the country had greatly risen. In 2009, the year that Slovakia joined the euro zone, its economy was jolted by an economic crisis that afflicted much of Europe. That year industrial production and exports fell, while unemployment jumped to more than 12 percent. The Slovak economy turned around quickly, however, and by 2011 it was experiencing one of the fastest growth rates in the EU.

AGRICULTURE AND FORESTRY

During communist rule, agriculture in the Slovak lands was subordinate to industrialization, and today only about one-third of Slovakia's territory is cultivated. On the fertile lowlands, wheat, barley, sugar beets, corn (maize), and fodder crops are the most important crops, whereas on the relatively poor soils of the mountains the principal crops are rye, oats, potatoes, and flax. Tobacco and fruits are grown in the Váh valley, and vineyards thrive on the slopes of the Carpathian ranges in Západní Slovensko *kraj* (region). On the plains, farmers raise pigs and cattle. Sheep raising is prevalent in mountain valleys.

The harvesting of wood and the production of other forest products constitute a small part of the economy. About one-third of Slovakia's forests had been destroyed or seriously damaged by 1989, but reforestation efforts following independence resulted in a modest increase in forested areas.

RESOURCES AND POWER

Slovakia has limited reserves of brown coal and lignite, located in the foothills near Handlová to the west and Modrý Kameň to the south. The brown coal has been used in thermal power stations, as fuel in the home, and as raw material in the chemical industry. Pipelines import Russian oil (to a major refinery at Bratislava) and natural gas, the latter supplementing existing coal gas supplies. Natural gas began to be extracted near the western town of Gbely in 1985.

Substantial deposits of iron ore, copper, manganese, magnesite, lead, and zinc are mined in the Slovak Ore Mountains. Imported bauxite and nickel ore are refined at Žiar nad Hronom and Sered', respectively. Eastern Slovakia has some economically significant salt deposits.

The chief energy source is nuclear power, followed by fossil fuels and hydroelectric power; the latter is generated by a series of dams on the Váh, Orava, Hornád, Slaná, and Danube rivers. In 1977 the Czechoslovak and Hungarian governments signed an agreement to build a major hydroelectric project on the Danube southeast of Bratislava at Gabčíkovo and Nagymaros. The project called for the diversion of the Danube and the construction of two dams to be built by each of the partners. In 1989 Hungary withdrew from the Nagymaros venture because of environmental and other concerns. Slovakia's completion of the project on its own led to a dispute between the two countries that persisted into the 21st century.

MANUFACTURING

Prior to independence, Slovakia was the location of some of the least effective state-run industries in Czechoslovakia. By the early 21st century, however, successful manufacturing industries produced a substantial proportion of

A view of Gabcikovo Dam in southern Slovakia. Hydroelectric power generated by various dams is one of the top three energy sources in the country. Sean Gallup/Getty Images

Slovakia's GDP, and manufacturing workers constituted a significant portion of the labour force. Bratislava, Košice, and the towns along the Váh River are Slovakia's main manufacturing centres. Important industries include automobiles, machinery, steel, ceramics, chemicals, textiles, food and beverage processing, arms, and petroleum products. The former East Slovakian Iron and Steel Works in Košice—one of the last monuments of large-scale Soviet industrial planning in central Europe—was privatized in 1992 after a considerable fall in steel output; in 2000, U.S. Steel purchased the firm's steel-related assets. Slovakia's armaments industry has revived since 1993 and produces military equipment primarily for export. Environmental pollution—the legacy of communist-era industrialization—remains a pressing concern.

FINANCE

The National Bank of Slovakia succeeded the Czech and Slovak central bank on January 1, 1993, as the republic's principal financial institution. The bank's first major accomplishment was its conversion to the new republican monetary system, with the koruna as the national currency (replaced in 2009 by the euro). Following decentralization of the banking system, a number of commercial and joint-venture banks came into being. A stock exchange operates in Bratislava.

KOŠICE

One of Slovakia's major industrial centres is Košice (German: Kaschau; Hungarian: Kassa), located in the eastern part of the country. It lies on the Hornád River, south of Prešov.

Košice originated in the 9th century and was chartered in 1241. In the late Middle Ages it was one of the 24 trading settlements of the Polish-Slovak frontier, in which immigrant German merchants were prominent. In 1660 Benedict Kischdy, the Hungarian bishop of Eger, founded a university at Košice that was later suppressed by the Austrians. There are remnants of the city's stout 17th-century fortifications, built as a defense against the Turks; particularly well preserved are the Hangman's Bastion, now a museum, and the Mikluš Prison. The long medieval street known as Hlavná Ulica is still the centre of the city. Along it stand the great Gothic Cathedral of St. Elizabeth, St. Michael's Chapel, Levoča House (the former warehouse of the trading-settlement merchants), and several other churches and palaces.

Košice developed rapidly after it became a part of Czechoslovakia in 1920. In 1938 the city was occupied by the Hungarians; after liberation in 1945, it became the first seat of the postwar Czechoslovakian government and of the Slovak National Council. Šafařík University (1959) and several scientific and research institutes were founded in the city in the decades after World War II. Since 1945 Košice's population has more than doubled, and the city is now the political, economic, and cultural centre of southeastern Slovakia.

Košice lies between the mineral-rich Slovak Ore Mountains to the west (with iron ore, magnesite, and limestone) and a fertile agricultural plain to the east. It is both a centre for heavy industry and a market for farm products. One of eastern Europe's largest integrated iron and steel complexes is at Huko, just south of Košice. Nearby are several spas and villages, notably Herlany, Jasov, Jahodná, and Štós. The city is home to the Eastern Slovakia Museum.

Slovakia's well-educated labour force helps attract foreign investors from the Netherlands, Germany, and Austria, as well as other Western countries. For much of the 1990s, foreign investment in Slovakia lagged behind that of other former Soviet satellites, owing to a lack of confidence in Slovakia's financial leadership and institutions as well as to the Mečiar government's restrictive policies toward foreign investment in formerly state-owned properties. In 1998, however, the government announced tax incentives designed to stimulate foreign investment in Slovak enterprises, such as tax grants or credits for every new job created in the country. Consequently, in the early 21st century direct foreign investment increased greatly.

TRADE

Slovakia has depended on foreign trade to boost economic growth. Following the breakup of Czechoslovakia, trade with eastern European countries declined, while that with Western countries expanded. After joining the EU in 2004, Slovakia traded principally with other EU states. The volume and profile of trade between Slovakia and the Czech Republic remain significant in spite of occasional disruptions stemming from political squabbles. Other important trade partners are Germany, Italy, Poland, Austria, Hungary, and the United States. Slovakia's main exports include automobiles, machinery, and iron and steel. Major imports include machinery, automobiles, and mineral fuels.

SERVICES

Service industries, an increasingly important part of Slovakia's economy, account for more than two-thirds of GDP. Since the 1990s tourism has undergone considerable growth. During the communist period, most visitors to the Slovak lands were from other eastern European countries. Since independence, however, many more visitors from western Europe and North America travel to Slovakia. Tourist attractions include spectacular mountain scenery, caves, castles, other historic buildings and monuments, arts festivals, and numerous thermal and mineral springs.

LABOUR AND TAXATION

The vast majority of Slovak workers are employed in the manufacturing and service industries. The participation rate of women in the workforce is just under half. Most Slovak employees are members of trade unions, which prior to 1989 were controlled by the Communist Party of Czechoslovakia. The 1992 constitution guarantees the right to form unions and the right to strike, and a sizable number of workers continue to pay their membership dues. A number of unions, representing workers in both manufacturing and service industries, are affiliated with the Confederation of Trade Unions of the Slovak Republic.

Higher wages prevail in the urban and industrial areas, but some inhabitants of less-developed rural areas live at the subsistence level. Unemployment is also a greater problem outside the major cities, though unemployment rates remain high throughout the country.

Slovakia derives the bulk of its revenue from corporate and personal income taxes and value-added tax (VAT). Taxes were simplified in 2005, when a flat rate was introduced for corporations, VAT, and individuals.

TRANSPORTATION AND TELECOMMUNICATIONS

Slovakia has a modernized but relatively low-density transport system. The most important element is the railways, which are especially significant in freight transport—notably of coal, ores, metals, and building materials. The basic network, which was taken over from the Hungarian state, followed a north-south pattern to connect with Budapest. Today, rail lines link Bratislava and the regional capitals, but the system is somewhat inefficient. Many of the lines follow river valleys through mountainous areas. During the communist era, rail links with the Soviet Union were improved by an extensive program of double-tracking and electrification. With assistance from the European Investment Bank, Slovakia further upgraded its rail system in the early 21st century. The work included increased track electrification as well as track modifications to allow high-speed train travel.

Development of the highway network proceeded at a slower pace than that of the railway system. A superhighway begun in 1938 but completed only in 1980 links Bratislava with Brno and Prague in the Czech Republic. After independence, increased freight transport and automobile traffic resulted in significant congestion in some areas. Slovakia constructed additional highways in the late 20th and early 21st centuries.

The Danube River, forming the western third of the border with Hungary, dominates Slovakia's water transport. Komárno and Bratislava are the country's principal ports. The Komárno road bridge between Hungary and Slovakia, destroyed in World War II, was rebuilt in the early 21st century, with Slovakia and Hungary sharing the construction costs. Slovakia's interior rivers are not navigable.

There are airports at Bratislava, Košice, Žilina, Poprad-Tatry, Sliač, and Piešt'any. Although the Bratislava and Košice airports are ranked as international, the smaller airports also can accommodate international traffic. Still, most international travelers to Bratislava arrive at and depart from Vienna's airport, some 40 miles (60 km) west of Slovakia's capital.

Slovakia expanded and modernized its telecommunications system in the early 21st century. Cellular telephones became increasingly popular, and cellular service is now widely available. The rates of personal computer ownership and Internet usage are comparable with those of nearby eastern European countries.

CHAPTER 22

SLOVAK GOVERNMENT AND SOCIETY

The Slovak National Council adopted a new constitution for the republic on September 1, 1992, four months before the partition of the federation. In general philosophy, this document—like its Czech counterpart—reflects the Charter of Fundamental Rights and Freedoms passed by the former Czechoslovak Federal Assembly in 1991. The constitution provides for a unicameral legislature (the National Council), consisting of deputies chosen by direct general election. The head of state, the president, is elected for a five-year term. The 1992 constitution specified that the president was to be elected by a three-fifths majority of the National Council; however, in 1999 the government approved a constitutional amendment that changed the procedure so that subsequent presidents would be directly elected. The supreme executive body of the republic is the government formed by the prime minister, whom the president appoints. The prime minister is usually the leader of the majority party or coalition in the National Council.

LOCAL GOVERNMENT

The constitution addresses the issue of local administration only cursorily, defining the single unit of municipality as a territorial and administrative entity exercising jurisdiction over its permanent residents. Actually, Slovakia is composed of eight administrative regions (including Greater Bratislava), with each region divided into a number of districts.

Political map of Slovakia. Encyclopædia Britannica, Inc.

In March 1996 the Mečiar government implemented a new scheme of local governments that resulted in a redrawing of the political borders of many southern districts, with borders running from north (where the population is solidly Slovak) to south. The ultimate aim of this reconfiguration was transparent: to reduce the number of ethnic Hungarians elected to the municipal and district councils. However, the reconfiguration of 15 existing southern districts and the creation of 37 new ones did not substantially change the ethnic balance in the southern councils, as was shown in subsequent elections. Mečiar's other attempt to introduce ethnic quotas in municipal elections procedures in 1998 was turned down by the Constitutional Court.

JUSTICE

The apex of the Slovak judicial system is the Supreme Court, to which district and regional courts are subordinated. The Constitutional Court, comprising a panel of judges appointed by the president, occupies a special position, as it deals with matters arising from the constitution and the application of international treaties. The lower courts of justice resolve civil and criminal matters and assess the legality of administrative rulings. Slovakia's civil law code is based on Austro-Hungarian codes, as amended after 1918 and 1945, but has been revised to eliminate language dating from the communist era and to comply with requirements set by the Organization for Security and Co-operation in Europe.

POLITICAL PROCESS

All Slovaks gain the right to vote at age 18. Because delegates to the National Council are elected through a system of proportional representation, many political parties combine in the legislature. Major parties include the populist Smer ("Direction"), the Slovak Democratic and Christian Union, the Slovak National Party, the Party of the Hungarian Coalition, the Movement for a Democratic Slovakia, and the Christian Democratic Movement.

SECURITY

In 1991, with the withdrawal of Soviet troops and the dissolution of the Warsaw Pact, federated Czechoslovakia assumed control of its own military affairs. This responsibility, in turn, devolved to Slovakia and the Czech Republic on January 1, 1993. The apportionment of formerly federal military property between the two new republics was a major hurdle in the partition process, as was the creation of separate armed forces.

Slovakia's armed forces comprise an army and an air force. The country also has separate civil defense troops and internal security forces. The right to conscientious objection is enshrined in the 1992 constitution; however, this right does not apply to those who are already serving in the military. In 2004 conscription was reduced from one year to six months of service; in 2006 it was phased out. The transformation from conscript army to professional army was undertaken to comply with the standards of the North Atlantic Treaty Organization (NATO), which Slovakia joined in 2004.

Since the late 1990s, Slovakia has participated in many NATO and United Nations peacekeeping forces. Slovakia also supported the 2003 U.S.-led invasion of Iraq with a small contingent.

National and local police forces enforce the law. As in the Czech Republic, democratization and liberalization precipitated an increase in crime, which overburdened the existing police forces for a time. Since independence, Slovak police also have had to contend with international criminal gangs.

HEALTH AND WELFARE

The 1992 constitution retains the federal guarantees of free health care under a public insurance program. The health care system remains largely under state control, though private facilities and private medical insurance have been introduced. Factory and community clinics, first aid stations, and other outpatient facilities supplement the national system of hospitals. In addition, spas such as those at Piešt'any and Bardejov and sanatoria in the High Tatras long have been a feature of Slovak health care.

An act introduced in 2003 required employers to contribute a percentage of their payroll and the self-employed to contribute a portion of their earnings toward social insurance. Old-age pensions are paid to both men and women.

Most employed Slovaks enjoy an adequate standard of living. However, members of the Roma minority frequently have a much lower standard of living than the general population, owing to high unemployment and instances of discrimination.

HOUSING

A housing shortage continues to be one of the most severe problems affecting the country. In addition, many of the urban high-rise housing estates dating from the 1970s are badly in need of repair. In the cities and towns, almost all housing units are supplied with electricity, water, and bathrooms. Housing in some rural areas is considerably inferior.

EDUCATION

The Slovak constitution guarantees free public education at the primary and secondary levels for all citizens. There are also a number of private and church-affiliated schools. Kindergartens are available for children ages 3 to 6. Education is compulsory between the ages of 6 and 15 and usually includes instruction in a major foreign language. General secondary schools offer preparation for university study. Vocational secondary schools provide training in technical and clerical fields and the service industries.

Slovakia has a number of institutions of higher education, of which the largest and oldest is Comenius University in Bratislava (founded 1919). Also in

JOHN COMENIUS

The educational reformer and religious leader John Comenius (born Jan Ámos Komenský, March 28, 1592, Nivnice, Moravia [now in Czech Republic]—died November 15, 1670, Amsterdam, the Netherlands) is remembered mainly for his innovations in methods of teaching, especially languages. He believed that teachers should understand how a child's mind develops and learns, and he advocated full-time schooling for all the youth of the nation and maintained that they should be taught both their native culture and the culture of Europe.

His parents were members of a Protestant group called the Bohemian Brethren. They died when he was 10 years old, and after four unhappy years spent living with his aunt in Stránice, he was sent to a secondary school at Prerov. Though the teaching methods there were poor, he was befriended by a headmaster who recognized his gifts and encouraged him to train for the ministry. He studied at Heidelberg University in Germany and became a clergyman.

A great part of his adult life was disrupted by the Thirty Years' War from 1618 to 1648. He and some fellow Brethren fled their homeland in 1628 and settled in Leszno, Poland. There he wrote his first books calling for the reform of the educational system: *The Great Didactic*, *The School of Infancy*, and *Janua Linguarum Reserata* (1632; *The Gate of Tongues Unlocked*). These earned him a reputation in other countries, and he was invited first to England, then Sweden and Hungary to reform school systems. While the changes he made in the school systems were short-lived, his approach to learning was lasting. Back in Leszno in about 1654, he wrote a picture textbook, *Orbis Sensualium Pictus* (1658; *The Visible World in Pictures*), that remained in use for two centuries. War in Poland caused him to flee to Amsterdam, where he remained until his death.

Portrait of John Comenius on a Czechoslovak banknote of the 1980's. Georgios Kollidas

Bratislava are the Slovak University of Technology, the University of Economics, and several arts academies. Košice also has universities and a school of veterinary medicine. Since independence, additional colleges and universities have opened in Trnava, Banská Bystrica, Nitra, Prešov, Zvolen, and Trenčín. There is a Roman Catholic university in Ruomberok.

The significant Hungarian minority in Slovakia has been provided with primary, secondary, and vocational schools. The training of Hungarian schoolteachers in Slovakia is secured through special classes at the Bratislava and Nitra universities. For the first time, a Hungarian-language university opened in 2004 in Komárno.

CHAPTER 23

SLOVAK CULTURAL LIFE

The antecedents of a distinct Slovak culture date from the Christian mission sent to Moravia in 863 CE by the Byzantine emperor Michael III at the request of the Moravian prince Rostislav; the Moravian state then encompassed at least part of the territory of present-day Slovakia. Byzantine influence was short-lived, however, and did not survive the competition with Latinized western Christianity. Slavic liturgy disappeared from the region after the invasions by nomadic Magyar (Hungarian) tribes toward the end of the 9th century. These Magyar invasions also succeeded in separating the West Slavic ancestors of today's Slovaks, living north of the Danube River, from the South Slavs. Thereafter, until the founding of Czechoslovakia in 1918, the history of the Slovaks was closely connected with that of Hungary.

Slovak culture, particularly the Slovak language, survived despite Hungarian hegemony and the widespread use of Czech, Latin, and German. In the 15th century, Hussites from Bohemia brought the Czech language and culture to Slovakia, and Slovak Lutherans used Czech as both their liturgical and literary language, but they remained a distinct minority. Roman Catholicism continued as the majority religion, and Latin was used not only for liturgical purposes but also as the main administrative language until almost the mid-19th century, when it was replaced by Hungarian. German was widely used by the aristocracy and the urban middle class, owing to the influence of the Habsburg monarchy. The first Slovak intellectuals to be concerned with the preservation of the Slovak language and culture emerged during the Enlightenment and the French revolutionary wars. Although primarily educated in Hungarian, the Slovak intelligentsia—whether priests, lawyers, or doctors—communicated with Slovak peasants and servants in their language and helped to accelerate the spread of modern Slovak literacy. Hungarian nationalists reacted by enforcing Magyarization at every level of education beyond primary school; contemporary experts predicted the extinction of the Slovak nation within a generation. Nevertheless, the number of Slovaks attending secondary schools and colleges in Hungary continued to increase, and selective censorship could not stop the spread of Slovak newspapers and books. With the creation of Slovakia within the new country of Czechoslovakia, the durability of the Slovak language and culture was confirmed. Shortly after Slovakia's independence, Slovak became enshrined as the country's official language.

DAILY LIFE AND SOCIAL CUSTOMS

The rich folklore and customs of many Slovak regions have survived into modern times. They are on full display in the Catholic parishes, especially during the two main Christian holidays. A genuine Roman Catholic Christmas in Slovakia includes the three days of Christmas (December 24–26) and is carried over to Three Kings' Day (January 6). Traditional Christmas carols are typically a part of the festivities. In some regions Easter,

particularly Good Friday, is the biggest religious holiday of the year. Apart from religious celebrations, numerous folk music festivals take place in Slovakia. These may feature both Slovak and Roma performers.

Slovak food and drink have been influenced by the surrounding, mostly Hungarian and German, cuisine. Traditional Slovak food consists of a wide range of soups, gruels, boiled and stewed vegetables, roasted and smoked meats, and dairy products, especially sheep's milk cheese (*bryndza*). *Bryndzové halušky*, small potato dumplings mixed with *bryndza*, is a Slovak specialty. Viticulture was brought to Slovakia by the ancient Romans as they advanced along the Danube 2,000 years ago, and vineyards still are found along the Danube and Váh rivers. In addition to wine, brandy is a popular drink in Slovakia. Typical Slovak brandies include the plum-based *slivovica* and the juniper-based *borovička*.

THE ARTS

Historically, the arts in Slovakia were generally closely bound up with those of its regional neighbours, and artistic expression was strongly influenced by the prevalence of other languages and traditions. However, beginning in about the mid-19th century, toward the end of the period of Hungarian dominance, the perception of a Slovak national identity came to the fore. More-distinctly Slovak works of art, using the national language and Slovak cultural traditions, began to be created.

LITERATURE AND DRAMA

Although Slovak dialects had been distinct from Czech since the Middle Ages, a Slovak literary language did not develop until the late 18th century. The Catholic priest Ján Hollý (1785–1849) was the first Slovak writer to use the Slovak language successfully in his poetry. The language had been recently codified by another priest, Anton Bernolák, who had based his codification on the Western Slovak dialect. Yet Bernolák's Slovak failed to catch on, owing to a lack of followers and strong opposition by educated Slovak Lutherans, who used Czech as their literary language. Even Ján Kollár's *Slávy dcera* (1824; "The Daughter of Sláva"), considered a principal work of Slovak literature and among the impulses behind Pan-Slavism, was written in Czech. It was up to a younger group of Slovak Lutheran writers, headed by Ľudovít Štúr, to abandon Czech in favour of Slovak. This time the codification was based on the Central Slovak dialect. Later poets, using a refined form of literary Slovak, continued to produce nationalistic and Romantic works, such as *Marína* (1846), by Andrej Sládkovič (Andrej Braxatoris), and the ballads of Janko Kráľ, whose exploits in the Revolutions of 1848 made him a legend.

In the first half of the 20th century, poetry, particularly lyric poetry, continued to be the chief strength of Slovak literature. Notable poets included Hviezdoslav (Pavol Országh), Svetozár Hurban Vajanský, Ivan Krasko (Ján Botto), Martin Rázus, Janko Jesenský, and Emil Boleslav Lukáč. However, important Slovak novelists—such as Timrava (Božena Slančíková), Milo Urban, and Margita Figuli—also emerged.

With the foundation of Czechoslovakia and the further expansion of Slovak education, Slovak writings multiplied. The difficulties of World War II and its aftermath of communist rule found vivid, personal expression in the work of Ladislav Mňačko, Alfonz Bednár, and Dominik Tatarka. Mňačko was among the first eastern European writers to criticize Stalinism, in his popular novel *The Taste of Power* (1967), while Tatarka attacked the Gustav Husák regime's process of "normalization" in Czechoslovakia after 1969 in *Sám proti noci* (1984; "Alone Against the Night"). In the years leading up to the Velvet Revolution of 1989, such novelists as Ladislav Ballek, Vincent Šikula, and Ján Johanides asserted a distinct Slovak voice. During the late 20th and early 21st centuries, a new generation of writers—including Dušan Mitana, Pavel Vilikovský, Dušan Dušek, Michal Hvorecký, and Martin Šimečka—distinguished themselves.

Slovak drama developed at about the same time as Slovak literature; Juraj Palkovič's play *Dva buchy a tri šuchy* (1800; "Two Bumps and Three Rubs") is considered the first example. Ján Chalupka produced a lively satire, *Kocúrkovo*, in 1830, while Ján

HVIEZDOSLAV

One of the most powerful and versatile of Slovak poets was Hviezdoslav (the pseudonym of Pavol Országh, born February 2, 1849, Vyšný Kubín, Slovakia, Austrian Empire [now in Dolny Kubin, Slovakia]—died November 8, 1921, Dolny Kubin, Czechoslovakia). Hviezdoslav was a lawyer until he became able to devote himself to literature. He originally wrote in Hungarian and was a Hungarian patriot, but in the 1860s he switched both activities to Slovak. By the time of his death the Slovaks possessed an extensive poetic literature of a high order.

Hviezdoslav's contribution to this development was of decisive importance. In his main epics—*Hájnikova žena* (1886; "The Gamekeeper's Wife") and *Ežo Vlkolinský* (1890)—he treated local themes in a style that combined realistic descriptive power with lyric echoes from folk song. In his voluminous lyric output he experimented with a variety of metrical forms and forged a characteristic style, interwoven with neologisms and dialect elements. Most memorable are his moving *Krvavé sonety* (1919; "Blood-Red Sonnets"), which embody his attitude toward World War I. He also translated much Hungarian, Russian, German, and English literature into Slovak.

Sculpture of Hviezdoslav in Kiskőrös, Hung. Csanády

Palárik wrote popular comedies, including *Inkognito* (1857; "Incognito") and *Zmierenie* (1862; "The Reconciliation"). The best-known Slovak playwright of the 20th century was Peter Karvaš, author of *The Diplomats*, *The Midnight Mass*, and *Antigone and the Others*, among many other plays.

MUSIC

Music occupies an important place in Slovak cultural life. Its development has been traced to Roman times, and it was nurtured by the Roman Catholic Church and by the Magyar nobility. In addition, a strong folk tradition developed; this became an object of scholarly interest in the first half of the 19th century, when a separate national musical tradition began to emerge under the influence of such composers as Frico Kafenda. Modern Slovak music has drawn from both classical and folk traditions, particularly with such 20th-century composers as Ján Cikker, Gejza Dusík, Eugen Suchoň, Andrej Očenáš, and Alexander Moyzes. Slovak opera singer Lucia Popp performed internationally during the 1970s and 1980s. Bratislava and Košice have symphony orchestras and opera ensembles.

PAINTING

Slovak painters typically have looked outside the country for inspiration, particularly to Prague. At the end of the 19th century, however, Slovakia was "discovered" by Mikoláš Aleš from Bohemia and Jóža Úprka from Moravia. At the same time, a national school of Slovak painters emerged with Peter Michal Bohúň and Jozef Boetech Klemens. After 1918 a number of Slovak painters studying in Prague developed the "descriptive realism" school. In the 1950s and '60s a younger generation of painters began to leave this school behind and follow other European trends. Among the early 20th-century painters, Dominik Skutecký, Lajos Csordák, Július Jakoby, Martin Benka, Mikuláš Galanda, Ľudovít Fulla, and Cyprián Majerník became prominent. By the end of the 20th century the following painters made their imprint: Daniel Brunovský, Stano Bubán, Laco Teren, and Ivan Csudai.

MOTION PICTURES

The Slovak motion picture industry emerged in the 1920s. Notable from this period is the silent film *Jánošík* (1921), based on the life and legend of the so-named Slovak folk hero. Of the films produced after World War II, perhaps the best known internationally is *The Shop on Main Street* (1965), directed by Ján Kadár and Elmar Klos. It received an Academy Award (for best foreign-language film), the first ever awarded to a Czechoslovakian production. Among internationally recognized Slovak film directors is Juraj Jakubisko, who first gained acclaim during the late 1960s as part of the Czech New Wave. His strongly visual, metaphorical films include *It's Better to Be Healthy and Wealthy Than Poor and Ill* (1993) and *An Ambiguous Report About the End of the World* (1997). Other Slovak directors who have received international attention include Martin Sulik and Dušan Hanák, best known for their documentary *Paper Heads* (1995). Film continued to be a respected art form in Slovakia in the early 21st century, as evidenced by the country's film festivals and the work of the Slovak Film Institute. Slovak animation also gained in importance.

CULTURAL INSTITUTIONS

The Slovak National Library is in the city of Martin, which is also the seat of the foremost Slovak cultural society, the Matica Slovenská (founded 1863). The

JÁN KADÁR

The motion-picture director Ján Kadár (born April 1, 1918, Budapest, Hungary—died June 1, 1979, Los Angeles, California, U.S.) was important in the "New Wave" of Czechoslovak cinema of the early 1960s. Kadár attended Charles University in Prague and the Film School in Bratislava, Czechoslovakia (1938). During World War II he was interned in a Nazi labour camp, after which he worked as a scriptwriter and assistant director, first at the Koliba Studios in Bratislava and from 1947 at the Barrandov Studios, Prague. While at Bratislava he made the outstanding documentary *Life Is Rising from the Ruins* (1945). In 1950 Kadár directed the comedy *Katka* (U.S. title, Katya), his first independent feature and a milestone in the postwar Czechoslovak cinema. It was followed by a series of films codirected with Elmar Klos. They include *Únos* (1952; Kidnap); *Smrt si říká Engelchen* (1963; *Death Is Called Engelchen*), which won first prize at the Moscow Film Festival; *Obžlovaný* (1964; *The Accused*, or *The Defendant*); and *Obchod na korze* (1965; U.S. title, *The Shop on Main Street*; U.K. title, *The Shop on High Street*), the drama of an ordinary Czechoslovak citizen who is confronted with a personal moral decision regarding the Nazi persecution of the Jews. This film won the New York Film Critics Award and the Academy Award for best foreign-language film.

Kadár immigrated to the United States in 1968. His later films include *The Angel Levine* (1970), based on a story by Bernard Malamud; *Adrift* (1971); and *Lies My Father Told Me* (1975). In 1976 he was made dean of the American Film Institute's film school.

Slovak Centre of Scientific and Technical Information (formerly the Slovak Technical Library) and the University Library are in Bratislava. The last, founded in 1919, is the oldest and largest academic library in Slovakia. In addition, Slovakia has a large network of smaller public libraries and branch libraries.

Most major museums, including the Slovak National Museum (founded 1893) and the Slovak National Gallery (founded 1948) are located in Bratislava. The Museum of Jewish Culture, a part of the Slovak National Museum, opened in 1991. The Museum of Carpathian German Culture and the Museum of Hungarian Culture in Slovakia are both in Bratislava, while other regional ethnographic museums are located throughout the country—for example, the Museum of Ukrainian-Ruthenian Culture in Svidník. Other noteworthy museums include the Slovak Museum of Mining in Banská Štiavnica and the Slovak Agricultural Museum in Nitra. A unique museum of visual arts, the Warhol Family Museum of Modern Art, opened in Medzilaborce in 1991; its collection includes a number of works by Andy Warhol, whose parents were from the region.

The first professional theatre featuring performances in the Slovak language was the Slovak National Theatre in Bratislava, established in 1920. In addition

Danubiana Meulensteen Art Museum, near Bratislava, Slovakia. © Lisa Lubin - www.llworldtour.com

to plays, the theatre also mounts ballets and operas. A new theatre building was built in 2007, but productions also continued to be mounted at the original Neo-Renaissance theatre built in 1886. The state subsidizes a number of theatre companies, including professional companies focused on ethnic minorities. The Slovak Folk Artistic Ensemble and the dance ensemble Lúčnica perform programs of traditional Slovak music and dance; both have played a role in disseminating Slovak folk culture to other parts of the world. Slovakia's leading orchestra is the Slovak Philharmonic.

Slovakia boasts several UNESCO World Heritage sites, including Spiš Castle, one of the largest castle complexes in central Europe. Among the other sites are the wonderfully well-preserved village of Vlkolínec, the medieval town of Bardejov, the historic town centre of Levoča, and the traditional wooden churches in the Carpathian Mountains.

SPORTS AND RECREATION

Slovaks take full advantage of the mountainous terrain of their country; hiking, mountaineering, downhill skiing, and rock climbing are popular pursuits. Other outdoor recreational activities—such as fishing, white-water rafting, ice skating, cycling, spelunking, horseback riding, and bathing in thermal or mineral water—also attract large numbers of enthusiasts. Among spectator sports, football (soccer) and ice hockey draw the largest crowds. Slovak athletes participated in the Olympics as members of the Czechoslovak team until 1994, when the republic first competed as a separate country at the Winter Olympics in Lillehammer, Nor. Slovakia won its first Olympic medals in canoe events at the 1996 Olympic Games in Atlanta.

The republic has several national parks. Two of these, the Tatry (High Tatras) and the Pieniny national parks, are situated along the Polish border and are administered in cooperation with Polish authorities; the Low Tatras National Park is located in the interior. These areas feature glacial landscapes, alpine flora and fauna, and relict species from the Pleistocene Epoch (about 2,600,000 to 11,700 years ago). Smaller nature reserves also protect distinctive wilderness areas.

MEDIA AND PUBLISHING

Slovakia has a number of daily Slovak-language newspapers. *SME* and *Pravda*, the latter formerly the organ of the Communist Party but now independent, have large circulations. The state subsidizes a number of periodicals in such minority languages as Hungarian, Czech, Ukrainian, German, and Romany. The number of book publishers in Slovakia increased dramatically following the collapse of communism, but a substantial number did not survive their first book launchings.

The state-controlled monopolies on newspaper and book publishing were broken up with greater ease in Czechoslovakia after 1989 than was the monopoly in broadcasting. The division of Czechoslovakia, however, brought about the collapse of the federal broadcasting system, which ended on January 1, 1993. Both state-sponsored and commercial radio and television stations operate in Slovakia.

CHAPTER 24

CZECH AND SLOVAK HISTORY

The Czechoslovak region lay across the great ancient trade routes of Europe, and, by virtue of its position at the heart of the continent, it was a place where the most varied of traditions and influences encountered each other. The Czechs and the Slovaks traditionally shared many cultural and linguistic affinities, but they nonetheless developed distinct national identities. The emergence of separatist tendencies in the early 1990s, following the loosening of Soviet hegemony over eastern Europe, ultimately led to the breakup of the federation.

THE HISTORICAL REGIONS TO 1918

During the many centuries preceding the formation of the modern state of Czechoslovakia in the early 20th century, each of the major political and historical regions that had emerged in the area—Bohemia, Moravia, and Slovakia—had been subject to conquest; each underwent frequent shifts of population and periodic religious upheavals; and at times at least two of the three were governed by rival rulers. Bohemia and Moravia—the constituent regions of the Czech Republic—maintained close cultural and political ties and in fact were governed jointly during much of their history. Slovakia, however, which bordered on the Little Alfold (Little Hungarian Plain), was ruled by Hungary for almost 1,000 years and was known as Upper Hungary for much of the period before 1918. Thus, the division of Czechoslovakia at the end of 1992 was based on long-standing historical differences.

ORIGINS AND EARLY HISTORY

The part of Europe that constitutes the modern states of the Czech Republic and Slovakia was settled first by Celtic, then by Germanic, and finally by Slavic tribes over the course of several hundred years. The three regions of Bohemia, Moravia, and Slovakia coexisted, with a constantly changing degree of political interdependence, for more than a millennium before combining as Czechoslovakia in 1918.

BOHEMIA

The prehistoric people of Bohemia, north of the middle Danube River, were of uncertain origin. The Boii, a Celtic people, left distinct marks of a fairly long stay, but its time cannot be firmly established. (The name Bohemia is derived through Latin from Celtic origins.) The Celtic population was supplanted by Germanic tribes. One of them, the Marcomanni, inhabited Bohemia, while others settled in adjacent territories. No outstanding event marked the Marcomanni departure.

Archaeological discoveries and incidental references to Bohemia in written sources indicate that the movements of ethnic groups were not always abrupt and turbulent but that the new settlers began to enter the territory before the earlier inhabitants had left it. It can be assumed, therefore, that the Slavic people were coming in groups before the southward migration of the Germanic tribes. In the 6th century CE, Bohemia and the neighbouring territories were inhabited by the Slavs.

While mountains and forests offered protection to Bohemia, the tribes in the lowlands north of the Danube and along its tributaries were hard-pressed by the Avars of the Hungarian plains. Attempts to unite the Slavic tribes against the Avars were successful only when directed by such personalities as the Frankish merchant Samo, who gained control of a large territory in which at least part of Bohemia was included. His death in 658 ended the loosely knit state. A more auspicious era dawned after the Frankish king Charlemagne defeated the Avars in the 8th century.

There followed a period of comparative security, in which the concentration of the Slavs into political organizations advanced more promisingly. Soon after 800 three areas emerged as potential centres: the lowlands along the Nitra River, the territory on both sides of the lower Morava (German: March) River, and central Bohemia, inhabited by the Czech tribe. In time the Czechs, protected from foreign intruders, rose to a dominant position. Governed by rulers claiming descent from the legendary plowman Přemysl and his consort Libuše, the Czechs brought much of Bohemia under their control before 800 but failed to defeat the tribes in the east and northeast. Apart from occasional disturbances, such as Charlemagne's invasions (805), the Czech domain was not exposed to war and devastation, and little of the life

AVARS

The Avars were a people of undetermined origin and language, who, playing an important role in eastern Europe (6th–9th century), built an empire in the area between the Adriatic and the Baltic Sea and between the Elbe and Dnieper rivers (6th–8th century). Inhabiting an area in the Caucasus region in 558, they intervened in Germanic tribal wars, allied with the Lombards to overthrow the Gepidae (allies of Byzantium), and between 550 and 575 established themselves in the Hungarian plain between the Danube and Tisza rivers. This area became the centre of their empire, which reached its peak at the end of the 6th century.

The Avars engaged in wars against Byzantium, almost occupying Constantinople in 626, and against the Merovingians; they also were partly responsible for the southward migration of the Serbs and the Croats. In the second half of the 7th century, internal discord resulted in the expulsion of about 9,000 dissidents from the Avar empire. The state, further weakened by a revolt precipitated by the creation of the Bulgarian state in the Balkans (680), survived until 805 when it submitted to Charlemagne.

there came to the notice of clerics who were recording contemporary events in central Europe.

MORAVIA

The earliest known inhabitants of Moravia, situated to the east of Bohemia, were the Boii and the Cotini, another Celtic tribe. These were succeeded about 15–10 BCE by the Germanic Quadi. The Germanic peoples were pushed back from the middle Danube by the coming of the Avars in 567 CE. The exact date of the arrival of the Slavs in Moravia, as in Bohemia, is uncertain; but by the late 8th century Moravia was settled by the Slavs, who acknowledged no particular tribe but took the general name of Moravians from the Morava River. An important trade route from the Baltic to the Adriatic Sea developed through the Morava River basin.

When Charlemagne destroyed the Avar empire about 796, he rewarded the Moravians for their help by giving them a part of it, which they held as a fief from him. They thus became loosely tributary to him for all their lands. By contrast, Bohemia's princes, who enjoyed independence, often made war on Charlemagne and on his successors, Louis I (the Pious) and Louis II (the German). By the first half of the 9th century, Moravia had become a united kingdom under Prince Mojmír I (ruled c. 818–c. 846).

About 833 Mojmír attached the Nitra region (the western part of modern Slovakia) to his domain. His successor (after 846), Rostislav, consolidated the country and defended it successfully. His relations with the East Frankish empire

Statue commemorating the clerics Cyril and Methodius, brothers who preached in Moravia's native Slavic tongue. The first Slavic alphabet, Cyrillic, is named for Cyril, who is credited with its creation.
zprecech/Shutterstock.com

(since 843 under Louis the German) were determined by political considerations and by the advance of Christianity into the Slavic areas. The bishoprics of Regensburg, Passau, and Salzburg, all in East Frankish lands (the first two now in Germany and the third now in Austria), competed in trying to convert the central European Slavs but achieved only limited success. The archbishop of Salzburg consecrated a church at Nitra about 828, and in 845 Regensburg baptized 14 chieftains from Bohemia, while Mojmír's Moravia apparently had fairly frequent contacts with Passau. Missionaries in Moravia made noticeable progress before 860; stone churches were built as places of Christian worship at Mikulčice and elsewhere.

But Rostislav was dissatisfied with the Latin-speaking Frankish clergy and asked the Byzantine emperor Michael III for Slavic-speaking preachers. A group of clerics headed by two brothers of Macedonian origin, Cyril and Methodius, arrived from Constantinople (now Istanbul) in 863. They not only preached in a Slavic language, Old Church Slavonic, but also translated portions of the Christian scriptures into that language and used them in divine services. To Cyril is attributed the creation of the first Slavic alphabet; its final form, Cyrillic, is named for him. After some two and a half years, the two brothers journeyed to Rome to ask for papal support for their work and their use of Slavic. Cyril died there in 869, but Methodius received the pope's sanction for his work

in Moravia as well as farther south in Pannonia. The two territories were organized as a province and connected with the ancient archbishopric of Sirmium, restored by the pope. Methodius's elevation to archbishop angered the Frankish clergy, who regarded his archdiocese as their missionary field. He was captured and imprisoned. In 873 the pope ordered Methodius's release, but he banned the Slavic liturgy. Methodius then returned to Moravia and put himself under the protection of Rostislav's successor, Svatopluk. Clerics of the Latin rite continued to interfere with the archbishop's work until 880, when, in a compromise struck with Rome, Methodius obtained from Pope John VIII a formal sanction of his work, including the Slavic liturgy.

Svatopluk distinguished himself in the conduct of political affairs. After the death of Louis the German (876), he acquired large territories with Slavic populations. The kingdom that he created, known as Great Moravia, included all of Bohemia, the southern part of modern Poland, and the western part of modern Hungary. He annexed some territories and left local princes who recognized his suzerainty in others. The latter arrangement was apparently the case of the Czech prince Bořivoj I.

Propagation of Christianity followed Svatopluk's advances. According to legends, Bořivoj was baptized by Methodius and then admitted clerics of the Slavic rite to his principality. While Methodius was engaged in missionary work in the annexed territories, however, advocates of the Latin rite, headed by a Frankish cleric, Wiching, bishop of Nitra (in Slovakia), strengthened their position in Moravia. During Methodius's lifetime the Slavic clergy had the upper hand; after his death in 884, though, Wiching banned Methodius's disciples from Moravia, and most of them moved to Bulgaria. Furthermore, Pope Stephen V reversed his predecessor's policy and forbade the Slavic liturgy. Notwithstanding the collapse of the Byzantine mission to Greater Moravia, the Slavic liturgy, with its Cyrillic script, spread not only to Bulgaria but also to Ukraine, to Russia, and back to the Balkans.

Svatopluk continued his policy of expansion for several more years, but soon after 890 he made the East Frankish (German) king Arnulf his enemy. Arnulf's expedition into Moravia in 892 opened a period of troubles, which increased when Arnulf made an alliance with the Magyars of Hungary. Svatopluk's successor, Mojmír II, tried unsuccessfully to protect his patrimony; in 906 Great Moravia ceased to exist as an independent country.

SLOVAKIA

Slovakia was inhabited in the first centuries CE by Illyrian, Celtic, and then Germanic tribes. The Slovaks—Slavs closely akin to, but possibly distinct from, the Czechs—probably entered it from Silesia in the 6th or 7th century. For a time they were subject to the Avars, but in the 9th century the area between the Morava River and the central highlands formed part of Great Moravia, when the Slovak population accepted Christianity from Cyril and Methodius. In the 890s, however, the German king Arnulf called in the Magyars to help him against Moravia. As Slovakia lay in their path, they overran it. The Moravian state was destroyed in the first decade of the 10th century, and, after a period of disorder in the 11th century, Slovakia found itself incorporated as one of the lands of the Hungarian crown.

The main ethnic frontier between Magyars and Slovaks ran along the line where the foothills of the Western Carpathians merge into the lowland plains. Nevertheless, the landlord class of Slovakia was Magyar, and much of the urban population was German. (German settlers—tradesmen, craftsmen, and miners—largely founded the towns in Slovakia.) On the other hand, as the country suffered from chronic overpopulation, a constant stream of Slovak peasants moved down into the plains, where they usually were Magyarized in two or three generations.

THE PŘEMYSLID RULERS OF BOHEMIA (895–1306)

In 895 the prince of Bohemia made an accord with Arnulf, the German king who had attacked Moravia, and thereby warded off the danger of invasion. The domain over which the house of Přemysl ruled from Prague was in the early 10th century the largest political unit in Bohemia. Hostile tribal chieftains controlled the eastern and northeastern districts, but the extent of their power is not known. The most powerful of them, the Slavníks residing at Libice, remained defiant until the end of the 10th century.

At first Bohemia maintained close relations with neighbouring Bavaria. Both countries were threatened for several decades by the Magyars and by the rise in Germany of the Saxon dynasty, which began with Henry I (the Fowler) in 918 and reached its climax with the imperial coronation of Otto I in Rome in 962. (This coronation marked the restitution of the Holy Roman Empire, with which Bohemia was linked thereafter for many centuries.)

Bohemia's orientation toward the Saxon dynasty began in the 920s under Wenceslas I (Czech: Václav), the grandson of the Czech prince Bořivoj. It was symbolized by the dedication of a stone church at the Prague castle to a Saxon saint, Vitus. Both Slavic and Latin legends praise Wenceslas and his grandmother St. Ludmila as fervent Christian believers but tell little about his political activities. After Wenceslas was murdered in 929 or 935—according to legend, by his younger brother and successor, Boleslav I—the prince became regarded as the patron saint of Bohemia. The legends present the murder as an outburst against Wenceslas's devotion to the new

WENCESLAS I

The patron saint of the Czech Republic and, formerly, Czechoslovakia was Wenceslas I (Czech: Svatý Václav; born c. 907, Stochov, near Prague—died September 28, 929, Stará Boleslav, Bohemia; feast day September 28), a prince of Bohemia and a martyr. Wencelas was raised a Christian by his grandmother St. Ludmila, but his ambitious mother, Drahomíra (Dragomir), a pagan, had her murdered and acted as regent herself, until Wenceslas came of age in 924 or 925. Her court intrigues and the wishes of the people to end the conflicts between Christian and non-Christian factions in Bohemia led Wenceslas to take the reins of government. As duke he was pious, reportedly taking the vow of virginity, and encouraged the work of German missionary priests in the Christianization of Bohemia. His zeal in spreading Christianity, however, antagonized his non-Christian opponents.

Faced with German invasions in 929, Wenceslas submitted to the German king Henry I the Fowler. His submission provoked some of the nobles to conspire against him, and they prompted his younger brother, Boleslav (Boleslaus), to murder him. Waylaid by Boleslav en route to mass, Wenceslas was killed at the church door. Frightened by the reports of miracles occurring at Wenceslas's tomb, Boleslav had his remains transferred in 932 to the Church of St. Vitus, Prague, which became a great pilgrimage site during the medieval period. Wenceslas was regarded as Bohemia's patron saint almost immediately after his assassination. His virtues are sung in the Christmas carol (19th century) "Good King Wenceslas."

faith, but the conspiracy probably had a strong political motivation—namely, the payment of annual tribute to the king of Germany.

Boleslav I attempted, unsuccessfully, to loosen the ties Wenceslas had made with the Saxon dynasty. Like his brother, however, he reigned as a Christian prince; his daughter married Prince Mieszko I of Poland and helped to spread Christianity in that country. His son and successor, Boleslav II, used his friendly relations with the pope and the emperor to enhance his prestige. He attached new territories east of Bohemia to his father's annexations. In 973 a bishopric for the entire principality was founded in Prague. Bohemia was thus taken off the Bavarian metropolitan jurisdiction and subordinated to the geographically distant archbishop of Mainz. The first bishop of Prague, Thietmar, was from the Saxon land but knew the Slavic language. He was succeeded in 982 by Adalbert (Vojtěch), a member of the Slavník family, the second most powerful princely clan in the land. In 995 Boleslav II moved against the Slavníks and slaughtered the whole clan. Adalbert survived because he had gone abroad to spread Christianity. (In Hungary he baptized the country's future patron saint, King Stephen I, but in 997, on the shores of the Baltic Sea, he was killed by heathens.)

Struggles among the descendants of Boleslav II plagued Bohemia for the first three decades of the 11th century and considerably reduced its power. Most of the territories that had been attached to the country in the 10th century were lost. Bohemia's fortunes improved when Prince Břetislav I, a grandson of Boleslav II, led a successful expedition into Moravia; he conquered only a minor portion of the former Great Moravia, but it was large enough to constitute a province, and it was linked from then on with Bohemia.

The ambitions of Břetislav, who was enthroned in 1034, ran higher, and he invaded Poland in 1039—with only temporary success. Incurring the indignation of the German king Henry III, he was forced to evacuate the conquered territory and to make an oath of fealty (1041). In the latter part of his reign, Břetislav cooperated with Henry III (who was crowned Holy Roman emperor in 1046), thus protecting his domain against armed intervention. Břetislav's submission marked the end of Bohemian attempts to break out from the hegemony of Germany and the Holy Roman Empire.

The entire territory of Bohemia and Moravia was regarded as a patrimony of the house of Přemysl, and no emperor attempted to put a foreign prince of his own choice on the throne. But the ruling family grew large, and after Břetislav's death (1055) it became entangled in competition for primacy. For about 150 years the course of public life in Bohemia was largely determined by dissensions among the adult princes, some of whom ruled in portions of Moravia under Prague's suzerainty. The emperor and the feudal lords exploited the conflicts to promote their selfish interests. A key problem was the absence of any strict law of succession; the principle of seniority usually clashed with the reigning prince's desire to secure the throne for his oldest son.

The territory's minor obligations toward the emperors were a handicap under weak princes or when the male members of the ruling family were at odds, but a strong prince could turn friendly relations with the empire to his advantage. Břetislav's second son, Vratislav II (ruled 1061–92), as a compensation for services rendered, obtained from Emperor Henry IV the title of king of Bohemia (1085). Another ruler, Vladislav I, became the "supreme cupbearer" to the emperor (1114), one of the highest court offices, which entitled him to participate as one of seven electors in choosing the head of the Holy Roman Empire. Vladislav II (ruled 1140–73) participated in the campaigns of Emperor Frederick I (Barbarossa) in Italy. He was named king and crowned by the emperor at Milan in 1158.

Active participation in imperial policies and military campaigns reduced markedly the Czechs' isolation, caused by Bohemia's geographic position. Other contacts were made with foreign merchants and with clerics who came from abroad or who were traveling from Bohemia to Rome and to famous shrines. By the early 11th century the Latin rite prevailed. Cosmas of Prague, who recorded in his chronicle the history of Bohemia to 1125, was an ardent supporter of the Latin liturgy. Western orientation of the hierarchy and of the monastic orders

was documented by the prevalence of Romanesque architecture, of which notable examples could be found in Prague and in the residences of the ruling family. In social stratification and in economy, the country reached such a degree of consolidation that it withstood, without serious damage, the political struggles that ravaged it in the late 12th century.

Frederick I helped to foment the discord among Přemysl's descendants during this era. In 1182 he reduced the dependence of Moravia on the Prague princes and subordinated that province to his imperial authority. In 1187 he exempted the Prague bishop, a member of the Přemysl family, from the jurisdiction of the ruling prince and made the bishopric an imperial fief. These decisions had no lasting significance, however, and the Přemysl patrimony survived. The period of trials closed with Frederick's death (1190).

Subsequently, frequent changes on the imperial throne lessened the danger of intervention. During the same period the Přemysl family was reduced to one branch, so the problem of succession lost its pressing importance. In 1198 the Bohemian duke Přemysl Otakar I received the title of king of Bohemia for himself and his descendants from one of the competitors for the imperial crown. A solemn confirmation occurred in 1212, when Frederick II (crowned emperor in 1220) issued a charter known as the Golden Bull of Sicily, which regulated the relationship between Bohemia and the empire. The Bohemian king's obligations were reduced to a minimum, but, as elector, he ranked first among the four secular members of the college of electors.

Under Otakar I and his successors, Bohemia moved from depression to political prominence and economic prosperity. The clergy gained independence from secular lords in 1221. The landowning class, made up of wealthy barons and less-propertied squires, claimed freedom in administering its domains and a more active role in public affairs. In the early 13th century the population of Bohemia and Moravia increased noticeably through immigration from overpopulated areas in Germany.

Many of the German-speaking newcomers, especially miners, were encouraged by the king to establish new boroughs, endowed with royal privileges under the more advanced German city laws of the period. The newly founded royal town of Kutná Hora (German: Kuttenberg), for example, soon grew into the second city of Bohemia, and its royal mint supplied the kingdom's treasury with silver coins. Bohemia's urban settlers, called burghers, enjoyed valuable privileges, especially the use of German city law. Considered free citizens, the burghers paid taxes to the king but handled their own affairs in matters of criminal and property law as well as defense. In the future they would form the nucleus of the third estate (one of the three traditional political orders; the barons and the lesser nobility constituted the first two, respectively). In addition to the townsfolk, German farmers settled in the border districts of the kingdom. German immigration continued under Otakar I's successor, Wenceslas I (ruled 1230–53), and reached its peak under Otakar II (ruled 1253–78). Bishop Bruno of Olomouc, in cooperation with the latter king, promoted the colonization of large tracts of land in northern Moravia. (A similar pattern of colonization occurred in the Slovak lands, where mining towns such as Banská Štiavnica and Kremnica prospered.)

Otakar II, whom Dante described in his *Divine Comedy* as one of the great Christian rulers, was a strong and capable king who obtained possession of Austrian lands through marriage, and in 1260 he was invited by the nobility of Steiermark (Styria) to become their overlord. Personal bravery and financial resources facilitated his penetration into other Alpine provinces. Before his opponents could combine forces to check his advance, Otakar had exercised influence in Kärnten (Carinthia) as well as in some territories along the Adriatic coast. By then, Otakar, known throughout Europe as the "king of iron and gold," aspired to the imperial crown as well.

Otakar's expansion aroused the hostility of the kings of Hungary, but even more dangerous was Count Rudolf of Habsburg, who, following his election as King Rudolf I of Germany in 1273, claimed the Austrian lands as vacant fiefs of the empire. War ensued and ended in Otakar's defeat in 1276. Otakar was unwilling to accept the loss of Austria as final and began a new campaign. Not only Rudolf's army but also Hungarian troops moved against the Czech forces, and a group of noblemen, most of them from southern Bohemia, sided with the enemy. Otakar was too weak to resist the unexpected coalition against him, and, on August 26, 1278, at Dürnkrut, Austria, he lost both the battle and his life. (In the same period Hungary underwent its own disintegration, and strong feudal warlords ruled over its different parts. Most of Slovakia was then controlled by the mighty Matúš Čak, lord of Trenčín.)

Otakar's only son, Wenceslas II (ruled 1278–1305), was too young to take control immediately. During the period following Otakar's death (remembered as the "evil years"), Wenceslas was a mere puppet in the hands of ambitious lords, but in 1290 he emancipated himself from the tutelage and ruled with more success than had his father. The country was slowly recovering from both political and economic depression, and it again played an active role in international relations. Instead of resorting to wars, Wenceslas engaged in negotiations and soon achieved success in Upper Silesia. This was a prelude to his penetration into Poland, which culminated in 1300 with his coronation as its king. Diplomatic dexterity and enormous wealth quickly enhanced Wenceslas's prestige. In 1301 he was considered a candidate for the vacant throne of Hungary, but instead he recommended his son Wenceslas, who ruled Hungary until 1304. Wenceslas II's acquisitions, however, were lost soon after his death; his son, as King Wenceslas III,

took over Bohemia but was assassinated on his way to Poland (1306). Thus ended the long rule of the Přemyslid dynasty by the male line.

THE LATE MIDDLE AGES (1306–1526)

After a four-year struggle for the throne, in 1310 the Bohemian magnates decided for John of Luxembourg, son of Henry VII, the Holy Roman emperor from 1312. John, who married Elizabeth (Eliška), the second daughter of Wenceslas II, was only 14 when he was named king.

THE LUXEMBOURG DYNASTY

John of Luxembourg confirmed the freedoms that the Bohemian and Moravian nobles had usurped during the interregnum and pledged not to appoint aliens to high offices. Nevertheless, a group of advisers, headed by Archbishop Petr of Aspelt, tried to uphold the royal authority. In the resulting conflict, a powerful aristocratic faction scored a decisive victory in 1318. Its leader, Jindřich of Lípa, virtually ruled over Bohemia until his death in 1329. Meanwhile, John found satisfaction in tournaments and military expeditions. He succeeded in attaching to Bohemia some adjacent territories; the extension of suzerainty over the Silesian principalities was his most significant achievement. He was assisted late in his reign by his oldest son, Wenceslas, who was brought up at the French royal court, where he changed his name to Charles. In 1346 both John, then blind, and Charles joined the French in an expedition against the English, during which John fell at the Battle of Crécy.

John and Charles benefited from friendly relations with the popes at Avignon. In 1344 Pope Clement VI elevated the see of Prague and made Arnošt of Pardubice its first archbishop.

The pope also promoted the election of Charles as German king (1346). In Bohemia, Charles ruled by hereditary right. To raise the prestige of the monarchy, he cooperated with the nobility and the hierarchy. He made Bohemia the cornerstone of his power and, by a series of charters (1348), settled relations between

GOLDEN BULL OF EMPEROR CHARLES IV

In 1356 the emperor Charles IV promulgated a constitution for the Holy Roman Empire known as the Golden Bull. It was intended to eliminate papal interference in German political affairs and to recognize the importance of the princes, especially the electors, of the empire. Its name, like that of other "golden bulls," derived from its authentication with a golden seal (Latin *bulla*).

Returning to Germany in July 1355 after his coronation as emperor in Rome, Charles IV summoned the princes to deliberations at Nürnberg, which resulted in the promulgation of the first 23 chapters of the Golden Bull on January 10, 1356; the concluding 8 chapters were added after further negotiation with the princes in Metz on December 25, 1356. The purpose was to place the election of the German ruler firmly in the hands of the seven electors and to ensure that the candidate elected by the majority should succeed without dispute. That the electoral college consisted of three ecclesiastical and four lay princes had been established since 1273, but it was not always clear who these seven were. Therefore, the Saxon vote was now attached to the Wittenberg (not the Lauenburg) branch of the Saxon dynasty; the vote was given to the count Palatine (not to the duke of Bavaria); and the special position of Bohemia, of which Charles himself was king, was expressly recognized. In addition Charles established succession by primogeniture, attached the electoral vote to the possession of certain lands, and decreed that these territories should never be divided. The candidate elected by the majority was regarded as unanimously elected and entitled to exercise his royal rights immediately. Thus the pope's claim to examine rival candidates and to approve the election was ignored. Also, by instituting the duke of Saxony and the count Palatine as regents during the vacancy, the Golden Bull excluded the pope's claim to act as vicar.

These results were achieved only by concessions to the electoral princes, who were given sovereign rights, including tallage and coinage, in their principalities. Appeals by their subjects were severely curtailed; conspiracies against them incurred the penalties of treason. Moreover, the efforts of cities to ensure autonomous development were repressed, with serious and long-lasting consequences for the future of the German middle classes. In theory, these privileges were confined to the seven electors; in practice, all the princes quickly adopted them.

Bohemia, Moravia, and other portions of his patrimony. He acquired several territories in the vicinity at opportune times by purchase or other peaceful means. At the end of his reign, four incorporated provinces existed in union with Bohemia: Moravia, Silesia, and Upper and Lower Lusatia. Charles also confirmed earlier documents defining the position of Bohemia in relation to the empire. In 1355 he was crowned emperor in Rome as Charles IV. After consultation with the electors, Charles issued the Golden Bull, which remedied some of the political problems of the empire, especially the election of the emperor.

Under Charles, Prague became the headquarters of the imperial administration. He doubled the size of the city by attaching a new borough, Nové město (New Town), which increased the population to about 30,000. In 1348 he founded in Prague the first university in the empire. It consisted of four traditional faculties (theology, law, medicine, and liberal arts), and its members were grouped into four nations (Bohemian, Bavarian, Saxon, and Silesian Polish). Prague attracted scholars, architects, sculptors, and painters from France and Italy and from German lands; the most distinguished among them was the architect Petr Parléř, a native of Swabia. The flourishing of the late Gothic architectural style left a deep mark on the city and its environs, as exemplified by the Charles Bridge, St. Vitus's Cathedral, and Karlštein Castle.

During this period Bohemia was spared entanglements in wars and reached a relative prosperity, shared by the upper classes and the peasantry. Charles was eager to save the power and possessions accumulated since 1346. He succeeded in getting his son Wenceslas crowned as king of the Romans (meaning, essentially, Holy Roman emperor-elect) in 1376. He also made provisions for dividing the Luxembourg patrimony, with the understanding that its male members would respect Wenceslas as their head. After Charles's death (1378), a smooth transition to Wenceslas's reign appeared to be assured. The country mourned Charles as "the father of the country."

Charles's heir ruled Bohemia, without opposition, as Wenceslas IV. Although not without talents, he lacked his father's tenacity and skill in arranging compromise, and in less than a decade the delicate balance between the throne, the nobility, and the church hierarchy was upset. In a conflict with the church, represented by Jan of Jenštein, archbishop of Prague, the king achieved temporary success; the archbishop resigned and died in Rome (1400). The nobility's dissatisfaction with Wenceslas's regime was serious; it developed mainly over the selection of candidates for high offices, which noble families regarded as their domain and to which Wenceslas preferred to appoint lower noblemen or even commoners. The struggle was complicated by the participation of other Luxembourg princes, especially Wenceslas's younger brother

Sigismund. The nobles twice captured the king and released him after promises of concessions. But Wenceslas never took his pledges seriously, and the conflict continued. Simultaneously with the troubles in Bohemia, discontent with Wenceslas was growing in Germany. In 1400 the opposition closed ranks; the German princes deposed Wenceslas as king of the Romans and elected Rupert of the Palatinate in his place.

Meanwhile, a religious reform movement had been growing since about 1360. It arose from various causes, one of which was the uneven distribution of the enormous wealth accumulated by the church in a comparatively short time. Moral corruption had infected a large percentage of the clergy and spread also among the laity. Prague, with its large number of clerics, suffered more corruption than the countryside. Both the king and the archbishop showed favour to zealous reformist preachers such as Conrad Waldhauser and Jan Milíč of Kroměříž, but exhortations from the pulpit failed to turn the tide. After 1378 the Great Schism in Western Christendom—the period when rival popes reigned in Avignon and in Rome—weakened the central authority. Disharmony between King Wenceslas and Archbishop Jan of Jenštein also hindered the application of effective remedies. By the late 14th century the reform movement was centred at Prague's Bethlehem Chapel, where preaching was done in Czech.

The second, more dramatic, period of the religious reform movement began with the appointment in 1402 of the Czech university scholar Jan Hus to the pulpit at Bethlehem Chapel. Hus combined preaching with academic activities, and he was able to reach the Czech-speaking masses as well as an international audience through his use of Latin. The university was split in its support of Hus; while Czech scholars tended to agree with his reformist agenda, foreign members followed the conservative line. Another cause of division was the popularity of the teachings of John Wycliffe, an English ecclesiastical reformer of the previous century, among the Czech masters and students. Hus did not follow Wycliffe slavishly but shared with him the conviction that the Western church had deviated from its original course and was in urgent need of reform. The atmosphere in Prague deteriorated rapidly as the German members of the university allied with Czech conservative prelates, led by Jan Železný ("the Iron"), bishop of Litomyšl. Because Wenceslas favoured the reform party, its opponents pinned hopes on the king's half brother Sigismund, then king of Hungary; Wenceslas was childless, and Sigismund had a fair chance of inheriting the Bohemian crown.

In the winter of 1408–09, a strong group of cardinals convened a general council at Pisa and elected a third pope (or antipope), Alexander (V), in the hope of ending the schism. Wenceslas sympathized with the cardinals and invited the university to join him. When the German university members did not respond favourably, he issued, in January 1409 at Kutná Hora (Kuttenberg), a decree reversing the university's traditional voting process, used to decide important issues. Thereafter, the three "foreign" nations of the university (Bavarian, Saxon, and Silesian) had one vote together, and the Bohemian nation had three. The German masters and students protested by moving to Leipzig, Germany, where they founded a new university. Some of them unleashed a polemical campaign attributing to Hus more influence on the king than he actually had and depicting Hus as the chief champion of Wycliffe's ideas.

During this time the antipope Alexander (V) issued a bull virtually outlawing Hus's sermons in Bethlehem Chapel and authorizing rigid measures against discussing Wycliffe's ideas. Hus and his collaborators continued their activities nevertheless. Neither Wenceslas nor any of the Czech prelates was experienced enough to achieve reconciliation between the church authorities and the reform party, and Bohemia was drawn into a sharp conflict. In 1412 Alexander's successor, the antipope John (XXIII), offered indulgences for contributions to the papal treasury. When Hus and his friends attacked the questionable practices of papal collectors in Prague, John put Prague under interdict. Hit by the sentence of excommunication, Hus left Prague and moved to the countryside under the protection of his noble friends.

In 1414 John, acting in harmony with Sigismund (who since 1411 had been the German king), called the Council of Constance (German: Konstanz). The aim of the council was mainly to abolish the threefold papal schism but also to examine the teachings of Hus and Wycliffe. Hus went there hoping to defend himself against accusations of heresy and disobedience. A safe conduct from Sigismund, however, did not protect him in Constance. Late in November he was imprisoned and was kept there even after John, who had lost control of the council, had fled and been condemned by the cardinals. In the spring of 1415, Hus was called three times before the council to hear charges, supported by depositions of the witnesses and by excerpts from his own writing. The council paid no attention to Hus's protests that many of the charges were exaggerated or false. Hus refused to sign a formula of abjuration; he was then condemned as a Wycliffite heretic and burned at the stake on July 6.

THE HUSSITE WARS

By killing Hus, the church authorities provided the Czech reformers with a martyr. From then on, the movement, hitherto known as Wycliffite, took the name Hussite, and it grew rapidly. The Hussites reacted emotionally against the Council of Constance, the German king Sigismund, and the conservative clergy. A letter of protest, signed by 452 members of the nobility, was dispatched to Constance in September 1415. The contemptuous reaction of the council, which indicted all the Bohemian signatories, increased the Hussites' discontent, as did the burning at the stake of another reformer, Hus's friend Jerome of Prague, in May 1416.

Hus had not developed a system of doctrine, nor had he designated his successor. The most faithful of his disciples, Jakoubek of Stříbro, was not strong enough to keep the movement under his control. Ideological differentiation set in and resulted in divisions and polemics. The moderate Utraquists (or Calixtins; respectively, from the Latin *utraque*, "each of two," and *calix*, "chalice"), named after the Hussite practice of serving laypersons the Eucharist under the forms of both bread and wine, were entrenched in Prague. The radicals came mostly from smaller boroughs and the countryside. The Germans in Bohemia and in the incorporated provinces remained faithful to the Roman Catholic Church, and, thus, the deep-seated ethnic antagonism was accentuated.

The death of the Bohemian king Wenceslas IV in 1419 hastened the political crisis. The Hussites were resolutely opposed to Sigismund's inheritance of the Bohemian throne, but the Czech Catholics and the Germans were willing to recognize him. Sigismund, determined to break the Hussite opposition, initiated a period of bitter struggles that lasted more than 10 years. He had the support of opponents of Hussitism within the kingdom, of many German princes, and of the papacy. Invasions of Bohemia assumed the character of crusades but were successfully repelled by the Hussites, who pulled together in times of danger.

In 1420 the radical Hussites—who by this time were centred at a fortified settlement called Tábor in southern Bohemia—reached agreement with the moderate Utraquists on the fundamental articles of their faith. The accord, which became known as the Four Articles of Prague, stressed that (1) the word of God should be preached freely, (2) Communion should be administered in both kinds (i.e., both bread and wine, rather than bread only) to laypersons as well as to clerics, (3) worldly possessions of the clergy should be abolished, and (4) public sins should be exposed and punished. However, a wide range of disagreements between the Utraquists in Prague and the radicals (known as Taborites) at Tábor was left open, often resulting in mutual accusations and embitterment. A third party of Hussites arose in northeastern Bohemia, around a newly founded centre at Oreb, but it had a much smaller following than those of Prague or Tábor.

Meetings were held at which attempts were made to give the country a national government; the most significant was an assembly at the city of Čáslav (June 1421). A regency council was set up, but it lacked sufficient authority, and the virtual master of the country was the leader of the "warriors of God," Jan Žižka. He was originally attached to Tábor, but he became disgusted with the endless disputes of its theologians and left the radical stronghold to organize a military brotherhood in northeastern Bohemia (1422); its members became so devoted to Žižka that after his death in 1424 they called themselves the Orphans.

Žižka strove tenaciously for two goals: the protection of Bohemia from Sigismund and the suppression of those whom he perceived as enemies of the law of God within Bohemia and Moravia. He scored brilliant victories in battles against Sigismund's forces but could not unite the country under his banner. A Roman Catholic minority, stronger in Moravia than in Bohemia, resisted the overtures of the Hussite theologians and Žižka's attacks. After Žižka's death, his heirs, headed by the preacher Prokop the Bald, lost interest in protracted warfare with Catholic lords at home and undertook instead highly successful foraging raids into the German territories bordering on Bohemia. In response, the Roman Catholic Church mounted altogether five abortive crusades against the Hussites. Whenever a crusade menaced Bohemia, however, the radical military brotherhoods joined the conservative forces to push back the invader. The last encounter at Domažlice in 1431 was bloodless; the crusaders reportedly fled in panic upon hearing the Hussites singing their chorals.

Meanwhile, a general council of the church opened in 1431 at Basel, Switzerland, and determined to find a peaceful settlement. At a conference at Cheb (German: Eger) in Bohemia the following year, delegates from Basel and the Hussite spokesmen resolved that in controversial matters "the law of God, the practice of Christ, of the apostles and of the primitive church" would be used to determine which party held the truth.

The Hussite envoys reached Basel and opened debate on the cardinal points of their doctrine. It soon became clear, however, that the council was unwilling to abide by the Cheb agreement and that theologians representing the Tábor and Orphan brotherhoods would not acquiesce to a lean compromise. The Utraquists ultimately joined forces with the Catholics to defeat the radical Hussites in a fratricidal battle at Lipany in May 1434.

Under the leadership of Jan Rokycana, the future archbishop of the Hussite church, the Hussites' dealings with the Council of Basel advanced markedly after the battle. The final agreement came to be known as the Compacts (Compactata) of Basel. The agreement followed the Four Articles of Prague but weakened them with subtle clauses (e.g., the council granted the Czechs the Communion in both kinds but under vaguely defined conditions). After the promulgation of the compacts in 1436, an agreement followed with Sigismund, now accepted as the legitimate king of Bohemia. But he died in 1437, and Bohemia was neither united in religion nor consolidated politically.

Various forces hindered religious pacification. The Catholic clergy refused to respect the Compacts of Basel because they were not sanctioned by the pope; the Catholics would not accept Rokycana as archbishop of the Hussite church either. The radical parties, although gravely weakened at Lipany, also stood in uncompromising opposition to Rokycana. His bid for recognition was defied as well by the Utraquist wing, which had seized key positions during Sigismund's brief reign.

THE HUSSITE PREPONDERANCE

Sigismund had no son, and the problem of succession to the Bohemian throne caused a split among the nobility, which had been enriched during the Hussite wars by the secularization of church properties and which had grown accustomed to the absence of monarchy. The conservatives accepted Sigismund's son-in-law Albert II of the Austrian house of Habsburg, but the more resolute Hussites favoured a Polish candidate. Albert's death in 1439 ushered in another interregnum. In January 1440 an assembly was held to set up provincial administration for Bohemia; its composition demonstrated clearly the steady rise in the importance of the wealthy barons, who functioned as the first estate. The lesser nobility, large in number, was considered the second estate. The upper classes recognized the royal boroughs as the third estate but were reluctant to share power with them. In the January assembly the political alignments were not identical with religious divisions; nonetheless, the first estate included a powerful Catholic faction, and the second estate was predominantly Hussite. The assembly did not elect a governor of Bohemia. Instead, in the counties into which Bohemia was subdivided, leagues were organized to promote the cooperation of local lords, knights, and royal boroughs, irrespective of religious orientation.

The problem of succession became urgent when Albert's widow, Elizabeth, gave birth to a boy called Ladislas Posthumus (the future Ladislas V). Several foreign princes challenged this Habsburg claim, but in 1443 the estates recognized Ladislas as the legitimate heir to the throne of Bohemia. As he resided at the court of his guardian, the German king and future Holy Roman emperor Frederick III, the interregnum was extended. The barons voted George of Poděbrady as their leader, but for several years the destiny of Bohemia was determined by the efforts of Oldřich of Rožmberk, the most powerful Bohemian magnate, and his allies, who undermined George's plans.

Apart from political and economic consolidation, George strove for a papal sanction of the Compacts of Basel and for the confirmation of the Hussite leader Rokycana as archbishop. In 1448 George decided to act. He seized Prague and appointed Rokycana head of the Utraquist consistory. Although Frederick III was, like Rožmberk, a Roman Catholic, he realized that an alliance with the Hussite George would strengthen Ladislas's chances of succession. In 1451 Frederick designated George governor of Bohemia. From that position of strength, George moved energetically against both the Rožmberk coterie and the remnants of the radicals, entrenched at Tábor.

In October 1453 the teenage Ladislas, German-speaking and brought up as a Roman Catholic, was crowned king of Bohemia in St. Vitus's Cathedral. George served as his chief adviser. (Analogous arrangements existed in Hungary, where the minor Ladislas also was king, but the authority lay in the hands of his guardian, the general János Hunyadi.) Above all, George hoped the king could reestablish Bohemia's connection with the crown provinces, especially the populous and rich Silesia, that had deteriorated during the Hussite wars. But in 1457 Ladislas suddenly died. Although several foreign princes competed for the throne, the estates of Bohemia reaffirmed the elective principle and decided unanimously for George, who became king in 1458.

Although attached to the Utraquist party, for George the Hussite revolution was finished. He endeavoured to rule as a king of "two peoples": the Utraquists and the Catholics; the Czechs and the Germans. As he was eager to be crowned according to the rites prescribed by Emperor Charles IV, in the presence of two foreign bishops he obliged himself to defend the true faith and to lead his people from errors, sects, and heresies. Because the Compacts of Basel were not mentioned, George did not hesitate to make his pledge; since the agreement with the Council of Basel, the Utraquists considered the Communion in both kinds as a lawful concession and not a heresy. Both the election and coronation took place in Prague, and so George's principal

concern was to have his title recognized by the estates of the incorporated provinces. He was mostly successful, but he had to accept the friendly help of papal envoys to obtain in 1459 a provisional recognition by the Catholic and predominantly German city of Breslau (modern Wrocław, Pol.) in Silesia.

During the next three years, thanks to his superior diplomatic skills, George enhanced his prestige both at home and abroad. Feeling that no lasting peace could be achieved without the speedy settlement of religious issues, George attempted in 1462 to have the Compacts of Basel sanctioned by Pope Pius II. Instead of approving the compacts, however, the pope declared them null and void. When informed of the pope's action, George affirmed his devotion to the Hussite practice of Communion in both kinds. Although neither the pope nor the king showed any intention of retreating, armed conflict did not take place, and several princes, including Frederick III, were willing to use their influence to arrange a compromise.

But a new pope, Paul II, elected in 1464, soon adopted an aggressive policy that encouraged George's foes, especially the city of Breslau. A group of Catholic noblemen from Bohemia, headed by Zdeněk of Šternberk, formed a hostile league at Zelená Hora (1465) and entered into negotiations with Breslau and other Catholic centres. Shortly before Christmas 1466, the pope excommunicated George and released his Catholic subjects from their oath of allegiance. In the spring of 1467 George's troops attacked the rebel forces. George was, on the whole, successful in desultory campaigns against the insurgents' strongholds, but his position became more awkward in the spring of 1468, when Matthias I of Hungary, his son-in-law and rival, brought support to the Czech rebels. Matthias claimed that he needed the resources of the imperial and Bohemian crowns in order to launch a great crusade against the Turks. The Hungarians invaded Moravia, and, by tying down a considerable portion of the Bohemian army, they facilitated rebel successes in other parts of the kingdom. In May 1469 the opposition, controlling all provinces except Bohemia, proclaimed Matthias king of Bohemia. In 1470 George achieved some successes over his rivals, but he was unable to consolidate them because of deteriorating health. He died in March 1471, mourned by both the Utraquists and loyal Catholics.

THE JAGIELLONIAN KINGS

After the death of King George, the Holy Roman emperor Frederick III and the Polish king Casimir IV of the Jagiellon dynasty observed benevolent neutrality toward Bohemia. But George's rival, the Hungarian king Matthias I, continued to claim the Bohemian throne and to control the provinces of Moravia, Silesia, and Upper and Lower Lusatia. In May 1471 Casimir's son Vladislas II was elected king of Bohemia. Though he had been

raised as a Catholic, he was supported by George's adherents, irrespective of their religious affiliation, while George's foes adhered to Matthias. Vladislas's forces were not strong enough to defeat Matthias; an agreement concluded in 1478 enabled Vladislas to strengthen his position in Bohemia but left Matthias in temporary possession of the remaining crown provinces. After Matthias's death in 1490, however, Vladislas was elected king of Hungary (as Ulászló II) and thus finally reunited the provinces with Bohemia. Vladislas's successor was his only son, Louis II, who became king of Hungary and Bohemia upon his father's death in 1516.

The reigns of Vladislas and Louis brought Bohemia and Hungary under the rule of the Jagiellon dynasty, which had ruled Lithuania and Poland since the late 14th century. Despite the successful consolidation of the four realms under one dynasty, this period was marked by the decline of royal authority in Bohemia. After 1490 Vladislas spent more time in Hungary than in Bohemia, as did Louis. Meanwhile, the Catholic lords attached themselves to the Bohemian court and exercised strong influence on the kingdom's public affairs. An exemplarily weak monarch, Vladislas was nicknamed Dobzse (meaning "very well," or "all right") after his habit of signing with that word every document laid before him.

Vladislas made no secret of his dislike of the Utraquist rites, but, by his coronation oath, he obligated himself to respect the basic Hussite tenets outlined in the

Compacts of Basel. As the king stood aloof, the Catholic and Utraquist factions of the Bohemian estates concluded an agreement at Kutná Hora (March 1485) that reaffirmed the compacts, recognized the existing religious divisions in Bohemia, and forbade attempts by either party to extend its sphere of influence at the expense of the other. The accord lasted until 1516 but was renewed in 1512 as "of perpetual duration." The Hussite group known as the Unitas Fratrum (Unity of the Czech Brethren) was not granted legal protection, however. In 1508 Vladislas sanctioned the persecution of the group, but his decree was not applied too rigidly.

Provincial assemblies, or diets, rather than the royal court held primacy under the Jagiellonian kings, especially when they resided at Buda (modern Budapest). Each of the kingdom's provinces—Moravia, Silesia, Upper and Lower Lusatia, and Bohemia itself—had a diet. (The Bohemian diet often carried decisions for the entire kingdom.) The lords dominated the diets and were supported by the lesser nobility when attempting to limit royal power or when introducing restrictive measures against the lower classes. Both the mighty barons and the less propertied knights viewed with displeasure the political aspirations of the royal boroughs. The diets passed several resolutions to remove the third estate from the positions acquired during the Hussite revolution. Because the boroughs obtained little help from the sovereign, the nobility encountered little resistance.

A land ordinance adopted in 1500 limited considerably the participation of the boroughs in the diets. The boroughs also were hit by several decrees, approved by the diets (notably in 1487 and 1497), by which landowners attached peasants to their lands, thus further reducing the peasants' ability to migrate to towns.

Nevertheless, the royal boroughs, prosperous and self-confident, resisted the limitations and sought allies wherever they could find them. They obtained some concessions under Vladislas, but in 1517 they had to surrender some of the earlier privileges on which their economic prosperity was based. The higher estates tacitly recognized the right of the royal boroughs to participate in the diets as the third estate but reserved for themselves the positions on the board of provincial officers, including that of the vice chamberlain, who, in the king's name, supervised municipal administration. Although the boroughs gained some reasonable satisfaction, the landowning nobility was permitted to engage in the production of articles that were previously the monopoly of the royal boroughs.

The agreement of 1517 did not end feuds and conflicts among the aristocratic factions and their supporters in the lower classes. In 1522 Louis II left for Prague, intending to strengthen the royal authority. With the help of loyal lords, he relieved Zdeněk Lev of Rožmitál of the office of supreme burgrave in February 1523 and appointed Prince Karel of Minstrberk, a grandson of George of Poděbrady, to that key position in provincial administration. Religious controversies that flared up soon after Martin Luther's attack on indulgences (October 1517) increased tensions in Bohemia. Rožmitál, posing as a staunch supporter of the old faith, ingratiated himself with the king and regained his office. Meanwhile, Louis, fully occupied with Hungarian affairs, was preparing for a campaign against the Turks. Meeting the Ottoman army at the Battle of Mohács with inadequate forces, Louis was defeated and drowned in the marshes while fleeing from the battlefield (August 1526).

HABSBURG RULE

Ferdinand I of Habsburg, the husband of Louis's sister Anne, presented his claims to the vacant thrones of Bohemia and Hungary. He made substantial concessions to the Bohemian magnates and was elected king in October 1526; the coronation took place in February 1527. Ferdinand also ruled in other countries, and beginning in 1531 he assisted his brother, the emperor Charles V, in the affairs of the Holy Roman Empire. After Charles's resignation (1558) Ferdinand himself was elected emperor. He considered Bohemia his most precious possession.

With the ascension of Ferdinand to the Hungarian throne, the Slovak lands, which had been ruled by Hungary since the 11th century, came under Habsburg rule. After the Hungarian defeat at the Battle of Mohács, the Ottoman Empire took over much of Hungary; the remainder of the Hungarian lands, including Slovakia, were known as Royal Hungary. Pozsony (now Bratislava, Slovakia) became the administrative capital of Royal Hungary, and Nagyszombat (Trnava, Slovakia), a centre of Roman Catholicism, became the see of the bishop of Esztergom.

RELIGIOUS TENSIONS IN BOHEMIA

As king of Bohemia, the Roman Catholic Ferdinand I was obliged by the coronation oath to observe the Compacts of Basel and to treat the Utraquists as equal to the Catholics. But since 1517, when Luther sparked the religious revolution that became known as the Reformation, Bohemia had been open to Protestant ideas emanating from Wittenberg (Germany) and other centres of Lutheranism. Lutheranism gained adherents among the Utraquists and among the German-speaking inhabitants of Bohemia and Moravia. As Lutheranism grew, the Unitas Fratrum also increased in numbers. Shielded by sympathetic landowners, some of whom became members, the Hussite group successfully resisted repeated attempts at its extermination.

As religious tensions persisted, Ferdinand endeavoured to dilute his precoronation pledges to the Bohemian magnates and to curtail the privileges of the estates. An opportunity to settle these problems arose during the Schmalkaldic War (1546–47), fought between the Habsburgs and the Schmalkaldic League, a defensive alliance formed by Protestant

SCHMALKALDIC LEAGUE

The Schmalkaldic League was a defensive alliance formed during the Reformation by Protestant territories of the Holy Roman Empire. Their object was to defend themselves collectively against any attempt to enforce the recess of the Diet of Augsburg in 1530, which gave the Protestant territories a deadline by which to return to Catholic practices. Established in February 1531 at Schmalkalden, Germany, the league was led by Landgrave Philip the Magnanimous of Hesse and John Frederick I of Saxony. Among its other original members were Brunswick, Anhalt, and the cities of Mansfeld, Magdeburg, Bremen, Strassburg, and Ulm. The league had a timeline of six years but was regularly extended.

Fearing that the league would ally itself with his enemy, Francis I of France, the emperor Charles V was forced to grant it de facto recognition until 1544, when he made peace with Francis. He then began military operations against the league in 1546—the Schmalkaldic War—and effectively defeated it in 1547.

territories of the Holy Roman Empire. The Bohemian estates wavered considerably in their loyalty to the empire, and so, after the Habsburg victory at Mühlberg (April 1547), Ferdinand quickly moved against them. The high nobility and the knights suffered comparatively mild losses, but the royal boroughs virtually lost their political power and were subordinated more rigidly to the crown. Another target of the king's wrath was the Unitas Fratrum, many of whose members were driven from Bohemia into Moravia and Poland. Significantly, Ferdinand's vindictive policies did not apply to Moravia, whose estates had been more cooperative during the Schmalkaldic War.

Ferdinand supported a scheme of religious reunion on the basis of the Compacts of Basel, but he soon realized that few Utraquists still adhered to that outdated document. The majority, called Neo-Utraquists by modern historians, professed Lutheran tenets as formulated by Luther's associate Philipp Melanchthon. Disheartened by the meagre results of his policy, Ferdinand threw his full support behind the Catholic party. In 1556 he introduced the newly founded and militant Society of Jesus (Jesuits) into Bohemia. Shortly before his death in 1564, Ferdinand obtained from Pope Pius IV a sanction of the Utraquist practice of Communion in both kinds, but the pope insisted on so many restrictions that his bull satisfied only the Utraquist extreme right.

Ferdinand's firstborn son, Maximilian II, became Holy Roman emperor in 1564. Though sympathetic to Protestantism, he was reluctant to grant free exercise of the Lutheran faith, which the majority of the Bohemian estates requested in 1571. After several years of futile efforts, the estates adopted a more flexible policy. Both the Czech Neo-Utraquists and the German-speaking Lutherans came together and prepared a summary of their faith, known as the Bohemian Confession, which agreed in the main points with the Lutheran Augsburg Confession. The members of the Unitas Fratrum cooperated with the adherents of the Bohemian Confession but preserved both their doctrine and their organization. In 1575 Maximilian approved the Bohemian Confession, but only orally; it was commonly assumed that his oldest son, Rudolf, who was present at the session, would respect his father's pledge.

THE COUNTER-REFORMATION AND PROTESTANT REBELLION

The early stage of Rudolf II's long reign as Holy Roman emperor (1576–1612) was simply an extension of Maximilian's regime. But in 1583 Rudolf transferred his court from Vienna to Prague, and the Bohemian capital became once more an imperial residence and a lively political and cultural centre. A passionate patron of the arts and sciences, Rudolf brought with him the alchemist Edward Kelly and the astronomers Johannes Kepler and Tycho Brahe. However, the emperor, brought up in Spain, had sympathy only for the Roman Catholic faith.

Because of its long antipapal tradition and its political prominence, Bohemia had an important place in the strategy of the Counter-Reformation, the Roman Catholic Church's effort to combat the rise of Protestantism. Because the crown possessions were too small to yield adequate income and because only the provincial diets had the power to approve increased taxation, Rudolf depended on the mostly Protestant Bohemian estates. But during his reign, the Catholic minority—stronger among the lords than among the lesser nobility and burghers—came under the influence of militant elements, trained in Jesuit schools, and listened attentively to the papal nuncios and Spanish ambassadors. The Catholics singled out the Unitas Fratrum as their first target. Although numerically weak, the Hussite group exercised a strong influence on Czech religious life and developed lively literary activities (e.g., during Rudolf's reign they produced a Czech translation of the Bible, which came to be known as the Kralice Bible). Thus, the Catholics sought to create a breach between the Unitas Fratrum and the Protestant majority, who adhered to the Bohemian Confession.

In 1602 Rudolf issued a rigid decree against the Unitas Fratrum that was enforced not only in the royal boroughs but also on the domains of fervent Catholic lords. The Unitas Fratrum and also the more resolute adherents of the Bohemian Confession realized that the days of peaceful coexistence with Catholics were gone. They closed ranks under the leadership of Lord Václav Budovec, a prominent member of the Unitas Fratrum. Meanwhile, dissatisfaction with Rudolf's regime was growing rapidly in other Habsburg domains as well. His younger brother, Matthias, made contacts with the Austrian and Hungarian opposition; the Moravian estates, headed by Karel the Elder of Žerotín, joined Matthias.

In 1608 Protestant rebel forces advanced to Bohemia. The Protestant estates there used Rudolf's weakness to force concessions. In July 1609 Rudolf reluctantly issued a charter of religious freedoms (the Letter of Majesty) that granted freedom of worship to both the Catholics and the party of the Bohemian Confession. Some passages of the charter were vague, and so the Protestant and Catholic estates concluded an agreement stipulating that future conflicts should be settled by negotiation. The Catholic radicals, too weak to upset the agreement, were unwilling to accept the charter as the final word in religious controversies.

In 1611 Rudolf was deposed, and Matthias was crowned king of Bohemia; he succeeded to the imperial throne the following year. Because he was childless, Matthias presented in 1617 to the diet of Bohemia his nephew Ferdinand of Steiermark (Styria) as his successor. The Protestant faction was caught unprepared and acquiesced in Ferdinand's candidacy; he was crowned king of Bohemia in St. Vitus's Cathedral. Opposition grew quickly to Ferdinand, who was suspected of cooperation with the irreconcilable opponents of the charter of religious freedoms.

In the spring of 1618 the Protestant estates decided on action. Two governors of Bohemia, William Slavata and Jaroslav Martinic, were accused of violating the charter. After an improvised trial, they were thrown from the windows of the Royal Chancellery at the Prague Castle (May 23, 1618) but escaped unharmed. This act of violence, usually referred to as the Defenestration of Prague, sparked a larger Protestant rebellion against the Habsburgs in Bohemia and opened the Thirty Years' War. The Bohemian estates established a new government steered by 30 directors, who assembled troops and gained allies in the predominantly Lutheran Silesia and in the Lusatias; the estates of Moravia, however, were reluctant to join at first.

The death of Matthias (March 1619) accelerated the rebellion. The directors of Bohemia refused to admit Ferdinand II as the legitimate Bohemian king. In Moravia the militant Protestant party overthrew the provincial government, elected its own directors, and made an accord with Bohemia. At a general assembly of representatives of all five provinces, a decision was made to form a federal system. Ferdinand II was deposed, and Frederick V, elector of the Rhine Palatinate and a son-in-law of James I, king of England and Scotland, was offered the crown. He accepted and early in November 1619 was crowned king according to an improvised Protestant rite.

Frederick's chances for success were slight; the population of Bohemia, especially the peasantry, was unenthusiastic in its support of the rebellion. Frederick received some financial help from the Netherlands, but German Protestant princes hesitated to become involved in a conflict with the Habsburgs, among whose allies were not only Catholic Bavaria but also Lutheran Saxony, whose ruler, the elector John George I, desired land in the Bohemian provinces.

In late summer 1620 Duke Maximilian I of Bavaria led the army of the Catholic League—a military alliance of the Catholic powers in Germany—into Bohemia. On November 8, 1620, in the short Battle of White Mountain at the gates of Prague, Catholic troops defeated the Protestant army. Frederick and his chief advisers fled the kingdom, and Ferdinand II retook possession of Bohemia.

In imposing penalties, the victorious Ferdinand treated Bohemia more harshly than he did other provinces. In June 1621, 27 of the rebellion's leaders (3 lords, 7 knights, and 17 burghers) were executed. Landowners who had participated in any manner in the rebellion had much of their property confiscated. The upper estates and the royal boroughs were ruined; they ceased to function as centres of economic and cultural activities. Ferdinand rescinded Rudolf's charter of religious freedoms and began a program of vigorous re-Catholicization of Bohemia and Moravia. The Jesuits, banned in 1618 by the Bohemian directors, returned triumphantly and acted as the vanguard in the systematic drive against the non-Catholics, including the moderate Utraquists.

RE-CATHOLICIZATION AND ABSOLUTIST RULE

In 1627 Ferdinand II promulgated the Renewed Land Ordinance, a collection of basic laws for Bohemia that remained valid, with some modifications, until 1848; he issued a similar document for Moravia in 1628. The Habsburg Ferdinand settled, in favour of his dynasty, issues that had disturbed Bohemian public life since 1526: the Bohemian crown (and consequently the much desired seat of one of the electors of the Holy Roman emperor) was declared hereditary in the Habsburg family; no election or even formal acceptance by the estates was required for the succession; the king had the right to appoint supreme administrators; in the provincial diets the higher clergy was constituted as the first estate, and all the royal boroughs were represented by one delegate only; the Bohemian diet lost legislative initiative and could meet only upon the king's authorization to approve his requests for taxes and other financial subsidies; the king could admit foreigners to permanent residence; and the use of the German language, in addition to the traditional Czech, was authorized. Roman Catholicism was the sole Christian faith permitted. (The only non-Catholics allowed to remain in Bohemia after 1627 were Jews, who nonetheless faced harsh discrimination. Although Jews were not numerous in the Bohemian lands, Prague was home to one of the largest Jewish communities in Europe.)

Royal decrees pertaining to religion granted Protestant lords, knights, and burghers the right to choose either conversion or emigration. Only about one-quarter of the noble families living in Bohemia and Moravia prior to 1620 remained; the majority emigrated to the Lusatias (both annexed by Saxony in 1635) and Silesia, which was the only Bohemian province allowed to retain the Lutheran confession after the Thirty Years' War. Many peasants also left the country, though illegally, especially during the rebellion itself. The Czechs' most significant representative abroad was the scholar John Amos Comenius (Jan Ámos Komenský). The emigrations devastated Bohemia and Moravia, which may have lost as much as one-half of their population.

Many of those remaining in the homeland were gradually converted to Roman Catholicism. The re-Catholicization required substantial educational and missionary efforts, and the Jesuits ultimately became the most conspicuous force in Czech cultural life. In 1654 their leading college, the Clementinum, was united with the remnants of Charles University. The Jesuits controlled not only higher education but also literary production.

Meanwhile, the Habsburgs filled the vacated places among the upper social classes with newcomers, who often were adventurers serving in the imperial army and most of whom obtained land as a compensation for services rendered to Ferdinand II and his successor, Ferdinand III (emperor from 1637 to 1657), during or after the Thirty Years' War. The remaining old families (e.g., the Lobkovic [Lobkowicz], Kinský, and Sternberg lines) and the newcomers (e.g., the Piccolomini, Colloredo, Buquoy, Clam-Gallas, Schwarzenberg, and Liechtenstein lines) had in common their attachment to the Roman Catholic Church and to the Habsburg dynasty; they intermarried and became amalgamated over the next several decades. The growth of the German-speaking nobility led German to become the language in which public affairs were transacted.

Language was not the only barrier separating the peasantry and lower middle class from the propertied noblemen and burghers. Both the victorious Catholic Church and the wealthy laymen regarded the Baroque style as the most faithful expression of their religious convictions and their worldly ambitions. For about 100 years, the Baroque dominated in architecture, sculpture, and painting and influenced literature, drama, and music. The external appearance of Prague and the smaller boroughs and towns changed markedly.

The emperor Leopold I (ruled 1658–1705) soon became involved in long and costly wars against the Turks and the French. Although Bohemia was not threatened by either of these enemies, its population had to share the financial burdens. The landed nobility was reluctant to accept financial obligation, so the major part of the contributions was expected to come from the burghers and the peasants. The urban communities, which had been impoverished during the Thirty Years' War, made no progress toward social and economic recovery. The lot of the peasantry was so heavy that uprisings occasionally took place, though with no chance of success. For the common people, the short reign of Emperor Joseph I (ruled 1705–11) brought some relief, but under his brother and successor, Charles VI (ruled 1711–40), their plight reached appalling dimensions. The court and the residences of the ranking aristocrats consumed vast sums of money, which had to be squeezed from the depopulated towns and poorly managed domains.

During this period, especially from the reign of Leopold I, the Habsburg emperors strove to increase their authority over the imperial lands, and their rule became more absolutist in nature and more administratively centralized. Nevertheless, the kingdom of Bohemia retained its very limited autonomy. The Habsburgs did not insist on incorporating the Bohemian lands into their other domains: although the two Lusatias were ceded to Saxony in 1635, Bohemia, Moravia, and Silesia (until 1742) retained their provincial administration. Members of the local nobility were appointed to high offices. The supreme

Depiction of a clash in 1762 at Teplitz, (now Teplice, Czech Republic) during the Seven Years' War in the reign of the Habsburg empress Maria Theresa. The war was costly; sections of Habsburg territories were lost to Prussia. Imagno/Hulton Fine Art Collection/Getty Images

chancellor of Bohemia served as a link between the kingdom and the emperor; he resided in Vienna to facilitate communication with the court and the various central agencies attached to it.

The accession of Charles VI's daughter Maria Theresa (ruled 1740–80) sparked the War of the Austrian Succession. Bavaria and Prussia invaded the Habsburg territories. Charles Albert, elector of Bavaria, occupied with French assistance a major part of Bohemia and was acclaimed Emperor Charles VII, but he could not establish himself permanently, and in 1742 he pulled his forces back. Three wars fought against Frederick II (the Great) of Prussia in 1741–63, mostly in Bohemia and Moravia, were more serious and costly. Finally, Maria Theresa acquiesced in the loss of the major part of Silesia. Small duchies that she was able to retain were constituted as a crown land of Silesia and remained closely connected with Moravia and Bohemia.

In 1749 Maria Theresa launched an ambitious program of administrative reforms; its principal point was a closer union of the Bohemian crown land with the Alpine provinces in order to create a fiscally more efficient unit. The queen's staunchest opponents were members of the landowning nobility who, up to that time, had controlled the provincial administration. In 1763 Maria Theresa made some concessions but would not abandon her centralist policy. Her hope was that the opposition would split. While the conservative faction remained unreconciled to the new course, more-flexible individuals accepted high positions in Vienna or in the provincial capitals and helped to build up the system, which the emperor Joseph II (coruler, 1765–80; sole ruler, 1780–90) inherited from his mother and subordinated more rigidly to the sovereign's will and discretion.

Joseph II adopted Maria Theresa's idea of curtailing the privileges of the upper social classes, so as not to conflict with the interest of the state, of which the ruler—the "enlightened despot"—was the supreme representative. The administrative reforms continued, and the judicial and fiscal systems were revamped to serve the monarch more adequately. The state extended its influence in such other fields as education, landowner-tenant relationships, the economic recovery of the royal boroughs, and a more adequate distribution of the burden of taxes. The reforms did not aim at a total abolition of social and economic distinctions, but they generally improved the lot of the lower middle class and of the peasantry. Two decrees of 1781 made Joseph popular among the commoners: he abolished restrictions on the personal freedom (serfdom) of the peasants, and he granted religious toleration. After the long period of oppression, these were hailed as beacons of light, although they did not go as far as enlightened minds expected. In fact, Joseph's Edict of Toleration was not followed by a mass defection from the Roman Catholic Church in Bohemia and Moravia, partly because it did not refer to either Utraquism or the Unitas Fratrum; rather, it authorized adherence to the Augsburg (Lutheran) or Gallican (Reformed) confessions.

Joseph's conservative successors, Leopold II (ruled 1790–92), Francis II (the last Holy Roman emperor and, as Francis I, the first emperor of Austria; ruled 1792–1835), and Ferdinand (I) of Austria (ruled 1835–48), left intact the centralistic system inherited from Maria Theresa and Joseph II, but they did engineer a gradual transition from the manorial system to the full ownership of land by the peasants.

In the late 18th and early 19th centuries the French Revolutionary and Napoleonic wars had embroiled most of Europe. Some of the military campaigns and peace negotiations between Austria and France took place on Czech and Slovak lands—for example, the Battle of Austerlitz (now Slavkov u Brna, Czech Republic) and the Treaty of Pressburg (now Bratislava, Slovakia). During this time, provincial loyalties remained stronger than ethnic nationalism. Nevertheless, Czech nationalism began to emerge in Bohemia about 1800, partly out of opposition to the centralistic tendencies of the Vienna court and partly under the impact of the ideals of the French Revolution. Institutions destined to play an important role in the Czech national renascence, such as the Royal Bohemian Society of Sciences and the National Museum (1818)—which used the German language at first but later admitted Czech to foster Bohemian

patriotism—drew support both from the propertied German population and from those Czechs who became more conscious of their origins and of their kinship with other Slavic peoples.

NATIONAL AWAKENING AND THE RISE OF CONSTITUTIONALISM

In 1848 the German speakers of Bohemia and Moravia (about one-third of the population) had a distinct advantage over the Czechs. Germans constituted nearly the entirety of the upper classes of the two provinces and prevailed in most towns. There were ostensibly no barriers to social advancement for Czechs of middle-class or peasant origin, but they needed to communicate in German. Imbued with ideas of national emancipation—taken from the French Revolution and the writings of German intellectuals—scholars, writers, clergymen, and schoolmasters of Czech origin began to stir a national consciousness among the common people. Not only the countryside but also the urban communities witnessed an awakening. Habsburg centralism, symbolized by the Austrian chancellor Prince von Metternich, tolerated no political activities but did not hinder cultural activities, such as the printing and distribution of nonpolitical books in Czech, theatrical performances, and social gatherings. The Czechs had their intellectual elite, small in number but devoted to the national cause, and they were shielded by a group of sympathetic aristocrats.

Similar conditions, though on a much reduced scale, existed in the Hungarian counties inhabited by the Slovaks, who lacked not only their own aristocracy but a middle class as well. Up to 1840 the Czech language, regenerated by such eminent linguists as Josef Dobrovský and Josef Jungmann, was used by both Czech and Slovak authors, especially Protestants. But the growing national awareness among the Slovak intellectual elite led to the development of a Slovak literary language for the sake of reaching more Slovaks, including those with no more than an elementary education. The work of Slovak intellectuals such as Ľudovít Štúr, a teacher at the Pressburg Lutheran Lyceum who further refined literary Slovak and published a Slovak newspaper (1845), collided sharply with the trend advocated by Hungarian nationalists, who aimed to replace Latin with Hungarian throughout the kingdom. Nonetheless, the Slovak literary language gradually replaced Czech among Slovak authors. Thus, the mounting wave of nationalism among Slovaks as well as Czechs created conditions for the eventual establishment of two closely related but distinct political units.

The Czechs soon looked to the historian František Palacký, who had written a history of the Czech nation, as their political leader. Palacký was assisted by the able journalist Karel Havlíček Borovský and by František Ladislav Rieger, a student of political science and economics. In opposing Metternich's oppressive regime, the Czechs sought alliance with German liberals. When the Revolutions of 1848 reached Bohemia in March of that year, Czech and German leaders collaborated in their attempt to bring down absolutism through constitutional reform.

Both parties had a vague notion that Bohemia should return to its autonomous status and become a constituent part of the regenerated Habsburg monarchy, but they could not resolve some specific problems of a common political future. The Germans saw advantages in cooperating with their kinsmen in other Habsburg lands and in Germany proper; after all, Austria was the leading power within the German Confederation, the loose political organization that had replaced the Holy Roman Empire. The Czech leaders, however, sensed danger in the German unification schemes debated in the German constituent assembly in Frankfurt and in plans for a modernized but highly centralized Austria. Their primary concern was the diet of Bohemia, and at times they included among their desiderata a general assembly of deputies from Bohemia, Moravia, and Silesia to stress a continuity of modern political efforts with the ancient kingdom. Thus, the Czechs pursued two contrasting aims that were not easy to reconcile: the liberal ideal of "natural rights," combined with the conservative aim of preserving the ancient legal prerogatives of the Bohemian crown.

A good deal of vacillation in and after 1848 was caused by the inability of Palacký and others to harmonize the emphasis on historical rights with genuine devotion to the modern principles of Czech nationalism and Slavic solidarity. In late spring 1848 the idea of a newly elected diet for Bohemia was obscured by a loftier project, an assembly of spokesmen of the Slavic peoples from all parts of the Habsburg empire. Yet no matter how sincerely Palacký and other prominent figures professed their loyalty to the ruling house, the first historical Slavic congress in Prague found only hostile reception among the Germans and Hungarians. In May 1848 the Slav delegates were finally dispersed by Austrian troops commanded by Alfred, prince zu Windischgrätz, who also cancelled elections for the provincial diet in response to an abortive uprising in Prague launched by students.

Consequently, the Czech leaders were forced to recognize that the constituent assembly meeting in July 1848 in Vienna was the only representative body before which they could express their aspirations. When the assembly reconvened at the Czech city of Kroměříž (German: Kremsier), they made themselves allies of all factions that attempted to prepare the ground for a constitutional and federal system. Rieger, in particular, rose to the occasion when defending the principle that all power comes from the people.

But the draft of a constitution for the Habsburg monarchy ran counter to ideas prevailing among the advisers of the new Austrian emperor, Francis Joseph (ruled 1848–1916). Early in March 1849 the Kroměříž assembly was dispersed. On December 31, 1851, Francis Joseph abolished the last vestiges of constitutionalism and began to rule as absolute master.

The absolutist regime, headed by the prime minister Alexander Bach, was rigid and tolerated no opposition (the popular Czech journalist Havlícek was arrested and deported, for example). Nevertheless, the regime abolished the robot (compulsory labour service by peasants), returned to the old provincial administration that benefited the smaller nationalities, and promoted the teaching of national languages in public schools, among other reforms. However, Austria's military defeat in 1859 by Sardinia, aided by France, revealed the weakness of the government. The defeat resulted in the loss of Lombardy, and the Bach government had to resign. In the October Diploma of 1860 and the February Patent of 1861, Francis Joseph declared the end of neoabsolutism and his readiness to adopt a constitution.

NATIONAL TURMOIL UNDER THE DUAL MONARCHY

The regime failed to implement a system acceptable to all the various nationalities, and the Austrian Empire remained in a state of crisis through 1866, when it went to war with Italy and Prussia. After a disastrous defeat by Prussia in the Battle of Königgrätz (now Hradec Králové, Czech

AUSGLEICH

The Ausgleich (German: "compromise"), also called the Compromise of 1867, was a compact, finally concluded on February 8, 1867, that regulated the relations between Austria and Hungary and established the Dual Monarchy of Austria-Hungary. The kingdom of Hungary had desired equal status with the Austrian Empire, which was weakened by its defeat in the Seven Weeks' War (Austro-Prussian War) of 1866. The Austrian emperor Francis Joseph gave Hungary full internal autonomy together with a responsible ministry, and in return Hungary agreed that the empire should still be a single great state for purposes of war and foreign affairs, thus maintaining its dynastic prestige abroad.

Republic), Francis Joseph sought a solution that would promise speedy recovery and the stabilization of internal affairs. In 1867 he negotiated a compromise (the Ausgleich) with the unrepentant Hungarians, and the Austrian monarchy was transformed into a dual monarchy— the empire of Austria-Hungary.

In Hungary the dominant Hungarians systematically suppressed Slovak ethnic identity. This was achieved primarily through a policy of Magyarization, which made the Hungarian language paramount in administration, education, and business. In the Austrian half of the empire, Germans remained the strongest single group, followed by Czechs, Poles, and other nationalities. The dual system passed through successive crises but survived and remained in existence until 1918.

Like other nationalities, the Czechs resumed political activities after the promulgation of the October Diploma of 1860. Palacký was recognized as a dominant figure, but the actual leadership passed into Rieger's hands. Palacký's ideal scenario was to reconcile the conflicting principles of Czech nationalism and historical continuity (the so-called Bohemian historical rights) in a forward-looking federal scheme. The more practical politician Rieger, who found support among some Bohemian aristocrats, decided to emphasize the historical rights while maintaining loyalty to the Habsburg monarchy. However, Rieger's progressive opponents exploited his alliance with the conservative aristocracy. Meanwhile, differentiation within the National Party (the main Czech political party) began in 1863 and continued more rapidly after 1867.

Irrespective of ideological orientation, the Czechs opposed the dual monarchy. After the promulgation of a new liberal constitution in December 1867, the Czech politicians led by Rieger set out to obtain privileges similar to those that the Hungarians now enjoyed. Following negotiations with Vienna in 1871, the Czechs agreed to a constitutional program called the Fundamental Articles, which proposed giving Bohemia a status equal to that of Hungary. The articles predictably encountered not only an angry Hungarian opposition but also heavy pressure from Austria's other provinces, and they were never implemented.

The Czechs did not abandon the idea of the restitution of the kingdom of Bohemia to its former rank, similar to that of Hungary, but its chances of realization declined with the consolidation of the dual monarchy. Moreover, Francis Joseph showed no intention of going to Prague to be crowned with the ancient crown of St. Wenceslas—one of the Czechs' historical demands. After 1871 the Czech political leadership was confronted with a dilemma: whether to boycott the Reichsrat (the imperial parliament in Vienna, to which Austria's provinces sent deputies) and the Bohemian diet or to join the government majority for concessions in education and economic life. Rieger decided to institute the boycott.

In 1874 the National Party split; the progressive wing (commonly called the Young Czechs), which was gaining popularity among the urban middle class and well-to-do peasants, advocated ending the parliamentary boycott. Meanwhile, Rieger found it increasingly difficult to defend his boycott policy as well as the alliance with the big landowners; they brought no tangible results and

obstructed the flow of progressive ideas. Once the Young Czech deputies insisted on the dissolution of the boycott, they were applauded by their supporters—including Tomáš Masaryk, the future first president of Czechoslovakia—to whom progress in education, emancipation from clerical influences, and improvement of living standards were more vital than the continued emphasis on unforfeited historical rights. The so-called Old Czechs lost ground in the 1880s and suffered a total defeat in the parliamentary election of 1891.

The most determined opponents of the Bohemians' schemes were the representatives of the German-speaking population of Bohemia and Moravia, later known as the Sudeten Germans. An 1879 alliance between Austria-Hungary and the recently founded German Empire increased their sense of belonging to one of Europe's dominant cultures, but they viewed with alarm Czech economic competition, particularly the migration of Czech workers into German-speaking districts, as well as other gains made by Czechs during the late 19th century. In 1880 the government of the Austrian prime minister Eduard, count von Taaffe, made Czech a language of administration in Bohemia and Moravia. Two years later the German-language university in Prague (Charles University) was split into two institutions, with the Czech university assuming the prime position. Finally, reforms of the franchise gave the Czechs a majority in the Bohemian diet. Growing disquiet among the German-speaking politicians, especially those from Bohemia, exploded in 1897 when the Austrian prime minister Kasimir Felix, count von Badeni—in order to win Czech votes to renew the compromise with Hungary—agreed to make Czech equal to German as the internal language of administration in Bohemia and Moravia. This meant that all German civil servants would henceforth have to be bilingual. Badeni encountered such a vigorous opposition, organized by German nationalists, that he lost the emperor's confidence. He resigned, and his successor recognized the futility of trying to adjust the outdated laws in favour of the Czechs.

The changing social and economic stratification also sped the decline of the Young Czechs. Mass political parties, such as the Agrarians and the Social Democrats, arrived on the scene; these groups appealed to the peasant and working-class voters, who enjoyed voting rights after the introduction of universal manhood suffrage in 1906. Yet instead of helping to consolidate the parliament, as many had hoped, universal suffrage increased divisions and made it increasingly difficult for prime ministers to form a solid majority bloc. Thus, from the election in 1907 to the outbreak of World War I in 1914, the Vienna parliament could easily be bypassed by the imperial court and by the ministries of foreign affairs and war, over which Francis Joseph exercised strong control.

During this period, in the Hungarian portion of the empire, the Slovaks continued to experience ever-increasing Magyarization. By the end of the 19th century no Slovak secondary schools remained. Linguistic oppression also extended to religion: in 1907 at Černová (now Stará Černová, Slovakia), some 15 Slovak demonstrators demanding that a new church be consecrated by the Slovak nationalist priest Andrej Hlinka were shot by police. In politics, only the Social Democrats and the nationalistic Slovak People's Party, led by Hlinka, took interest in the Slovak people. Certain Slovak intellectuals associated with the periodical *Hlas* chose a pro-Czech orientation in their search for political allies. The percentage of Slovaks in the region declined steadily. Many, in search of work, migrated to other parts of the empire. By World War I about half a million Slovaks had emigrated abroad, mostly to the United States.

STRUGGLE FOR INDEPENDENCE

World War I deepened the antagonism between the Germans and the Czechs within the Czech Lands. The Germans lent full support to the war effort of the Central Powers, but among the Czechs the war was unpopular, because they realized that a German victory would terminate their hopes for political autonomy. However, Czech opposition to the war was uncoordinated. The Young Czech leader Karel Kramář, a neo-Pan-Slavist himself, desired Russian troops to occupy the Czech Lands and install a Russian grand duke as the future king

PAN-SLAVISM

The 19th-century movement known as Pan-Slavism recognized a common ethnic background among the various Slav peoples of eastern and east-central Europe and sought to unite those peoples for the achievement of common cultural and political goals. The Pan-Slav movement originally was formed in the first half of the 19th century by West and South Slav intellectuals, scholars, and poets, whose peoples were at that time also developing their sense of national identity. The Pan-Slavists engaged in studying folk songs, folklore, and peasant vernaculars of the Slav peoples, in demonstrating the similarities among them, and in trying to stimulate a sense of Slav unity. As such activities were conducted mainly in Prague, that city became the first Pan-Slav centre for studying Slav antiquities and philology.

The Pan-Slavism movement soon took on political overtones, and in June 1848, while the Austrian Empire was weakened by revolution, the Czech historian František Palacký convened a Slav congress in Prague. Consisting of representatives of all Slav nationalities ruled by the Austrians, the congress was intended to organize cooperative efforts among them for the purpose of compelling the Emperor to transform his monarchy into a federation of equal peoples under a democratic Habsburg rule.

Although the congress had little practical effect, the movement remained active, and by the 1860s it became particularly popular in Russia, to which many Pan-Slavs looked for leadership as well as for protection from Austro-Hungarian and Turkish rule. Russian Pan-Slavists, however, altered the theoretical bases of the movement. Adopting the Slavophile notion that western Europe was spiritually and culturally bankrupt and that it was Russia's historic mission to rejuvenate Europe by gaining political dominance over it, the Pan-Slavists added the concept that Russia's mission could not be fulfilled without the support of other Slav peoples, who must be liberated from their Austrian and Turkish masters and united into a Russian-dominated Slav confederation.

Although the Russian government did not officially support this view, some important members of its foreign department, including its representatives at Constantinople and Belgrade, were ardent Pan-Slavists and succeeded in drawing both Serbia and Russia into wars against the Ottoman Empire in 1876–77.

When efforts were made in the early 20th century to call new Pan-Slav congresses and revive the movement, the nationalistic rivalries among the various Slav peoples prevented their effective collaboration.

of Bohemia. His future political rival, Tomáš Masaryk, preferred a pro-Western orientation.

In exile in western Europe, Masaryk was joined by Edvard Beneš and Milan Štefánik. Masaryk, envisioning a political union of the Czechs and the Slovaks, established contacts with Czech and Slovak emigrants living in Allied and neutral countries, especially the United States. In

October 1915, in a public lecture at King's College, London, he called for the establishment of small states in east-central Europe, based on the principles of nationality and democracy and directed against German plans for European hegemony. He argued that divided nationalities, such as the Poles living in three countries and the Czechs and Slovaks living in two, should be allowed to form nation-states and become allies of the West. In 1916 the Czech National Council (later renamed the Czechoslovak National Council) was established in Paris under Masaryk's chairmanship. Its members were eager to maintain contacts with the leaders at home in order to avoid disharmony, and an underground organization called the "Maffia" served as a liaison between them.

At home under Austrian rule the influence of the military increased. The press was heavily censored, public meetings were forbidden, and those suspected of disloyalty were imprisoned. Among the leading politicians who were arrested and received suspended death sentences were Karel Kramář and Alois Rašín. Dissatisfaction among the Czech soldiers on the Eastern Front became more articulate in 1915, and whole units often went over to the Russian side.

Francis Joseph died in November 1916 and was succeeded by Charles (I). The new emperor called the parliament to session in Vienna and granted amnesty to political prisoners such as Kramář and Rašín. Charles's reforms, although in many respects gratifying, called for more-intensive activities abroad in order to convince the Allied leaders that partial concessions to the Czechs were inadequate to the problems of postwar reconstruction. The position of the Slovaks was not improving either, as the Hungarian government refused to respect the principle of nationality.

Two major events coincided with Charles's new course in home affairs and with his discreet exploration of the chances of a separate peace: the Russian Revolution (March 1917) and the U.S. declaration of war on Germany (April). In May 1917 Masaryk left London for Russia to speed up organization of a Czechoslovak army. While small units of volunteers had been formed in the Allied countries during the early part of the war, thousands of prisoners of war were now released from Russian camps and trained for service on the Allied side. A Czechoslovak brigade participated in the last Russian offensive and distinguished itself at Zborov (Ukraine) in July 1917. From the United States came material help and moral encouragement, though U.S. Pres. Woodrow Wilson's early statements pertaining to the peace aims were rather hazy. But several weeks after the United States declared war on Austria-Hungary, President Wilson promulgated his celebrated Fourteen Points (January 1918), the 10th of which called for "the freest opportunity of the autonomous development" of the peoples of the Austro-Hungarian Empire.

After the Bolsheviks seized power in Russia, they made a separate peace settlement with Germany. The Bolshevik government then granted the Czechoslovak

Legion—made up of those Czechs and Slovaks who had been fighting on the side of Russia—the freedom to leave Russia, but violent incidents that occurred during the evacuation led the Bolsheviks to order the legion's disarmament. The legionnaires rebelled, however, and took over the Trans-Siberian Railroad. By challenging Bolshevik power, the legion contributed to the outbreak of the Russian Civil War.

The achievements of the Czechoslovak Legion, noticed favourably by the Western governments and press, gave the Czechoslovak cause wide publicity and helped its leaders to gain official recognition. Masaryk left Russia for the United States, where, in May 1918, he gained solid support from Czech and Slovak organizations. A declaration in favour of a political union of the Czechs and the Slovaks, containing a guarantee of Slovak rights to their own parliament, legislation, and administrative language, was issued at Pittsburgh, Pennsylvania, on May 31, 1918.

Throughout 1918, dealings with the Allies progressed more successfully. Added to the favourable publicity of the Siberian campaigns were increased activities at home demanding a sovereign state "within the historic frontiers of the Bohemian lands and of Slovakia" (the Epiphany Declaration; January 1918). An anti-Austrian resolution adopted at the Congress of Oppressed Nationalities, held in Rome in April, helped to disarm conservative circles in Allied countries that had opposed a total reorganization of the Danubian region. Eventually,

France recognized the Czechoslovak National Council as the supreme body controlling Czechoslovak national interests; the other Allies soon followed the French initiative. On September 28 Beneš signed a treaty whereby France agreed to support the Czechoslovak program in the postwar peace conference. To preclude a retreat from the earlier Allied declarations, the Czechoslovak National Council constituted itself as a provisional government on October 14. Four days later, Masaryk and Beneš issued a declaration of independence simultaneously in Washington, D.C., and Paris.

Meanwhile, events were moving rapidly toward total collapse of the Habsburg monarchy. The last attempt to avert it, a manifesto issued by Charles on October 16, brought no positive results. Afterward, Vienna had no choice but to accept Wilson's terms. A domestic political group called the Prague National Committee proclaimed a republic on October 28, and two days later at Turčiansky Svätý Martin (now Martin, Slovakia) a Slovak counterpart, the Slovak National Council, acceded to the Prague proclamation.

CZECHOSLOVAKIA TO 1945

When the new country of Czechoslovakia was proclaimed on October 28, 1918, its leaders were still in exile. Masaryk was chosen as president on November 14, while he was still in the United States; he did not arrive in Prague until December. Beneš, the country's foreign minister,

Map of Czechoslovakia. Encyclopaedia Britannica, Inc.

was in Paris for the upcoming peace conference, as was Karel Kramář, who had become Czechoslovakia's first prime minister. (The Slovak leader and first war minister Štefánik died in an airplane crash in May 1919.) Masaryk and Beneš remained in charge of foreign relations, and the leaders of five major parties dealt with home affairs.

THE ESTABLISHMENT OF THE REPUBLIC

The first task of the new state, to establish its borders, was undertaken at the Paris Peace Conference, where the historical frontiers separating Bohemia and Moravia from Germany and Austria were approved, with minor rectifications, in favour of the new republic. Several disputes soon surfaced, however. The political spokesmen of the Germans in Bohemia and Moravia advocated cession of the area known as the Sudetenland to Germany or Austria, but, because neither Germany nor Austria was in a position to intervene with armed troops, the Czechs, backed by the Allies, occupied without much bloodshed the seditious German-speaking provinces.

The delineation of the Slovak boundary was another serious problem, as there was no recognized linguistic frontier between the Hungarian and Slovak populations in the south. Since none of the successive Hungarian governments was prepared to give up what they considered ancient Magyar lands, the new frontier had to be redrawn by the force of arms. Hungary's communist government—which in March 1919 had taken power in Budapest under the leadership of Béla Kun—sent troops to eastern Slovakia, where a sister communist republic was proclaimed. The Hungarian communists and their Slovak allies wished to reattach the Slovak "Upper Lands" to a multiethnic communist Hungary, to which the Russian Bolsheviks promised military assistance. With Allied help, however, the Czech military asserted itself in Slovakia as well as in the new province of Subcarpathian Ruthenia (comprising the mostly Slavic northeastern portion of prewar Hungary), and those two ex-Hungarian provinces were attached to Czechoslovakia.

A dispute over the duchy of Teschen strained relations with Poland, which claimed the territory on ethnic grounds (more than half the inhabitants were Poles). Czechoslovakia desired it for historical reasons and because it was a coal-rich area, through which ran an important railway link to Slovakia. The duchy was partitioned between the two countries in 1920, with Czechoslovakia receiving the larger, economically valuable western portion.

The second task of the new government, to secure the loyalty of its approximately 15 million citizens, proved onerous as well. The borders of Czechoslovakia encompassed not only Czechs and Slovaks but also Germans, Hungarians, Ruthenians, and Poles. About 15 percent of the people were Slovaks; they were a valuable asset to the Czechs, who made up about half the population. Together, these two linguistically close groups constituted a healthy majority in the cobbled-together state. However, the Czechs and Slovaks had vastly different experiences to bring to the process of state building. The Czech intellectual elite could look back at a thousand years of state history, first as a principality and then as a kingdom, while Slovakia had never existed as a separate geopolitical unit. The Czechs also were better educated and considerably more urbanized, industrialized, and secularized than the Slovaks, who had suffered from Magyarization efforts under Hungarian rule, particularly the lack of Slovak-language schooling above the elementary level.

Consolidation of internal affairs proceeded slowly while the government worked to replace the wartime economy with a new system. A threatening financial crisis was averted by the country's first minister of finance, Alois Rašín. A relatively far-reaching land reform program was carried out: the first estates to be confiscated and partitioned were those belonging to German and Hungarian aristocracy, and those who benefited were Czech and Slovak farmers. In addition, the network of railroads and highways had to be adjusted to the new shape of the republic, which stretched from the German-speaking Cheb (German: Eger) region in western Bohemia to the Ukrainian Carpathians in the east.

In the chaotic conditions prevailing in central Europe after the armistice, a parliamentary election appeared to be impossible. The Czech and Slovak leaders agreed among themselves on the composition of a constituent assembly, which excluded Germans, Hungarians, Ruthenians, and Poles. The assembly adopted a new, democratic constitution, modeled largely on that of the French Third Republic, in February 1920. Supreme power was vested in a bicameral National Assembly. Its two houses, the Chamber of Deputies and the Senate, had the right to elect, in a joint session, the president of the republic for a term of seven years. The cabinet was made responsible to the assembly. Despite the exclusion of minority groups from the writing of the constitution, the document generously defined the fundamental rights of Czechoslovakia's citizens, irrespective of ethnic origin, religion, and social status.

The most resolute opposition to the new constitution came from both German nationalist parties, which called for increased autonomy or the right to be incorporated into Germany, and the newly constituted Communist Party, whose chief aim (at least until 1935) was the destruction of the bourgeois republic and the establishment of a communist dictatorship. Although the Germans issued protests against the constitution, they participated in parliamentary and other elections. In 1925 two German parties, the Agrarians and the Christian Socialists, joined the government majority, thus breaking a deadlock. Disagreement with the trend toward centralism was the main source of dissatisfaction among the Slovak Populists, a clerical party headed by Andrej Hlinka. Calls for Slovak autonomy were counterbalanced by other parties seeking closer contacts with the corresponding Czech groups; the most significant contribution to that effort was made by two Slovak parties, the Agrarians under Milan Hodža and the Social Democrats under Ivan Dérer. The strongest single party in Czechoslovakia's opening period, the Social Democracy, was split in 1920 by internal struggles; in 1921 its left wing constituted itself as the Czechoslovak section of the Comintern (Third International). After the separation of the communists, the Social Democracy yielded primacy to the Czech Agrarians, or Republicans, as the latter party was officially renamed. The Agrarians were the backbone of government coalitions until the disruption of the republic during World War II; from its ranks came Antonín Švehla (prime minister, 1921–29) and his successors.

Foreign relations were largely determined by wartime agreements. Czechoslovakia adhered loyally to the League of Nations. In 1920 Foreign Minister Beneš initiated treaties with Yugoslavia and Romania that gave rise to the Little Entente—a defensive military pact against German and Hungarian aggression. France was the only major power that concluded an alliance with Czechoslovakia (January 1924). Relations with Italy, originally friendly, deteriorated after Benito Mussolini's rise to power in 1922. Czech anticlerical feeling precluded the negotiation of a concordat with the papacy until 1928, when an agreement settled the most serious disputes between church and state. Ultimately, it was Germany that most strongly influenced the course of Czechoslovak foreign affairs. One of Beneš's highest priorities was to prevent the union of Austria and Germany. Nevertheless, the relations between Czechoslovakia and Germany improved slightly after the Locarno Pact of 1925.

THE CRISIS OF GERMAN NATIONALISM

When the impact of the Great Depression reached Czechoslovakia soon after 1930, the highly industrialized German-speaking districts of the Sudetenland—a section of land in the vicinity of the Sudeten mountain ranges—were hit more severely than the rest of the country. The grievances of the Germans, who felt that the Prague government was offering the Czech areas a disproportionate amount of unemployment relief, contributed to the rise of militant German nationalism in Czechoslovakia, especially after Adolf Hitler's rise to power in Germany. In

October 1933 Konrad Henlein, a furtive supporter of Hitler, launched his Sudeten German Home Front. Professing loyalty to the democratic system, he called for recognition of the German minority as an autonomous body. In 1935 Henlein changed the name of his movement to the Sudeten German Party (Sudetendeutsche Partei; SdP) so that the group could take part in the parliamentary election (May 1935). The party also capitalized on discontent of Sudeten Germans over the ethnic discrimination practiced in the region by Czech officials. The SdP captured nearly two-thirds of the Sudeten German vote and became a political force second only to the Czech Agrarians.

A tense interlude of little more than two years followed the landslide victory of the SdP. In December 1935 Masaryk retired from the presidency, and Beneš was elected his successor by an overwhelming majority, including Hlinka's party. Under Beneš the country followed a rigorous course of rearmament, and a fortification system was built along the frontier with Germany. A military assistance treaty with the Soviet Union in 1935 enhanced the false sense of national security. The program of the Czechoslovak Communist Party was determined not only by this treaty but also by the general reorientation of the Comintern, which now urged cooperation with antifascist forces in popular fronts.

Meanwhile, Hitler embarked on his program of eastward expansion. As early as November 5, 1937, he informed his military chiefs of his intention to move against Austria and Czechoslovakia at the next opportunity. Two weeks later Henlein, anticipating that Czechoslovakia would be defeated militarily within a few months, offered Hitler the SdP as an instrument to break up the country from the inside. Earlier that year Prime Minister Milan Hodža had made significant progress toward gaining the cooperation of those segments of the German population that were attached to the principles of democracy, but the Anschluss (annexation) of Austria to Germany the following spring unleashed a nationalistic frenzy among Czechoslovakia's Sudeten Germans.

As the international crisis deepened, Czechoslovak politics became further polarized. The political right, led by the Agrarians, worked to win the support of the Sudeten Germans; the political left was prepared to cooperate with the Soviet Union. Henlein, meanwhile, played his hand so skillfully that influential foreign circles, especially in London, believed that he was not Hitler's stooge but a free agent merely demanding self-determination for Czechoslovakia's oppressed Germans. The advocates of the "appeasement" of Germany, an idea rapidly gaining ground in Britain and France, failed to realize that the Sudeten German negotiators acted on instructions from Berlin. Indeed, the main task of Henlein's party was to give Hitler a better chance to dislocate the republic without recourse to war. To invalidate critical comments from London and

Paris, Beneš consented late in July 1938 to the mission of Lord Runciman, whose avowed purpose was to observe and report on conditions within the country.

The political crisis culminated in September 1938. Armed with information supplied by Lord Runciman, the British prime minister Neville Chamberlain visited Hitler at Obersalzberg, where he assured Hitler that the German objectives could be achieved without fighting. On September 21 Beneš was forced by Paris and London to accept the British plan of ceding the frontier regions that had a German-speaking majority—the Sudetenland—to Hitler. The French consented to Chamberlain's policy, thus abandoning their former commitments, and the Soviet Union was under treaty obligation to assist Czechoslovakia only if the French would honour their pledges first.

But Hitler wanted war against Czechoslovakia, and he rejected the British plan when Chamberlain visited him for the second time, at Bad Godesberg. For several days Europe stood on the verge of war; Czechoslovakia announced general mobilization, which was followed in France and Britain with partial call-ups. In the end the appeasers won the day. On September 29 Hitler agreed to receive Mussolini, Chamberlain, and the French premier Édouard Daladier in Munich. In the resulting Munich agreement, the Prague government was forced to relinquish to Germany all frontier districts with populations that were 50 percent or more German by October 10. Beneš resigned the presidency on October 5 and went into his second political exile.

THE BREAKUP OF THE REPUBLIC

The annexation of the Sudetenland, completed according to the Munich timetable, was not Czechoslovakia's only territorial loss. Shortly after the Munich verdict, Poland sent troops to annex the Teschen region. By the Vienna Award (November 2, 1938), Hungary was granted one-quarter of Slovak and Ruthenian territories. By all these amputations Czechoslovakia lost about one-third of its population, and the country was rendered defenseless.

As the country lost its German, Polish, and Hungarian minorities, the Czechs reluctantly agreed to change the centralistic constitution into a federalist one. The Slovak Populists, headed since Hlinka's death by Jozef Tiso, pressed Prague for full Slovak autonomy, which was proclaimed in ilina on October 6. Subcarpathian Ruthenia was also granted autonomous status. A cumbersome system composed of three autonomous units (the Czech Lands, Slovakia, and Ruthenia) was introduced late in the fall. On November 30 the respected lawyer Emil Hácha was elected president, and Rudolf Beran, the leader of the Agrarian Party, was appointed federal prime minister. Under German pressure the complicated party system was changed drastically. The right and centre parties in the Czech Lands formed the Party of National Unity, while the Socialists organized the Party of Labour. In Slovakia the

Populists absorbed all the other political groups.

Meanwhile, the public knew little of the confidential negotiations being conducted in Vienna and Berlin by Tiso's aides, who went along with Hitler's preparation for the final takeover of Slovakia. On March 14, 1939, immediately after Tiso's return to Bratislava from talks with Hitler in Berlin, all Slovak parliamentarians voted for independence. On the following day, Bohemia and Moravia were occupied and proclaimed a protectorate of the German Third Reich, while Slovakia became a nominally independent state under Tiso as president. Although under German control and forced to participate in the German attack on the Soviet Union with a token military force, Slovakia was able to retain a certain degree of independence in internal matters. This fact, however, did not stop the authorities from sending Slovakia's Jewish citizens to Nazi extermination camps, where most of them perished; between 1942 and 1944, approximately 70,000 of Slovakia's roughly 87,000 Jews were deported.

WORLD WAR II

In exile in Chicago, the former Czechoslovak president Beneš appealed to the Great Powers and the League of Nations to denounce German aggression and the breach of the Munich agreement. France, Britain, and the United States raised formal protests against Hitler's takeover of the Czech Lands (the "rape of

Prague"); a strong protest also was voiced by Maksim Litvinov, the Soviet foreign minister. In July 1939 Beneš returned from Chicago to London to force his leadership upon the Czechoslovak movement in exile, which threatened to be divided between Paris and Warsaw. Until the fall of France in June 1940, Beneš could not assert himself, but in July the British government under Winston Churchill granted Beneš's Czechoslovak National Committee the status of a provisional government in exile; it was to receive regular British subsidies until the end of the war. In July 1941 the Soviet Union and Britain jointly granted the Beneš government in exile full recognition; U.S. recognition arrived only in October 1942. Along with seeking recognition for his government, Beneš devoted his efforts to getting the Munich agreement annulled.

In Prague Hitler installed as a Reich protector the former German foreign minister Konstantin von Neurath. Hácha remained president, but his cabinet operated with limited powers. For some two years the Czech protectorate kept the semblance of an autonomous body, but in September 1941 Reinhard Heydrich, the head of German secret police, replaced Neurath as Reich protector and inaugurated a reign of terror. In retaliation, Czech agents, perhaps acting on the orders of Beneš's government in exile, bombed and shot Heydrich in May 1942 (he died in June). After the assassination, the Nazis proclaimed martial law, executed hundreds of Czechs without trial, and destroyed the village of Lidice near Prague. Within a few weeks, the entire Czech underground network was wiped out. Hácha did not have the strength to resign and, trying to mitigate the brutality of German rule, stayed on as president. Martial law ultimately was lifted only because the Germans needed Czech workers to maintain productivity in the armaments industry. Consignment of young people for work in Germany continued without much resistance until the collapse of the Nazi regime.

In December 1943 Beneš visited Moscow and signed a 20-year treaty of alliance, in which the Soviets recognized Czechoslovakia's pre-Munich agreement borders. This treaty, as well as agreements made with Klement Gottwald, the leader of the Czechoslovak communists exiled in Moscow, thenceforth determined Beneš's policies toward the Czech protectorate and Slovakia.

In Slovakia in late August 1944 a popular uprising, planned by officers of the Slovak army, broke out following clashes between German troops and Slovak partisans under Soviet commanders. In contrast with the Warsaw Uprising, which also took place that August, the Soviets were directly supporting the Slovak rebels. Although the rebel Slovak army was fighting for the Czechoslovak cause, Slovak communists (among them the future Czechoslovak leader Gustav Husák) drafted schemes suggesting the incorporation of Slovakia into the Soviet Union after the war. The Nazis crushed the uprising at the end of October, before Soviet troops were able to cross the

Carpathians. Nevertheless, the advance of the Red Army through Slovakia—several months before the Western Allies were able to advance closer to the Czech border—became of decisive importance.

In March 1945 Beneš and his government in exile journeyed from London to Moscow to make a final accord with Soviet premier Joseph Stalin and Gottwald. A program of postwar reconstruction was worked out under decisive communist influence. Zdeněk Fierlinger, a former Czechoslovak diplomat and communist ally, became prime minister of a new provisional government, set up at Košice in Slovakia on April 3.

The new Košice government exercised jurisdiction in the eastern portion of Czechoslovakia while fighting continued in Moravia and Bohemia until early May 1945. On May 5 an uprising against the German troops concentrated in central Bohemia started in Prague. Appeals for Allied help were largely ignored. Troops under U.S. Gen. George S. Patton reached Plzeň (Pilsen) but, complying with instructions from Gen. Dwight D. Eisenhower, did not advance to Prague. Finally, on May 9, Soviet troops under Marshal Ivan Konev entered the Czech capital, liberating it from German occupation.

COMMUNIST CZECHOSLOVAKIA

It was thus with Soviet assistance that President Beneš and his government returned to Prague on May 16, 1945, after nearly seven years of exile. It was believed that his intention was to restore in Czechoslovakia the liberal democratic regime that had collapsed under Nazi assault in 1938. It would not be an exact replica but an "improved" version adapted to the new circumstances. In particular, the Czechoslovak state was to be more ethnically homogeneous: the problem of minorities was to be resolved by large-scale expulsions of Germans and Hungarians from the country. (In the end Beneš did not achieve the expulsion of the Hungarians, merely the confiscation of their property.) The country was to remain a republic whose president would retain considerable constitutional and executive power; a government based on the electoral performance of select political parties would run the country by means of a professional civil service, while the judiciary would enforce laws passed by parliament—the National Assembly.

THE PROVISIONAL REGIME

In his search for improvement, Beneš decided to limit the number of political parties to six. (Subsequently, two additional parties were permitted in Slovakia, but too late for the election in 1946.) In the autumn of 1945 Beneš nominated the Provisional National Assembly, which reelected him president and confirmed in office the provisional government, headed by Fierlinger, that he had appointed in April. The vice premier was Gottwald,

JAN MASARYK

The statesman and diplomat Jan Garrigue Masaryk (born September 14, 1886, Prague, Bohemia, Austria-Hungary [now in Czech Republic]—died March 10, 1948, Prague, Czechoslovakia) served as foreign minister in both the Czechoslovak émigré government in London during World War II and the postwar coalition government of Czechoslovakia. The son of the statesman Tomáš Masaryk, Jan served in a Hungarian regiment during World War I, entered the foreign office of the newly independent Czechoslovakia in 1919, and served in Washington, D.C., and London before becoming secretary to the foreign minister Edvard Beneš in 1921.

From 1925 to 1938 Masaryk was ambassador to Great Britain. During World War II he was foreign minister of the Czechoslovak émigré regime in London. A leading spokesman for that government, Masaryk made wartime broadcasts to occupied Czechoslovakia, published in English in 1944 under the title *Speaking to My Country*, and became a popular figure at home. Retaining the portfolio

Jan Masaryk. Encyclopædia Britannica, Inc.

of foreign minister after his government's return to Prague in 1945, he accompanied Beneš to Moscow and also participated in the inauguration of the United Nations in San Francisco. He was convinced that Czechoslovakia must remain friendly to the Soviet Union, and he was greatly disappointed by the Soviet veto of Czechoslovak acceptance of postwar U.S. reconstruction aid under the Marshall Plan.

At the request of President Beneš, Masaryk remained at his post after the Communist takeover of February 25, 1948. A few weeks later, however, he either committed suicide by throwing himself out of a window at the foreign office or was murdered by being thrown out.

and the leaders of the other political parties also held vice premierships. A general election was scheduled to legitimize the provisional regime as well as to test the nation's acceptance of this new order, in compliance with the agreement of the Allies at the Yalta Conference in February 1945.

On May 26, 1946, the Communist Party of Czechoslovakia won a great victory in the general election, polling 2,695,293 votes—38.7 percent of the total. Several factors contributed to the success of the communists, particularly the Western powers' betrayal of Czechoslovakia in the Munich agreement and a resuscitated sense of Pan-Slavic solidarity, fed by strong anti-German feelings. Gottwald became premier, and the communists took control of most of the key ministries, including interior, information, agriculture, and finance. Jan Masaryk (the son of Tomáš Masaryk) retained foreign affairs, however, and Gen. Ludvík Svoboda remained minister of defense.

Although the political parties formed a coalition called the National Front, collaboration between the communists and noncommunists was difficult from the beginning. While all parties agreed that economic recovery should remain the priority, and while a two-year plan was launched to carry it out, they began to differ as to the means to be employed. The noncommunists wanted no further nationalizations or land confiscations, no special taxation of the rich, raises in pay for the civil service, and, above all,

economic aid from the United States by way of the Marshall Plan. The conflict sharpened in the summer of 1947 when the government first accepted Marshall Plan aid but then rejected it because of pressure from the Soviet Union. Although the noncommunists blocked communist policies within the government throughout 1947, they had no common strategy regarding the next election—only a common desire to defeat the communists decisively. The communists, on the other hand, envisioned gaining an absolute majority in the next election with the help of the Social Democrats.

The tension between the two factions developed into a crisis over the question of who was to control the police. The communist interior minister objected to the appointment of noncommunist officials for senior police posts. In protest, most of the noncommunist ministers resigned on February 20, 1948; they hoped the government paralysis would force Gottwald and the communist ministers to resign as well. Instead, the communists seized the ministries held by the resigning ministers as well as the headquarters of the parties now in opposition.

Following mass demonstrations in the streets of Prague of communist-led workers, many armed with rifles, President Beneš yielded. On February 25 he allowed the formation of a new government, in which the communists and left-wing Social Democrats held the key posts. The other parties of the National Front were nominally represented by individual members chosen not by the parties themselves but by the communists. The Provisional National Assembly overwhelmingly endorsed the new government and its program.

Most of the noncommunist political leaders, risking imprisonment, fled the country; they were joined by many ordinary people who headed to the West to avoid living under communism. As a sign of their triumphant strength, the communists retained Masaryk as foreign minister, but on March 10 his body was found beneath a window of the foreign ministry. Overnight the Communist Party had become the only organized body left to run the country.

STALINISM IN CZECHOSLOVAKIA

After February 1948 Czechoslovakia belonged to the Communist Party apparatus. The economy was subject to further nationalization, and all agricultural land became state or collective farms. When a new constitution declaring the country to be a "people's republic" (i.e., a communist state) was promulgated on May 9, Beneš, though seriously incapacitated by illness, finally displayed signs of resistance; he refused to undersign the constitution and resigned as president. Under a new electoral law and with a single list of candidates, a general election was held on May 30, and the new National Assembly elected Gottwald president. Antonín Zápotocký succeeded him as premier, while Rudolf Slánský retained

the powerful post of secretary general of the Czechoslovak Communist Party.

With the communists firmly in power, the will of Soviet Premier Joseph Stalin was soon imposed on Czechoslovakia. In 1947 Moscow had set up the Cominform (Communist Information Bureau) to tighten discipline within the socialist camp; in the autumn of 1949 Soviet advisers were sent to Czechoslovakia. In 1950 the outbreak of the Korean War initiated, under Soviet pressure, a vast rearmament program in the country.

Meanwhile, the communists had begun purging the armed forces of officers suspected of being pro-Western. As an example, Gen. Heliodor Pika, deputy chief of staff of the Czechoslovak army and Beneš's wartime military representative in the Soviet Union, was arrested on trumped-up charges of espionage in May 1948; he was executed in June 1949. His trial was followed by a witch hunt inside the entire officer corps.

Another target of the party was religion, especially the Roman Catholic Church. Church dignitaries were interned; monasteries and religious orders were dissolved; and a state office for church affairs was set up to bring churches under communist control. Soviet security advisers helped to prepare the trials of clergy who refused to cooperate with the communist authorities, and an effort was made to organize a group of collaborationist clergy.

In a series of purges beginning in 1950, noncommunists were charged with various antistate activities. In June Milada Horáková, a former member of the National Assembly, and other politicians from the right and the left were tried for espionage. She and several others were sentenced to death. Gottwald also was put under pressure to uncover ideological opponents in the Czechoslovak Communist Party, which Soviet advisers now began to scrutinize. Charges of "nationalistic deviationism" and "Titoism" (referring to Josip Broz Tito, the renegade communist leader of Yugoslavia) were leveled against the foreign minister, Vladimír Clementis, who was dismissed from office, as were the Slovak regional premier, Gustav Husák, and several other Slovaks; all were accused of "bourgeois nationalism." In February 1951 Clementis, Husák, and several others were arrested, and in December 1952 Clementis was executed. Additionally, First Secretary Rudolf Slánský and 10 other high party officials, mostly Jewish, were sentenced to death in a trial considered by some to be the climax of the communist purges in eastern Europe. All together, some 180 politicians were executed in these purges, and thousands were held in prisons and labour camps.

In March 1953, a few days after Stalin's funeral, Gottwald unexpectedly died. Antonín Zápotocký was elected president, while Viliám Široký, a Slovak, became premier; the powerful post of the party's first secretary went to Antonín Novotný, who had played a very active role in conducting the purges. That May a monetary reform, which effectively deprived the farmers and better-paid workers of all their savings, led to sporadic riots against the communist authorities. The riots gave Novotný, backed by Moscow, an excuse to check any attempt by Zápotocký and Široký to ease government repression. In 1957, when Zápotocký died, Novotný combined the party secretaryship with the presidency. His faction—mostly mediocre apparatchiks—became supreme and remained so until 1968. Novotný kept Stalinism alive. Show trials continued until 1955, after which administrative sanctions began to be employed.

THE GROWING REFORM MOVEMENT

By the early 1960s Novotný faced acute economic problems. The communists' industrial and agricultural plans had failed to bolster the economy, and stagnation had set in. In industry, production costs remained high, fuel supplies were short, the quality of goods was poor, and absenteeism was widespread. Production began to fall. In agriculture, the situation was worse: collectivized agriculture produced less in 1960 than had been produced in the prewar years.

In September 1964 the government was forced to accept a new set of economic principles put forward by a group of reformers who had advanced through the party ranks. Prominent among them was economics professor Ota Šik, who advocated replacing the country's rigid command economy with a mixed economy. Managers of enterprises would have a free hand in production and trading, and the efficiency of each enterprise would be measured by its "profitability" in terms of the labour and capital invested. Wholesale prices were to be overhauled in 1967 and 1968. Reform in agriculture was also attempted in 1966, with a cutback in central planning and the introduction of marketing principles. To attract Western currency, tourism was to be encouraged by doubling the old tourist rate of exchange. Novotný, however, refused to seek credit from the West for fear of becoming too dependent on capitalism, and in the end few of the proposed economic changes were implemented. Novotný's timid reforms thus satisfied no one, resolved no serious problems, and brought into existence a conspicuous pressure group (known as the "economists") within the party leadership.

A Slovak pressure group emerged as well. Although Novotný agreed to the rehabilitation of the Slovaks purged in the 1950s, a new constitution in 1960 further restricted Slovak autonomy. By 1963, new leaders had moved into power in Slovakia; Karol Bacílek, who was compromised by the purges in the 1950s, was replaced as first secretary of the Slovak Communist Party by Alexander Dubček. When the rehabilitated Slovaks, among whom was Gustav Husák, began to clamour for a federal solution to their problem, Novotný could propose nothing

better than disciplinary measures. The Slovaks turned against him—contributing to his imminent downfall.

The immediate cause of Novotný's downfall, however, was unrest in the public and cultural spheres, particularly among students and writers. The young generation, raised under the communist regime and educated according to the Soviet model, had tired of restrictions on personal freedom and was critical of the country's low standard of living. Students were restless throughout the 1960s, and the traditional student festival, the Majáles, in 1966 became a riot against the regime. Then in 1967, dissatisfied with the conditions in their dormitories, students gathered in the streets demanding "more light." The party felt challenged and sent in the police. In the end the minister of the interior apologized for police brutality against the students. Meanwhile, since 1962 the country's writers, despite the imposition of Socialist Realism as the official literary style, had produced some remarkable works that had escaped censorship. In 1967, at a congress of Czechoslovak writers, many refused to conform to the standards demanded by the Communist Party. Novotný answered this rebellion with sanctions: Jan Beneš was sent to prison for antistate propaganda; Ludvík Vaculík, Antonín J. Liehm, and Ivan Klíma were expelled from the party; and Jan Procházka was dismissed from the party's Central Committee, of which he was a candidate member. This repression merely strengthened opposition to Novotný, however.

During the session of the Central Committee in October 1967, an open clash occurred between Novotný and the Slovaks. When Novotný hinted that Dubček and the rest of the Slovak opposition were tainted with "bourgeois nationalism," he sealed his fate as a leader. Novotný invited Leonid Brezhnev, first secretary of the Communist Party of the Soviet Union, to Prague to help him quash the dissension, but Brezhnev refused to get involved. Novotný, now deserted, faced another hostile session in December. After Šik's demand that the presidency be separated from the party office, Novotný offered his resignation as first secretary. This was accepted at the next session, and in January 1968 Novotný himself recommended as his successor his Slovak opponent Dubček, who was elected unanimously after the Central Committee failed to agree on the other candidates.

THE PRAGUE SPRING OF 1968

As the new first secretary of the Communist Party of Czechoslovakia, Dubček was propelled into the role of chief reformer, even though he was not particularly qualified for it. He was a young Slovak who had spent his political life in the party apparat, and, because he was a compromise candidate, people did not expect much from him. Yet in the effort of ridding the government of the old guard, Dubček was aided by the pressure of public opinion, which was growing stronger, especially after members of the press became determined to express themselves more freely in early March 1968.

By April the old apparat had crumbled, and the reformers held sway. Several diehards attempted suicide, but on the whole the transfer of power was peaceful. Oldřich Černík became prime minister, and Šik and Husák became vice premiers in charge of reforms in the economy and Slovakia, respectively. From March 30, Czechoslovakia also had a new president, Ludvík Svoboda, who had been minister of defense in the first postwar government. He had aided the communists during the 1948 coup but was himself purged in the 1950s and had lived in retirement since then. The interior ministry came under the control of another purge victim, Josef Pavel. The newly elected Presidium, the policy-making body of the Czechoslovak Communist Party, consisted largely of newcomers.

The crown achievement of the new reformist government was the Action Program, adopted by the party's Central Committee in April 1968. The program embodied reform ideas of the several preceding years; it encompassed not only economic reforms but also the democratization of Czechoslovak political life. Among its most important points were the promotion of Slovakia to full parity within a new Czechoslovak federation, long overdue industrial and agricultural reforms, a revised constitution that would guarantee civil rights and liberties, and complete rehabilitation of all citizens whose rights had been infringed in the past. The program also envisaged a strict division of powers: the National Assembly, not the Communist Party, would be in control of the government, which in turn would become a real executive body and not a party branch; courts were to become independent and act as arbiters between the legislative and executive branches. Political pluralism was not recommended, but the Communist Party would have to justify its leading role by competing freely for supremacy with other organizations in the process of formation. International opinion saw Dubček as offering "socialism with a human face."

The effect of the liberalization movement—which became known as the Prague Spring—on the Czechoslovak public was unprecedented and quite unexpected. Alternative forms of political organization quickly emerged. Former political prisoners founded K 231, a group named after the article of the criminal code under which they had been sentenced; a number of prominent intellectuals formed KAN, a club for committed non-Communist Party members; and there even were efforts to reestablish the Social Democratic Party, forcibly fused with the Communist Party in 1948. With the collapse of the official communist youth movement, youth clubs and the Boy Scouts were resurrected. Christian churches, national minority associations, human rights groups, and other long-forgotten societies became active as well.

On June 27, 1968, the dissident writer Ludvík Vaculík published a document signed by a large number of people representing all walks of Czechoslovak life. This document, dubbed the "Two Thousand Words" manifesto, constituted a watershed in the evolution of the Prague Spring: it urged mass action to demand real democracy. Though shocked by the proclamation, Dubček was convinced that he could control the transformation of Czechoslovakia.

The Soviet Union and the other Warsaw Pact allies were far more alarmed. After Dubček declined to participate in a special meeting of the Warsaw Pact powers, they sent him a letter on July 15 saying that his country was on the verge of counterrevolution and that they considered it their duty to protect it. Nevertheless, Dubček remained confident that he could talk himself out of any difficulties with his fellow communist leaders. He accepted an invitation by Brezhnev to a conference at Čierná-nad-Tisou (a small town on the Soviet border with Slovakia), where the Soviet Politburo and the Czechoslovak leaders tried to resolve their problems. On August 3, representatives of the Soviet, East German, Polish, Bulgarian, Hungarian, and Czechoslovak Communist parties met again at Bratislava; the communiqué issued after that meeting gave the impression that pressure would be eased on Czechoslovakia in return for somewhat tighter control over the press.

WARSAW PACT

The treaty known formally as the Warsaw Treaty of Friendship, Cooperation, and Mutual Assistance, or the Warsaw Pact, was in existence from May 14, 1955 to July 1, 1991. The treaty established a mutual-defense organization (Warsaw Treaty Organization) during the Cold War that was composed originally of the Soviet Union and Albania, Bulgaria, Czechoslovakia, East Germany, Hungary, Poland, and Romania. (Albania withdrew in 1968, and East Germany did so in 1990.) The treaty (which was renewed on April 26, 1985) provided for a unified military command and for the maintenance of Soviet military units on the territories of the other participating states.

The immediate occasion for the Warsaw Pact was the Paris agreement among the Western powers admitting West Germany to the North Atlantic Treaty Organization. The Warsaw Pact was, however, the first step in a more systematic plan to strengthen the Soviet hold over its satellites, a program undertaken by the Soviet leaders Nikita Khrushchev and Nikolay Bulganin after their assumption of power early in 1955. The treaty also served as a lever to enhance the bargaining position of the Soviet Union in international diplomacy, an inference that may be drawn by the concluding article of the treaty, which stipulated that the Warsaw agreement would lapse when a general East-West collective-security pact should come into force.

The Warsaw Pact, particularly its provision for the garrisoning of Soviet troops in satellite territory, became a target of nationalist hostility in Poland and Hungary during the uprisings in those two countries in 1956. The Soviet Union invoked the treaty when it decided to move Warsaw Pact troops into Czechoslovakia in August 1968 to bring the Czechoslovak regime back into the fold after it had begun lifting restraints on freedom of expression and had sought closer relations with the West. (Only Albania and Romania refused to join in the Czechoslovak repression.)

After the democratic revolutions of 1989 in eastern Europe, the Warsaw Pact became moribund and was formally declared "nonexistent" on July 1, 1991, at a final summit meeting of Warsaw Pact leaders in Prague, Czechoslovakia. Deployed Soviet troops were gradually withdrawn from the former satellite countries, now politically independent countries; and the decades-long confrontation between eastern and western Europe was formally rejected by members of the Warsaw Pact.

However, on the evening of August 20, 1968, Soviet-led armed forces invaded the country. The Soviet authorities seized Dubček, Černík, and several other leaders and secretly took them to Moscow. Meanwhile, the population spontaneously reacted against the invasion through acts of passive resistance and improvisation (e.g., road signs were removed so that the invading troops would get lost). Although communications were disrupted and supplies were held up, the people went on with life at the local level. Even the scheduled 14th Communist Party Congress took place on August 22; it elected a pro-Dubček Central Committee and Presidium—the very things the invasion had been timed to prevent. The National Assembly, declaring its loyalty to Dubček, continued its plenary sessions. On August 23 President Svoboda, accompanied by Husák, left for Moscow to negotiate an end to the occupation. But by August 27 the Czechoslovaks had been compelled to yield to the Soviets' demands in an agreement known as the Moscow Protocol. Svoboda, bringing with him Dubček and the other leaders, returned to Prague to tell the population what price they would have to pay for their "socialism with a human face": Soviet troops were going to stay in Czechoslovakia for the time being, and the leaders had agreed to tighter controls over political and cultural activities.

The continued presence of Soviet troops helped the communist hard-liners, who were joined by Husák, to defeat Dubček and the reformers. First of all, the 14th Party Congress was declared invalid, as required by the Moscow Protocol; hard-liners were thus able to occupy positions of power. Czechoslovakia was proclaimed a federal republic, with two autonomous units—the Czech Lands (Bohemia and Moravia) forming the Czech Socialist Republic and Slovakia the Slovak Socialist Republic, respectively—each with national parliaments and governments. A federal arrangement was the one concession the hard-liners

were ready to make, and, indeed, many citizens (particularly the Slovaks) had desired it. Nonetheless, protests against the curtailing of reforms—such as the dramatic suicide of Jan Palach, a student who on January 16, 1969, set himself on fire—were what held the country's attention.

Gradually, Dubček either dismissed his friends and allies or forced them to resign, and on April 17, 1969, Husák replaced him as first secretary. Dubček continued for a while as chairman (speaker) of the parliament and then became ambassador to Turkey. After his recall in 1970 he was stripped of his party membership. The victorious Husák declared the Dubček experiment to be finished and promptly initiated a process of "normalization."

"NORMALIZATION" AND POLITICAL DISSIDENCE

As first secretary, Husák patiently tried to persuade Soviet leaders that Czechoslovakia was a loyal member of the Warsaw Pact. He had the constitution amended to embody the newly proclaimed Brezhnev Doctrine, which asserted the right of the Soviet Union to intervene militarily if it perceived socialism anywhere to be under threat, and in 1971 he repudiated the Prague Spring—declaring that "in 1968 socialism was in danger in Czechoslovakia, and the armed intervention helped to save it." In 1970 Oldřich Černík was finally forced to resign the premiership; he was succeeded by Husák's Czech rival, Lubomír Štrougal. In 1975, when President Svoboda retired because of ill health, Husák once again fused the two most important offices in Czechoslovakia and became, with full Soviet approval, president himself.

Having purged the reformists during 1969–71, Husák concentrated almost exclusively on the economy. In the short term, Czechoslovakia did not suffer significantly, even from the disruption caused by the military occupation in 1968. The country undertook important infrastructure improvement projects, notably the construction of the Prague metro and a major motorway connecting Prague with Bratislava in Slovakia. Husák, however, did not permit the industrial and agricultural reforms from the Action Program to be applied and so failed to cure the country's long-term economic problems. The achievements of the mid- to late 1970s were modest, and by the early 1980s Czechoslovakia was experiencing a serious economic downturn, caused by a decline in markets for its products, burdensome terms of trade with several of its supplier countries, and a surplus of outdated machinery and technology.

Although Husák had avoided the bloodletting of his predecessors, his party purges had damaged Czechoslovak cultural and scientific life, since positions in these two areas depended on membership in the party. Numerous writers, composers, journalists, historians, and scientists found themselves unemployed and forced to accept menial jobs to earn a living. Many of these disappointed intellectuals tried to continue the struggle against the regime, but they were indicted for committing criminal acts in pursuance of political objectives. Though these trials could not be compared to the Stalinist show trials, they kept discontent among the intellectuals simmering, even if the mass of the population was indifferent. Intellectual discontent gathered strength in January 1977, when a group of intellectuals signed a petition, known as Charter 77, in which they urged the government to observe human rights as outlined in the Helsinki Accords of 1975. Many intellectuals and activists who signed the petition subsequently were arrested and detained, but their efforts continued throughout the following decade. Among the victims of the crackdown was the philosopher Jan Patocka, who died on March 13, 1977, after a number of police interrogations.

Several mass demonstrations took place in the country during the 1980s. The largest protest gathering in Slovakia since the Prague Spring occurred on March 25, 1988: during this so-called "Candle Demonstration" in Bratislava, thousands of Slovaks quietly held burning candles to show their support for religious freedom and human rights. Police dispersed the demonstration with water cannons and made numerous arrests.

VELVET REVOLUTION AND VELVET DIVORCE

In 1989 a wave of protests against communist rule erupted in eastern Europe;

among the most significant events were the culmination of the Polish Solidarity movement, the adoption of a democratic constitution in Hungary, and the mass exodus of thousands of freedom-seeking East Germans, some via Prague, after Hungary opened its border with Austria. Despite the momentous events in surrounding countries, the Czechoslovak people took little action until late in the fall of 1989. On November 16, students in Bratislava gathered for a peaceful demonstration; the next day a student march, approved by the authorities, took place in Prague. The Prague march was intended to commemorate the 50th anniversary of the suppression of a student demonstration in German-occupied Prague, but students soon began criticizing the regime, and the police reacted with brutality.

This incident set off a nationwide protest movement—dubbed the Velvet Revolution—that gained particular strength in the country's industrial centres. Prodemocracy demonstrations and strikes took place under the makeshift leadership of the Civic Forum, an opposition group for which the dissident playwright and Charter 77 coauthor Václav Havel served as chief spokesman. In Slovakia a parallel group named Public Against Violence was founded. Daily mass gatherings culminated in a general strike on November 27, during which the people demanded free elections and an end to one-party rule.

The communist authorities were forced to negotiate with the opposition, and, as a result, a transition government incorporating members of the Civic Forum and Public Against Violence was formed. Husák resigned in December 1989, and Havel was chosen to succeed him as Czechoslovakia's first noncommunist president in more than 40 years. The former party leader Alexander Dubček returned to political life as the new speaker of the Federal Assembly. In June 1990, in the first free elections held in Czechoslovakia since 1946, the Civic Forum and Public Against Violence won decisive majorities; in July Havel was reelected as president.

The new government undertook the multifarious tasks of the transition from communism to democracy, beginning with privatizing businesses, revamping foreign policy, and writing a new constitution. The last Soviet troops were withdrawn from Czechoslovakia in June 1991, and the Warsaw Pact was disbanded the following month, thus completing Czechoslovakia's separation from the Soviet bloc. However, the drafting of a new constitution was hindered by differences between political parties, Czech-Slovak tensions, and power struggles. Another serious obstacle was the cumbersome federal structure inherited from the communists. When issues dividing Czechs and Slovaks were discussed, the existence of multiple ministerial cabinets and diets made it extremely difficult to achieve the prescribed majority on the federal level. Moreover, the minority bloc of Slovak deputies had disproportionate veto power.

The Czechoslovak federation began to appear increasingly fragile in 1991–92, and separatism became a momentous issue. Parliamentary elections in June 1992 gave the Czech premiership to Václav Klaus, an economist by training and finance minister since 1989. Klaus headed a centre-right coalition that included the Civic Democratic Party, which he had cofounded. The Slovak premiership went to Vladimir Mečiar, a vocal Slovak nationalist and prominent member of Public Against Violence who had served briefly as Slovak prime minister in 1990–91. Mečiar headed his Movement for a Democratic Slovakia party. The parties led by Klaus and Mečiar were supported by about one-third of the electorate in their respective republics, but the differences between the two were so great that a lasting federal government could not be formed.

After Havel's resignation on July 20, 1992, no suitable candidate for the federal presidency emerged; Czechoslovakia now lacked a symbol of unity as well as a convincing advocate. Thus, the assumption was readily made, at least in political circles, that the Czechoslovak state would have to be divided. There was little evidence of public enthusiasm for the split, but neither Klaus nor Mečiar wished to ask the population for a verdict through a referendum. The two republics proceeded with separation negotiations in an atmosphere of peace and cooperation. By late November, members of the National Assembly had voted Czechoslovakia out of existence. Both republics promulgated new constitutions, and at midnight on December 31, 1992, after 74 years of joint existence disrupted only by World War II, Czechoslovakia was formally dissolved. With the completion of this so-called Velvet Divorce, the independent countries of Slovakia and the Czech Republic were created on January 1, 1993.

THE CZECH REPUBLIC: 1993 TO THE PRESENT

The former president of Czechoslovakia, Václav Havel, was elected president of the new Czech Republic in January 1993, and Václav Klaus became prime minister. Because there was as yet no Senate, the election was conducted only by the Chamber of Deputies, thus contravening the republic's new constitution. Although the separation with Slovakia proceeded amicably, customs posts were erected along the Czech-Slovak border, and signs of rising national tempers were briefly noted on both sides of the new frontier.

Under a centre-right coalition government—composed of the Civic Democratic Party, the Civic Democratic Alliance, and the Christian and Democratic Union-Czech People's Party—the new Czech Republic pursued a fairly aggressive policy of political and economic reform, the cornerstone of which was a program of rapid privatization. On May 31–June 1, 1996, the Czech Republic held its first general election since the country had become a separate entity. The coalition government lost its parliamentary majority when the centre-left Czech Social Democratic Party nearly quadrupled the number of seats it had previously held in

VÁCLAV HAVEL

The Czech playwright, poet, and political dissident Václav Havel (born October 5, 1936, Prague, Czechoslovakia [now in Czech Republic]—died December 18, 2011, Hrádecek, Czech Republic) became a political leader after the fall of communism. He served as president of Czechoslovakia (1989–92) and of the Czech Republic (1993–2003).

Havel was the son of a wealthy restaurateur whose property was confiscated by the communist government of Czechoslovakia in 1948. As the son of bourgeois parents, Havel was denied easy access to education but managed to finish high school and study on the university level. He found work as a stagehand in a Prague theatrical company in 1959 and soon began writing plays with Ivan Vyskocil. By 1968 Havel had progressed to the position of resident playwright of the Theatre of the Balustrade company. He was a prominent participant in the liberal reforms of 1968 (known as the Prague Spring), and, after the Soviet clampdown on Czechoslovakia that year, his plays were banned and his passport was confiscated. During the 1970s and '80s he was repeatedly arrested and served four years in prison (1979–83) for his activities on behalf of human rights in Czechoslovakia. After his release from prison Havel remained in his homeland.

Havel's first solo play, *Zahradní slavnost* (1963; *The Garden Party*), typified his work in its absurdist, satirical examination of bureaucratic routines and their dehumanizing effects. In his best-known play, *Vyrozumění* (1965; *The Memorandum*), an incomprehensible artificial language is imposed on a large bureaucratic enterprise, causing the breakdown of human relationships and their replacement by unscrupulous struggles for power. In these and subsequent works Havel explored the self-deluding rationalizations and moral compromises that characterize life under a totalitarian political system. Havel continued to write plays steadily until the late 1980s; these works include *Ztížená možnost soustředění* (1968; *The Increased Difficulty of Concentration*); *Spiklenci* (1971; *The Conspirators*); the three one-act plays *Audience* (1975), *Vernisáž* (1975; *Private View*), and *Protest* (1978); *Largo Desolato* (1985); and *Zítra to Spustíme* (1988; *Tomorrow*).

When massive antigovernment demonstrations erupted in Prague in November 1989, Havel became the leading figure in the Civic Forum, a new coalition of noncommunist opposition groups pressing for democratic reforms. In early December the Communist Party capitulated and formed a coalition government with the Civic Forum. As a result of an agreement between the partners in this bloodless "Velvet Revolution," Havel was elected to the post of interim president of Czechoslovakia on December 29, 1989, and he was reelected to the presidency in July 1990, becoming the country's first noncommunist leader since 1948. As the Czechoslovak union faced dissolution in 1992, Havel, who opposed the division, resigned from office. The following year he was elected president of the new Czech Republic. His political role, however, was limited, as Prime Minister Václav Klaus (1993–97) commanded much of the power. In 1998 Havel was reelected by a narrow margin, and, under his presidency, the Czech Republic joined the North Atlantic Treaty Organization (NATO) in 1999. Barred constitutionally from seeking a third term, he stepped down as president in 2003.

Havel's first new play in more than 20 years—*Odcházení* (*Leaving*), a tragicomedy that draws on his experiences as president and presents a chancellor leaving his post while grappling with a political enemy—premiered in 2008. Havel subsequently directed its film adaptation (2011).

the Chamber of Deputies. Nevertheless, the coalition headed by Klaus and Havel remained in power, with a pledge of support from the Social Democrats. However, major economic problems, serious rifts within the ruling coalition, and public dissatisfaction with Klaus's leadership and economic policy forced the prime minister's resignation in November 1997. Klaus's Civic Democratic Party then split into two factions. Jan Ruml, a former interior minister, founded a new conservative party, the Freedom Union, to which almost half of the Civic Democrat deputies defected.

Klaus, however, remained a political force and shortly after his resignation was reelected party chairman of the Civic Democratic Party. At the June 1998 elections his party won more than one-fourth of the votes; the Social Democrats won nearly one-third. President Havel, who had been reelected by a slim margin to a second term in January, called upon Social Democrat chairman Miloš Zeman (as the leader of the party with the largest number of seats in the Chamber of Deputies) to form a government, which was not initially successful. Eventually Zeman was installed as prime minister, and Klaus was elected to the chairmanship of the Chamber of Deputies.

The country's domestic troubles during the mid- to late 1990s were to some extent mitigated by its acceptance into NATO. However, by the end of the 1990s, public dissatisfaction with the political leadership was growing. In early 1999, a group of prominent political writers issued "Impuls 99," a declaration calling for decisive social, moral, and political change that would ensure the country's rapid accession to the European Union (EU), to which it had formally applied for membership in 1996. In November 1999 activists who had been leaders during the 1989 revolution circulated a more radical manifesto, "Thank You! Now Leave!," demanding the resignations of the leaders of all the major political parties for jeopardizing the Czech Republic's acceptance into the EU. Tens of thousands of citizens took to the streets of Prague and other cities to demonstrate against the government. Another cause for concern was the spread of racial violence against the Roma (Gypsies).

On the other hand, in the realm of foreign policy, the Czech Republic experienced considerable success during the 1990s. In January 1997 Germany and the Czech Republic signed a document of reconciliation in which Germany acknowledged regret for its treatment of Czechs during the Nazi era, and the Czech Republic expressed remorse for Czechoslovakia's expulsion of some three million Germans from the Sudeten region following World War II. Relations between Slovakia and the Czech Republic, however, remained tense for most of the 1990s, with some improvement in the early 21st century.

Klaus regained the political spotlight in 2003 when he became president at the conclusion of Havel's decade-long tenure. Klaus, who was narrowly reelected by the Czech Parliament in February

2008, served alongside a series of prime ministers and cabinets beset by political infighting. Meanwhile, the Czech Republic had taken a historic step on May 1, 2004, when it became a member of the EU, and during the first half of 2009 the country assumed the rotating EU presidency. Some observers questioned the republic's fitness to lead the EU when, in March 2009, the centre-right Czech government collapsed after losing a parliamentary vote of confidence. A nonpartisan interim prime minister, Jan Fischer, took power in May.

In the same month, the Czech Senate voted in favour of the EU's Lisbon Treaty (an agreement to reform certain EU institutions), which the lower house had already approved. Klaus, however, claimed that the treaty was not in the best interests of the Czech Republic and refused to sign it until November 2009, when the Czech Constitutional Court ruled that the treaty did not threaten the Czech constitution. Klaus then reluctantly endorsed the treaty, completing the country's ratification process. The Czech Republic thus became the last of the 27 EU members to ratify the Lisbon Treaty.

Meanwhile, the country's interim government remained in power for more than a year, until July 2010, when President Klaus appointed a fellow Civic Democrat, Petr Nečas, as prime minister. Nečas headed a new coalition government comprising the Civic Democratic Party and two other right-of-centre parties. Although the Czech Social

Democratic Party had garnered the most votes in the parliamentary elections held in late May, the three centre-right parties together had won a majority.

SLOVAKIA: 1993 TO THE PRESENT

The Slovak Republic came into being on January 1, 1993, following the dissolution of the Czechoslovak federation. The new prime minister, Vladimír Mečiar, and his Czech counterpart, Václav Klaus, had been among the strongest proponents of separation, but their enthusiasm did not extend to the general populace. Although a renewed sense of national pride welled up in Slovakia, so, too, did a feeling of apprehension about the republic's future. This sense of uneasiness was manifested in the large numbers of Slovaks who began applying for Czech citizenship immediately after partition.

Slovakia generally had been perceived as the junior partner in the federation, but that arrangement also had provided the republic with a degree of political security and economic stability that became less certain with independence. Long-standing political differences and tensions with neighbouring countries that had been suppressed during the period of Soviet hegemony reemerged; notable among these were Hungary's concerns about the future of the large Hungarian minority in southern Slovakia. In addition, economic forecasts for Slovakia generally were less optimistic than those for the Czech Republic.

Slovakia inherited an economy dependent on large-scale but obsolete heavy industry, and the country faced rising unemployment and poor prospects for foreign investment. Furthermore, since Czechs had long dominated the federal leadership of Czechoslovakia, the Slovak regional leaders lacked experience at the national level.

In February 1993 Michal Kováč, the deputy chairman of the Movement for a Democratic Slovakia (Hnutie Za Democratické Slovensko; HZDS), became president of the republic. Difficulties immediately arose in maintaining a coalition government, with the result that the HZDS and the rather autocratic figure of Mečiar tended to dominate. Mečiar favoured a brand of populist nationalism that left Slovakia's minorities at a disadvantage. He was neither overly interested in forging alliances with western Europe nor in tolerating dissenting voices from the opposition parties. In March 1994 Mečiar lost a vote of confidence and was forced to resign. A new five-party interim

VLADIMIR MEČIAR

The political leader Vladimir Mečiar (born July 26, 1942, Zvolen, Czechoslovakia [now Slovakia]) served as prime minister of Slovakia (1990–91, 1992–94, and 1994–98) and worked to establish it as a republic separate from the Czech Republic, its partner in the federation of Czechoslovakia, in 1993. His leadership was later associated with autocratic policies and failing economic conditions.

In his youth, Mečiar competed as an amateur boxer. He was educated at Comenius University in Bratislava. He served in various posts in the pro-communist Union of Slovak Youth and apparently backed Alexander Dubček during the Prague Spring of 1968. His opposition to Communist Party hard-liners cost him his party membership in 1969, and he slipped into relative obscurity for the next two decades.

Mečiar reemerged as a prominent member of Public Against Violence, an anticommunist opposition group, and became interim minister of the interior following the 1989 Velvet Revolution, which toppled communist rule in Czechoslovakia. In the June 1990 elections, Public Against Violence won a clear victory in Slovakia, and Mečiar became Slovak prime minister. Mečiar was ousted from his post as prime minister in April 1991, partly because of accusations of having collaborated with the secret police during the communist era. Instead of diminishing his power, however, Mečiar's reversal boosted his popularity among Slovaks, who viewed their former premier as a martyr.

Out of office but riding a crest of popular acclaim, Mečiar then formed the Movement for a Democratic Slovakia (Hnutie Za Democratické Slovensko; HZDS). Seeing Slovak nationalism as his path to power, he pledged to stand up to Prague and its fast-paced program of free-market reforms. The HZDS finished first in the June 1992 regional parliamentary elections, and Mečiar again became the Slovak prime minister. With the division of Czechoslovakia into two independent republics in January 1993, Mečiar became the head of government of a sovereign country.

In his first year as leader of independent Slovakia, Mečiar faced a host of difficulties. A large Hungarian minority turned restive. Some observers saw autocratic tendencies in the HZDS regime. More seriously, the economy stumbled as Mečiar's plan for a gentle transition from socialism to capitalism did little to reduce the nation's dependence on the weakening arms industry. By midyear, unemployment had reached 11.5 percent and was rising, and foreign investment was dropping precipitously. The HZDS government adopted an austerity budget with reduced spending for social programs. Not surprisingly, Mečiar's popularity plummeted, and he was defeated in a parliamentary nonconfidence vote in March 1994. Nevertheless, he returned to power for his third term as prime minister after elections that fall.

Mečiar's very name became associated with corruption and economic stagnation. Western countries viewed his leadership as undemocratic, and the North Atlantic Treaty Organization (NATO) and the European Union were wary of dealing with Slovakia because of his influence. In the elections of 1998—as Slovakia endured a 22 percent unemployment rate—Mečiar was again voted out of office when Mikulas Dzurinda won a majority. In 2000 Meciar was arrested for having ordered the 1995 kidnapping of the son of the president of Slovakia and after allegations that he had bribed cabinet members. This news came in the wake of his 1998 decision to give amnesty to the man who had previously been charged with the kidnapping. Dzurinda tried to abolish that amnesty shortly after taking office, but in 2008 the European Court of Human Rights declared Dzurinda's action illegal.

Despite vowing in 1998 that he would never return to politics again, Mečiar ran unsuccessfully for office in 1999, 2002, and 2004. His connection to the 1995 kidnapping has never been proven.

coalition headed by a new prime minister, Jozef Moravčík, adopted a policy of closer alignment with western Europe.

In the September 1994 elections, however, the HZDS regained power, and Mečiar was reinstalled as prime minister, forming in mid-December a coalition composed of the HZDS, the right-wing Slovak National Party, and the leftist Association of Workers of Slovakia. Once back in office, Mečiar attempted to recentralize state authority by blocking further privatization of state-owned companies. In addition, the rivalry between Mečiar and Kováč, who had never seen eye to eye, deepened. The Mečiar government's stance toward Slovakia's minorities and its tenuous commitment to democratic principles did not go unnoticed by the international community, and in March 1995, under pressure from Western powers, Slovakia and Hungary signed the Treaty of Friendship and Cooperation, in which the Slovak government pledged to protect minority rights. The commitment was called into question, however, when in November the government made Slovak the republic's official language, a move that caused great consternation among the nation's Hungarian minority. The Hungarian government declared the policy to be in violation of the treaty. Throughout 1996 there was increasing concern over the Mečiar government's antidemocratic direction, which included a so-called antisubversion law that would curb freedom of expression, which Kováč refused to sign. The law later passed in an amended form.

In June 1997 a European Union–Slovakia parliamentary committee made it clear that, in order for Slovakia to qualify for EU membership, the government would have to make adjustments in its policy toward the opposition and its treatment of minorities. Kováč and Mečiar agreed to the stipulations in October. However, at an EU summit held in December, it became evident that Slovakia would not be among the first wave of former Soviet-bloc countries admitted to the union.

During the early part of 1998, several attempts to elect a new president failed, and on March 2, when Kováč's term expired, a number of presidential duties devolved to Mečiar, in accordance with the Slovak constitution. Mečiar immediately made several unilateral decisions that clearly benefited his own interests. His actions, condemned by the EU and the United States, spawned a series

of protests in Slovakia. The country remained without a president for much of the year. Parliamentary elections held in September resulted in the removal of the HZDS from power. A four-party coalition composed of the centre-right Slovak Democratic Coalition, the Party of the Democratic Left, the centre-left Party of Civic Understanding, and the Party of the Hungarian Coalition took over the reins of government, with Mikuláš Dzurinda, the chairman of the Slovak Democratic Coalition, as prime minister.

Mečiar offered his name as a presidential candidate in the election held on May 29, 1999, but he was defeated decisively by Rudolf Schuster, a member of the Carpathian-German minority and the chairman of the Party for Civic Understanding. The new ruling coalition declared its intention to ready the country for membership in the EU and NATO, to take measures to halt environmental degradation, and to crack down on organized crime, which had become an increasingly worrisome problem in the latter part of the 1990s. The coalition also introduced a wide-ranging austerity program intended to arrest Slovakia's economic decline. The program met with a wave of protests and strikes but was favourably received by the Organisation for Economic Co-operation and Development (OECD), which Slovakia joined in 2000.

Political difficulties continued into the 21st century; however, the economy began to turn around, and the government continued the privatization of state-owned industries. After parliamentary elections in 2002, Dzurinda retained his post as prime minister. The new centre-right ruling coalition approved additional economic and social reforms but lost its parliamentary majority in 2003. The year 2004 was a momentous one, as the country joined both NATO and the EU. Ivan Gašparovič of the Movement for Democracy party defeated Mečiar in the presidential election that year, and the economy continued to grow. Parliamentary elections in 2006 resulted in yet another coalition of ruling parties, with the leader of the populist party Smer, Robert Fico, becoming prime minister.

Slovakia did not escape the global economic downturn that began in 2008, but public support for Prime Minister Fico remained high, thanks partly to Slovakia's adoption of the euro at the beginning of 2009. It was the second country in the former communist bloc (after Slovenia) to do so. That April Gašparovič defeated Iveta Radičová, of the Slovak Democratic and Christian Union (SDKU), to be reelected president. A significant issue leading up to the June 2010 parliamentary elections was the question of Slovakia's role in the bailout of debt-laden euro zone countries. The four-party centre-right coalition government that emerged from those elections was headed by Radičová, who became the first woman to serve as Slovakia's prime minister. In August 2010 the Slovak parliament refused to pay the €816 million ($1.1 billion) that constituted the country's share of the bailout fund for Greece organized by the EU and the International Monetary Fund. Slovak politicians argued that their country was one of the poorest in the euro zone and should not be expected to finance the mismanagement of its richer neighbours. This sentiment came to the fore in October 2011, when a no-confidence vote over the expansion of the European Financial Stability Facility (EFSF), the euro zone's primary bailout mechanism, toppled the Radičová government. After the government's collapse, Radičová opened talks with Smer, and Fico pledged his support for the EFSF in exchange for early elections.

When Slovaks headed to the polls in March 2012, they resoundingly rejected the Radičová coalition. Smer, with Fico at its head, collected 83 of 150 seats, becoming the first single party to win a clear majority in the Slovak parliament since the fall of communism. Allegations of corruption against centre-right politicians, as well as frustration with austerity measures, soured voters on the SDKU, and the party barely obtained the number of votes necessary for representation in the parliament. Fico pledged that his government would adhere to the deficit-control regulations of the EU's new fiscal compact by raising the tax rates of wealthy individuals and corporations.

CONCLUSION

The countries of central and eastern Europe in this volume—Bulgaria, Hungary, Romania, and the Czech Republic and Slovakia—have been a historical crossroads for the people and civilizations of the so-called "West" and "East" (the latter of which might be more accurately described geographically as located to the north, south, and east). Bulgaria was for centuries part of the Byzantine Empire and, later, the Ottoman Empire. The territories that became Romania were at times under the control or strong influence of Russia, Hungary, and the Ottoman and Roman empires. Hungary and the lands that became the Czech Republic and Slovakia were more Western in their orientation, with connections to the Roman and Holy Roman empires, Hungary, Austria, Germany, and Poland. In the 20th century, all became communist countries and were part of the eastern European Soviet-aligned bloc for decades until the fall of communism in the late 1980s and early 1990s.

Through the centuries, music, literature, and other artistic forms have flourished in the region. In Bulgaria, folk culture has been particularly strong, and some of its traditional music achieved worldwide fame in the late 20th century. In Hungary, high culture has dominated, especially in music, exemplified best by classical composers Franz Liszt and Béla Bartók. Many of Romania's most noted artists did their greatest work after emigrating, including playwright Eugene Ionesco, sculptor Constantin Brancusi, and writer Tristan Tzara, the founder of the 20th-century revolutionary movement in the arts known as Dada. Czech culture centred on Prague. In the 20th century that country gave birth to many great writers, including Franz Kafka, Rainer Maria Rilke, Milan Kundera, and Václav Havel, who became the Czech Republic's first president. In Slovakia, writing and filmmaking have arguably been the most prominent art forms, although even their most notable practitioners, such as poet Hviezdoslav and motion-picture directors Ján Kadár and Dušan Hanák, have not achieved as great of international fame as have the artists of the Czech Republic.

Overall, the countries of the region have made great contributions to world culture and intellectual discourse. As members of the European Union and other international organizations, they are integral players on the world stage.

GLOSSARY

ALLUVIAL Composed of or containing clay, silt, or other deposits contained in runoff from moving water, such as rivers.

ASSIMILATE To absorb into the culture of a population or group.

ATTAR A fragrant essential oil used in the making of perfume and other products.

AUTOCEPHALOUS Refers to independence from external authority, especially in regard to Eastern national churches.

BOYAR A member of the Russian aristocracy, a step below a ruling prince.

DE FACTO A term used to describe someone or something that, in effect, is in control or has power but is not officially recognized as such.

ECCLESIASTICAL Of or relating to the church.

EGALITARIAN Of or relating to a belief in human equality, especially with respect to social, political, and economic affairs.

ETHNOGENESIS The origin and development of an ethnic or national group.

EXARCHATE An area overseen by the bishop of an independent Eastern church.

FIEF Something over which one has rights or control, especially with regard to a feudal estate.

GUILD An association of people with similar interests or beliefs , such as artisans and merchants.

GYMNASIUM A term used in some European countries to describe a secondary or college preparatory school.

HOMOGENEOUS Of the same or similar nature.

KARST An irregular limestone region with sinkholes, underground streams, and caverns.

KOLKHOZ A collective farm found in the former Union of Soviet Socialist Republics.

LAGOON A shallow body of water located near or communicating with a larger body of water.

MAGNATE A person of rank, power, influence, or distinction.

OMBUDSMAN A government official appointed to receive and investigate complaints made by individuals against public officials.

PAGAN One who follows a polytheistic religion.

PASTORAL Of or relating to rural life or an economy based on the raising of livestock.

PATRIARCHAL Of or relating to the male line of descent , or male-dominated; also, having to do with a jurisdiction in an Eastern Orthodox church.

PRIVATIZATION The state of being changed from public (government) to private control or ownership.

SPAHI One of a former corps of irregular Turkish cavalry.

SUFFRAGAN A bishop of a church who is subordinate to an archbishop or another official in the hierarchy

SURREPTITIOUS A word to describe something done or accomplished by stealth or in secret.

SUZERAINTY An area overseen by a feudal lord.

URBANIZATION The process of becoming a city , or city-like, greatly increasing in population density.

BIBLIOGRAPHY

BULGARIA

GEOGRAPHY

A general work is Emil Giatzidis, *An Introduction to Post-Communist Bulgaria: Political, Economic, and Social Transformations* (2002). Economic and social policies are discussed in Robert J. McIntyre, *Bulgaria: Politics, Economics, and Society* (1988); John R. Lampe, *The Bulgarian Economy in the Twentieth Century* (1986); and George R. Feiwel, *Growth and Reforms in Centrally Planned Economies: The Lessons of the Bulgarian Experience* (1977). Bulgaria's cultural heritage is surveyed in Machiel Kiel, *Art and Society of Bulgaria in the Turkish Period* (1985), an extensive survey of Turkish influences on Bulgaria and on Christian art and symbolism, 1360–1700.

HISTORY

A general overview of Bulgarian history is provided by Richard J. Crampton, *A Concise History of Bulgaria*, 2nd ed. (2010). Coverage of specific periods of history may be found in Robert Browning, *Byzantium and Bulgaria: A Comparative Study Across the Early Medieval Frontier* (1975); Assen Nicoloff, *The Bulgarian Resurgence* (1987); John D. Bell, *Peasants in Power: Alexander Stamboliski and the Bulgarian Agrarian National Union,* *1899–1923* (1977); Stéphane Groueff, *Crown of Thorns* (1987, reissued 1997), covering the reign of Boris III (1918–43); Marshall Lee Miller, *Bulgaria During the Second World War* (1975); and John D. Bell, *The Bulgarian Communist Party from Blagoev to Zhivkov* (1986). Stefanos Katsikas (ed.), *Bulgaria and Europe: Shifting Identities* (2010), examines Bulgaria's place within Europe.

HUNGARY

GEOGRAPHY

Overviews of the history, geography, and people of Hungary and its social, economic, and cultural life are provided by Ferenc Erdei (ed.), *Information Hungary* (1968), for the communist era; and Éva Molnár (ed.), *Hungary: Essential Facts, Figures, and Pictures* (1995), for the post-communist era.

Cultural topics are considered in Francis S. Wagner, *Hungarian Contributions to World Civilization*, 2nd ed. (1991); and András Gerö and János Poór (eds.), *Budapest: A History from Its Beginnings to 1998*, trans. from Hungarian (1997).

Hungarians in the surrounding states are profiled in Stephen Borsody (ed.), *The Hungarians: A Divided Nation* (1988); and László Szarka (ed.), *Hungary and the Hungarian Minorities*, trans. from Hungarian (2004).

HISTORY

Overviews of Hungarian history include Peter F. Sugar, Péter Hanák, and Tibor Frank (eds.), *A History of Hungary* (1990); *Stephen Sisa, The Spirit of Hungary*, 4th ed. (1999); László Kontler, *Millennium in Central Europe: A History of Hungary* (1999; reissued as *A History of Hungary: Millennium in Central Europe*, 2002); and Paul Lendvai, *The Hungarians: A Thousand Years of Victory in Defeat* (2003; originally published in German, 1999). Another useful historical reference is S.B. Várdy, *Historical Dictionary of Hungary*, 2nd ed. (1997).

ROMANIA

GEOGRAPHY

General overviews of Romania are presented in Peter Siani-Davies and Mary Siani-Davies (compilers), *Romania*, rev. ed. (1998). Economic aspects are discussed in David Turnock, *The Romanian Economy in the Twentieth Century* (1986); and Walt Patterson, *Rebuilding Romania: Energy, Efficiency, and the Economic Transition* (1994). Trond Gilberg, *Nationalism and Communism in Romania: The Rise and Fall of Ceaușescu's Personal Dictatorship* (1990), explores the devastating effects of the Ceaușescu regime on the people and country of Romania. Tom Gallagher, *Romania After Ceaușescu* (1995), delineates the challenges of Romania's transition from a closed to an open political system.

HISTORY

A general survey of Romanian history is Lucian Boia, *Romania: Borderland of Europe*, trans. from Romanian (2001). Dumitru Berciu, *Romania* (1967), covers the prehistory of the Carpathian-Danube region. Dumitru Berciu and Bucur Mitrea, *Daco-Romania* (1978; originally published in French, 1976), describes the origins and continuity of the Daco-Romans in Dacia. On the modern period, Keith Hitchins, *The Romanians, 1774–1866* (1996), and *Rumania, 1866–1947* (1994), analyze the emergence and development of modern Romania. Robert R. King, *A History of the Romanian Communist Party* (1980), traces the evolution of communism from insignificance to dominance. Mary Ellen Fischer, *Nicolae Ceaușescu: A Study in Political Leadership* (1989), analyzes the formation and nature of the communist dictatorship.

CZECH AND SLOVAK HISTORY

Hugh LeCaine Agnew, *The Czechs and the Lands of the Bohemian Crown* (2004), may be considered the first synthetic, full-length history of the Czechoslovak region in English. The best economic survey is Alice Teichová, *The Czechoslovak Economy, 1918–1980* (1988).

The kingdom of Bohemia in the 14th and 15th centuries, and especially the

Hussite movement and its aftermath, are discussed in Howard Kaminsky, *A History of the Hussite Revolution* (1967). An excellent treatment of Bohemia's role in the 17th century is Josef Polišenský, *The Thirty Years War* (1971; originally published in Czech). The history of the region under Habsburg rule is found in R.J.W. Evans, *The Making of the Habsburg Monarchy, 1550–1700: An Interpretation* (1979, reissued 1991). The development of modern Czech nationalism and of the Czechoslovak state are explored in Hugh LeCaine Agnew, *Origins of the Czech National Renascence* (1993).

The formation of the Czechoslovak republic is addressed in Z.A.B. Zeman, *The Masaryks: The Making of Czechoslovakia* (1976, reissued 1990), and *The Break-Up of the Habsburg Empire, 1914–1918: A Study in National and Social Revolution* (1961, reprinted 1977). Czechoslovakia's fate through the presidency of Edvard Beneš and World War II is addressed by Beneš's former secretary in Edward Taborsky, *President Beneš: Between East and West, 1938–1948* (1981). The painful history of the Nazi occupation is examined in Vojtech Mastny, *The Czechs Under Nazi Rule: The Failure of National Resistance, 1939–1942* (1971). The communist capture of power is described in Karel Kaplan, *The Short March: The Communist Takeover in Czechoslovakia, 1945–1948* (1987; originally published in German). The most detailed study on the Prague Spring of 1968 is H. Gordon Skilling, *Czechoslovakia's Interrupted Revolution* (1976). Bernard Wheaton and Zdeněk Kavan, *The Velvet Revolution: Czechoslovakia, 1988–1991* (1992), describes the popular revolution of 1989 and subsequent events. Later works include Carol Skalnik Leff, *The Czech and Slovak Republics: Nation Versus State* (1996).

THE CZECH REPUBLIC

GEOGRAPHY

A brief guide containing all the essentials is Jiri Hochman, *Historical Dictionary of the Czech State* (1998). Also informative is Daniel Miller, "Czech Republic," in Richard Frucht (ed.), *Eastern Europe: An Introduction to the People, Lands, and Culture*, vol. 2, (2005). Milan Holeček et al., *The Czech Republic in Brief* (1995) is a geographical guide. The history of the Roma minority is addressed in Renata Weinerova (eds.), *Roma Migration in Europe* (2004).

Jaroslav Krejčn *Social Change and Stratification in Postwar Czechoslovakia* (1972), is a socioeconomic study of Czechoslovak life in the communist period. The companion volume by the same author, *Czechoslovakia 1918–92: A Laboratory for Social Change* (1996), should be consulted for its discussion of socioeconomic analysis of the early post-communist years. Miloslav Rechcigl, Jr. (ed.), *The Czechoslovak Contribution to World Culture* (1964), is a collection of essays on all aspects of intellectual life, with an extensive bibliography.

HISTORY

Concise historical information can be found in Jiří Hochman, *Historical Dictionary of the Czech State* (1998); and Petr Ornyj, *A Brief History of the Czech Lands to 2004* (2003). A notable history of the country's transition to a market economy and accession to NATO and the EU is Václav Klaus, *Renaissance—The Rebirth of Liberty in the Heart of Europe* (1997).

SLOVAKIA

GEOGRAPHY

Milan Strhan and David P. Daniel (eds.), *Slovakia and the Slovaks: A Concise Encyclopedia* (1994), is a useful English-language reference work. Richard C. Frucht (ed.), *Eastern Europe: An Introduction to the People, Lands, and Culture*, 3 vol. (2005), offers a geographic survey. Stefan Auer, *Liberal Nationalism in Central Europe* (2004), is a solid analysis with rich material on Slovakia. The government's role in health care is discussed in Svätopluk Hlavacka, Róbert Wágner, and Annette Riesberg, *Health Care Systems in Transition: Slovakia* (2004). Peter Petro, *A History of Slovak Literature* (1995), addresses Slovak literature from medieval to recent times. Specific studies of music include Oskár Elschek (ed.), *A History of Slovak Music: From the Earliest Times to the Present* (2003).

HISTORY

Very useful reference books are Stanislav J. Kirschbaum, *Historical Dictionary of Slovakia*, 2nd ed. (2007); and Július Bartl, *Slovak History: Chronology and Lexicon*, 1st Eng. ed. (2002). The new standard history is Peter A. Toma and Dušan Kováč, *Slovakia: From Samo to Dzurinda* (2001). Slovak nationalism is covered in Peter Brock, *The Slovak National Awakening* (1976); and Yeshayahu A. Jelinek, *The Lust for Power: Nationalism, Slovakia, and the Communists, 1918–1948* (1983).

INDEX

943.7   Bulgaria, Hungary, Romania,
BUL   the Czech Republic, and
        Slovakia

$45.00   07/15